D0340288

TAKING
LIBERTIES

A HISTORY OF HUMAN RIGHTS IN CANADA

Edited by

**David Goutor and
Stephen Heathorn**

OXFORD
UNIVERSITY PRESS

OXFORD
UNIVERSITY PRESS

Oxford University Press is a department of the University of Oxford.
It furthers the University's objective of excellence in research, scholarship,
and education by publishing worldwide. Oxford is a registered trade mark of
Oxford University Press in the UK and in certain other countries.

Published in Canada by
Oxford University Press
8 Sampson Mews, Suite 204,
Don Mills, Ontario M3C 0H5 Canada

www.oupcanada.com

Library and Archives Canada Cataloguing in Publication

Taking liberties : a history of human rights in
Canada / edited by David Goutor and Stephen Heathorn.

Includes bibliographical references and index.
ISBN 978-0-19-900479-9 (bound)

1. Human rights—Canada—History. I. Goutor,
David, 1969–, editor of compilation II. Heathorn,
Stephen J., 1965– , editor of compilation

JC599.C3T288 2013   323.0971   C2013-902500-6

Cover image: Aleksander Velasevic/iStockphoto

Printed and bound in the United States of America.

1 2 3 4 — 16 15 14 13

CONTENTS

PREFACE   v

Michael Ignatieff

Acknowledgements   *xi*

INTRODUCTION   1

Stephen Heathorn and David Goutor

CHAPTER 1   29

Decoding the Rights Revolution: Lessons from the Canadian Experience

James W. St. G. Walker

CHAPTER 2   59

Where Do We Begin? Human Rights, Public History, and the Challenge of Conceptualization

Bonny Ibhawoh

CHAPTER 3   88

The Rights Revolution in Canada and Australia: International Politics, Social Movements, and Domestic Law

Dominique Clément

CHAPTER 4   114

"Their Equality Is My Equality": F. Andrew Brewin and Human Rights Activism, 1940s–1970s

Stephanie Bangarth

CHAPTER 5   139
Transnational Links and Citizens' Rights: Canadian Jewish Human Rights Activists and Their American Allies in the 1940s and 1950s
Ruth A. Frager and Carmela Patrias

CHAPTER 6   166
A Limited Vision: Canadian Participation in the Adoption of the International Covenants on Human Rights
Jennifer Tunnicliffe

CHAPTER 7   190
Children's Rights from Below: Canadian and Transnational Actions, Beliefs, and Discourses, 1900–1989
Dominique Marshall

CHAPTER 8   213
Social Movements and Human Rights: Gender, Sexuality, and the Charter in English-Speaking Canada
Miriam Smith

CHAPTER 9   233
Human Rights for Some: First Nations Rights in Twentieth-Century Canada
J.R. Miller

AFTERWORD   261
Rights, History, and Turning Points
William Schabas

Select Bibliography   272

Contributors   282

Index   285

Preface

◦—◦

Michael Ignatieff

The subject of this path-breaking collection of historical essays is how human rights language has changed Canada—and the modern world. Rights are legal claims, moral norms, and political demands. As legal claims, they are codified in international conventions and state constitutions enforceable at law. As moral norms, they express core standards that define how human beings should treat each other. As political demands, rights offer legitimacy to campaigns for social justice around the world.

Each of these three dimensions—as law, ethics, and politics—is in dynamic tension with the other. Human rights lawyers like to think of human rights law as a securely anchored international legal realm that is above the rough and tumble of power, requiring no further political justification for its legitimacy. In reality, both rights-respecting and rights-violating states repeatedly challenge the remit of international human rights law. Its status as a legal standard above the competition of states is anything but uncontested. Similarly, human rights activists are constantly telling us they do not do "politics," and yet their activity is inescapably political. For fifty years Amnesty International has mobilized citizens to demand the release of prisoners in other states: what is this but transnational political activism? It does not become less political because it is in the name of moral and legal universals, though the universals help to keep human rights from succumbing to the partisanship and partiality that drives normal politics.

When activists and theorists use human rights as an ethics, they are articulating a political claim for justice that goes beyond narrow compliance with black-letter law. They appeal instead to moral claims about human equality and dignity that have a resonance and power distinct from the authority human rights possesses as law. The historical diffusion of human rights is inexplicable if it is seen merely as a legal discourse. It is the powerful attraction of its moral appeal to human dignity and human agency that needs to be at the centre of any historical story about the hold human rights has acquired in the moral imagination.

In the battle for power, activists deploy the legal and moral dimensions of human rights to de-legitimize political excuses for abuse while legitimizing their own campaigns to bring such abuses to an end. Thus human rights functions as law and a critique of law; operates as an ethics for everyday life; and provides the legitimizing arguments for a politics directed against cruelty, inequality, and injustice. Each of these dimensions must figure in the story we tell about how human rights consciousness has shaped the modern world.

Human rights has shaped our time because it is protean, because it can serve many masters and many purposes. Because it is protean, it is also deeply contested. The international lawyers want to keep it disinfested of politics, while activists on the ground believe human rights campaigns must become political in order to succeed. Ethicists want us to take care lest rights talk swallows up the entirety of our conception of what human beings owe each other. The right is not the entirety of the good and the good cannot be described only in the language of rights. No one, for example, has a right to love, but love figures in anyone's idea of the human good. The most contested use of human rights is as a language of power. It is used by states to justify coercive interventions in other states and as such arouses deep anger when it appears to be an apologia for imperialism. When powerful states use human rights to condemn their enemies, while pardoning the abuses of their friends, the discourse itself loses legitimacy for appearing to permit double standards.

As the globalization of markets, labour, and capital draws distant societies into the orbit of global power centres, human rights has become the most influential example of the globalization of ethical language itself. Human rights has gone global by going local, by working its way into the moral language and political demands for justice in societies the world over. But at every point in this process, conflict has arisen between the local and the global. Local activists who use universal human rights to confront practices that assign women to inferior spheres must answer this question: What gives them the right, exactly, to proclaim the superiority of the universal over the local? The answer, in practice, has been that the women subjected to humiliating or confining social practices—purdah, arranged marriage, bride price—have sought the protection—and the voice—that universal human rights language provides them. Indeed, it is the way human rights has empowered victims and enabled them to rise above victimhood that has been human rights' most remarkable achievement since 1945. The historical diffusion of human rights language from Europe and North America to the rest of the world is often viewed as an exercise in Western moral imperialism, but its reception in developing societies cannot be explained in these terms. It would not have become so resonant among women and subjugated minorities in developing societies if it was an alien and Western imposition. It has been successful because it has given these groups a language in which to advance their claims and find their political voice. Those who have criticized human rights for its individualistic bias—for its supposedly Western focus on an individual rights-bearer—are criticizing precisely what has been so popular about the discourse when it enters patriarchal, patrimonial, and tribal societies where the individual is subordinated to coercive social, religious, and moral codes. It is a language that enables subjected groups to see themselves, sometimes for the first time, as agents and actors, persons entitled to dignity and rights and therefore capable of acting politically to improve their lives. The individual character of rights claims is precisely what has made human rights such a pervasive and influential language of human agency, especially for women and oppressed and excluded minorities.

At the same time as human rights has become the *lingua franca* of moral claims the world over, the same discourse has offered Western liberal democracies a redeeming definition of who they are and what they stand for. Human rights has become a saving source of legitimacy for Western societies that have seen the end of their empires, the decline of their hegemonic influence and the erosion of their moral self-confidence. The idea that human rights serves as a legitimizing ideology for Western states makes human rights lawyers, activists, and theorists uneasy and with good reason. Human rights ought not to be an ideology at all, but a moral practice, the stubborn and unending work of protecting victims without regard to their ideological label. Human rights ought to be disciplined by consistency, impartiality, and neutrality toward all states, cultures, and traditions. Such a moral practice cannot give moral comfort to any state or ideology. Indeed, a consistent human rights practice means turning the spotlight of scrutiny not only upon tyrannical, corrupt, or failing states but also upon those Western states that wrap themselves in the moral prestige of their own rule of law.

Canada is one of those liberal democracies that has vested its self-image in the language of human rights and defined its global role as a defender of these universal values. Unlike its neighbour next door, Canada has deliberately refused an exceptionalist self-definition, one that celebrates the unique distinctiveness of its rights tradition and therefore defends its prerogative to pick and choose which international instruments it subscribes to. In contrast, Canada likes to think of itself not as exceptional but as an exemplary global citizen, one of the founders of the post-1945 human rights order.

This volume of essays is at its most interesting—and most consistent with the moral discipline of human rights itself—when it subjects this Canadian self-image to critical historical scrutiny. Thanks to John Humphrey's role in drafting the Universal Declaration of Human Rights, Canadians like to think they were present at the creation of international human rights. The historical reality is considerably more complicated. In fact, Canada's history as a British parliamentary democracy, ordered by the British common law, made Canadian elites reluctant to embrace a human rights language that seemed to owe more to continental European traditions than their own. These essays lay bare a notable paradox in the historical diffusion of human rights. The language itself originates in British and American revolts against monarchical absolutism, and yet the common law and parliamentary sovereignty traditions especially in Britain, but also in Canada, have become resilient sources of resistance to the transnational authority of international rights instruments. Canadian rights traditions did not provide a ready home for international human rights and to this day, when United Nations human rights bodies dare criticize Canada's record, the hostile reaction tells you how strongly many Canadians believe that they have nothing to learn from international rights norms. The Canadian Charter of Rights and Freedoms incorporates these norms into the Canadian constitutional framework and yet in doing so says to Canadians, in effect, you need look no further than Canadian law for remedy.

The same complex, ambivalent story can be told in relation to Canada's treatment of political and ethnic minorities. From the War Measures Act to Japanese internment and the exclusion of Jewish refugees from Europe, Canada's actual rights observance does not fit easily with its self-image as an open and tolerant society. Thanks to the work of Canadian historians—and community activists as well—we now include these incidents, together with many others—from the mistreatment of British Sikh subjects aboard the Komagata Maru in Vancouver harbour to the century-long scandal of Aboriginal residential schools—in any honest account of who we are as a people. Like any society, Canada needs to live in truth. Achieving historical truth is a struggle, a battle between memory and forgetting, between those who want the hurt to be buried and those who want to heal the hurt by surfacing it into public memory. Thanks to these struggles, some recalled in this book, we are much closer to the truth than we were fifty years ago, and our country's human rights performance is stronger because of it.

Human rights is not an ideology any more than history is an ideology. Neither discourse should be in the service of patriotism and self-congratulation. Both are critical disciplines in the strict sense of the word, requiring those who practise them to follow the path to truth wherever it may lead. These essays are in the best traditions of both disciplines: they try to follow the truth so that we can see ourselves as we are, citizens of a divided world and citizens of a country that can always stand to be a bit better than it actually is.

Acknowledgements

As editors, we would like to thank the Wilson Institute and its director, Viv Nelles, for supporting the Taking Liberties workshop in March 2012, from which this collection derives, and Lynton "Red" Wilson, the chancellor of McMaster University, for his vision in funding the Wilson Institute in the first place. The president of McMaster University, Patrick Deane, and the dean of humanities, Suzanne Crosta, supported our efforts and offered gracious welcomes at the workshop events. A number of people in the Department of History at McMaster were also crucial in making the workshop a success, particularly the chair of the department, Pamela Swett, who always offered positive advice, and Edita Marinc, Wendy Benedetti, and Debbie Lobban, who provided the essential administrative support. However, Stephen Heathorn's co-organizer of the event, Jennifer Tunnicliffe, deserves most of credit for the design of the original workshop. This volume could not have come together without the excellent work and generous attitudes of all its contributors, and we appreciate their good-natured responses to our queries and quick deadlines. Viv Nelles was especially key to the development of this volume, providing advice and help at critical moments in the process. We are also deeply appreciative of the assistance and enthusiastic encouragement provided by the editorial staff at Oxford University Press Canada, especially Jen Rubio and Katie Scott, and for the sensitive, thorough read by the copy editor, Leslie Saffrey. Working with OUP has been a delight. Lastly, David Goutor would like to thank his wife Lisa for her love, her patience, and her support. He would also like to thank Lisa and his two little kids, Madeleine and Max, for making every day that much brighter. Stephen Heathorn would like to thank Sherisse for her forbearance and support, and Nigel and Adrienne for just being themselves.

David Goutor
Stephen Heathorn
June 2013

Introduction

•—◆—•

Stephen Heathorn and David Goutor

We are living in the age of human rights. In recent decades, the idea of human rights has become what Michael Ignatieff calls the "*lingua franca of global moral thought.*"[1] And this has not been merely talk: elaborate institutional structures have been built to defend human rights, and governments around the world find themselves answering to rights campaigns and legal challenges coming from both their own citizens and international bodies. Human rights today are widely viewed as embodying "the highest moral precepts and political ideals"[2]—they are universal and inherent properties of human beings, regardless of their circumstances. Small wonder, then, that both our popular understanding and the academic study of human rights often cast the emergence of the rights age as the inevitable product of human progress, as the march of enlightenment.[3]

However, another characteristic of human rights has been just as widely noted: determining what constitutes a human right, how to protect it, and how to deal with those who violate it, is an endlessly complex and often divisive process. For some commentators, the most remarkable attributes of rights discourse are vagueness and malleability. Supposedly inviolable human rights frequently conflict—one famous example is the right to free speech versus the right to protection against discrimination and hate speech. Moreover, regardless of whether they are discussed in terms of abstract ideas or legal entities, human rights have developed in profoundly contingent ways and at different rates in different places.

Indeed, today human rights may be typically framed in terms of universal concepts, but they are in fact profoundly historical constructs. The very idea of human rights has been contested and had to be fought for, including in developed Western democracies. Local contexts have been especially important to the development of "universal" human rights. This paradox—that the local contestations of rights have been key to their broader acceptance—underpins many of the essays in this collection and demonstrates the fundamental importance of the historical analysis of human rights. There was nothing inevitable about the emergence of human rights.

And yet, as a number of contributors to this volume suggest, the discussion of human rights has suffered from a "lack of historicity" (see Ibhawoh, p. 59). Human rights has long been the domain of political scientists, legal scholars, and philosophers, all of who aim at providing the normative and legal grounding to the limits of human rights in the present.[4] This is an important goal to be sure. But achieving a fuller understanding of the meaning of human rights requires examining its historical development: not in a teleological fashion or the vain search for precise "origins," but rather understanding how and why human rights as a concept was advanced, was fought for and against, and what historical baggage aided or impeded the concept's ultimate acceptance (see Ibhawoh, pp. 59–62 and Walker, pp. 48–52 A number of historians around the world are now doing exactly that. Indeed, the last ten years has seen an explosion in the historical scholarship on human rights.[5] This volume contributes to the growing historiographical debate about universal human rights by concentrating on Canada's relationship to human rights both domestically and in the international sphere.

Historicizing the debate about human rights is as important a mission in Canada as it is anywhere. Canada has embraced human rights recently to a remarkable degree, developing what Dominique Clément calls in this volume "the most sophisticated human rights legal regime in the world." (p. 102). Nevertheless, Canadians are generally unaware of the struggles by different minority groups to gain protections against discrimination in the form of human rights legislation.[6] Similarly, the widespread acceptance of human rights is now often cited as something that makes Canada distinctive on the world stage.[7] In *The Rights Revolution*, Michael Ignatieff contends that "Canada has shown the way" regarding how to solve the "fundamental problem facing humanity," namely "how to create stable political order among people of different religions, cultures, and economic classes."[8] But there is little awareness of how Canada's experience fits into the international development of human rights discourse. In fact, Canada's relationship to human rights since the 1940s has been complex and uneven, in part due to conflicting influences from British traditions of civil liberties and parliamentary democracy and the rights culture of Canada's neighbour, the United States.

This volume seeks to broaden and deepen the historiography on Canada's relationship with human rights, analyzing the development of rights discourse and activism in Canada and putting it within the contexts of (1) the historical traditions that Canada inherited, (2) the post–Second World War universalizing claims, and (3) the domestic and international realms within which such rights have been promoted. The following sections of the introduction will set the stage for the examination of each of these themes, before briefly outlining the state of the literature on human rights and the contributions of the particular articles.

CANADA WITHIN THE BRITISH TRADITION

Much of Canada's pre–human rights tradition was inherited from British law, political custom, and practice; this had a profound impact on how human rights developed in Canada. From Britain (or more accurately from England), Canada inherited a national political system based upon the dual principles of parliamentary supremacy and the rule of law; statutes passed by Parliament acted as the highest and final source of law, and all citizens were technically subject to and had equal protection under this law. For just as in Britain and in many of its former colonies (see Clément, pp. 88–113). Canada's government traditionally had little role to play in the protection of its citizens' rights—or *liberties* as they were more usually referred to prior to the Second World War. Unlike in the United States, where rights were incorporated as guiding principles in the founding documents of the republic (and the supposed practice of its government), civil liberties in Britain and Canada were purely customary and protected by the historical (but changeable) precedents of the common law.

The expansion of civil liberties and the development of the language of natural rights in Britain were products of an evolution which took centuries but did not take a linear path. Indeed the British legacy evident in the civil liberties tradition and the assumption of natural rights expressed in the American Declaration of Independence came from a shared political and religious history.[9] Debates about the abstract nature and actual manifestations of liberty, republican and liberal, characterized seventeenth-century modern political discourse culminating in the thought of John Locke.[10] A more abstract notion of natural rights emerged as a source of contention in the eighteenth-century transatlantic Enlightenment-inspired revolutionary movements. Some of the most influential social and cultural historians of eighteenth-century Britain have concerned themselves with explaining why these political discourses diverged; the language of historical liberties remained predominant in

England while that of natural rights found its home across the Atlantic and the English Channel. This was not a clean or simple break either, for the suppression of Thomas Paine's *The Rights of Man* (1791) occurred at the same moment that purely customary liberties were codified into written law.[11]

Liberties within England owed much to the libertarian political culture that flourished under an established church that allowed (severely) limited toleration of other faiths and a political regime that had rejected rigidly centralized government.[12] Restraints on central government were strengthened by the Union of England and Scotland in 1707, and, though less voluntary and more divisive, by the Union with Ireland in 1800. As the central state was thought to be limited, it was also not obliged to protect the liberties that its citizens were presumed to hold. British civil liberties were thus, as human rights lawyer Geoffrey Robertson notes, a "state of mind rather than a set of legal rules."[13] By the mid-nineteenth century, natural rights talk had largely disappeared from British political culture (except on its republican fringes), and found no home in legislation, unlike in the United States where they remained foundational.

In the US tradition, natural rights came first, then came government. Certainly the American authors of the Declaration of Independence drew on existing English tradition (especially the 1689 Bill of Rights)[14] but for them the rights of individuals did not originate with any government, but pre-existed its formation. Thus the protection of these rights was the first *duty* of government and even after government was formed, rights provided a standard by which its performance was to be measured. Of course, the fact that the framers of the Declaration of Independence and US Constitution and many Americans thereafter had a rather limited view of who counted as a person helps explain the tortured history of race and gender relations in the United States.

This "natural rights" view of citizens in relation to their government was not the case in the nineteenth century in Britain. Civil liberties as they continued to develop in Britain remained related to political participation and the ability to live freely from government restrictions and the unwanted actions of others; while still thought to be rooted in the individual, they were subject to limitations by the state through the exercise of parliamentary sovereignty. Civil liberties were understood as a product of a specific history and custom rather than derived from abstract principles. They were not conceived of, in law or in practice, as universal nor absolute rights. This understanding can be seen in Albert W. Dicey's influential *Introduction to the Study of the Law and the Constitution* (1885).[15]

Dicey, a constitutional lawyer and legal scholar, explained that a codified set of individual rights was unnecessary because Britain's rule of law provided inherently for civil liberties that could and would be upheld by Parliament.[16] As a number of scholars have shown, Dicey explained that civil liberties were not "so much guaranteed by statute as allowed to exist merely because no law has prohibited them."[17] Therefore, "freedom is not something that can be asserted in opposition to law; it is the residue of conduct permitted in the sense that no statute or common law rule prohibits it."[18] Thus activism against discrimination and for advancing particular rights prior to the Second World War tended to reflect the customary-law/civil-liberties regime of Britain. Many advocates of citizenship rights for women in the nineteenth century, for instance, claimed their efforts at changing the common law precedents that underpinned discrimination against them were nothing more than the necessary extension (or reclamation) of traditional British liberties, rather than being grounded in abstract arguments about women's equality (as Mary Wollstonecraft had done in the late eighteenth century).[19] While such rhetoric was perhaps an attempt to diminish the perceived radicalism of their claims in the face of late-Victorian gender norms,[20] it is the case that nineteenth-century feminists first concentrated on removing the discrimination in property laws, specifically around marriage, before then moving onto claiming equal political rights for women under the law.[21] Similarly, when *Lascars*—sailors from Britain's colonies in the Indian subcontinent or the Caribbean—challenged the discriminatory Coloured Seaman's Order of 1926, they did so on the basis of the liberties protected by traditional "British justice" rather than through appeals to specific rights, abstract or otherwise.[22]

From Confederation through the early twentieth century, Canada's legal system followed the British model, and its elites rigorously embraced established British notions about civil liberties and the law. Suggestions of creating constitutional protections of individual rights were dismissed using the principle of parliamentary supremacy, and as one human rights advocate lamented, Canadian lawyers tended to be "reared in the Diceyan gospel."[23] Similarly, as James Walker notes, there was a strong sense that entrenched principles of "Anglo-Canadian law" provided enough protection for members of society, and if minorities wanted "legal refinements, this was simply a case of a special interest seeking special treatment for its own members."[24]

In general, agitation against social inequalities by women and minorities received a cold reception in Canada. The discriminatory "isms"— including racism, sexism, and heterosexism—were so widely accepted that they were seen as "common sense."[25] There was an established social hierarchy that placed white, heterosexual, British (or in some cases French), able-bodied men at the top. To be sure, Canadians also felt that the plight of marginalized groups was not as desperate as it was in many other places. They were especially certain that Canada did not have the United States' abrasive and often violent history of racial and ethnic relations.[26] Yet this sense also fostered an especially strong culture of denial about the existence of discrimination. Certainly such denial also existed elsewhere in the world; but a number of scholars have noted "an almost willful blindness" about social inequities in Canada.[27]

In Britain, the government's ability to uphold the Victorian liberal notion of citizen civil liberties was tested by two world wars, economic depression, the rise in Europe of powerful anti-liberal ideologies, the Cold War, increasing levels of migration, the loss of empire, the consequences of a new united Europe, and the challenge of maintaining Britain's place in a new global world. Indeed, one of the last influential embodiments of the Victorian liberal view and an influential rights activist in his own right, Bertrand Russell, despaired in his memoirs that the "Communists, Fascists and Nazis have successively challenged all that I thought good, and in defeating them much of what their opponents have sought to preserve is being lost. Freedom has come to be thought weakness, and tolerance has been compelled to wear the garb of treachery."[28]

This gloomy conclusion referred to the British state's passing of laws to limit the civil liberties of its citizens where it felt necessary—which it did on numerous occasions in the first half of the twentieth century. But a countervailing tendency to that of increased state restriction was the growth of organizations such as the National Council of Civil Liberties, which developed to promote liberty and to urge government to alter (or leave alone) its laws when civil liberties were deemed under threat.[29]

The Canadian government, meanwhile, proved all too willing to limit civil liberties through such actions as granting itself sweeping powers over citizens during the First World War by enacting the War Measures Act; using draconian laws to help crush the postwar labour revolt, especially the Winnipeg General Strike; and repressing political dissent, particularly during the early 1930s when "Iron Heel" R.B. Bennett was prime minister. In the late 1920s and through the 1930s, municipal and provincial governments also suppressed suspected radicalism, especially by recent immigrants. The most notorious example was Quebec Premier Maurice Duplessis's Padlock Law, which authorized police to close up any premises where they suspected communist material was being disseminated. Resistance to such measures was more limited in Canada than in Great Britain, as there were only some small and ineffective civil liberties organizations, which were often further weakened by divisions between communists and others.[30]

Hostility toward immigrants, racialized peoples, and women increased in Canada during the Great Depression; there was a deep sense that white, Anglo-Canadian men should have first claim on any available work.[31] Anti-Semitism also escalated, and Canada had an abysmal record regarding Jewish refugees fleeing Hitler, keeping its gates shut as firmly as any Western democracy.[32] During the Second World War, a new wave of hostility against "enemy aliens" and the government's re-imposition of the War Measures Act produced further violations of individual freedoms. The government displayed a tendency toward "incarcerative overkill," detaining political subversives (especially communists until Hitler's Germany invaded the Soviet Union in the fall of 1941) and "suspicious" members of the Italian and German communities.[33] After Pearl Harbor, Japanese Canadians were especially targeted: the government disfranchised more than twenty thousand, removed them by force from British Columbia, confiscated their property, and then auctioned it off. These moves led to new protests and mobilizing, yet it was not until the late stages of the war, and especially the postwar period, that human rights activism gained significant momentum. This growing strength of Canadian human rights campaigns was part of a broader international trend.

HUMAN RIGHTS AS A GLOBAL PHENOMENON

The adoption of the United Nations' Universal Declaration of Human Rights (UDHR) of 1948 both reflected the growing interest in much of the world in human rights and signalled the arrival of human rights as

a global issue. A number of factors are commonly cited as giving impetus to human rights campaigns in the 1940s, including the idealism of
much of the wartime propaganda, and particularly the declaration of the
Atlantic Charter; revulsion against the racism of the Nazis and particularly "discovery" of the Holocaust in 1944–5; and the hopes for international co-operation fostered by the creation of the UN.

The UDHR's definition of human rights included both the traditional civil liberties found in democracies and more egalitarian rights,
and can also include collective as opposed to merely individual rights.[34]
As already noted, this expansive notion of universal human rights has
relatively recent origins, although there is yet to be consensus on the
nature of those origins or their precise antecedents (see Ibhawoh and
Walker in this volume).

As soon as "rights talk" spread, so did the fierce contestation about
what counted as a human right. In particular, the struggle for human
rights in the postwar era was almost immediately complicated by the
politics of the Cold War. Transnational debates about racial discrimination, colonialism, and national self-determination; the denial of political
participation; and the continuance of social and economic inequalities
could not escape the polarizing pull of East versus West, of communism versus capitalist democracy. The West charged the communist bloc
with widespread violation of individual human rights; communist states
countered that the West deployed human rights rhetoric as a cover for
economic exploitation, and that human rights were selectively and hypo-
critically applied by the West, given their own imperialist history and the
ongoing racial discrimination in the remaining colonies of the European
states and in the United States.

The Cold War, moreover, exacerbated differences over the conceptualization of rights among activists in various domestic contexts too.
In opposition to what had been hoped by the drafters of the UDHR,
ideological distinctions grew particularly sharp.[35] The tendency of civil
liberties groups in the 1930s and early 1940s to divide between anti-to-
talitarian and pro-communist positions became much more pronounced
in the Cold War context.[36] This had consequences for the types of rights
advocated by such groups. Partly as a result of such tensions, by 1952 the
UN had decided to separate civil and political rights from economic and
social rights. Two distinct International Covenants were formalized after
nearly a decade and a half of further wrangling in 1966.[37]

The struggle of the global South for independence from European imperial powers further complicated the emergence of human rights in the 1950s and 1960s. Newly independent states that emerged from decolonization had a political stake in defining human rights primarily in terms of collective self-determination. This was affirmed at the Bandung Conference in 1955 where African and Asian nations officially declared self-determination as the "first" right, thereby asserting—despite some stinging criticism from conference delegates—that for developing nations there was a primacy of collective over individual rights.[38] The states of the global South also tended to put a higher value on economic and social rights, for developmental reasons, than did the states of most developed countries. But the contestation between those who advocated collective over individual rights, and vice versa, was not limited to newly independent and former colonized nations.

In Western democracies, a major wave of activism among minorities, feminists, and environmentalists expanded the human rights agenda by the 1970s. These campaigns implicitly challenged both state governments and the principle of national sovereignty on which the United Nations itself had been founded.[39] According to Samuel Moyn's influential and extremely provocative study, it was not until this surge in activity that human rights became an important global force; he argues that historians have seriously overstated the impact of earlier efforts, usually in a misguided effort to find a progression leading to the rights consciousness of recent decades.[40] The advocates of these rights tended to be nongovernmental organizations (NGOs): the 1960s witnessed an explosion of social movements around the world that put the attainment of particular rights at the core of their mission. Amnesty International (AI), founded in 1961, is one of the more famous examples; an NGO founded in Britain but with a global perspective, it advocated for the rights of individual political prisoners, but later expanded its remit to the protection of all prisoners from torture, and the rights of children and women.[41] AI deliberately concentrated on individuals and individual rights in an effort to get widespread public support for its campaigns, much to the annoyance of its critics: social and economic rights were added to AI's mission statement only in 2001. The flowering of NGOs in the 1960 and early 1970s challenged the existing rights status quo both in domestic and international arenas, especially as many of these NGOs and social movements aimed to rise above Cold War politics, although they were nonetheless labeled subversive in the West and agents of capitalism in the East.

It has been suggested by some scholars that the Helsinki Accords in 1975 marked a turning point in the global remit of human rights. For in return for the acceptance of the territorial status quo in Europe, Western Europe demanded that Eastern Europe sign agreements to respect individual human rights and freedoms, particularly of thought, conscience, religion, and belief, with no denial of rights on the basis of race, sex, language, or religion. National self-determination was also to be respected.[42] The Accords led to the creation of Helsinki Watch groups, NGOs dedicated to monitoring the compliance of the Accords by all signatories. Over time, these de facto Cold War instruments encouraged the dissidents within communist states to challenge their governments, but also eventually put pressure on Western states to live up to their rights rhetoric too. Yet the difficulty of enforcing human rights on regimes reluctant to abide by the UDHR or the various subsequent international conventions and accords was a perpetual one. The first global effort to enforce international human rights laws came only in the 1990s when the United Nations set up ad hoc courts to deal with war crimes committed in the break-up of Yugoslavia and the ethnic conflict in Rwanda.[43] This was followed in 1998 by the setting up of the permanent International Criminal Court, although certain key states who refused to join the new court included the United States and Israel.[44]

CANADA AND UNIVERSAL HUMAN RIGHTS

Much of the impetus for the first major Canadian human rights campaigns came from the international forces noted above. Moreover, as Ruth Frager and Carmela Patrias show in this volume, many Canadian human rights activists—especially Jewish activists—drew heavily on larger and more sophisticated American rights groups for ideas, materials, and organizational models. But domestic events and indigenous human rights activism were also crucial. The authorities' excessive anti-espionage campaign after the Gouzenko affair—which uncovered a Soviet spy ring at work in Canada—prompted a wave of mobilization to protect civil liberties.[45] A complex set of changes in the labour movement turned Canadian labour from one of the strongest opponents of immigration into a key supporter of human rights campaigns.[46] In addition, a number of communities became more active in response to the oppression they faced during the period. Japanese Canadians and their supporters organized to resist their treatment at the hands of the government, particularly the efforts to deport them to Japan after the war.[47] Canadian Jews became especially mobilized in response not only to the horrors suffered by Jews in Europe, but to Canada's continuing restrictive policies toward Jewish refugees—which persisted even after the end of the war.[48]

This "awakening" to human rights issues produced some notable legislative and policy breakthroughs near the end of the decade and especially in the 1950s. For the first time, laws were passed that framed discrimination as a social and moral wrong serious enough to warrant state intervention against it. In 1958 Prime Minister John Diefenbaker introduced a Bill of Rights to the House of Commons (as a statute, not a constitutional amendment), and it passed in 1960. Lambertson characterizes 1960 as the end point of early wave of human rights activism, as many of the key goals of rights advocates, such as anti-discrimination legislation and a Bill of Rights, were finally achieved.[49] But scholars disagree regarding just how much change human rights activists achieved in this period. For Walker, the new approach in legislation and the rights culture that surrounded it constituted a "fundamental shift" away from the traditional (and dismissive) approach to discrimination of earlier periods.[50] In this volume, Walker suggests these moves might constitute one of the three key rights revolutions in Canada's history. Clément, on the other hand, calls the changes in the 1940s and 1950s "baby steps," and (including in this volume) characterizes legislation enacted in this period as weak and ineffective.[51]

Although Moyn's study has certainly helped to draw attention to such questions over the relative significance of different waves of activism, a major controversy has not (yet) developed in Canadian scholarship over the periodization of the growth of human rights consciousness.[52] There is certainly general agreement that much of the Canadian elite remained committed to traditional notions of British liberties and skeptical toward the emerging rights talk in the 1940s and 1950s. These attitudes among the elites were evident during the creation of the UDHR. A Canadian, John P. Humphrey, was the principle author of the UDHR, yet as Clément and Jennifer Tunnicliffe show in this volume, Canada not only was a reluctant signatory, but remained cool for years afterward toward the process of drafting of its related covenants and generally making human rights a consideration in foreign policy.

Moreover, it is generally agreed that the Diefenbaker Bill of Rights did not bring much change to the legal system. The very act of codifying some rights into law was a departure from the traditional British approach, as the protection of liberties was no longer left entirely up to the wisdom of Parliament to handle at any moment. Yet the principle of parliamentary supremacy remained intact, as the Bill put no limits on the power of Parliament to amend the Bill or simply override its provisions in the future. Diefenbaker would later pose himself as a having been a long-time champion of human rights, but in fact his primary motives in creating the Bill were nation-building—as the Bill would grant Canadians rights as citizens, no matter where they resided in the country—and partisan outrage over the Liberals' abuses of executive power during the Second World War and the Gouzenko affair.[53] There is also consensus that the Bill failed to serve as an effective shield for Canadians against discrimination, especially because the judiciary remained tied to traditional, narrow views of rights.[54] This was evident in the ongoing practical application of Section 133 of the British North America Act (1867), which recognized a limited administrative and judicial role for French/English bilingualism rather than granting fundamental language rights.

The second wave of rights activism in the 1960s and 1970s was especially strong in Canada. The remarkable growth of social movements internationally inspired Canadian human rights campaigns. But scholars have also emphasized that rights activism was driven by the agency of Canadians who developed new organizations that spoke out against forms of discrimination that used to have "common sense" status, and demanded legislative protection for various marginalized groups. Clément has argued that social movements of different kinds were so important and influential that their activism "defined the sixties and seventies."[55] The emergence of the "Quiet Revolution" in Quebec, for instance, raised the issue of minority rights within Canada to prominence as a new territorial conception of "Québécois" identity as a "distinct society" based principally on language emerged. Moreover, a new episode of the Canadian government wielding excessive and arbitrary power—when Prime Minister Pierre Trudeau invoked the War Measures Act in response to the October Crisis of 1970—sparked new efforts to defend civil liberties.[56]

This phase of the rights revolution produced a series of major legislative breakthroughs. Many provinces went beyond enacting laws that addressed overtly discriminatory acts by individuals and took a proactive approach, launching educational programs and implementing policies that targeted systematic discrimination.[57] This processes in many ways culminated in the Charter of Rights and Freedoms that was adopted in 1982, enshrining human rights in the patriated Constitution. The enactment of the Charter was a seminal moment in the history of rights in Canada for another reason: it signalled that previously entrenched principles such as parliamentary supremacy had been abandoned in favour of codifying rights in the legal system. This shift reflected and furthered the establishment of a vigorous "rights culture" in Canada.[58]

The continued expansion of rights activism and rights culture through the late twentieth century and into the twenty-first has brought Canada to the point where it is considered a global leader in human rights. A growing number of groups have launched legal challenges to gain protection or expand protections for their rights under the Charter. Clément and Walker note in this volume that the rights legal systems became still more expansive in scope and proactive in approach to eliminate discrimination and the conditions where it could occur. The systems have particularly intervened to a considerable extent to create accommodations for equity-seeking groups (especially the disabled) in Canadian workplaces, from where the majority of human rights complaints have consistently originated.[59] Moreover, human rights became an increasingly important priority in Canadian foreign policy—a considerable departure from the frosty attitude toward the UDHR and its covenants from the late 1940s through the mid-1960s (see Tunnicliffe, this volume). Human rights consciousness also led to growing concern with the policies toward refugees. In profiling the pioneering human rights work of Andrew Brewin, Stephanie Bangarth's article in this volume also explores the first instances when the plight of refugees engaging sustained attention from Canadian policy-makers and the public: the crisis in Biafra and the military coup in Chile.

Momentous as these changes have been, scholars have also highlighted the limits of Canada's "rights revolution." Its focus in Canada has been overwhelmingly on protecting individuals against discrimination or infringements of personal freedom; there has been much less progress—or even attention—regarding social or economic rights, or remedying income and wealth inequalities in general.[60] There is considerable doubt among labour scholars as to whether the individualistic rights discourse that has emerged in Canada offers anything of use to the union movement and the struggle for economic justice.[61] Historians have also argued that human rights advocates since the 1940s have consistently adopted a conservative approach to activism, relying on what Lambertson calls "reasoned argument and moral suasion" and avoiding broad-based mobilizations or mass protests.[62] Other scholars, including Miriam Smith in this volume, contend that the range of issues activists can address become severely constricted when they decide to work within the legal framework of the Charter and human rights legislation.

Moreover, there has been no pretense that discrimination has been eliminated, especially in the economy or with regard to cultural minorities. As Walker's essay in this volume emphasizes, the vast gulfs in income—between men and women, recent immigrants and those born in Canada, and the "white" population and racialized groups—highlight that the social hierarchy has hardly disappeared.[63] A culture of denial persists about social inequality, which has particularly encouraged the public ignorance about the history of struggles of human rights activists in Canada. There has also been considerable tension between the application of enshrined individual rights in the Charter and cultural/collective rights. The language laws in Quebec since the 1970s are a case in point. The Charte de la langue française (Bill 101, 1977) decreed that all children in state education, except those whose parents had themselves been taught in English in Quebec, hence forth had to attend francophone schools, thereby curtailing freedom of choice with respect to language of instruction for many people. All commercial signage was required to be only in French, and businesses with over fifty employees had to undertake "francization" programs. Some aspects of this law would be ruled unconstitutional under the terms of the 1982 Charter of Rights and Freedoms. The educational policy was deemed by the Canadian Supreme Court in 1984 to contravene Article 23 of the Charter and the commercial signage restrictions were also found to be discriminatory by the Supreme Court in *Ford v. Québec* (1988). In contrast, in another case brought before the United Nations Human Rights Committee (UNHRC) the following year, *Ballantyne, Davidson and McIntyre v. Canada*, the UNHRC acknowledged that, under Article 27 of the International Covenant on Civil and Political Rights, the Quebec government had a right to protect the French language within Quebec as long as such a policy was not used to limit the use of other minority languages in the private domain. In the event, the Quebec government initially disregarded the Canadian Supreme Court's rulings by invoking the de facto provincial veto—the "notwithstanding clause" of Canada's patriated Constitution—while making the case that the Charte de la langue française was in the best interests of Quebec's social and economic well-being.[64] Language restrictions were gradually relaxed thereafter, however, and most of the machinery for enforcing francization was subsequently abolished in 1993, along with many of the provisions restricting non-French advertising. Thus in the Quebec situation, cultural nationalism and the government assertion of distinctive rights based on identity politics was in clear tension with individual rights as defined in the 1982 Charter; both sides of the debate had clear and coherent grounds for their arguments. However, Jim Miller contends in his article in this volume that both the federal government's propaganda about its policies and the pervasive "myth of moral superiority" regarding the treatment of minorities helped Canada pursue a "policy of human rights for some" in relation to First Nations people (p. 233), leading to both the denial of cultural distinctiveness and the application of individual rights. Altogether, the "Church historian" approach to human rights and the "celebratory attitude toward the emergence and progress of human rights" that—according to Moyn—pervades the international (especially American) literature has been much less evident in the recent Canadian historical literature.[65]

Expanding the Literature on Human Rights in Canada

The overall development of the scholarly literature on human rights in Canada has been more or less consistent with international trends. There was little interest among historians in human rights up to almost the end of the twentieth century; as was the case elsewhere, human rights was primarily an area of interest for legal scholars and political scientists. Starting around the beginning of the twenty-first century, there was a flowering of scholarship on human rights, which has continued to the point that it is currently one of the most vibrant areas of Canadian historiography.[66]

This growing interest has also brought a shift in focus. The early literature on the development of human rights not only lacked a historical dimension, it also focused on the state and the roles of political and legal elites in shaping policy. Recent historical scholarship has taken a much more bottom-up approach, focusing on the communities, organizations, and activists that helped create Canada's "rights revolution." This new approach has been consistent with the heavy emphasis on social history in Canada in roughly the last three decades—the kind of history that generally challenges portrayals of marginalized peoples as victims awaiting assistance from the state and instead highlights their agency and autonomy. It has also enhanced the local, and indeed personal, dimension of the historical scholarship on human rights. Recent scholarship has introduced readers to figures such as Kalmen Kaplansky, who immigrated from Poland in 1929, became a skilled worker in the printing trade, got active in labour and social democratic politics, took charge of the Jewish Labour Committee in 1946 and became one of the most important human rights campaigners in Canada in the late 1940s and 1950s.[67] We have also learned about the impact of local events and campaigns, such as the Kenora Project, launched by the Canadian Jewish Congress in 1968 to combat discrimination against Aboriginals in the Northwestern Ontario town, or the backlash against the actions of police during the 1971 Gastown Riots in Vancouver.[68]

The flexible, subjective, and "inherently debatable" (Walker, p. 29) nature of rights talk has been another important theme of recent scholarship. Interpreting the terminology in the Canadian context can be a particular challenge, as historians seek to navigate the interplay of the inherited language of British liberties, or civil liberties, with the rights culture of the United States and the rights talk that emerged internationally. But another key theme—in Canada as elsewhere—has been that human rights are not merely discourses, and the struggles to protect human rights are hardly theoretical exercises. The influential post-colonial critic Edward Said repeatedly affirmed that human rights "are not cultural and grammatical things, and when violated they are as real as anything we can encounter."[69] Moreover, as British historian Stephen Brooke perceptively noted at the workshop on which this volume is based, human rights are not merely abstract ideals that bestow dignity, they have demonstrable material consequences of great import, such as access to social services and benefits and to opportunities in housing and the workplace. Canadian scholars have often focused on small organizations, local events, and particular conceptions of rights, but they have also certainly highlighted that the goal of rights activism is to make government produce concrete legislative changes—to make the state protect certain rights and freedoms. This rich interplay of contexts—international, national, and local—and of fields—political, legal, and social—has given a notably rich texture to much of the recent literature on human rights in Canada.

THE TAKING LIBERTIES WORKSHOP AND THIS VOLUME

Another sign of the maturation of the historical scholarship on human rights is the organizing of workshops and publication of collections of articles on the subject. In 2009, Janet Miron edited an introductory volume that outlines different forms of discrimination encountered in Canada, the campaigns to combat them, and the legal remedies that have been implemented. The goal of her diverse collection was to "incite interest and encourage readers to pursue further study into the growing number of publications that focus on human rights."[70] In contrast, the Taking Liberties workshop on which this present volume is based brought together scholars with the explicit aim of deeply historicizing human rights in Canada within a broader international context, and with the benefit of a rapidly expanding published corpus of contextual scholarship. Hosted by McMaster University's L.R. Wilson Institute for Canadian History, which has as its mission the rethinking of Canadian history within a global framework, this two-day workshop featured scholars of both Canadian history and of the wider "British world." Some of the results of this remarkably productive interchange of ideas are to be found in this volume. Regrettably, not all the contributions at the workshop could fit within the covers of one book, and in order to make coherent the issues at stake the editors decided to concentrate on those papers most pertinent to Canada rather than the entire wider British world—although it will be apparent that the included contributors have benefited from considering that wider perspective. One of the consequences of this decision, however, is the admittedly Anglo-centric nature of the available papers for this volume. And a key rights issue in Canadian history—language rights—is thereby unavoidably absent. The editors understand and regret the significance of this omission, but it was deemed equally important for the volume to remain true to the spirit of the workshop, in which everyone benefited from the expertise of those present, and so no non-participants in the workshop were commissioned for essays. In addition to presenters, the workshop also benefited tremendously from the perspectives of the session commentators, Sascha Auerbach, Karen Balcom, Stephanie Bangarth, David Goutor, and Viv Nelles, the comments of the assembled audience, and from the contributions of the two keynote speakers, Michael Ignatieff and William Schabas. The latter two contributors also agreed to offer reflections on the event and the revised papers selected for this volume, and these appear in the form of a preface and an afterword.

This volume is organized, much as the workshop was, by moving from general considerations of human rights rhetoric and action in Canada, to examining Canada's role within the international realm of universal human rights discourse, and then onto specific cases in which human rights have been prominent (or indeed strikingly absent) in the Canadian context. All the contributors, in one way or another, have addressed the paradoxes inherent within the universalizing claims of human rights and the distinctiveness of the Canadian situation.

The interaction between rhetoric about universality and human rights agitation at the local and community level is a particularly prominent theme in James Walker's article which leads off the collection. He shows how activists at these levels took terms such as "universal human rights" from broader national and indeed international settings, deployed them in their campaigns against the discrimination and marginalization they suffered, and in the process helped to create new understandings of rights discourse. Hence historians of human rights must examine local contexts, yet at the same time, he holds, "the local experience has necessarily to be approached through a transnational perspective." In developing this argument, Walker reviews the recent scholarly debates over the evolution of human rights discourse globally, looking particularly at the changing definitions of "rights" and "liberties," before turning to the experience "on the ground" in Canada stretching back to the late nineteenth century. Walker's focus on local activism illuminates another key point: that human rights be understood as "not a *gift* but a *prize*" (italics in original). In other words, human rights were not handed to people by political elites, the grand unfolding of some idea, or any other abstract process; rather they were won through the agency and creativity of average people demanding an end to injustice and the marginalization of certain groups. Ambitious in scope and sprinkled with thought-provoking musings—such as the possibility that "the international human rights revolution was simply a rhetorical splurge"—Walker's piece presents an important challenge to previous understandings of rights discourse.

The challenge of how to present the place and progress of human rights in Canada to the wider public is taken up in Bonny Ibhawoh's essay on the competing historical narratives about rights in public spaces—most specifically the new (and to some, controversial) national human rights museum in Winnipeg. Ibhawoh notes that academic debates need to be clarified for presentation in museums, which presents particular problems for a museum about human rights. He dismisses concerns about identifying the "true" origins of human rights, or presenting them as a teleological progression, and instead argues that human rights are best represented in public history through drawing connections between the historical epochs and episodes that have shaped the human rights idea. In doing so, he makes clear that it is important to leave open the possibility that the peoples and societies represented may not themselves have understood or constructed rights in the precise sense and terms used today. A public history of human rights should convey the multiple strands in the evolving human rights story: of human rights as "at once a historical product of the modern age and the outcome of cumulative human experiences; an assertion of individual liberties but also an affirmation of collective entitlements; a means of breaking down the impunity of rulers but also a way of forging relationships; a resource for civil repair but also a transcendent norm of resistance: an effect of power and resistance but also a form of freedom and discipline." For Ibhawoh, the public history of human rights should aspire to capture and reflect these complexities, rather than simply reflect today's presumptions about the universality of such rights.

The notion that key moments or historical episodes defined the universalization of human rights is taken up by Dominique Clément, who argues that the 1970s rather than the 1940s was the key decade in the development of postwar human rights in Canada. Here he is in line with some of the revisionist views of global human rights historians at Columbia University.[71] Using a comparison of two former British dominions Clément argues that when rights ideals were championed, partly as a consequence of the explosion of rights-focused social movements in the later 1960s, they came to be more contested in Australia than they were in Canada. Clément's essay also demonstrates the interrelationship between the passing of international human rights treaties and domestic human rights legislation, which in Canada led to the supplanting of the existing weak anti-discrimination laws with rigorous rights codes. Indeed, Clément argues that from the 1970s onward the new Canadian human rights legal regime was the most sophisticated in the world. In his view, Canada exemplifies the shift away from the entrenched civil liberties tradition and the influence of Cold War politics to a broader human rights discourse. Australia also engaged in national debates surrounding civil liberties in the post–Second World War period, but the Australian rights revolution in the 1970s was more restrained, and both governments' rights associations in Australia remained dedicated to a narrow conception of civil liberties.

The extent to which the growth of rights consciousness and the development of a human rights legal system depended on the efforts of dedicated individuals is a central theme of Stephanie Bangarth's article. She explores the work of Andrew Brewin, a key figure in the history of rights in Canada over four decades starting in the 1940s. As a lawyer, campaigner in groups such as the Co-operative Committee on Japanese Canadians, government official, political activist with the Co-operative Commonwealth Federation (CCF), and eventually a Member of Parliament for the New Democratic Party (NDP), Brewin helped not only to raise awareness about rights issues, but also to write some important pieces of rights legislation and defend human rights in court. Bangarth uses Brewin's career as a lens through which to examine the thinking of a rights campaigner who first became active in the 1940s, and particularly key influences such Christian socialism, which shaped the politics of many CCFers of Brewin's generation. She analyzes the mix of causes that were characteristic of what she calls a "modern Christian activist" working in the CCF in the 1940s and 1950s: labour law reform, the rights of Japanese Canadians, and the creation of a Bill of Rights. Yet Brewin's career had such longevity that he was also a major contributor to the wave of rights activism in the 1960s and 1970s. In particular, Bangarth's article shows Brewin's role in making human rights more than merely a domestic issue, in getting Canada involved in protecting the rights of people either caught in or trying to get away from crisis-stricken areas such as Chile and Biafra. Brewin was thus important in turning Canadians' attention toward the "politics of suffering abroad" (to use Moyn's terminology), which became a key part of human rights consciousness generally in this period.[72]

Activism of individuals and groups for the attainment of human rights is also at the core of the next essay in the collection. Ruth Frager and Carmela Patrias's article challenges the myth of Canada's moral superiority and greater tolerance of diversity (particularly compared to the United States), and addresses the blind spot the myth creates to the major American influences on Canadian human rights activism. Their paper aspires to push Canadian scholars to explore in depth the prevalence and power of American ideas about human rights in Canada. They particularly explore the "central role of Canadian Jews" in bringing American influences northward, as Jewish activists followed examples from the larger and better organized American Jewish community throughout the 1940s and 1950s. Frager and Patrias thus build a more transnational understanding of Canadian ethnic—particularly Jewish—history. Much of the existing literature has emphasized the distinctiveness of the Canadian Jewish community—but their examination of the migration of ideas across the border demonstrates the importance of international influences on that community. As with any migration, new ideas about rights did not move into Canada without undergoing significant change; Frager and Patrias explore in detail how Canadian Jewish activists dealt with the challenge of adapting American ideas to the Canadian context. Their article thus highlights the richness and depth of the Jewish community's contribution to Canadian society: Canadian Jews not only brought social, cultural, and political influences from their homeland, but also served as "conduits" for ideas from Jewish communities elsewhere, in this case human rights ideas championed by American Jews.

The next essay in the volume also addresses a myth about Canada and the promotion of human rights. The website for Foreign Affairs and International Trade Canada proclaimed in 2012 that, "Canada has been a consistently strong voice for the protection of human rights and the advancement of democratic values, from our central role in the drafting of the Universal Declaration of Human Rights in 1947/1948 to our work at the United Nations today." Jennifer Tunnicliffe demonstrates the extent to which this sweeping statement falls short of the mark. For the concept of universal rights was opposed within the Canadian government, and efforts at the United Nations to introduce an International Bill of Rights were resisted by Canadian policy-makers, throughout the late 1940s and 1950s. Tunnicliffe concentrates on Canada's participation in the debates over the development of the International Covenants on Human Rights, from 1949 to 1966, showing how a severely limited vision of rights held by Canadian politicians and policy-makers prevented Canada from contributing in a positive way to the development of early international human rights law. For the Canadian government, participation in the drafting of the Declaration and the Covenants was shaped by a limited understanding of civil liberties, rights, and freedoms inherited from Britain. The dilemma Canada faced was how to publicly support the United Nations' work in human rights without committing to an international human rights regime that conflicted with the government's own ideas about rights. These prevaricating tactics pursued by the Canadian government led to a delay in the embracing of human rights language by governments through to the 1960s.

If the Canadian government's involvement with human rights has been far more uneven than current popular and official memory allows, the championing of children's rights both by Canada and by NGOs and international organizations illustrates how contingent human rights talk has been. As Dominique Marshall demonstrates, children's rights were both front-and-centre and invisible in the international rights regime that developed in the twentieth century. Her paper is based on a re-examination of various case studies, including the propagation of the Declaration of the Rights of the Child of 1924, authored by the Save the Children International Union, and adopted unanimously by the Assembly of the League of Nations; the adoption and implementation of the Canadian "Children's Charter"; the Conference on the African Child of 1931 organized by the Save the Children International Union in Geneva; and the federal program of universal family allowances with Canada. It is especially attentive to the many groups in civil society which were involved in the writing and the uses of instruments of children's rights. It shows the circumstances in which the notion of children's rights offered a legitimate idiom of choice to talk about equality and universal entitlements for all generations. Conversely, it shows how the notion of children's rights has provided a powerful way to restrict discussions on equality and entitlements for all. This paradoxical legacy of children's rights suggests that the early ideas of rights for children deserve to be taken more seriously than they have recently been in histories of universal human rights, for they illuminate and complicate that broader story, both internationally and in Canada.

Miriam Smith's essay also focuses on a specific group integral to the development of human rights in Canada: the women's movement and the lesbian and gay movement (or later the LGBT—lesbian-gay-bisexual-transgender—movement), which have been especially active in human rights agitation since the 1970s. Smith uses historical institutionalism—a theoretical model from political science—to analyze the complex relationship between these social movements and state structures such as political institutions, current policies, and the "legacies of previous policies." In particular, she argues that social movements do not simply work to challenge and change state structures; the structures can exert as much or more influence on the character of social movements. Mobilization by the women's movement achieved some remarkable successes in getting strong provisions into the Charter of Rights and Freedoms (particularly sections 15 and 28) for equality rights and specifically for equality between men and women. Once the Charter was entrenched, the women's movement was "arguably the most important player" in the early court cases on equality rights, and more recently the LGBT movement used Charter-based legal challenges to significantly expand the rights of sexual minorities in Canada, especially when it comes to marriage. But Smith also contends that by focusing on legal activism, these social movements were effectively "boxed in" by the narrow categories imposed by the Charter. This is in turn thwarted prospects for political mobilization that took a broader-based approach toward social justice and equity issues, and that especially dealt with the interconnections among race, class, gender, and sexuality. Smith thus suggests that the women's and LGBT movements have lost the capacity to take on neo-liberalism and economic inequality.

The last paper in the collection makes the vitally important point that not all Canadians have experienced a "rights revolution" at all. Canada's First Nations have largely been excluded from the remit of human rights. Jim Miller's contribution, a landmark essay about the unique place of Aboriginal rights in Canada, asks how and why it has been that First Nations peoples have generally (at least until very recently) *not* used human rights discourse in their struggles for cultural recognition and in their legal claims; and he also investigates how Euro-Canadians have generally subordinated both the rights and the interests of Aboriginal peoples to their own. Consequently, while Canadians have come to believe that they have been superior to others, especially their American neighbours, in how they treat minorities, in fact the historical record belies this belief. Miller argues that First Nations have generally not accepted non-Natives' approach to protecting human rights because it was culturally inappropriate for their own societies. The protection of rights in Native communities has been a matter of kinship obligation, not state action. But for Euro-Canadians, individual as opposed to community rights have been more often proposed as in need of protection: indeed, the elevating of the solitary person's rights above those of the community helps mark out the distinctiveness of the human rights regime in Canada. But while there has thus been a disconnect between First Nations' and Euro-Canadian's view of rights, the sad fact is that official Canadian Indian policy has not held to a Euro-Canadian view of Native rights either. Indeed, Canada's record illustrates clearly that non-Native Canadians have engaged in a systematic, continuous, and enduring refusal to recognize First Nations' human rights even on a Euro-Canadian understanding of what constitutes them.

Hence a number of the contributors question the orthodox chronology of the acceptance and operationalization of human rights claims in Canada. Indeed, a running debate runs through these contributions on the key moment or moments for the "triumph" of human rights claims in Canada—or, especially in Miller's article, whether they "triumphed" at all. Together the papers in this volume force us to question some widely held beliefs about Canada and its historical record with regard to rights. For while Canada has indeed followed a distinctive path and has embraced the rhetoric of universal human rights more than other nation-states, its actual implementation of a human rights world view has been uneven and more qualified than popular and contemporary government sentiments today suggest. While far from dismissing either the importance of the idea of human rights or the real achievements made in Canada, the papers here suggest that examining Canada's history with regards to human rights should make us pause before trumpeting Canada as a beacon of human rights practice. They show also the intense and difficult struggles that have been undertaken by a wide variety of individuals and groups to attain the (imperfect) human rights regime that has been so far accomplished. Those struggles are worth celebrating, just as the limits of the progress of rights talk in Canada must be recognized.

NOTES

1. Michael Ignatieff, *Human Rights as Politics and Idolatry* (Princeton: Princeton University Press, 2001), 53.
2. Samuel Moyn, *The Last Utopia: Human Rights in History* (Cambridge, MA: Belknap Press, 2010), 1.
3. Paul Gordon Lauren, *The Evolution of International Human Rights: Visions Seen* (Philadelphia: University of Pennsylvania Press, 1998); Lynn Hunt, *Inventing Human Rights: A History* (New York: W.W. Norton, 2007). See the critiques by Kirstin Sellars, *The Rise and Rise of Human Rights* (Stroud, UK: Sutton Publishing, 2002); Kenneth Cmiel, "The Recent History of Human Rights," *American Historical Review* 109, no 1 (2004): 117–35.
4. Joseph Morsink, *The Universal Declaration of Human Rights: Origins, Drafting and Intent* (Philadelphia: University of Pennsylvania Press, 1999); William Schabas, *Genocide in International Law* (Cambridge: Cambridge University Press, 2000); Mary Ann Glendon, *A World Made New: Eleanor Roosevelt and the Universal Declaration of Human Rights* (New York: Random House, 2001); Daniel Thomas, *The Helsinki Effect: International Norms, Human Rights and the Demise of Communism* (Princeton: Princeton University Press, 2001); Martti Koskenniemi, *The Gentle Civilizer of Nations: The Rise and Fall of International Law, 1870–1960* (Cambridge: Cambridge University Press, 2002); Roger Normand and Sarah Zaidi, *Human Rights at the UN: The Political History of Universal Justice* (Bloomington, IN: Indiana University Press, 2008).
5. Akirie Iriye, Petra Goedde, and William I. Hitchcock, eds, *The Human Rights Revolution: An International History* (Oxford: Oxford University Press, 2012); Stefan-Ludwig Hoffmann, ed., *Human Rights in the Twentieth Century* (Cambridge: Cambridge University Press, 2011).
6. Dominque Clément, *Canada's Rights Revolution: Social Movements and Social Change, 1937–82* (Vancouver: University of British Columbia Press, 2008), 43.
7. See in particular, Michael Ignatieff, *The Rights Revolution* (Toronto: House of Anansi, 2000), 12–15.
8. Ignatieff, *Rights Revolution*, viii.
9. J.C.D. Clark, *The Language of Liberty, 1660–1832* (Cambridge: Cambridge University Press, 1994).
10. Steven Pincus, *1688: The First Modern Revolution* (New Haven, CT: Yale University Press, 2009).
11. This concern fundamentally underpins much of the work of E.P. Thompson. See his *The Making of the English Working Class* (Harmondsworth: Vintage, 1963) and *Customs In Common* (New York: Merlin Press, 1991). An excellent synthesis of eighteenth-century work on customary rights and the contested transition to codified legal tradition is Douglas Hay and Nicholas Rogers, *Eighteenth-Century English Society* (Oxford: Oxford University Press, 1998). For work that studies the eighteenth century in terms of the development of a public sphere embracing political rights and liberties, see Kathleen Wilson, *The Sense of the People* (Cambridge: Cambridge University Press, 1994).
12. Clark, *The Language of Liberty*; Geoffrey Holmes, *The Making of a Great Power: Late Stuart and Early Georgian Britain, 1660–1722* (London: Longman, 1993); Julian Hoppit, *Land of Liberty? England 1689–1727* (Oxford, 2002); Tim Harris, *Revolution: the Great Crisis of the British Monarchy, 1685–1720* (London: Allen Lane, 2006).
13. Geoffrey Robertson, *Freedom, The Individual and the Law* (London: Penguin, 1993), xiii.
14. Michael Zuckert, "Natural Rights in the American Revolution: The American Amalgam," in *Human Rights and Revolutions*, ed. Jeffrey Wasserman et al. (Latham, MD: Rowman & Littlefield, 2000), 59–76.
15. For a discussion of Dicey's influence on the understanding of British constitutionalism, see A.W. Brian Simpson, *Human Rights and the End of Empire: Britain and the Genesis of the European Convention* (Oxford: Oxford University Press, 2001), 33–37.

16. A. V. Dicey, *Introduction to the Study of the Law and the Constitution* (London, 1902), 198, 194.

17. Conor Gearty, *European Civil Liberties and the European Convention on Human Rights: A Comparative Study* (The Hague: Martinus Nijhoff Publishers, 1997), 64.

18. K.D. Ewing and C.A. Gearty, *Freedom Under Thatcher: Civil Liberties in Modern Britain* (Oxford: Clarendon Press, 1990), 9.

19. See for an example, C.C. Stopes, *British Freewomen: Their Historical Privilege* (London: Swan, 1894). Wollstonecraft remained a key feminist intellectual for many Victorian feminists, however.

20. E.J. Yeo, ed., *Radical Femininity: Women's Self-Representation in Nineteenth and Twentieth Century Social Movements* (Manchester: Manchester University Press, 1998).

21. Lee Holcombe, *Wives and Property: Reform of the Married Women's Property Law in Nineteenth Century England* (Toronto: University of Toronto Press, 1983); Mary Lyndon Shanley, *Feminism, Marriage, and the Law in Victorian England, 1850–1895* (Princeton: Princeton University Press, 1989).

22. Laura Tabili, *We Ask for British Justice: Workers and Racial Difference in Late Imperial Britain* (Ithaca, NY: Cornell University Press, 1994).

23. Frank Scott as quoted in Ross Lambertson, *Repression and Resistance: Canadian Human Rights Activists, 1930–1960* (Toronto: University of Toronto Press, 2005), 319.

24. James Walker, "The 'Jewish Phase' in the Movement for Racial Equity in Canada," *Canadian Ethnic Studies* 34, no.1 (2002): 6.

25. Ross Lambertson, "Domination and Dissent: Equality Rights before World War II," in *A History of Human Rights in Canada: Essential Issues*, ed. Janet Miron (Toronto: Canadian Scholars' Press, 2009), 14.

26. David Goutor, "A Different Perspective on the 'Labor Rights as Human Rights' Debate: Organized Labor and Human Rights Activism in Canada, 1939–1952," *Labor Studies Journal* 36, no. 3 (2011): 408–27.

27. Lambertson, *Repression and Resistance*, 199. See also Ruth Frager and Carmela Patrias, "'This Is Our Country, These Are Our Rights': Minorities and the Origins of Ontario's Human Rights Campaigns," *Canadian Historical Review* 82 (March 2001): 8–9.

28. Bertrand Russell, *Autobiography of Bertrand Russell*, vol. III, 1944–1967 (London: Allen & Unwin, 1971), 222.

29. Christopher Moores, "From Civil Liberties to Human Rights? British Civil Liberties Activism and Universal Human Rights," *Contemporary European History* 21, no. 2 (2012): 169–92, and "The Progressive Professionals: The National Council for Civil Liberties and the Politics of Political Activism in the 1960s," *20th Century British History* 20, no. 4 (2009): 538–60.

30. Lambertson, *Repression and Resistance*, Chap. 1, "Civil Libertarians and the Padlock Law."

31. Goutor, "A Different Perspective," 412; Katrina Srigley, "In Case You Hadn't Noticed!: Race, Ethnicity and Women's Wage Earning in a Depression-Era City," *Labour/le Travail* 55 (Spring 2005): 83–114.

32. Irving Abella and Harold Troper, *None is Too Many—Canada and the Jews of Europe* (Toronto: Lester & Orpen Dennys, 1982).

33. Lamberston, *Repression and Resistance,* Chap. 2, "The Second World War: Civil Liberties at Risk." It should be noted that Franca Iacovetta and Roberto Ventresca argue that many Italians interned by the government were undeniably open supporters of Fascism. See Franca Iacovetta and Robert Ventresca, "Redress, Collective Memory, and the Politics of History," in *Enemies Within: Italian and Other Internees in Canada and Abroad*, ed. Franca Iacovetta, Roberto Perin, and Angelo Principe (Toronto: University of Toronto Press, 2000), 379–414.

34. For a more thorough definition of civil liberties as they relate to Britain, see Conor Gearty, *Civil Liberties, Clarendon Law Series* (Oxford: Clarendon Press, 2007), 1; for a discussion of the difference between civil liberties and human rights in Britain, see David Feldman, *Civil Liberties and Human Rights in England and Wales*, 2nd ed. (Oxford: Clarendon Press, 2002), 4.

35. P. Coleman, *The Liberal Conspiracy: The Congress for Cultural Freedom and the Struggle for the Mind of Postwar Europe* (London: Collier Macmillan, 1989).

36. Susan Pennybacker, *From Scottsboro to Munich* (Princeton: Princeton University Press, 2009).

37. Paul Kennedy, *The Parliament of Man: The Past, Present, and Future of the United Nations* (New York: Random House, 2006), 183–84.

38. Roland Burke, "'The Compelling Dialogue of Freedom': Human Rights at the Bandung Conference," *Human Rights Quarterly* 28, no. 4 (2006): 951.

39. Iriye, Goedde, Hitchcock, eds, *The Human Rights Revolution*, 8; Samuel Moyn, *The Last Utopia*, 84–89; R. Burke, *Decolonization and the Evolution of International Human Rights* (Philadelphia: University of Pennsylvania Press, 2010).

40. Moyn, *The Last Utopia*.

41. Sellars, *The Rise and Rise of Human Rights*, 97–113.

42. William Korey, *The Promises We Keep: Human Rights, the Helsinki Process, and American Foreign Policy* (New York: St. Martin's Press, 1993), 5–9.

43. Samantha Power, *"A Problem from Hell": America and the Age of Genocide* (New York: HarperCollins, 2002), 475–86.

44. Iriye, Goedde, and Hitchcock, eds, *Human Rights Revolution*, 14.

45. Clément, *Canada's Rights Revolution*, 41–45.

46. Goutor, "A Different Perspective," 410–15, 417–23 ; Frager and Patrias, "This Is Our Country," 4–5, 11–12; Lambertson, *Repression and Resistance*, 286–87.

47. The government used the term *repatriation* to describe its efforts to send Japanese-Canadians to Japan. But as Stephanie Bangarth observes, since many of these candidates for "repatriation" were actually born in Canada, or were Canadian citizens, *deportation* or *expatriation* are likely more appropriate terms. Stephanie Bangarth, *Voices Raised in Protest: Defending North American Citizens of Japanese Ancestry, 1942–49* (Vancouver: UBC Press, 2008).

48. Walker, "The Jewish Phase," 2–7; Frager and Patrias, "This Is Our Country," 10–11.

49. Lambertson, *Repression and Resistance*, 371.

50. Walker, "The Jewish Phase," 17–18.

51. See also Dominique Clément, "'Rights without the Sword are but Mere Words': The Limits of Canada's Rights Revolution," in Miron, *A History of Human Rights*, 48.

52. Moyn, *The Last Utopia*. There was much discussion about Moyn and his views on the limits of rights consciousness in the 1940s and indeed all periods up until the "sudden" outbreak of interest in the 1970s, particularly among British historians.

53. Lambertson, *Repression and Resistance*, 328–31, 367–71.

54. Clément, *Canada's Rights Revolution*, 26.

55. *Ibid.*, 1.

56. *Ibid.*, 73–75, 105–16.

57. Walker describes policies against discrimination as aiming to "correct systemic conditions that produce discriminatory results even in the apparent absence of overt prejudicial acts." Walker, "The 'Jewish Phase,'" 2. See also Clément, *Canada's Rights Revolution*, 54.

58. Clément, "'Rights without the Sword'", 53.

59. See for instance Michael Lynk, "Disability and Work: The Transformation of the Legal Status of Employees with Disabilities in the Canadian Workplace" in *Law Society of Upper Canada Special Lectures 2007: Employment Law*, ed. R. Echlin and C. Paliare (Toronto: Irwin Law, 2008).

60. Clément, *Canada's Rights Revolution*, 210–11.

61. Michael Ignatieff made this point at his keynote address to the Taking Liberties Workshop at McMaster in March 2012. See Larry Savage, "Workers' Rights as Human Rights: Organized Labor and Rights Discourse in Canada," *Labor Studies Journal* 34, no. 1 (2009): 8–20; Eric Tucker, "The Constitutional Right To Bargain Collectively: The Ironies of Labour History in the Supreme Court of Canada," *Labour/Le Travail* 61 (2008): 151–80.

62. Lambertson, *Repression and Resistance*, 381. See also Clément, *Canada's Rights Revolution*, 208–9.

63. See also Grace Edward Galabuzi, *Canada's Economic Apartheid: The Social Exclusion of Racialized Groups in the New Century* (Toronto: Canadian Scholars' Press, 2006).

64. Pierre Columbe, *Language Rights in French Canada* (New York: P. Lang, 1995).

65. Moyn, *The Last Utopia*, 5.

66. James Walker's study of race and human rights was seminal in the development of human rights literature in Canada. James Walker, *"Race," Rights and the Law in the Supreme Court of Canada* (Waterloo, ON: Wilfrid Laurier University Press, 1997).

67. Frager and Patrias, "This Is Our Country," 17–19; Ross Lambertson, "The Dresden Story": Racism, Human Rights, and the Jewish Labour Committee of Canada," *Labour/Le Travail* 47 (2001): 43–82.

68. Clément, *Canada's Rights Revolution*, 51–53 and 75–78.

69. Edward Said, *Humanism and Democratic Criticism* (New York: Columbia University Press, 2004), 136.

70. Miron, *A History of Human Rights in Canada*, 2–3.

71. Notably Samuel Moyn and Mark Mazower.

72. Moyn, *The Last Utopia*, 12. See also Bonny Ibhawoh's essay in this volume, pp. 59–87.

Chapter 1

◦◆◦

Decoding the Rights Revolution:
Lessons from the Canadian Experience

James W. St. G. Walker

In 1999 political scientist Neil Stammers lamented the fact that so few historians were engaged in the study of human rights. He forcefully argued the need for "detailed and specific historical research" which "is notable only by its absence." This absence resulted, Stammers continued, "in the analytical inadequacies of the dominant discourses on human rights," generated by legal scholars and philosophers who ignore context and agency.[1] Disappointed at the apparently poor response to his appeal, Stammers was still complaining a decade later about "the absence of history as a discipline," because historical analysis could investigate how human rights emerge and demonstrate the role of social movements in their development. "The significant involvement of historians in the field of human rights could sensitise scholars from other disciplines to the importance of such issues."[2]

While it is true that historians came to this field rather late, the dearth that concerned Stammers is finally being addressed. In November 2011 the University of Toronto held a workshop on "Rethinking Human Rights." It was intended as a debate between Lynn Hunt and Samuel Moyn, but illness kept Hunt from attending so her position was represented by Andrew Jainskill of Queen's University.[3] The debate among the platform participants, and the audience, was lucid and informed, revealing that there is currently an abundance of historical interpretation confronting issues related to human rights. That there is little agreement among scholars is testimony to the complexity of those issues and the subjectivity imposed by an inherently debatable idiom.

This chapter begins with a brief examination of some of the recent historical writings on international human rights, seeking in particular their answer to the question "Where do human rights come from?", and assessing their contribution to our understanding of how human rights develop. The chapter will then turn to the Canadian experience with human rights, primarily since the Second World War, paying attention to the transition from traditional English rights to the universal rhetoric of human rights. The intention is to test the answers found in the current literature against events "on the ground" in Canada. Can a piece of local research contribute to a broader understanding of how human rights have emerged? Has there been a Canadian "rights revolution" and, if so, how do we account for it? Finally, the chapter will offer some reflections on any lessons suggested by this examination. Do origins even matter? Is there a DNA code for human rights that can be discovered through historical research?

READING THE RIGHTS REVOLUTION

A Question of Origins: Recent Literature

Perhaps the most significant Big Question agitating the current literature is "when": When did human rights appear on the scene and how did they develop thereafter? It is "origins" that seem to attract the historical mind as it launches a relatively new endeavour. One view, firmly in place in the most substantial textbook in the field, is Paul Gordon Lauren's explanation that human rights evolved over the centuries, in a linear and incremental progression.[4] His method, as Reza Afshari puts it, was to cast "a searching light around the world and throughout history to locate those who, driven by compassion, altruism, and pity, have objected to injustice and exploitation. He refers to them all as human rights visionaries."[5] The world's great religions and civilizations play an initiating role, but the mainstream follows a channel already familiar from "rights of man" scholarship: from the Stoics and other classical sages, through Thomas Aquinas, John Locke, the English Bill of Rights, the American and French Revolutions and abolitionism, to the Universal Declaration and beyond. There is a cumulative inevitability to Lauren's account, with properties that could be termed organic (human rights grow from a seed planted at some decisive moment[s] in the past), and genealogical (passing from one great mind to another, elaborating en route). In an earlier analysis, written while the Covenants were still under consideration, Evan Luard proffered much the same list of stages through which international human rights have evolved.[6]

Lynn Hunt wants us to understand that our modern conception of human rights originates in the eighteenth-century Enlightenment, being "incarnated" in the French Revolution. The population was prepared through an expansion of "empathy" earlier in the century, promulgated in particular through the reading of epistolary novels that encouraged an ability to identify with other human beings. Once planted, human rights followed "an inner logic," an inevitable development that, after a gap in the nineteenth century, "crystallized" in the Universal Declaration. En route the French ideas inspired others; for example in Haiti they "ineluctably galvanized the free men of color and slaves themselves to make new demands and fight fiercely for them."[7] At the Toronto Workshop, Andrew Jainskill, representing Hunt's interpretation, referred to the "bulldozer effect" of human rights following the Revolution, operating like "a runaway train."[8]

This triumphalist version of the history of human rights is eschewed emphatically by Samuel Moyn. Moyn launches his argument with a disparagement of the historiography that has engaged in a "quixotic search for deep roots" of contemporary human rights. Only very recently have historians, or philosophers for that matter, sought to trace a consistent trajectory for human rights to the ancient Greeks or Jews, to medieval Christians or Enlightenment scholars or eighteenth-century revolutionaries. He even dismisses the impact of the Second World War and the Holocaust, popularly assumed, with considerable academic support, to have produced a reaction that led to the adoption of the Universal Declaration in 1948. The Declaration, he contends, was "dead at birth," neither representing nor inspiring any genuine human rights activity. Instead Moyn argues that during the 1970s other utopian visions—communism, nationalism, anti-colonialism, popular revolution—either self-destructed or were discredited, leaving human rights as the only available ideology. Human rights did not triumph; they simply survived when other visions failed. Moyn amasses considerable evidence to demonstrate a blossoming of human rights interest in certain quarters in the late 1970s, culminating in what he calls the "breakthrough year" of 1977. He discovers that a "true" commitment to human rights, that is, "supranational governance through law," appeared just over three decades ago, whereby entitlements were disconnected finally from their former "umbilical cord" to nation-states.[9]

Moyn is not the first or only scholar to recognize discontinuity in the history of rights, or to identify a more recent origin than Hunt or Lauren would accept. Mark Mazower rejects evolutionary progression, maintaining that human rights are "little more than half a century old," and he dismisses the "Eleanor" versus "Hitler" hypotheses that seek to explain the postwar appearance of human rights as either the product of vision-ary individuals (e.g., Eleanor Roosevelt) or revulsion at Nazi wickedness (personified in Adolf Hitler). Mazower concludes that Great Power in-terests favoured a declaration of human rights but not an effective re-gime, partly to avoid any complicating adoption of minority rights as had happened under the League of Nations.[10] For Elizabeth Borgwardt, it was the Atlantic Charter that "marked a defining, inaugural moment for what we now know as the modern doctrine of human rights."[11] Roland Burke's search for "the key point of origin for the human rights agenda" leads him to the role of what we now call the global South in setting and then implementing the human rights system adopted by the United Nations especially in the 1960s, ironic in the sense that the standards they designed were in direct contradiction to the authoritarian regimes that dominated much of the "Third World" at about the same time. In any case, "The struggle against colonialism had set the legal contours for a much more universalist program than might otherwise have emerged."[12] Several of the articles in Stefan-Ludwig Hoffmann's recent collection, in-cluding his own introduction, identify different points of departure for the spread of human rights ideology and instruments. Looking primarily at Europe, Mikael Rask Madsen defies conventional wisdom by confirm-ing "the paramount importance of Cold War politics on the development of human rights"; he means development in the sense of expansion.[13] And writing before any of these, Michael Ignatieff acknowledges the de-scent of human rights from the tradition of natural law but recognizes a fundamental revolution in the wake of the Second World War. It was in the context of the Holocaust, he writes, that human rights emerged. "Without the Holocaust, then, no [Universal] Declaration," he concludes; it was "the Ground Zero, or the starting point, for postwar human rights." Henceforth human rights became a self-directing agency, "embedding it-self in the soil" of cultures around the world. Emanating from this defin-ing moment were colonial revolutions and civil rights movements, and everywhere it gave "ordinary human beings the capacity to recognize evil when they see it, as well as the authority to denounce and oppose it."[14]

Despite radical differences in their interpretations, it would seem that all the historians under examination are in quest of a DNA-like code to explain either an abrupt revolutionary origin for human rights or a gradual accumulation. They all agree that human rights appear in time and are not the creation of a metaphysical agent such as God or nature, that an understanding of origins helps to explain their later development, and that rights consciousness has become a notable feature and power-ful force in contemporary life. But to complicate their differences further, they do not all seem to mean the same thing by "human rights." "The language of human rights is fluid," Kenneth Cmiel has reminded us. "The term has meant widely different things at different points in time. . . . [It] can mean diametrically opposed things."[15] Or as Morton Winston puts it colourfully, the term "human rights" is a "collective noun covering a number of distinct sorts of things, rather like the term 'furniture.'"[16]

A Matter of Definitions

Lauren's inclusive understanding of human rights allows him to place everything related to justice or social progress into a historical trajectory leading to the present. It is undeniable that the motifs currently found in human rights doctrine can be recognized in virtually every religion and civilization in world history. The Ten Commandments, like their coun-terparts in other religions, *imply* certain rights, but they directly articu-late a set of duties. Human dignity, justice, and fellowship may provide a universal cultural receptivity to the idea that there are fundamental rights, but they are not in themselves conceptualizations of human rights. Furthermore those same religious traditions contained elements antithetical to the current understanding of human rights, slavery and a subordinate position for women prominent among them. The cam-paigners for the abolition of the slave trade and slavery, and for reform in King Leopold's Congo, certainly expressed a deep empathy for the suf-fering of others, and they recognized the humanity of the victims of the wrongs they were trying to correct. "Am I not a man and a brother?" was no doubt a major conceptual breakthrough, but the abolitionists and re-formers did not call for an equality of *rights* such as would be considered fundamental to human rights today.[17]

Hunt does provide a much more specific description of what she considers essential in the definition of human rights. In a word, it is universality. She makes an abrupt distinction between the "ancient rights and liberties" derived from English experience and preserved for Englishmen in the 1689 Bill of Rights, and the framing of rights as uni-versal in the American and French Declarations. "Sometime between 1689 and 1776 rights that had been viewed most often as the rights of particular people . . . were transformed into human rights, universal natural rights."[18] But even Hunt's own evidence suggests that this distinction is not as meaningful as she intends. In the first place, the *application* of local and universal rights was almost identical, as indeed was their content: security of person, security of property, impartial justice, the right to participate in government. And so were the limitations, again noting in particular the position of women and the continuation of slavery, the latter supported by the claim of a right to property ownership. Whatever the French Revolution accomplished in these areas did not survive. Rather than being a complete abandonment of existing patterns, universality was the theory on which a claim to particularistic or citizenship rights could be made. The purpose behind the universal idiom is illustrated in the Americans' demand in the mid-1760s for their rights as British subjects. As they moved toward independence, universal rights gave a better rationale; they could hardly rely on "British rights" if they were rejecting British jurisdiction. The shift between the 1760s and 1770s was entirely practical: the American Founders were employing these rights, claiming them for themselves, not just proclaiming their existence. Similarly the French could not invoke a tradition of domestic rights; as the Americans substituted one rationalization for another, the French had to appeal beyond their national experience to justify their claim to certain rights.[19] Hunt's "transformation" seems to have been strategic and linguistic. As Aristotle reportedly advised, "If the written law tells against our case, clearly we must appeal to the universal law."[20]

Moyn is even more adamant in drawing a sharp distinction between domestic and universal rights. Indeed, his very definition depends on this division, as he locates the breakthrough to "true" human rights in "supranational governance through law" and a break with national governments. He quotes Malcolm X approvingly: "Civil rights means you're asking Uncle Sam to treat you right. Human rights are something you were born with." Apart from the metaphysical inclination in Malcolm's statement, the rights being claimed by the civil and human rights advocates were identical, as W.E.B. DuBois understood in his 1947 *Appeal to the World*. It is the foundation for the claim that differs.[21] Virtually all of the rights listed in the Universal Declaration, the Covenants, the many treaties and conventions, depend on a national government to put them into effect. Even "Responsibility to Protect" (R2P), arguably the most universalist enforcement mechanism to emerge since 1948, recognizes that it is the responsibility of nation-states to protect the rights of their citizens.[22] NGOs will campaign for an international standard and then use it to achieve a domestic reform through the apparatus of a nation-state, at which point it can be implemented. Apparently Moyn's distinction is more theoretical than real. Furthermore, even if the "universal" peaked in 1977 as he contends, at that very time "on the ground" atrocities proliferated in places such as Uganda, Cambodia, Ethiopia, and East Timor. From that perspective Roland Burke, who would have been writing at about the same time as Moyn, proposes that "1977 probably marked the nadir of the human rights program."[23] While Chile could serve as a target inspiring international denunciations, Pinochet remained in power from 1973 to 1989. Steven Pinker notwithstanding, gross violations continue to be perpetrated long after the "breakthrough."[24]

Is it possible then that the international human rights revolution has simply been a rhetorical splurge? In the French Revolution, in the Second World War, and in the 1970s, following the authors discussed above, we witness the emergence of a new language, a particular vocabulary of human rights, and it is the evolution of this new language that is being described in the literature.[25] A powerful discourse emerged from the Second World War (and the other tributaries identified in the literature), one that was employed strategically by activists for colonial independence, domestic civil rights, and international human rights instruments. The process of using currently available discourse to counter oppression has a long—and universal?—history. The Haitians Lynn Hunt refers to as having been "galvanized" by the Revolution "to make new demands" and to "fight" for their freedom did not learn that they were oppressed from the French Declaration, nor did it inspire them to act: the language ensuing from the Assembly discussions gave the Haitians an idiom in which to frame their demands as rights claims. A similar process is visible in 1689, when English reformers appealed to an English tradition to entrench their rights claims, an appeal that could resonate with their leaders and with the population generally. The Americans began their protest with this same strategy in the 1760s. In this respect Burke, who sees the anti-colonialists as using the language of human rights "as a weapon" to gain acceptability for self-determination, is more convincing than Ignatieff, who sees human rights as a motivating force in the anti-colonial movement.[26] What we can discern from the secondary literature is that the language of human rights is a utilitarian device, not a description of reality or even a program for reform. This does not render the "revolution" meaningless. In fact it could inject greater meaning into the changes that have taken place with the understanding that international proclamations and universal appeals must be picked up and used by activists on the ground.

Quentin Skinner has persuasively demonstrated that words change their meaning over time, and new terms come into usage to capture new meanings. Skinner also accepts the notion that certain *concepts* can have histories that extend beyond the terms that are used to express them. Human rights is just such a concept; as a linguistic entity our current expression of human rights came into effect about the Second World War, with some scattered usages apparent earlier in the century. The concepts captured by the term have a much longer history. We cannot today step outside the stream of history and offer a permanent and neutral definition of human rights. Words, Skinner argues, are "the wrong unit of analysis altogether."[27] The meaning is in how they are used.

ON THE GROUND": THE CANADIAN EXPERIENCE

The Canadian society entering the Second World War was exclusive and restrictive toward many people on grounds of "race." Canada's borders were closed to a range of prospective immigrants because of their alleged inability to assimilate, determined by their "racial" character. Employment discrimination was rife, it was legally admissible to discriminate in providing a service or accommodation, residential segregation was widespread, even the vote was denied to some Canadians due to their "race." Seventy years later much of that has changed. We have a Charter of Rights and Freedoms proclaiming racial equality, a Multiculturalism Act whose purpose is to promote that equality, provincial human rights codes and commissions to enforce it. Actions that once bore the stamp of morality and legality now require apology and redress. This has all the appearance of a revolution in our public policies and our cultural codes.

This section will assess this "revolution" in light of the literature discussed in the previous section, to see if we can determine where the impulse for rights-expansion was coming from, how the claimants defined the rights they were seeking, and why it should matter to us. It will do so through an examination of some "telling events"[28] in the Canadian history of human rights, organized in three generally chronological movements, each of which sought what was understood at the time to constitute equal rights. It will be argued that the Canadian experience offers not just an example of *what* happened, but lessons on *how* things happened. Although the narrative follows the efforts of racialized minorities to overcome disadvantageous relationships with their neighbours and their governments, related scholarship suggests that the events described here are consistent with the experience of other Canadian groups who perceived disadvantage and campaigned for the establishment of a right.[29]

As was seen in the international literature, the Second World War and the Holocaust also feature in explanations for domestic developments in Canada: Nazi atrocities led to the Universal Declaration, which in turn led UN members to bring their own legislation into line with their international commitments. For example William Schabas writes that the Declaration "compelled parliament to examine the issue of domestic implementation which led eventually to enactment of the Canadian Bill of Rights in 1960. The inadequacies of that legislation propelled legislators to prepare the Canadian Charter of Rights and Freedoms."[30] Even some human rights activists attribute the changes in Canada to the "compulsion" emanating from the Universal Declaration.[31] There is a liability in this line of reasoning, for it can subordinate Canadian agency in initiating Canadian human rights reforms, or assign that agency to courts and governments. Some legal analyses tend to lay out changes in the law without mentioning the background circumstances or public campaigns for the reforms in question, with chapter titles such as "The Rise and Spread of Anti-Discrimination Legislation."[32] These accounts do not match the historical record in at least two respects. First, there is a long pre-war history of attempts to overcome racial disadvantage, and there was nothing sudden or automatic about the reforms that were introduced after 1945. They were products of organized and sustained campaigns, contradicting any notion of a "paradigm shift" emerging out of the ashes of Auschwitz. Secondly, governments and courts have typically been quite reluctant to implement reforms and have retarded rather than advanced the "rights revolution."

Claiming Equality

As examples of the longevity of the demand for equality, one could cite the Black Loyalists who petitioned their governors in Nova Scotia in the 1780s, and eventually King George himself, complaining that they were not receiving the same treatment and rewards as other Loyalists. Insisting that "We are Britishers and we have the law and constitution of our glorious Empire to support us, and our rights we claim and our rights we will demand," their descendants in nineteenth-century Nova Scotia petitioned successfully for the franchise, and then used their votes strategically to gain support for their children's right to an education.[33] Legal challenges were also adopted to overcome racial boundaries. Mr. William Franklin, a black man ejected from a London, Ontario restaurant in 1923, sued the proprietors "for the establishment of what I believe to be a right as a Canadian citizen. I am not fighting to soothe my own injured feelings. I am taking this stand for the benefit of all peoples of color, for generations of colored children yet unborn. I want to prove to all the world that the majesty of the British law will brook no prejudice."[34] The most celebrated case occurred in 1936, when Mr. Fred Christie was refused service in a Montreal tavern. His community supporters declared that they were "firmly convinced that the Supreme Court of Canada will not uphold this malicious principle of racial discrimination, which is certainly contrary to British principles and traditions." Montreal's black newspaper agreed: "Unless we are prepared to fight for equal treatment under the law of the land, we ought not and will not be regarded or treated as responsible citizens." The fight was carried eventually to the Supreme Court of Canada, whose decision came down in December 1939. "Any merchant is free to deal as he may choose with any individual member of the public," Justice Rinfret wrote. "The only restriction to this general principle would be the existence of a specific law, or . . . the adoption of a rule contrary to good morals or public order."[35] The Court did not consider racial discrimination to be contrary to good morals or public order in 1939; like William Franklin, Fred Christie lost his case, indicating that it was the judiciary and not the disadvantaged group that needed to be taught how to recognize evil when they saw it.

Chinese Canadians, similarly, used the petition, the lawsuit, labour activism, and occasionally the boycott, to confront discriminatory taxation and other laws beginning in the 1880s. The Chinese community concentrated their reforming efforts on occupational restrictions and the immigration laws that excluded their family members from Canada. When the Saskatchewan legislature passed a law in 1912 making it illegal for Chinese men to employ white women, Moose Jaw restaurateur Quong Wing challenged the law in court, arguing that under the

Naturalization Act he was "entitled to all political and other rights, powers and privileges to which a natural-born British subject is entitled." But the courts, including the Supreme Court of Canada, decided that the restriction was constitutionally valid.[36] For Japanese Canadians the franchise became the special issue: petitions, delegations to Victoria and Ottawa, and a lawsuit to the Privy Council, were all utilized before the Second World War, unsuccessfully, in the effort to win the right to vote.[37]

South Asians also faced immigration and franchise restrictions. In March 1907 the British Columbia legislature unanimously passed a bill to exclude "Hindus" from the provincial franchise, and a 1908 federal order-in-council gave cabinet authority to reject immigrants who arrived other than by a continuous journey from their country of origin. This amounted to exclusion, for in 1908 there was no means to make such a journey between India and Canada. Omission from the provincial voters' list automatically meant federal disfranchisement and disqualification from many jobs, contracts, and licences as well as civil duties such as jury service. It was profoundly symbolic of the fact that persons from India (and China and Japan) and their Canadian-born descendants did not belong and were not to participate in Canadian democracy. An organization known as the Khalsa Diwan Society was founded in Vancouver in 1908 to confront these disabilities.[38]

The original tactic adopted in their campaign for equality was to appeal to "the Home Government" in London using petitions and personal delegations, basing their claim on their "birthright as British subjects" and "British fair play." They even claimed that the separation of families caused by immigration rules was immoral and a violation of their "natural human rights." When London failed to respond, appeals were made to Ottawa and to the Canadian public. Under the leadership of Dr. Sundar Singh and with the imprint of the "Canada India Committee," speakers went across the country to arouse church and community groups to support their demands with resolutions and letters to Members of Parliament. South Asians also published newspapers, in both English and Punjabi, to inform Canadians and people in India of their problems, winning supportive resolutions from the Indian National Congress in 1914 and 1915, the latter moved by Mohandas K. Gandhi. At Imperial Conferences beginning in 1917 and extending into the 1940s, Indian representatives brought pressure on Canadian and British delegations to remove the unequal disqualifications from South Asians in Canada.[39]

During the so-called Riot at Christie Pits in Toronto in 1933, one Jewish participant told a *Toronto Star* reporter: "These boys are all British. They have been brought up in Canadian schools, and have learned something of the British bulldog idea never to give up without a fight." And the League for the Defence of Jewish Rights, commenting on that same episode, said in a formal statement "Toronto cannot afford to act in the spirit which is contrary to the spirit and traditions of Great Britain. Hitlerism is subversive of Canadian ideals." This in 1933. In our post-colonial age it is easy to forget that Anglo-Canadian ideals *were* regarded as universal, and the British Empire as their vehicle. Also in the 1930s the Committee for Jewish–Gentile Relations published a pamphlet entitled "Facts and Fables About the Jews" which ended with the statement: "The British Empire and British democracy are based upon the principle of justice and toleration for all races and creeds. This is a principle to be cherished and preserved against the falsehoods of antisemitism."[40]

The Impact of the Second World War

Passionate appeals for equal rights as British subjects and for justice and fair play did not move either those in authority or the Canadian majority. A fundamental barrier was an almost universal belief that "races" were actual categories of humanity, each with its own qualities and faults. The notion that the law should accommodate these differences was not considered unreasonable. An associated barrier was the prevailing definition of individual rights. Traditional British rights included freedom of association and freedom of commerce, which could be interpreted as the right to refuse to associate with any class of person as neighbour, employee, or customer, and the right to free expression could mean the right to slander or threaten entire groups. These assumptions were "orienting notions" in Canadian culture at the time;[41] the "revolution" was not simply a matter of re-arranging public policy but of re-orienting the public mind.

It must be recognized that nothing happened suddenly or as an automatic consequence of the war. Initially, the military itself rejected volunteers on grounds of "race": the air force had a "whites-only" regulation until 1943, and the navy had a similar rule into 1944. Chinese and Japanese Canadians were openly excluded from all the armed services until 1944; confidential instructions were sent to army reception centres saying that South Asians should be summoned for the medical examination and then rejected as unfit for active service. There is a fascinating correspondence between Ottawa and Halifax, extending from September 1939 to May 1942, over how best to exclude African-Canadian volunteers from the army.[42] Nor did the uniform, once worn, mean equal treatment. Stan Grizzle of Toronto was put on permanent latrine-cleaning duty at Camp Borden when he refused to become batman to a white officer. He was reassigned only after he went on strike, demanding that the principles for which we were fighting must be applied to him.[43] Hugh Burnett of Dresden, Ontario, was refused service in every restaurant in his hometown, even though, as he put it, he was wearing "the king's uniform" at the time. In July 1943 he wrote a letter of complaint to Justice Minister Louis St. Laurent, fully expecting the restaurants would be required to admit him. But Mr. Burnett received a reply from the deputy minister stating that it would not be "fair" to force a merchant to serve just anyone who happened to come along.[44]

Legislatures and courts were no more likely to reflect a "war conscience" toward minorities. In March 1945, two months after the liberation of Auschwitz, the BC legislature rejected a CCF motion to enfranchise Asian Canadians.[45] That same month Justice Chevrier of Ontario lamented "the unchristian action of racial discrimination" and extended sympathy to the Jewish people for the atrocities "inflicted upon them by a satanic direction in this present war," yet he felt compelled, by his understanding of freedom of association, to uphold a property covenant that excluded Jews.[46] "Paradigm shift," apparently, is the wrong metaphor for what happened to rights-thinking during and immediately after the war, for that term implies a new way of seeing things. It might better be understood as a "sea change," that is a change in the environment or circumstances, to which the navigators could adjust their tactics. The war, in short, provided a new context, but direct action remained necessary.

There was in fact a perception that inequality and hostility actually increased during the war. Canadian Jews reported in May 1940 that anti-Semitism was on the rise, fuelled partly by a widespread assumption that Jews were shirking their responsibilities, and not volunteering for the Canadian forces.[47] In 1942 black and Jewish citizens complained that the National Selective Service (NSS) practised racial discrimination in assigning workers to wartime employment. The Canadian Jewish Congress mounted a systematic campaign to gather evidence, collecting sworn affidavits from Jews who had experienced discrimination by this government agency. And that evidence flowed in, overwhelmingly, as people related their heart-breaking encounters. Indignation resonates through the affidavits. In one typical statement a young woman protested: "I am a Canadian born British subject. I believe we are fighting a war at present to erase and prevent just such Nazi-ideas from becoming dominant in this country." The Jewish brief and public meetings in African-Canadian churches brought about a change in policy, and the NSS issued a statement that "discrimination impairs the war effort by preventing the most effective use of our total labour supply, and tends to defeat the democratic objectives for which we are fighting."[48] In 1944, following years of effort by the Canadian Jewish Congress (CJC), the Ontario legislature passed a Racial Discrimination Act to ban the public display of discriminatory signs and advertisements. With his minority government under intense pressure, Premier George Drew conceded that "If you discriminate against any person because of race or creed in respect to their ordinary rights as citizens, you deny that equality which is part and parcel of the very freedom we are fighting to preserve."[49]

The war was lending a moral base, and a publicly recognizable reference point, for campaigns against racial discrimination. South Asians, who were not aware of the secret instructions against their enlistment, held public meetings claiming that their war contribution entitled them to the right to vote.[50] When the federal government introduced a bill in 1944 to disfranchise Japanese Canadians who had been moved to other provinces where, until this time, they would have been entitled to vote, Liberal MP Arthur Roebuck denounced it as Nazi racism. "If you keep that up," he told the House of Commons, "it will not be long before Canada will be Hitlerized." MP Victor Quelch agreed: "It seems to me that this legislation is a negation of the principles contained in the Atlantic Charter."[51] The controversial measure did pass both Houses of Parliament, but the Canadian *public* was beginning to make the connection between racial discrimination and the wartime enemy. Letters and petitions from outraged citizens, church groups, and civil liberties organizations flowed to Ottawa, a dress rehearsal, as it were, for the widespread popular campaign by the Co-operative Committee on Japanese Canadians against the "deportation" of Japanese Canadians after the war. These events reveal that the rhetoric of a war fought for democracy could be a powerful tool, but it still required an organized and public campaign to accomplish a reform. As Stephanie Bangarth demonstrates, the Cooperative Committee employed the language of universal human rights from the Atlantic Charter and the UN Charter, given the absence of any suitable claims under the existing Canadian Constitution.[52] The universality of the new rhetoric had a certain tactical implication as well, or at least it lent itself to a revised tactic: that of broad coalitions of like-minded Canadians rather than complaints by victims of specific policies.

This does not mean that the Canadian agitators were motivated by the UN documents, for their activities began before those documents were formulated. Rather, these episodes are a reminder that rights activists were employing any available precedents, moral or legal declarations, or external examples that could support their claims. Universal rights were grasped as an opportunity to accomplish a domestic goal. In doing so, the Cooperative Committee effectively imported human rights rhetoric as a compensation for the denial of the rights of Japanese Canadians as British subjects. Canadian Jewry, too, adopted the idiom of human rights with enthusiasm. Delegates from the CJC attended the United Nations founding convention in San Francisco in 1945, attached to a delegation from the American Jewish Congress. In advance they submitted a brief to the federal government outlining their major concerns and objectives for the postwar world, foremost an International Bill of Rights that would guarantee "basic human rights," "full and complete protection of life and liberty," and "unequivocal equality of rights in law." The suddenness of the shift in language can be illustrated by two CJC briefs calling for action against employment discrimination. In the 1942 brief the case was made on grounds of British justice, fair play, economic self-interest, and wartime national unity. A brief in 1947, making virtually identical demands, justified its claim with reference to the human rights provisions in the United Nations Charter.[53]

The Committee for the Repeal of the Chinese Immigration Act neatly illustrates how the new environment was utilized by reformers. It was decidedly a broad coalition of Canadians from different backgrounds, religions, ethnicities, and regions. Their appeals to the government and to public opinion made a number of points that can be attributed to the wartime and postwar context. China was a gallant ally in the war; Chinese Canadians had participated in the Canadian war effort, sending over five hundred soldiers to active duty and subscribing to Victory bonds in the highest proportion of any Canadian community; Canada's war aims of freedom and democracy were violated by exclusion of immigrants on grounds of "race"; the new Citizenship Bill affirmed the equality of all Canadian citizens; and Canada's obligations under the UN Charter required the elimination of racist laws. Appeals of this kind, and the tremendous public support they generated, effected the repeal of the Chinese Immigration Act in 1947.[54]

In British Columbia in the same period South Asian and Chinese Canadians undertook a joint approach to the provincial legislature, where their appeals for equality stressed Canadian rather than British rights. By 1945 the United Nations' commitment to human rights and racial equality offered heavy ammunition to support the claim for equal participation in Canadian democracy. A committee of the legislature, conducting hearings in October and November 1946, received delegations from Indian- and Chinese-diaspora leaders, the Canadian Legion, churches, civil liberties groups, the United Nations Association and professional bodies challenging the voting regulations on grounds of human rights. Meanwhile the national conversation on the Canadian Citizenship Act during 1946 (proclaimed January 1, 1947) promoted the ideal of equal citizenship for all Canadians and drew the editorial comment that continued denial of the franchise would "sabotage" the new Act. The BC committee recommended unanimously that the legislature enfranchise Canadians of both Chinese and Indian origin, and this was accepted without dissent by the legislature on April 2, 1947.[55]

Defining Problems and Solutions:
From Protection to Remedial Programs

With the racial restriction eliminated from the franchise, and the most egregious example of immigration restriction repealed, the campaign for equality could be deemed a success.[56] Yet "the problem" as perceived by Canadian minorities had not been solved. *Private* discrimination remained untouched. Canadians could still be excluded from employment, services, accommodation, and property ownership because of "race," and these discriminatory individual practices were not only legal but could be enforced through the courts. This provoked a new set of questions concerning how to restrict discriminatory behaviour without violating individual rights. For this to succeed a different perspective on the notion of citizens' rights was necessary. Reinterpretation was facilitated by a postwar theory that racism was a pathological condition, practised by maladjusted individuals whose behaviour, on the one hand, was protected by traditional individual freedoms, and on the other hand set a negative standard for the behaviour of the rest of the majority population. By restricting the discriminatory actions of the pathological individuals, therefore, an immediate problem would be eliminated and a new environment created in which racism was unacceptable and even illegal.

The postwar campaign for protective legislation has been described in detail.[57] In Ontario, utilizing the discriminatory conditions that were brought into public awareness by Hugh Burnett and his National Unity Association of Chatham, Dresden, and North Buxton, a dynamic coalition led by the Jewish Labour Committee, the Canadian Jewish Congress, and the Association for Civil Liberties succeeded in convincing the government of Premier Leslie Frost to introduce Canada's first fair practices laws in the early 1950s. Although a change in the law was the ostensible goal of the campaign, the real target was the Ontario voter, and the challenge was to redefine, indeed to reverse, the prevailing concept of individual rights, to focus upon the excluded community as the bearer of the right to equality rather than upon the perpetrators of discrimination and their "rights" to exclude or malign their fellow citizens. It is clear that the Ontario cabinet was moved not by the arguments of the campaigners but by the support they garnered in the general population.[58] Mr. Frost was careful not to admit that racial boundaries actually existed in Ontario, explaining that an absence of protective legislation could be misinterpreted as *false* evidence of the existence of discrimination.[59] It is interesting to note that he cited the Universal Declaration as justification for the Fair Employment Practices Act in 1951, ignoring several years of coalition campaigning after the Declaration was endorsed. And while he explicitly rejected the inclusion of public accommodations when requested by Hugh Burnett in 1951,[60] after three more years of public agitation by the coalition Mr. Frost could discover justification for the Fair Accommodations Practices Act in the Universal Declaration as well. His own hard-line Conservative supporters could accept an international obligation more readily than a capitulation to a successful political movement.

While it is true that legislation protecting the victims of discrimination would become "common sense" across Canada during the next decade, it is certainly not the case that the Ontario formula simply "spread" from one provincial government to another. In Nova Scotia, for example, disillusionment with the law as it existed was prompted by the case of Viola Desmond, an African Canadian who was jailed and fined for sitting in a whites-only section of a New Glasgow cinema.[61] When provincial courts upheld her conviction in 1947, the Nova Scotia Association for the Advancement of Coloured People (NSAACP) joined a coalition movement with labour, church, and other groups to demand fair practices legislation. It was 1955 (Employment) and 1959 (Accommodations) before the province had its own Fair Practices Acts. Similar campaigns were held in other provinces; the initiative, repeatedly, came from concerned groups of citizens.

Once again the problem as defined could be considered solved. And, once again, Canadian minorities discovered that *their* problem continued. Some further refinement was required, some new conceptualization capable of addressing their perceived disadvantages. The African-Canadian population of Halifax, to continue this example, remained severely deprived with respect to employment, income, housing, and education, as revealed in a 1962 study.[62] The very boundaries that had been on the NSAACP agenda, that were supposed to be breached by legislation preventing discrimination, were described as deep-seated, and progress as distressingly slow. The legislative reforms of the 1950s and 1960s had not saved Africville from destruction, and had created no jobs, schools, or homes for African Canadians in Nova Scotia. Some community members, with some Dalhousie University students, began to reconsider the tactics they had been following for the past twenty years. Instead of fighting instances of discrimination case by case, they thought they should confront the underlying syndrome that seemed to generate another case every time one was solved. What was novel about this approach was that it identified the problem as "systemic," as the responsibility not just of a few overt racists but of society as a whole. The proposed solution was broad intervention in the economy and in society, to interrupt the self-perpetuating syndrome of racially defined boundaries. Black youth leader B.A. "Rocky" Jones demanded *affirmative* action, to give black initiatives a chance of success. The presence in Nova Scotia of Black Panthers from the United States lent a sense of urgency to the situation in the 1960s.[63]

One of those local initiatives was a special educational program for black school dropouts, using volunteer teachers and the facilities of the Dalhousie Student Union. After much community, student, and faculty lobbying, in 1970 the university officially adopted the program and its volunteer teachers as the Transition Year Program (TYP), the first such operation in Canada, admitting both African-Canadian and Mi'kmaq students for an intensive year of pre-university training. The TYP launched an experiment in affirmative action that was intended to break the vicious circle of poor education and restricted opportunity, and to produce a generation of young people better prepared to analyze and communicate the needs of their community. Since its inception about a thousand students have passed through the program, who now form a cadre of educated local black and Aboriginal leadership in the province.[64] This development occurred at the community level, before lawyers, courts, and governments recognized the concepts of systemic racism and affirmative action.

Though considered radical in the 1960s, the remedial approach became acceptable following the apparent failure of existing legislation to prevent a perceived "race crisis" in the second half of the 1970s. The problem had been revealed, quite simply, as far too widespread to be blamed exclusively on a few "rotten apples." A public outcry prompted a series of studies sponsored by governments and concerned associations, leading to an appreciation that new instruments were necessary to address systemic inequality.[65] Jennifer Tunnicliffe offers a detailed description of the Ontario Human Rights Commission's consequent review of the Ontario Human Rights Code, and of the extensive public consultation that accompanied it. The revised Code of 1981 adopted the conceptual orientation of pro-action and positive intervention, and the focus shifted away from the discriminator to the citizen's right to equality. The correction of unequal conditions, rather than punishment of offenders, became the human rights theme.[66] The 1982 Charter of Rights and Freedoms, and particularly the keystone section 15 on equality rights, was the federal government's commitment to the remedial concept.[67] Subsequent elaborations include the Employment Equity Act of 1986 and the Multiculturalism Act and the Japanese-Canadian Redress Settlement, both in 1988.[68] The Supreme Court of Canada offered its blessing when Justice William McIntyre wrote: "The promotion of equality entails the promotion of a society in which all are secure in the knowledge that they are recognized at law as human beings equally deserving of concern, and consideration. It has a large remedial component."[69]

And yet, once more . . . Thirty-plus years after the adoption of remedial action, it is obvious that essential problems are not being adequately addressed. Census data continue to indicate that "visible minorities," and especially African Canadians, have consistently lower than average incomes and higher levels of unemployment, even when qualifications, experience, and regional factors are considered. "Tests" conducted by citizen groups have suggested that racial discrimination must be considered among the reasons for these discrepancies. Housing discrimination, especially in rental accommodation, is far from eliminated. Racial profiling by police and other government officials is reportedly quite common. Statistics Canada reports an increase in "hate crimes," the highest number since they began collecting figures in 2005. Polls reveal that a majority of "visible" Canadians believe they have experienced racial discrimination or have witnessed a racist incident. Research by the Maytree Foundation and the Toronto City Summit Alliance shows that racialized minorities are seriously under-represented among leadership roles in every segment of the public and private sectors. A new analysis of the Ethnic Diversity Survey of over forty thousand people offered evidence that racial discrimination persists in applying for jobs, at work, in stores, banks, and restaurants, and that young black males are the most stigmatized group. Discouraging studies by the Toronto Board of Education showed that black school children were streamed into "basic" courses at a rate more than double that for white children and had a considerably higher drop-out rate.[70] New responses are being implemented, most dramatically the launching of an Africentric school in Toronto.[71]

REFLECTIONS

Has there been *a* rights revolution in Canada? Have there been, rather, three distinct revolutions, one for equal citizenship, one for protective legislation, and one for remedial programs? Certainly each represented a dramatically new way of seeing things and brought public policies with quite different approaches to the problem of inequality as it was then perceived. And even if the policies all turned out to be less than total solutions, the activists promoting them *believed* that the achievement of their immediate goal would lead to equal rights. Although the three movements discussed in this chapter were not designed as incremental stages in a grander plan, there was a cumulative impact on the Canadian people, their attitudes, and their behaviours. The political and legal format adopted for so many campaigns can imply that changes in the law were all that were demanded or necessary, but closer examination shows that effective reform meant first a conversion of the public mind and a reconceptualization of terms like *right*, *fair*, and *justice*. Certain groups were left out, and they wanted to be in, to belong, to be considered "normal" regardless of cultural or physiological differences. And inclusion cut both ways. When some people or some cultural characteristic became "normal," it required adjustment from the entire society, including its institutions; they participated in the creation of a new civic culture and civic structure. It seems most satisfactory to regard the events of the past half-century as a continuing revolution, affecting how people live their lives, how they relate to other members of their society, how they interpret their role as Canadian citizens, and their dignity as human beings. This is one conclusion derived from its historical analysis, and it suggests that the current situation, while still far from satisfactory, is not a final product but a moment in an ongoing process. That Canadians continue to grope for a solution is evidence that a problem has been recognized, and this is in itself a revolutionary development.

Rights, after all, have never been a fixed entity. In the English tradition, a right is defined as "a justifiable claim, on legal or moral grounds, to have or obtain something, or to act in a certain way."[72] In other words a right is an entitlement, and it has both legal and ethical connotations. Such entitlements have been part of human relationships throughout history, creating or recognizing distinctions among persons and setting standards for appropriate behaviour depending on one's level in the social order. *Human* rights, however else they might be defined, are entitlements eligible to be claimed by everyone; they are inclusive. Rights discourse enables an individual to make a claim as a rights-bearer, something far more powerful, and ultimately more dignified, than sympathy or charity. Framing the relationship in this way changes its nature, for rights are about relationships; they carry corresponding obligations. They measure the way we treat others as well as the treatment we claim for ourselves; they are social instruments, reciprocal, a process. Even when entrenched in the law, rights are values and as such are an expression of our culture. Like every other cultural component, they are not static or "discovered" but dynamic, generated over time in historical circumstances. Notice that the Supreme Court of Canada pronounced in 1939 that racial discrimination was not immoral. That morality has changed. New ways of seeing things prompt new impressions of what is wrong, opening space for the demand of a new right. It was the task of the rights activists to produce that new outlook, to revise conceptions of the problem and how it could be overcome. Most of the literature on rights, including the titles discussed earlier in this chapter, distinguish civil rights from human rights. Civil rights are those entitlements enjoyed by citizens of a given political entity; a human right is not restricted by membership in any nationality or group. But as the preceding narrative has shown, the actual rights involved were claimed under both labels depending on opportunity. The distinction is important theoretically, but on the ground the language could shift in both directions. And the embrace of citizenship rights has expanded; in Canada today, for example, they include employment insurance, health care, and numerous elements that would not have been considered "civil" rights a generation or two ago.

International, "universal" rights have undergone similar shifts, expansions, and reconfigurations. What was "self-evident" or "common sense" in one time or place was not always the same in another; pronouncements from New York or Geneva or Strasbourg may be given different meaning, or ignored altogether, depending on the receptive conditions in a given locality. To find that meaning, therefore, it is necessary to look to the local. Thomas Laqueur has written that the interpretation of human rights "depends on historically quite specific conditions of local political culture," and he is echoed by Kenneth Cmiel's warning to historians to "refuse to be tripped up by any universal/local divide" for we are "writing the local histories of universal claims." It is within local cultures and circumstances that the universal idiom becomes meaningful.[73] This may be the ultimate lesson from this examination of the Canadian experience. We learn to see ourselves as "a local example of the forms human life has locally taken, a case among cases, a world among worlds."[74]

The Canadian history of this phenomenon reveals the agency that has been behind our own rights revolution. We do not find a group of victims on the one hand and a group of fixers on the other. People who perceived a disadvantage sought to change the terms of an existing relationship through establishing their claim to equal treatment. Sometimes they were successful and sometimes they were not, and the degree of their success depended on a number of environmental or contextual factors. Even the urge to articulate dissatisfactions in terms of "rights" is context-based. Perhaps oppressed peoples always yearn for freedom, but they do not always demand a right to equality. Significantly, all the successful claims examined here were those that attracted allies from the mainstream population. The Second World War and its accompanying political, social, and economic changes provided an environment that was especially receptive to claims generated decades earlier by racialized minorities. Although the "Nazi atrocity" theory is unsustainable, the global settlement following the war did provide a universalist language to replace the "British justice" claims of previous generations, and it could be grasped along with the new language of Canadian citizenship as tools in the ongoing struggle for equality. External influences promoted the domestic transformation. The Indian independence movement, the role of China in the war, the African-American civil rights movement and the presence of Black Panthers in Nova Scotia all stimulated the aspiring Canadian minorities and the receptivity of the majority. Scientific innovations were casting doubts on the reality and meaning of "race," while colonial independence disproved the permanence of the racialized global hierarchy. Two of the supports for Canadian racial attitudes were being undermined. The local experience has necessarily to be approached through a transnational perspective. Context, both Canadian and international, has to be considered in assessing the success or failure of a bid for a change in prevailing relationships.

As historians, it seems, we have a challenge of our own, as Neil Stammers has insisted. For it is "the historian's task," to quote Quentin Skinner one last time, to understand "climates of opinion"; it is historians who analyze context and process.[75] Moments of significant advancements (or reversals) in human rights can be investigated as historical events on their own terms within their own circumstances, rather than as stages in a trajectory retroactively constructed. We have a responsibility to participate in and amend the dominant discourse, the one that has rights "appearing" or "spreading," or whose study begins with a text rather than with a political demand. This is potentially a highly significant contribution, because it can indicate not only how specific rights have arisen but what purpose they were intended to achieve and how further enhancements can be accomplished. This is the point in searching for "origins," even if the grand origin of so much of the international literature is chimerical. It is more helpful to speak of "beginnings," for it is a similar process being witnessed over and over again. Claiming precedents and traditional authority or universal principles for rights claims has been among the tools used to effect a desired reform; these utilitarian devices should not be confused with "causes." If there is a "DNA" it will be found in process, not in content, events, or ideologies, nor in lists or lexicons. From the Canadian experience it is clear that rights are the product of struggle, engaged by the groups who perceived the disadvantage. By acknowledging this we do more than pay tribute to the heroes who have built our human rights record: we identify the path by which human rights are created and maintained in our democratic society. Human rights policies are solutions to problems. How the problem is identified and articulated will shape the kind of solution that will be adopted. If the Canadian people believe that human rights are the surviving utopian vision by default; or firmly embedded in our civilization; or the product of an inexorable historical trajectory; or the gift of parliaments and leaders, of courts and international instruments, or even of the Almighty, we will be inclined to leave further developments in the capable hands of the relevant authorities. If, on the other hand, we understand that human rights are not a *gift* but a *prize*, and that it has been ordinary people like ourselves who launched most of our rights initiatives, we will be much more likely to remain alert to potential violations and to participate in the protection of our rights as Canadians and as human beings. The perspective that is taken will largely depend on how the history of human rights is presented.

NOTES

1.   Neil Stammers, "Social Movements and the Social Construction of Human Rights," *Human Rights Quarterly* 21 (1999): 989.

2.   Neil Stammers, *Human Rights and Social Movements* (London: Pluto Press, 2009), 12–14.

3.   "Rethinking Human Rights: Two Workshops," organized by the Centre for the Study of France and the Francophone World and sponsored by the Department of History, the Chair in Jewish History and the Faculty of Law, November 11, 2011. The morning session, "Human Rights in Historical Perspective: A Dialogue," was chaired by Michael Marrus, with Charles Walton as commentator.

4.   Paul Gordon Lauren, *The Evolution of International Human Rights: Visions Seen* (Philadelphia: University of Pennsylvania Press, 1998, 2003).

5.   Reza Afshari, "On Historiography of Human Rights: Reflections on Paul Gordon Lauren's *The Evolution of International Human Rights: Visions Seen*," *Human Rights Quarterly* 29 (2007): 2.

6.   Evan Luard, "The Origins of International Concern over Human Rights," in *The International Protection of Human Rights*, ed. Evan Luard (London: Thames and Hudson, 1967), 7–21.

7.   Lynn Hunt, *Inventing Human Rights: A History* (New York: W.W. Norton, 2007), 17, 35ff, 150, 166, 172, 176, 205.

8.   Opening comments, November 11, 2011.

9.   Samuel Moyn, *The Last Utopia: Human Rights in History* (Cambridge MA: Belknap Press, 2010), 5ff, 13, 38,44ff, 72,81, 129, 225, 311. In his opening remarks at the Toronto Workshop Moyn stated that the history of human rights had been "created *ex nihilo*" within little more than the past decade.

10.   Mark Mazower, "The Strange Triumph of Human Rights, 1933–1950," *The Historical Journal*

47, no. 2 (2004): 379–81, 387, 395–97.

11. Elizabeth Borgwardt, *A New Deal for the World. America's Vision for Human Rights* (Cambridge MA: Belknap Press, 2005), 4.

12. Roland Burke, *Decolonization and the Evolution of International Human Rights* (Philadelphia: University of Pennsylvania Press, 2010), 13–19, 34–36, 41, 55, 59, 69, 91, 121.

13. Stefan-Ludwig Hoffmann, "Genealogies of Human Rights," in *Human Rights in the Twentieth Century*, ed. Hoffman, 1–28 (Cambridge: Cambridge University Press, 2011); Mikael Rask Madsen, "'Legal Diplomacy'—Law, Politics and the Genesis of Postwar European Human Rights," 80.

14. Michael Ignatieff, *The Rights Revolution* (Toronto: House of Anansi, 2000), 43, 48–49; *Human Rights as Politics and Idolatry* (Princeton: Princeton University Press, 2001), 7, 81; *The Lesser Evil: Political Ethics in an Age of Terror* (Toronto: Penguin Canada, 2004), 44. Ignatieff is in good company, for there is a large literature presenting the Holocaust-origin argument. To take only one example, Johannes Morsink has provided an elaborate description of the articles in the Universal Declaration, linking each one to a specific atrocity committed by the Nazis between 1933 and 1945, in "World War Two and the Universal Declaration," *Human Rights Quarterly* 15 (1993): 357–405, and in his monumental *The Universal Declaration of Human Rights. Origins, Drafting, and Intent* (Philadelphia: University of Pennsylvania Press, 1999), Chap. 2, 36–91. This Holocaust-centric thesis is distinctly modified, if not refuted altogether, in G. Daniel Cohen, "The Holocaust and the 'Human Rights Revolution': A Reassessment," in *The Human Rights Revolution: An International History*, ed. Akira Iriye et al. (New York: Oxford University Press, 2012), 53–71.

15. Kenneth Cmiel, "The Recent History of Human Rights," *American Historical Review* 109, no. 1 (2004): 6. Cmiel has elsewhere argued that "the phrase 'human rights' can rally people to action around the world precisely because the term is not pressed into too definite a meaning, precisely because it does not need extensive context to be understood," "The Emergence of Human Rights Politics in the United States," *Journal of American History* 86, no. 3 (1999): 1249.

16. Morton Winston, "Human Rights as Moral Rebellion and Social Construction," *Journal of Human Rights* 6 (2007): 283.

17. Adam Hochschild argues that the British abolitionist campaign was history's first human rights movement, and next came the Congo Reform in the early twentieth century: *King Leopold's Ghost* (New York: Houghton Mifflin, 1999); *Bury the Chains: Prophets and Rebels in the Fight to Free an Empire's Slaves* (New York: Houghton Mifflin, 2005). Broadening her scope beyond the British movement, Jenny S. Martinez claims that "the nineteenth-century slavery abolition movement was the first successful international human rights campaign," *The Slave Trade and the Origins of International Human Rights Law* (New York: Oxford University Press, 2012), 13.

18. Hunt, *Inventing*, 21–22.

19. Ibid., Chap. 3.

20. Quoted in Alan Dershowitz, *Rights From Wrongs: A Secular Theory of the Origins of Rights* (New York: Basic Books, 2004), 89.

21. Moyn, *Last Utopia*, 12–13, 20, 38, 81, 101–6; W.E.B. DuBois, editorial supervisor, *An Appeal to the World: A Statement on the Denial of Human Rights to Minorities in the Case of Citizens of Negro Descent in the United States of America and an Appeal to the United Nations for Redress* (New York: National Association for the Advancement of Colored People, 1947).

22. *Report of the International Commission on State Sovereignty. The Responsibility to Protect* (Ottawa: International Development Research Centre, 2001). International intervention is authorized only when the state is "unwilling or unable" to protect its citizens.

23. Burke, *Decolonization*, 137.

24. Steven Pinker, *The Better Angels of Our Nature: Why Violence Has Declined* (New York: Viking, 2011).

25. Describing many of the same 1970s events as Moyn, Cmiel defines the "revolution" as one of communication, an explosion of information and images that became recognizable around the

world: "Emergence of Human Rights Politics," 1232–33.

26. Hunt, *Inventing*, 165, Burke, *Decolonization*, 34–36, Ignatieff, *Politics and Idolatry*, 6. Bonny Ibhawoh shows that the "weapon" of rights discourse could be used both ways: "Stronger than the Maxim Gun: Law, Human Rights and British Colonial Hegemony in Nigeria," *Africa* 72, no. 1 (2002): 55–83; and *Imperialism and Human Rights: Colonial Discourses of Rights and Liberties in African History* (Albany, NY: SUNY Press, 2007).

27. Quentin Skinner, "Language and Social Change," in James Tully, ed., *Meaning and Context. Quentin Skinner and his Critics* (Cambridge: Polity Press, 1988), 119–21; Kari Palonen, *Quentin Skinner. History, Politics, Rhetoric* (Cambridge: Polity Press, 2003), quoting Skinner, 21.

28. The term comes from Natalie Z. Davis, "The Shapes of Social History," *Storia Della Storiografia* 17 (1990): 28, 31.

29. E.g. Shirley Tillotson, "Human Rights Law as Prism: Women's Organizations, Unions, and Ontario's Female Employees Fair Remuneration Act, 1951," *Canadian Historical Review* 72, no. 4 (1991): 532–57, and for a subsequent stage in the same historical narrative C. Egri and W. Stanbury, "How Pay Equity Legislation Came to Ontario," *Canadian Public Administration* 32 (1989): 274–303; Dominique Marshall, "The Language of Children's Rights, the Formation of the Welfare State, and the Democratic Experience of Poor Families in Quebec, 1940–55," *Canadian Historical Review* 78, no. 3 (1997): 409–42; Rianne Mahon, "Child Care as Citizenship Right? Toronto in the 1970s and 1980s," *Canadian Historical Review* 86, no. 2 (2005): 285–315; Miriam Smith, "Social Movements and Equality Seeking: The Case of Gay Liberation in Canada," *Canadian Journal of Political Science* 31, no. 2 (1998): 285–309, on the pre-Charter movement, and "Social Movements and Judicial Empowerment: Courts, Public Policy, and Lesbian and Gay Organizing in Canada," *Politics and Society* 33, no. 2 (2005): 327–53, on the impact of the Charter. For a broader account of rights activism see Dominique Clément, *Canada's Rights Revolution. Social Movements and Social Change, 1937–82* (Vancouver: UBC Press, 2008).

30. William Schabas, "Canada and the Adoption of the Universal Declaration," *McGill Law Journal* 43 (1998): 405.

31. E.g. Daniel N. Paul, *We Were Not the Savages: A Mi'kmaq Perspective on the Collision of European and Native American Civilizations*, rev. ed. (Halifax: Fernwood, 2000), 294–95.

32. E.g. Walter S. Tarnopolsky and William Pentney, *Discrimination and the Law in Canada* (Don Mills: De Boo, 1985), Chap. 2.

33. Judith Fingard, "Race and Respectability in Victorian Halifax," *Journal of Imperial and Commonwealth History* 20 (1992): 169–195; David A. Sutherland, "Race Relations in Halifax, Nova Scotia, During the Mid-Victorian Quest for Reform," *Journal of the Canadian Historical Association* 7 (1996): 35–54; James W. St. G. Walker, *The Black Loyalists: The Search for a Promised Land in Nova Scotia and Sierra Leone*, 2nd ed. (Toronto: University of Toronto Press, 1992).

34. *Franklin v. Evans* (1924) 55 *Ontario Law Reports*, 349; *Dawn of Tomorrow*, February 2 and 9, 1924.

35. *Christie v. York*, [1940] *Supreme Court Reports*, 139; *Free Lance*, July 9, 1938. For discussions of this and many other court challenges brought by African Canadians see Constance Backhouse, *Colour-Coded: A Legal History of Racism in Canada, 1900–1950* (Toronto: Osgoode Society and University of Toronto Press, 1998), Chaps. 6 and 7, and James W. St. G. Walker, *"Race," Rights and the Law in the Supreme Court of Canada: Historical Case Studies* (Toronto and Waterloo: Osgoode Society and Wilfrid Laurier University Press, 1997), especially Chap. 3.

36. *Quong Wing v. The King* (1914), 39 *Supreme Court Reports*, 440; Gillian Creese, "Organizing Against Racism in the Workplace: Chinese Workers in Vancouver before the Second World War," *Canadian Ethnic Studies* 19 (1987): 35–46; John P.S. McLaren, "The Early British Columbia Supreme Court and the 'Chinese Question,'" *Manitoba Law Journal* 20 (1991): 107–47; Patricia E. Roy, *A White Man's Province: British Columbia Politicians and Chinese and Japanese Immigrants, 1858–1914* (Vancouver: UBC Press, 1989), and *The Oriental Question: Consolidating a White Man's Province, 1914–41* (Vancouver: UBC Press, 2003). There was also

an organized Chinese-Canadian response to an attempt to segregate their children in school. See Timothy J. Stanley, *Contesting White Supremacy: School Segregation, Anti-Racism, and the Making of Chinese Canadians* (Vancouver: UBC Press, 2011).

37. *Cunningham v. Tomey Homma*, [1903] *Appeal Cases* (Judicial Committee of the Privy Council), 151; Carol F. Lee, "The Road to Enfranchisement: Chinese and Japanese in British Columbia," *BC Studies* No. 30 (Summer 1976): 44–76.

38. "Hindu" was defined in the Provincial Elections Act as "any native of India not born of Anglo-Saxon parents." The term was retained in official documents until 1947, including the *Census of Canada. Vancouver Province*, March 27, 1907; W.L. Mackenzie King, *Report of Mr W.L. Mackenzie King on his Mission to England in connection with the Immigration of Asiatics into Canada* (London: HM Stationery Office, 1908); PC 27, January 8, 1908; British Columbia Archives (BCA), GR-1195, Legislative Assembly, Miscellaneous Correspondence, 1942–47, Box 1, file 1, Petition of the Khalsa Diwan Society, January 26, 1945; British North America Act, s. 41; The Electoral Franchise Act, *Statutes of Canada*, 1885, c. 40, s. 9.

39. The petitions and accounts of the delegations were published in several sources. See for example Nand Singh Sihra, Balwant Singh and Narain Singh, "Indians in Canada," *The Indian Review* (June 1913): 453–456; Isabella Ross Broad, *An Appeal for Fair Play for the Sikhs in Canada* (Victoria: N.p., 1913); Victoria Society of Friends of the Hindu, *A Summary of the Hindu Question* (Victoria: N.p., 1911); *The Aryan*, August 1911 to November 1912; Anon., *The Hindu Case* (Toronto: Canada India Committee, 1915); A Hindu-Canadian, *India's Appeal to Canada* (Toronto: Canada India Committee, 1916). Submissions by church and other support groups are in Library and Archives Canada (LAC), RG 76, Vol. 386, File 536999, Parts 9 and 10, and Imperial Conference reports are in Parts 11 to 15.

40. Cyril Levitt and William Shaffir, *The Riot at Christie Pits* (Toronto: Lester and Orpen Dennys, 1987), and "The Swastika as Dramatic Symbol: A Case-Study of Ethnic Violence in Canada," in Robert Brym et al., eds., *The Jews in Canada* (Toronto: Oxford University Press, 1993), 77–96; James Parkes, *Facts and Fables About the Jews* (Toronto: Committee on Jewish-Gentile Relationships), copy in United Church of Canada Archives, Claris Silcox Papers, Box 12, "Periodicals and Pamphlets."

41. As defined by Clifford Geertz, *Local Knowledge: Further Essays in Interpretive Anthropology* (New York: BasicBooks, 1983), 186–87.

42. *The King's Regulations and Orders for the Royal Canadian Air Force*, 1924, Paragraph 275, amended in 1943 edition, Article 171; *Regulations and Instructions for the Royal Canadian Navy*, 1942, Chapter 7, Article 144 (2), amended by PC 1944–4950 (June 30); Canada, Parliament, House of Commons, Special Committee on Orientals in British Columbia, *Report and Recommendations*, 1940; LAC, RG24 Vol. 2765, file 6615-4-A, Vol. 5, correspondence and committee minutes on "Enlistment of Asiatics"; RG27 Vol. 130, file 601–3–4, "Conscription of East Indians for Canadian Army"; Department of National Defence, Directorate of History, file HQ 504–1–7–1, Vol. 1, "Enlistment of Chinese," and file "Sorting out Coloured Soldiers."

43. Mr. Grizzle relates this story in the film *Journey to Justice*, directed by Roger McTair, National Film Board of Canada, 2000.

44. Buxton National Historic Site and Museum, National Unity Association Papers, F. P. Varcoe, Deputy Minister of Justice, to Hugh Burnett, August 3, 1943.

45. BC did not publish accounts of legislature debates, but a clipping file has been compiled from newspaper reports, often verbatim. A microfilmed copy is available at the UBC Library.

46. *Re: McDougall and Waddell*, [1945] 2 *Dominion Law Reports* (DLR), 244.

47. LAC, MG28 V133, B'nai Brith Fonds, Vol. 3, File 9, "Proceedings, 1940," Report of the Joint Public Relations Committee. Enlistment figures were quite contrary to the perception of Jewish reluctance to volunteer.

48. Canadian Jewish Congress Charities Committee and National Archives (CJCCCNA), ZA 1942, Box 5, File 63, "Discrimination—Selective Service," NSS Circular 81, November 7, 1942, Press Release, November 17, and "Brief Presented to the National Selective Service by the Canadian Jewish Congress in 1942"; ZA 1943, Box 3, File 26, Memorandum by H.M.

Caiserman, "Employment Discrimination in Canadian War Industries," and "Memorandum Re: Illegalization of Discrimination in Canada"; Douglas MacLennan, "Racial Discrimination in Canada," *Canadian Forum* (October 1943): 164–65. A subsequent order advised NSS managers to use "good sense" and not to take the non-discriminatory policy "literally" by sending applicants to jobs "where it may not be practical to employ certain types," NSS Confidential Circular 81A, December 9, 1943. Carmela Patrias sets this episode in its broader context in *Jobs and Justice: Fighting Discrimination in Wartime Canada, 1939–1945* (Toronto: University of Toronto Press, 2012).

49.   *Statutes of Ontario* 1944, c. 51; Ontario Legislature, *Debates*, March 7, 1944.

50.   *Vancouver Province*, March 30, 1940, January 14 and October 13, 1942, January 18 and March 2, 1943. Some South Asians had been accepted as volunteers, before or despite the general instruction, and some of them would appear in uniform at the rallies.

51.   Canada, House of Commons, *Debates*, July 17, 1944, 4925–26, 4935.

52.   Stephanie D. Bangarth, *Voices Raised in Protest: Defending North American Citizens of Japanese Ancestry, 1942–49* (Vancouver: UBC Press, 2008). See also Ross Lambertson, *Repression and Resistance: Canadian Human Rights Activists 1930–1960* (Toronto: University of Toronto Press, 2005), Chap. 3.

53.   CJCCCNA, Series CA, Box 89, File 1025, "Memorandum submitted by The Canadian Jewish Congress and The Zionist Organizations of Canada to the Canadian Delegates to the United Nations Conference on International Organization at San Francisco," April 1945; ZA 1942, Box 5, File 63, "Brief Presented to the National Selective Service . . . ," 1942, "Memorandum on Unequal Opportunity in Employment in the Province of Ontario and the Need for Fair Employment Practices Legislation," February 1947. Copies of both briefs are also in Archives of Ontario (AO), RG3–17, George Drew Papers, Box 436, File "Fair Employment Practices Act."

54.   Stephanie D. Bangarth, "'We Are Not Asking You To Open Wide the Gates for Chinese Immigration': The Committee for the Repeal of the Chinese Immigration Act and Early Human Rights Activism in Canada," *Canadian Historical Review* 84 (2003): 395–422; Lisa Rose Mar, "From Diaspora to North American Civil Rights: Chinese Canadian Ideas, Identities and Brokers in Vancouver, British Columbia, 1924 to 1960" (PhD thesis, University of Toronto, 2002), and *Brokering Belonging. Chinese in Canada's Exclusion Era, 1885–1945* (Toronto: University of Toronto Press, 2010); Patricia E. Roy, "Lessons in Citizenship, 1945–1949: The Delayed Return of the Japanese to Canada's Pacific Coast," *Pacific Northwest Quarterly* 93 (2002): 69–80; Lee, "The road to Enfranchisement"; F.J. McEvoy, "'A Symbol of Racial Discrimination': The Chinese Immigration Act and Canada's Relations with China, 1942–1947," *Canadian Ethnic Studies* 14 (1982): 24–42.

55.   *Victoria Times*, March 1, 1943; *Vancouver Province*, March 9, 1944, January 22, February 19, March 20, April 2, and September 7, 1947; *Vancouver Sun*, January 29, March 11, 1944, February 19, 1947; *Ottawa Citizen*, February 20, 1945; *Vancouver News-Herald*, July 12, 1945, January 25, September 17, 1947; Khalsa Diwan Society, "Report on Dominion, Provincial and Municipal Franchise for the Hindus in British Columbia," Victoria, November 1947; LAC, MG31 E87, Gordon Robertson Fonds, Memorandum, January 4, 1943, Vol. 2 file 12; RG 76, Vol. 387, file 536999, part 18; J.F. Hilliker, "The British Columbia Franchise and Canadian Relations with India in Wartime, 1939–1945," *BC Studies* No. 46 (Summer 1980): 40–60. In 1949 Japanese Canadians received full voting rights.

56.   Aboriginals living on reserves did not gain the franchise until 1960, and immigration restrictions based on "race" survived in various forms until 1967.

57.   Lambertson, *Repression and Resistance*, Chap. 7; Carmela Patrias and Ruth A. Frager, "'This Is Our Country, These Are Our Rights': Minorities and the Origins of Ontario's Human Rights Campaigns," *Canadian Historical Review* 82 (2001): 1–35; James W. St.G. Walker, "The 'Jewish Phase' in the Canadian Movement for Racial Equality," *Canadian Ethnic Studies* 34 (2002): 1–29.

58.   By 1947, a public opinion poll showed that 64 percent of Canadians approved of legislation to prevent employment discrimination (*Toronto Star*, June 19, 1947). The poll was financed

by the Canadian Jewish Congress, who disseminated the results widely and included them as an appendix in a brief to Premier Frost. LAC, MG28 I 173,Ontario Labour Committee for Human Rights Papers, vol. 9, "Brief in Respect to Legislation Dealing with Expressions of Racial and Religious Discrimination in Ontario," June 7, 1949.

59. AO, RG3, Leslie Frost Papers, Box 2, file "Discrimination Acts," speech notes.

60. Ibid., Box 48, file 87-G, Hugh Burnett to Premier Frost, February 6, 1951.

61. Backhouse, *Colour-Coded*, Chap. 7. Transcripts of the trial, including statements from all the witnesses and an affidavit from Mrs. Desmond, are in Nova Scotia Archives and Records Management, RG 39C, Vol. 937, file SC 13347. The *Halifax Chronicle* and the *Toronto Star* both carried descriptive reports on November 30, 1946.

62. Dalhousie Institute of Public Affairs, *The Condition of the Negroes of Halifax City, Nova Scotia* (Halifax: Dalhousie University, 1962).

63. A full discussion of these events is in James W. St. G. Walker, "Black Confrontation in 1960s Halifax," in *Debating Dissent: Canada and the Sixties*, ed. Lara Campbell, Dominique Clément, and Greg Kealey (Toronto: University of Toronto Press, 2012).

64. Articles inspired by the fortieth anniversary of the TYP include Stephen Kimber, "TYP: It All Began in a Duck Blind," *Metro*, Halifax, November 15, 2010, and Patricia Brooks Arenburg, "Transition Year Program: An Extended Family," *Dalhousie Magazine* 28, no. 2 (Fall 2011): 14–15.

65. E.g. Walter Pitman, *Now Is Not Too Late* (Toronto: City of Toronto, 1977); Frances Henry, *The Dynamics of Racism in Toronto: Research Report* (Ottawa: Department of the Secretary of State, 1978); Cardinal Carter, *Report to the Civic Authorities of Metropolitan Toronto and Its Citizens* (Toronto: Metropolitan Toronto, 1979); John McAlpine, *Report Arising Out of the Activities of the Ku Klux Klan in British Columbia* (Victoria: BC Ministry of Labour, 1981); Social Planning Council of Metropolitan Toronto, *Racial and Ethnic Discrimination in Employment* (Toronto: Social Planning Council, 1982).

66. Jennifer Tunnicliffe, "The Ontario Human Rights Code Review, 1975–1981: A New Understanding of Human Rights and its Meaning for Public Policy" (MA thesis, University of Waterloo, 2005); *Life Together: A Report on Human Rights in Ontario* (Toronto: Ontario Human Rights Commission, 1977); *Statutes of Ontario* 1981, c. 53.

67. Section 15 (2) gives constitutional authority to "any law, program or activity that has as its object the amelioration of conditions of disadvantaged individuals or groups including those that are disadvantaged because of race, national or ethnic origin, colour, religion, sex, age or mental or physical disability."

68. The redress settlement was reached only after a long struggle waged by the National Association of Japanese Canadians. See for example Audrey Kobayashi, "The Japanese-Canadian Redress Settlement and its Implications for 'Race Relations," *Canadian Ethnic Studies* 24 (1992): 1–19, and Roy Miki, *Redress: Inside the Japanese Canadian Call for Justice* (Vancouver: Raincoast Books, 2004).

69. [1989] 1 Supreme Court Reports 143.

70. E.g. Sheila Block and Grace-Edward Galabuzi, *Canada's Colour Coded Labour Market: The Gap for Racialized Workers* (Toronto: Wellesley Institute, 2011); Leslie Ciarula Taylor, "The Darker Your Skin . . . the Less You Fit In," *Toronto Star*, May 14, 2009, and "Racism Still with Us," editorial, *Toronto Star*, May 15, 2009; Jill Mahoney, "Hate-crime Reports the Highest since 2005, Statscan Reports," *Globe and Mail*, June 8, 2011; Canadian Race Relations Foundation and Association for Canadian Studies, "A Four Country Survey of Opinion on Racism and Prejudice in 2010," released January 21, 2011. The new study of the Ethnic Diversity Survey was conducted by University of Toronto sociologists Jeffrey Reitz and Rupa Banerjee, "Racial Inequality, Social Cohesion, and Policy Issues in Canada," pre-publication copy dated August 2006.

71. Experiments in restorative justice, especially with respect to Aboriginal communities in Canada, and the widespread reparations movement both internationally and domestically, may represent a new conceptual revolution: moving beyond remedial measures to address past injustices more directly.

72. *Oxford English Dictionary*, online edition.
73. Thomas W. Laqueur, "The Moral Imagination of Human Rights," in Ignatieff, *Politics and Idolatry*, 131; Cmiel, "Recent History", 6–7.
74. Geertz, *Local Knowledge*, 16.
75. Palonin, *Quentin Skinner*, 20, quoting Skinner.

Chapter 2

•◆•

Where Do We Begin? Human Rights, Public History, and the Challenge of Conceptualization

Bonny Ibhawoh

Contemporary human rights scholarship labours under a crisis of historicity. Historians have raised critical questions about the meanings and origins of human rights that challenge long-standing orthodoxies and conventional wisdom in the field. The main critique is that human rights scholarship is trapped in an intellectual tradition of presentism and linear progressivism that tends to hinder proper understanding of the tensions inherent in both human rights theory and praxis. The trend has been to present human rights—despite frequent setbacks and many contradictions—as part of a saga of relentless human progress. In a field long dominated by social science and legal scholars, this is the inevitable consequence of an ahistorical preoccupation with the "here and now" and a tendency to read history backward. The crisis of historicity in human rights scholarship is compounded by the problem of conceptualization. Human rights may have become a dominant concept in global discourses of morality and ethics; they may be seen as "trumps" and transcendental claims by many,[1] but to some, human rights remain "nonsense on stilts"[2] and only as real as unicorns.[3]

The growing involvement of historians has not resolved the crisis of historicity that confronts human rights scholarship. If anything, it appears only to have deepened it. In his radically revisionist history of human rights, Samuel Moyn accuses historians of adopting a largely celebratory attitude toward the emergence and progress of human rights, providing recent enthusiasms with uplifting back stories and differing primarily about where to locate the breakthroughs in the evolution of the human rights idea.[4] Historians, he claims, have used history to confirm the inevitable rise of human rights as the "last utopia" rather than an ideology, one of several utopias, shaped by conscious choices and historical accidents.[5]

This is not an entirely new charge. Historians themselves have previously critiqued other human rights scholars for not historicizing their subject enough. Contemporary human rights discourse has, for the most part, produced a triumphalist vision of the role of rights talk in securing progressive and transformative social change.[6] To exercise one's human rights has come to be taken as something inherently good; an objective index of social and political progress. What has not been sufficiently explored in the discussion are the ways in which rights talk has been deployed to further more complex and sometimes contradictory agendas—progressive and reactionary. Historians have therefore argued for some shift away from the linear progressivism that underlies contemporary human rights scholarship.[7] A different approach is needed to reveal the "true origins" of human rights not as some inevitable outcome of a trajectory of liberal idealism but as the most recent of several universalist utopian programs.[8] A "true history" of human rights, one historian has argued, matters most of all to confront the prospects of human rights today and the prospects for the future.[9]

There is some value in the call for restoring nuance, skepticism, and context to human rights scholarship. However, the seeming fixation with "true origins" and "true histories" is telling. For the human rights historian, I discern a certain proprietary concern with historical authenticity. As with the concept of *globalization*, historical contributions to human rights scholarship in the past decade have been concerned with not only the question of historicity but also that of authenticity. What might an "authentic" history of human rights look like?

Even before historians became actively involved in the field, legal and social science scholars recognized the need to historicize human rights. Across the disciplines, human rights textbooks typically include a chapter or section on "Historical Background" and "Origins," however fleeting or perfunctory. For the most part however, the concern with historicization has been at the margins rather than the centre of human rights scholarship. Although late to the game, historians have sought to fill in the missing link. Initial skepticism of "human rights" as a subject of historical inquiry or tool of historical analysis has given way to cautious engagement. There is increasing readiness to re-examine key historical events through a human rights lens—the antislavery movement,[10] Enlightenment liberalism, eighteenth-century Euro-American political revolutions,[11] colonialism,[12] and even decolonization.[13] As the president of the American Historical Association proclaimed a few years ago, we have indeed all become historians of human rights.[14]

What does the growing involvement of historians in human rights scholarship portend for this uniquely multidisciplinary discipline? For one, it suggests a shift in interest in the history of human rights from the margins toward the centre of human rights scholarship. It also suggests renewed focus on old questions about the origins and historical antecedence of contemporary human rights. Attention to historicization brings novel perspectives to long-standing human rights debates over questions of *origin* and *meaning, scope* and *context, ordering,* and *prioritization.*

Perhaps the most contentious of these key human rights questions is that of origin and meaning. While many scholars trace the philosophical foundations of modern notions of human rights to natural law and Western liberal traditions, others argue for a more eclectic understanding of the term, focusing on differing notions of rights within both Western and non-Western societies. Even more contentious is the debate over the *meaning* and appropriateness of employing the concept of human rights in pre-modern contexts. Some scholars argue for an essentialist and historically specific definition of human rights, distinct from historical notions of rights, equity and "distributive justice." They contend that the contemporary idea of "human rights" is uniquely founded on post–Second World War developments and specifically, the adoption of the Universal Declaration of Human Rights (UDHR) by the United Nations in 1948. Others argue for a more evolutionary definition of human rights hinged not so much on the restricted context of postwar usage as on the continuing ideas that have historically underlined notions of liberty and justice in various societies.

These are old and familiar debates to human rights scholars. However, when new concerns about "historical authenticity" intersect with old debates about the origins, meanings, and scope of human rights they take on added significance. The tenor of these debates also changes significantly when human rights shifts from the confines of academic discourse to the terrain of public history. This chapter reviews some of the dominant arguments in debates about the origins and meanings of human rights and explores their implications for constructing a public history of human rights. It argues that the growing interest in the public history of human rights offers historians, even as late entrants into the field, an opportunity to move history from the margins of human rights scholarship to its centre. It also argues that need for public histories of human rights to engage, yet transcend, polemical academic debates about the meaning and origins of human rights.

As discourses and representations of human rights expand from the confines of academic and policy think-tank framings to the public square, historical contributions will become more crucial. Historians will inevitably shape debates about how to commemorate and memorialize human rights ideas, events, and struggles for public consumption. In doing so, historians will have to temper fixations with "historical authenticity" with a willingness to engage other forms of understandings and dialogue about human rights. Historians who dabble into the novel terrain of public human rights history must be open to drawing on multiple and eclectic methodologies and speaking a uniquely multidisciplinary human rights vernacular that is accessible to other scholars and to public audiences. The goal should be not so much to present the public with a "true" history of human rights as to offer a relevant and engaging history of human rights.

Human rights scholars and historians in particular need to pay more attention to what has been described as the "vernacularizing" of human rights—the complex process by which external impulses intersected with local ideas and situations to produce hybridized understandings of rights.[15] This also refers to the course of interpreting and translating "universal" human rights language to local contexts and how this affects the application of human rights norms for better or worse. Understanding the divergent processes of vernacularization or domestication of universal human rights is crucial to telling the human rights story. After all, the "universal," properly so called, is meaningless if not the aggregate of local experiences.

HUMAN RIGHTS AND PUBLIC HISTORY

In recent years the debate over the origins of human rights has shifted from academic publications and conferences to the realm of public history. Public history as used here refers broadly to history as seen, heard, read, and interpreted by or for a popular audience. It is history that "belongs" to the public, differing essentially from academic history in its emphasis on the public context of scholarship.[16] The public historian's approach to historical research, documentation, and dissemination promotes the collaborative study and practice of history in ways that are accessible and useful to the public. Traditional forums for public history—museum presentations, audio-visual documentaries, and historic site preservation projects—now increasingly include open-access websites dedicated to documenting historical heritage and collective memories.

This is not the place to engage the debate over the value of public history. It suffices to note that not everyone is keen on public history. Some academic historians remain cynical about public history, seeing it as a dumbing down of historical scholarship or as an opportunistic enterprise.[17] What is indisputable however, is the relevance of, and interest in public history as evident in the ever-growing popularity of representations about the past. Museums, once synonymous with "dry as dust history" now enjoy high public regard as influential sources of national histories. When people in Australia and the United States were recently asked to rank the sources of information about the past that they trust, museums came close to the top, well ahead of history teachers.[18] In many parts of the world, public interest in museums appears to have grown along with mounting concern about globalization, illegal migration, terrorism, and other threats to the integrity of the nation-state.[19]

In Canada, where recent museums and heritage projects have been largely private ventures, the trend is slightly different. Heritage concerns have been driven more by identity politics as much as if not more than overarching national agendas. To be sure, some politicians see the boom in identity-centred heritage museums in Canada as a threat to their vision of the country; but this is hardly the view of those building the museums or, arguably, the majority of the population. Still, the question has been asked in Canada and elsewhere: Why is it that as the public appetite for history grows the audience for academic historical productions shrinks or remains stagnant? The answer may lie partly in the differing attitudes that academic historians, museum historians, and the public bring to the making of history.[20]

In recent years, there has been an explosion in interest in the public history of human rights. This interest is most evident in the documentation of historical heritage and the commemoration of collective memories. Museums and museology have become key spaces for human rights commemoration and memorialization projects.[21] If the second half of the twentieth century marked the age of the "human rights revolution," the first half of the twenty-first century is shaping up to be the age of human rights commemoration and memorialization.

By the nature of their collections and exhibitions, museums are integral sites in the representation of past abuses, and they are becoming increasingly responsive to human rights violations in their program-ming. Besides several museums across the world dedicated to memo-rializing the Holocaust and other genocides, there are now a growing number of museums dedicated to human rights issues—slavery, torture, and historical incidents of political or social oppression. Many of these are national museums, relating narratives that are geographically and time specific.[22] There is the International Slavery Museum in the United Kingdom; the National Slavery Museum, the Civil Rights Museum, and the Museum of Tolerance all in the United States; the Apartheid Museum in South Africa; the Museum of Genocide Victims in Lithuania; the Tuol Sleng Museum in Cambodia; the Kigali Genocide Memorial Centre in Rwanda; the Museum of Memory and Human Rights in Chile; the *Lugar de Memorial* in Peru; and the Museum of Terror in Hungary. Such is the growth in the number of museums dedicated to human rights commem-oration that there is now an umbrella organization called the Federation of International Human Rights Museums.[23]

A Global Museum of Human Rights

Add to this growing list, the Canadian Museum of Human Rights (CMHR). At its establishment in 2008, the CMHR was the first national museum created in Canada since the 1960s and the first to be located out-side the capital territory.[24] The museum is unique in its scope and man-date. Unlike other human rights–oriented museums that tend to have a national and geographically limited focus, the CMHR was conceived to be broadly dedicated to the subject of human rights in Canada and beyond.[25] Its aims, as mandated by the Museums Act, is to "inform visi-tors about human rights, promote respect for others, and to encourage reflection and dialogue."[26] Its stated approach is to "foster critical think-ing about the ways that large-scale human rights abuses unfold at home and *in the world*." Its goal is to inspire people to "take a stand for human rights in their community, their country, and beyond."[27] This aspiration toward supra-nationality and globality is what makes the CMHR a dis-tinctive human rights public history project.

The CMHR and other new generation human rights museums call into question the social purpose of public museums. Museums con-stantly deal with accusations of imposing their visions of the past on their public audience.[28] Scholars have drawn attention to how museums have been used historically to construct and promote specific social and political agendas within the public sphere. Studies have also emphasized the museum's role as a locus to which artifacts are transported into a constructed narrative as a manifestation of power.[29] Indeed, many human rights museums combine their traditional role of education and commemoration with an explicit activist mandate.[30]

There is recognition, and some cases, concern that human rights museums, like others, serve more than just archival and repository functions, becoming instead "advocacy organizations" and "social justice centres." It is a concern that human rights museums constantly struggle with. Faced with controversies over what to include in the museum and how, officials of the CMHR at its inception sought to position the museum not just as a memorial to the past but also as a window into the future and an agent of change.[31] They stressed that the purpose of the museum is not to be a memorial for the suffering of different groups but to be a learning experience for visitors. It is considered a "museum of ideas," not just a museum of past events.[32]

Apart from questions pertaining to their roles and relevance, human rights museums face the challenge of conceptualization in constructing human rights narratives. What are human rights and where does the human rights story begin? This question is central to the work of human rights museums. In the critical public spaces where museum researchers and curators do their work, the human rights story has to be told in ways that make practical sense. For the CMHR, telling the human rights story began with academic and public consultations. Public consultations were aimed at ascertaining what Canadians wanted to see in a human rights museum.[33] Academic consultations were aimed at addressing questions about the concept, origins, and evolution of human rights. One goal was to develop a comprehensive Global Human Rights Timeline to guide the museum's displays and inaugural exhibits. This timeline would analyze major events, documents, and personalities in the development of human rights ideas around the world. This was in line with the museum's vision of fostering critical thinking about human rights at home and in the world.[34]

In what follows, I examine the debates about the *meaning, origins,* and *scope* of human rights and the challenges they pose for constructing a public history of universal human rights. This chapter draws on my work with the Canadian Museum of Human Rights and the Global Human Rights Timeline.

QUESTIONS OF MEANING AND ORIGIN

For public history projects, questions of origins and scope have practical implications. Questions about the meaning and origins of human rights determine where museum displays begin. They also determine what to include or exclude, what to emphasize, how to order displays and make connections between them. For the historian engaged in constructing a public history of human rights, postmodernist ambiguities have limited appeal. Here, the familiar argument that "human rights are indeterminate and deeply contested" is of little value. Human rights may indeed be contested in an abstract sense but for the museum curator, a working historical timeline should provide some clarity on the meaning and scope of human rights. Constructing a public history of human rights therefore raises old questions in new ways and forces us to rethink old answers to these questions.

The universal human rights regime continues to be challenged and complicated on multiple fronts by proponents of varying degrees of cultural relativism; by positivists who refuse to recognize any human rights other than legally enforceable entitlements, and by "essentialists" who subscribe only to a post–Second World War United Nations–inspired definition of human rights. Marie-Bénédicte Dembour has offered an innovative proposal for making sense of these competing understandings of human rights—"natural scholars" conceive of human rights as given; "deliberative scholars" conceive of human rights as political values that liberal societies choose to adopt through agreement; "protest scholars" see human rights as something fought for, and "discourse scholars" see human rights as talked about.[35] This classification underscores the complexities of the human rights idea and holds both possibilities and challenges for constructing a public history of human rights.

Another schematization that I find useful is Michel Ignatieff's recent reimagining of his treatise *The Human Rights Revolution*. There was not, after all, a single rights revolution but three related but somewhat distinct revolutions in the post–Second World War era—a revolution of *self-determination*; a revolution of *democracy*, and a revolution of *equality*.[36] Each preceding revolution held the promise of ushering in the next one even though this did not always materialize.

The academic discourse on the origins and philosophical foundations of human rights has been characterized by what I call "defining episodes." These are the historic landmarks in the development of the human rights idea that various scholars have identified and emphasized. Most scholars agree that these defining episodes represent milestones in the development of contemporary notions of human rights. There is, however, substantial disagreement over which of these episodes marked the most significant turning point in the developments of the human rights idea. I have identified a number of these defining episodes: ancient religious and secular humanism; Western legal and philosophical traditions and Enlightenment liberalism; eighteenth-century Euro-American political revolutions; the antislavery movement; the Holocaust and the Universal Declaration of Human Rights (UDHR) epoch; anti-colonial movements; and the universalization agenda of the 1970s. An exhaustive discussion of each of these defining episodes is not possible within this limited space. Here, I examine the most dominant of these episodes in human rights scholarship.

FROM HUMANIST ANTIQUITY TO ENLIGHTENMENT LIBERALISM

The argument that human rights are as old as civilization has been made by many scholars.[37] Several accounts of the history of human rights begin with the Hammurabi Code; Buddhist, Hindu, and Confucian texts; the Torah, the Bible, and the Quran. Although few draw direct connections between these traditions and the modern concept of human rights, ancient discourses of justice have come to be seen as the normative seeds of contemporary universal human rights. Is this therefore the natural place to begin the human rights story? To be sure, many religious texts contain passages that can be read as being human rights–affirming. But questions persist as to the real links between these early traditions and contemporary human rights. The connections may simply be too tenuous to provide meaningful basis for defining contemporary human rights.

Although scholars are increasingly seeking human rights origins in ancient humanism, a dominant defining episode in the origins of human rights debate is Western legal and philosophical tradition: specifically, *natural law theory*. Most academic studies begin the human rights story here. They trace contemporary conceptions of rights and liberties from natural law and ancient Greek stoicism through the medieval period to the Enlightenment. Natural law philosophy, characterized by a belief that laws and rules of conduct are embedded and derivable from human nature, has become a secure place in antiquity to ground universal human rights. Since human nature is the same the world over, the laws derived from that nature are seen as universal and true to all people, at all times and places. Thus, they are objective and eternal and are neither changeable nor alterable.[38]

Some scholars suggest that the defining notion of natural law underlies the concept of rights as expressed in the socio-political and philosophical developments in fifteenth- and sixteenth-century Europe. The Renaissance and the decline of feudalism inaugurated a long period of transition to the liberal notions of freedom and equality, particularly in the use and ownership of property. This created an unprecedented commitment to individual expression and world experience which was subsequently reflected in diverse writings—from the teachings of Thomas Aquinas and Hugo Grotius to the Magna Carta, the Petition of Rights of 1628, and the English Bill of Rights of 1689.[39] Enlightenment thought founded on natural law theory, many argue, inaugurated a new intellectual and political tradition in which the individual as a political actor was abstracted from the holistic totality of medieval society.

Related to the privileging of Enlightenment liberalism in discourses about human rights origins is the emphasis on the wave of Euro-American revolutions of the eighteenth century. The revolutions and the documents they inspired are said to be central to this history of contemporary human rights because they were founded on the notion of the autonomous person endowed with certain inalienable rights.[40]

In *Inventing Human Rights*, Lynn Hunt locates the origin of the human rights idea firmly in the American and French Revolutions and the Declarations they inspired. Hunt traces the impact of Enlightenment ideas on the social and political expansion of human rights and argues that equality, universality, and naturalness of rights gained direct political expression for the first time in the American Declaration of Independence and the French Declaration of the Rights of Man and Citizen.[41] These developments underscore a "*sudden* crystallization of human rights claims at the end of the eighteenth century."[42] Is this then an appropriate place to begin a global history of human rights?

Privileging the Enlightenment as the origin of human rights may have gained currency in human rights scholarship but it remains a decidedly Eurocentric approach. Limiting the discussion on the "invention" of human rights to the history of the Western world lends credence to the notion, already deeply held in certain quarters, that human rights are a Western invention—an idea conceived in the West and exported to the rest of the world. It is an argument that hardly serves the cause of universal human rights and one that may be problematic for a constructing a global public history of human rights. Unless used figuratively, the term *invention* clearly gets in the way of a full historical understanding of the complex cross-cultural processes by which human rights ideas have evolved. It simply implies too one-sided a historical happening.

ANTISLAVERY

If the origins of the human rights idea cannot be narrowed to Enlightenment liberalism or eighteenth-century Euro-American revolutions, perhaps it can be located in a related movement with more global ramifications—the antislavery movement. Several scholars have pointed out that the defining character of universal human rights has been significantly shaped by key reformist impulses of the late nineteenth century— the abolition of the slave trade, the development of factory legislation, mass education, trade unionism, and universal suffrage.[43] These developments served to broaden the scope of individual rights and stimulate an increasing international interest in their protection.

In *Bury the Chains*, Adam Hochschild presents the eighteenth- century antislavery movement as a story of successful human rights struggles led by a few groups of men and women who took on the vested interests of state, church, and big business. With organization, enthusiasm, and imaginative campaigning that foreshadowed the work of present-day human rights organizations, these abolitionists forced the British Parliament to uphold the rights and humanity of the enslaved and accede to the will of the British people in their opposition to slavery. It was, as Hochschild put it, "the first time in history that a large number of people became outraged, and stayed outraged for many years over some- one else's rights."[44]

Challenging the view that human rights law is a post–Second World War invention, one legal scholar has argued that use of international law to promote human rights began more than a century earlier with the move- ment to ban the international slave trade. Abolitionists in Britain, spurred by both Enlightenment conceptions of natural rights and by religious beliefs, pushed their governments to make the suppression of the slave trade a focus of diplomacy and treaty-making. The result over the first few decades of the nineteenth century was a novel network of international treaties prohibiting the slave trade. These treaties crafted the world's first international human rights courts—admiralty tribunals and the Courts of Mixed Commission—empowered to confiscate ships engaged in the illegal slave trade and liberate Africans found onboard.[45]

The conceptualization of the slave trade as a crime against humanity, and of slave traders as *hostis humani generis* (enemies of mankind) helped lay the foundation for twentieth-century international human rights law. Legal action against the slave trade introduced into modern international legal discourse the idea that violations of human rights were offences of concern to humankind generally, not just between people and their sovereign. This is the key conceptual step that separates the contemporary world of international human rights law from the idea of natural and universal rights that arose during the Enlightenment and took national legal form in documents like the Declaration of Independence and the French Declaration of the Rights of Man.[46]

To the extent that contemporary human rights operate within a legal and state-centric framework, this argument is persuasive. There are obvious historical parallels between the contemporary human rights movement and the antislavery movement. The role of antislavery in shaping the discourse on ethics and morality in the nineteenth century was so far-reaching, it has been described as "anti-structural."[47] With the antislavery campaign, something new and permanent was attempted that represented a significant break with the old political morality. Antislavery did not guarantee freedom for everyone, and sometimes even created new orthodoxies that took on elements of older oppressive structures. However, the success of antislavery as "anti-structure" is that it provided new opportunities to former slaves and captives or those most at risk, to escape from old structural constraints. It was the ethics of a second chance for such former slaves and the stress put on individual responsibility and equality before the law that gave antislavery its anti-structural force and transformative power. This radically anti-structural force is what antislavery shares with human rights.

Beyond these connections, was the antislavery discourse really a discourse of human rights? Can the public historian begin the story of human rights with antislavery? There is the temptation to do so. Humanitarians and evangelicals at the forefront of the antislavery movement certainly thought and advocated in terms of a certain universal humanism. Within this context of humanism, antislavery became a universal movement of rights, and the structure of profit, domination, and advantage that lived off slavery was challenged by this new social radicalism.[48] Abolitionists, in Europe and across the Atlantic, employed the language of human rights to articulate their opposition to slavery. Nowhere was this more evident than in early missionary literature. In a special issue of its journal, *The Anti-Slavery Examiner*, the American Antislavery Society in 1838 challenged slavery, not just in terms of Christian ethics but also as a "human rights" issue.[49] The journal, aptly titled "The Bible Against Slavery: An Inquiry into the Patriarchal and Mosaic Systems on the Subjugation of Human Rights," has been described as one of the strongest contemporary intellectual statements that we possess on the human rights character of antislavery.[50]

Still, there are many reasons why the public historian may be skeptical of beginning the history of human rights with antislavery. The most compelling of these is the arguments that in spite of the universalist parallels with antislavery, contemporary human rights are a uniquely modern invention with roots in the Second World War. Among those who hold this view, there is disagreement over where precisely to place the origin of contemporary human rights in the tumultuous decade of the 1940s— either during the Second World War or just after it.[51]

The emerging consensus is that the post–Second World War notion of universal human rights is fundamentally different from anything that had come before. The rise and fall of Nazi Germany had a most profound impact on the idea of universal human rights in the twentieth century as the world united in horror and condemnation of the Holocaust. Nazi atrocities, more than any previous event, brought home the realization that law and morality cannot be grounded in any purely utilitarian, idealist, or positivist doctrines.[52] Certain actions are wrong, no matter the social or political context, and certain rights are inalienable no matter the social or political exigencies. It also led to a growing acknowledgement that all human beings are entitled to a basic level of rights and that it was the duty of both states and international community to protect and promote these rights.

Postwar international consciousness of the need to protect the basic rights of all peoples by means of some universally acceptable parameters is evident in the UN Charter's affirmation of fundamental human rights and the "dignity and worth of the human person."[53] This commitment to universal human rights was followed by the Universal Declaration of

Human Rights (UDHR) in 1948 and international human rights conventions that have come to be collectively known as the International Bill of Rights.[54] The UDHR and these conventions, many now contend, constitute the source and essence of human rights.[55]

THE UDHR EPOCH

The idea that the UDHR marked a paradigmatic shift in the understanding of the notion of the human in relation to historical rights discourses has become a canon of human rights scholarship. In one of the early contributions to the debate over conceptualizing human rights, the political scientist Jack Donnelly made the argument for distinguishing between the concepts of *distributive justice* and human rights. Distributive justice, he argued, involves giving a person that which he or she is entitled (his or her rights). Unless these rights are those to which the individual is entitled simply as a human being, the rights in question will not be human rights. In many pre-modern societies, rights were assigned on the basis of communal membership, family, status, or achievement. These were therefore, strictly speaking, "privileges" granted by ruling elites, not human rights.[56] The idea of human rights, properly so called, is firmly rooted in the adoption of the UDHR by the United Nations in 1948. Other historical thoughts or events may well have influenced contemporary human rights, but the UDHR created an entirely new and unprecedented concept of rights.

More recent contributors have made the same point. "There were no human rights prior to World War II except those concretized domestically by the state," one historian has argued.[57] The argument distinguishes between precursors that represent a "politics of citizenship at home" and post-1970s "politics of suffering abroad" in which the state is also the source of the abuses. One has a domestic scope with a discourse of justice while the other is universal in latitude, international in outlook with a connection with the UN human rights idea.[58] The UDHR is also seen as marking a "juridical revolution."[59] Its adoption by the United Nations General Assembly in 1948 was not simply another episode in the human rights story but was an epoch-making event that *created* the concept of human rights. The UDHR articulated for the first time in human history a regime of basic and inalienable rights to which all human beings are entitled simply by virtue of their humanity. This concept of unfettered rights contingent on a universalist humanism is a uniquely post–Second

World War invention. Thus, the argument goes, the UDHR should principally define our understanding of human rights.

At an abstract and intellectual level, this argument has undeniable appeal. It is clean and structured. It allows us to talk about human rights with almost clinical precision and with much less uncertainties and ambiguities. We can clearly map their parameters, date them, and measure their enforcement. Beyond these however, what are the implications for public history? Is the public historian then constrained to begin the human rights story in the tumult and uncertainties of postwar internationalism? Does this imply, as some have argued, that talking about human rights in pre-1940s contexts is historically anachronistic? Can pre-UDHR rights discourses be (re)constructed as human rights histories?

Admittedly, the UDHR was a ground-breaking document; perhaps indeed an epoch-making event. It heralded a global milestone in the long struggle for human rights, promising "a magna carta for all humanity."[60] Its language of universal rights provided a framework for articulating new and long-standing demands for fundamental freedoms and political autonomy across the globe. However, crediting the UDHR and its drafters with "inventing" the notion of human rights may be stretching its historical significance. The idea that human beings are born free and equal certainly did not emerge in 1948. The articulation of this universalist principle under the auspices of an institution representative of nations of the world is what is unique about 1948.[61] But even this process of articulating a universal humanity, like those before it, was profoundly flawed.

It is well documented that in the discussions leading to the establishment of the United Nation and adoption of the UDHR, representatives of the key players in the UN negotiated the meaning of human rights in such a way that it did not encroach upon their sovereignty and in some cases, the possession of colonies. Many of the states at the forefront of drafting the UDHR defended their sovereignty and evaded glaring contradictions such as their own colonialism. In some instances, the principle of sovereignty and the concept of human rights were viewed as fundamentally opposed to each other; one had to do with the rights of states and the other with the rights of individuals. The work of the Human Rights Commission was not free of the underlying struggles over which rights to include and which to leave out.[62] It was partly because all major powers had something to be ashamed of in their conduct of human rights at the time, at home and abroad, that in the UDHR they enunciated rights without explaining why people have them and agreed on high principles while leaving the matter of enforcement unresolved.[63] The United States government, for example, was keenly aware of the international embarrassment caused by Martin Luther King Jr and the civil rights movement, especially in Asia and Africa where it feared at the time that many countries were leaning toward communism.

One of the most persistent critiques of the postwar human rights movement is that it was, at least at inception, an essentially Western movement with spurious claims to universality. Makau Mutua has argued that the contemporary human rights corpus, only put into effect following the atrocities of the Second World War, has its theoretical underpinnings in Western colonial attitudes and that it continues to be driven by totalizing Eurocentric impulses.[64] The UDHR and the postwar human rights regime they ushered are seen as a product of Western ethnocentrism imposed progressively on the rest of the world. Such skepticism is not limited to "Southern" voices. In 1947, the American Anthropological Association famously asked how the proposed UDHR could be applicable to all human beings and not be a "statement of rights conceived only in terms of values prevalent in the countries of Western Europe and America?"[65]

Others have pointed to the deep skepticism that greeted the adoption of the UDHR in the colonized "Third World"—the sense that it "took the suffering of whites to force the powers that be into action . . . [whereas] slavery and colonialism [had] left the world largely indifferent."[66] Moreover, at the adoption of UDHR in 1948, key signatory nations were complicit in gross human rights violations. Racial segregation was constitutional in the United States; Aboriginal people were poorly treated in Canada; France and Britain still held on to their colonies in Africa and Asia. For many in the non-Western world, still under colonial domination in the 1940s, the adoption of the UDHR did not elicit much excitement.[67] Anti-colonial nationalists were generally ambivalent and even cynical about a declaration purportedly affirming the rights of all human beings, drawn up by the same imperialist powers that denied them their right to self-determination.[68]

To begin the history of human rights with the adoption of the UDHR in 1948 is to ignore other defining moments that have shaped the human rights idea particularly in non-Western contexts. Take the example of the African National Congress (ANC) in South Africa. From its formation in 1923 until the collapse of the apartheid state in the 1990s, the ANC waged a relentless struggle for democracy and against state-sanctioned racism and oppression. ANC struggles drew on multiple rights discourses including natural rights, Christian humanism, Marxist solidarity rights, cultural morality, and international law. By the 1940s these rights discourses expanded to include the universal human rights language of the emergent United Nations system. For ANC activists, the adoption of the UDHR in 1948 only provided one more legitimizing weapon in a long-standing struggle against white minority rule.

The difficulty with beginning the story of universal human rights with the UDHR is that its presumed epochal significance remains open to question. A global public history of human rights should consider the ground-breaking elements of the UDHR, but it must also be alert to historical and contemporary contestations of its claim to universality. A global human rights story that begins with the UDHR invariably privileges one narrative out of many on the origins of human rights. But perhaps a West-centric, UDHR-centred human rights story can be balanced by focusing also on anti-colonialism—a movement that developed contemporaneously with the UDHR but which, unlike the UDHR, involved many peoples and societies in the global South.

Anti-colonialism

Anti-colonial struggles for self-determination had a significant impact on the development of the idea of universal human rights. Colonized people drew on the language of rights emerging in the West in their ideological struggles against imperial powers and their demands for national self-government. Anti-colonial movements in Asia, Africa, and elsewhere in the colonized world were among the first mass movements to draw on the universal language of human rights of the post–Second World War era. The adoption of the UDHR and the signing of the European Convention on Human Rights (ECHR) in 1950 lent the moral legitimacy of human rights to long-standing anti-colonial struggles for self-determination.[69] Anti-colonial nationalists demanded that the ideals of freedom and self-determination advanced as the basis of Allied military campaigns against Nazism in Europe and Japanese imperialism in Asia be also extended to them. In India, nationalists led by Gandhi took advantage of the new international emphasis on the right to self-determination espoused in the UN Charter to demand independence from British colonial rule. On these grounds, I have argued elsewhere that anti-colonial struggles were not only nationalist movements but were also veritable human rights movements.[70]

For the public historian seeking to balance a Eurocentric UDHR-inspired human rights narrative with one that engages perspectives from the global South, reconstructing anti-colonial history as human rights history hold interesting possibilities. But even this approach runs into difficulties. Some scholars insist that anti-colonialism was not a human rights movement because it was "already fully formed before human rights rhetoric after World War II had a chance to impact it seriously."[71] Others argue that anti-colonialism was not in essence a human rights movement because its primary aim was not to reduce the power of the state over the individual which is "the defining character of all human rights activism."[72] Concern over the unfettered power of the state over the individual led to pressure for international mechanisms of human rights protection, for states cannot be trusted themselves to respect limitations to their power unless there exist external controls of one kind or another."[73] This argument is premised on the rather contentious assumption that human rights apply primarily to individuals rather than to groups or collectives. Self-determination, as a collective entitlement and a core feature of the broader struggle for decolonization, should therefore not be considered part of the human rights movement.[74]

I find these arguments unconvincing. The assumption that sociopolitical struggles are "human rights" struggles only when they focus explicitly on reducing state power over the individual privileges particular ideological strands in the conceptualization of human rights. The problem with excluding anti-colonialism from the human rights story is that it treats classical individual-centred, state-centric civil and political rights as paradigmatic and overlooks the tensions and complementarities with other understandings of human rights—communal, collective, shared, economic, and social rights.

Human rights are not just individual rights, they are also people's rights; they are not just entitlements that individuals hold against the state, they are also entitlements that individuals and communities hold in their relationships with each other. As Hannah Arendt famously argued, the rights of "man" are indistinguishable from the rights of peoples.[75] In the context of anti-colonialism, emancipation meant that not only individuals, but also peoples, were free to determine their own fate. The question of human rights, therefore, quickly and inextricably blended with the question of national emancipation; only the emancipated sovereignty of peoples seemed to be able to ensure them. The realization and import of this identification of individual rights with people's rights came to light only with the rise of rightless peoples, comprising those who were deprived en masse of human rights.[76]

The dominant theme in nationalist discourse was the right to national self-determination which was seen as the starting point and indispensable condition for all other rights and freedoms. As would be expected in such circumstances, collective rights expressed in terms of the right of peoples to national self-determination took precedence over individual rights. Kwame Nkrumah, the Ghanaian nationalist who became prime minister of Ghana at independence, famously enjoined his countrypeople: "Seek ye first *the political kingdom* and all other things shall be added unto you."[77] The clear emphasis in anti-colonial nationalist rights discourse was on the collective right to political self-determination which was considered a prerequisite for the observance of individual rights. Does this strategic linking of collective self-determination with individual liberties make anti-colonialism any less a human rights movement?

There are even more explicit connections between anti-colonialism and the postwar human rights movement. In 1960 the UN General Assembly issued the Declaration on the Granting of Independence to Colonial Countries and Peoples.[78] The Declaration reaffirmed the fundamental human rights, dignity, and worth of all humans, and the equal right of peoples of all nations to self-determination. It asserted that all peoples have an inalienable right to complete freedom, the exercise of their sovereignty, and the integrity of their national territory. It also firmly placed anti-colonialism within the emergent universal human rights corpus. In the UN debates on colonialism and human rights, the presumption was that national self-determination is the starting point and indispensable condition for all other rights and freedoms. Individual rights could only be fully achieved when the collective rights of nationhood and self-determination were attained. The adoption in 1966 of the United Nations International Covenant on Civil and Political Rights, which explicitly articulates the right to self-determination, also reflects the influence that self-determination and anti-colonialism had on the development of the human rights idea.

Beyond all these however, it is important to note that human rights claims and struggles do not always take the form of organized political or social movements. Long before the first anti-colonial and nationalist political organizations were formed, individuals and groups articulated rights claims and undertook actions aimed at fulfilling their rights as humans, as indigenous peoples, and as colonial subjects and "protected persons." These non-formal and non-structured struggles for freedom, equity, and justice were no less struggles for human rights.

In constructing a global public history of human rights, the question is not so much whether the story should begin with anti-colonialism as whether it should be included at all. At a theoretical level, the argument against reading anti-colonialism as a human rights movement is unconvincing; at a practical level it is untenable. Anti-colonialism did not develop in isolation from the universal human rights discourse. Rather, it was integral to the development, translation, and vernacularization of the postwar universal human rights language to colonial and post-colonial contexts. This is an important part of the human rights story.

THE UNIVERSALIZING AGENDA OF THE 1970S

More recently, some scholars have made arguments for placing the defining locus of human rights not in the developments of the 1940s or the UDHR but in the universalizing impulses of the 1970s onward. The argument runs thus: Contemporary human rights may have been articulated at the United Nations in the 1940s, but it only became truly universal in the 1970s as it captured the global imagination. During this period, human rights activism experienced a dramatic boom, reaching into the very areas where human rights infractions occurred most frequently and violently.[79] This, accordingly, is what allowed it to evolve into a global movement, becoming the standard discourse for engaging with situation of systematic injustice.

Arguments have also been made for a conceptual distinction between pre-1970s discourses that espoused citizenship rights under the state and post-1970s discourses about paradigmatic rights-holders—rights that people have simply by virtue of being human. The precursors represent a "politics of citizenship at home" while the 1970s represent the "politics of suffering abroad," in which the state is also the source of the abuses.[80] One has a domestic scope with a discourse of justice while the other is universal in latitude and international in outlook with a connection with the UN human rights idea.[81]

The argument for privileging the 1970s as a defining epoch of universalization in the human rights story may be contested on two grounds. First, the distinction made between the "politics of citizenship at home" and "politics of suffering abroad" creates a conceptual dichotomy, another of those Manichean taxonomies that human rights scholarship now seems so inextricably trapped in. One of the problems with these kinds of dualities is that they create a false, albeit tidy, dichotomy in which two alternatives are considered, when in fact there are many shades of grey between the extremes.[82] Secondly, inherent in this dichotomy is a conflation of internationalism and universalism. As has been noted in relation to the UDHR, the so-called "universalizing impulses" of the 1970s were not always universally shared. The projection of ideas from powerful and influential metropoles to diverse locales may indeed internationalize these ideas and foster certain cosmopolitanisms, but that alone does not make them universal. If by "universal" we mean that which affects, concerns, and involves *all*, then claims to universality must continually be measured by the extent to which they aggregate local perspectives and experiences.

The 1970s indeed ushered in an era in which the focus of human rights discourse in the West shifted from infractions at home to violations abroad. These shifts are evidenced by the decision of the Jimmy Carter administration in the late 1970s to make human rights the centrepiece of US foreign policy and by the establishment of organizations such as Helsinki Watch (now Human Rights Watch) in 1975 to monitor human rights violations in the Soviet bloc. However, these developments must be read within the context of the international ideological politics of the Cold War. One of the Cold War legacies for human rights was the creation and intensification of the boundaries between civil/political rights and economic/social rights; between domestic "civil rights" infractions and foreign "human rights" violations. These boundaries reflect the East versus West polarization in international relations, which reduced human rights to a weapon of propaganda and political ideology in a bipolar struggle. As one United Nations report stated:

> The West emphasized civil and political rights, pointing the finger at socialist countries for denying these rights. The socialist (and many developing) countries emphasized economic and social rights, criticizing the richest Western countries for failure to secure these rights for all its citizens.[83]

Cold War politics shaped the way human rights was understood and talked about in different countries, creating new epistemological and pedagogical fault lines. For many in the West, human rights violations became something that only happened abroad. When it involved "us" it was a civil rights issue but when it involved "others" it became a human rights issue. How else can one explain the persistent reference in history books to the struggles by blacks against Jim Crow segregation laws in United States as "civil rights" struggles whereas contemporaneous movements by black Africans against apartheid in South Africa are described in the same textbooks as "human rights" struggles?[84] The distinction between the "politics of citizenship at home" and "politics of suffering abroad" in the 1970s was an essentially ideological construct which makes sense only in specific historical contexts. It is problematic as defining global benchmark for human rights.

Besides, it has been suggested that the critical universalizing phase in the development of human rights was not the 1970s but the 1940s through the 1950s, when formerly colonized Asian and African voices became the most vocal champions of universality at international forums such as the United Nations.[85] Non-Western delegates made strident demands for universal application of rights a key plank in the attack on colonialism while colonial powers replied with well-crafted arguments about the essential cultural difference of their overseas territories. In what would today seem an ironic reversal of roles, Western nations argued for a restricted culturally relative interpretation of human rights while non-Western nationalists drew on universalist ideals of self-determination.

Yet, by the late 1960s and early 1970s, this universalist position began a precipitous reversal, coincident with the rise of authoritarian regimes in Asia and Africa. The 1970s saw the virtual abandonment of universality in many parts of the global South and the "decline of human rights."[86] Unlike the first wave of anti-colonial nationalist leaders, postcolonial governments denounced human rights as a Western imposition, and emphasized the need for different rights in developing countries. There were strident calls to consider Asian and African values in the interpretation and application of universal human rights standards. The most extreme voices even rejected the very possibility of universal human rights. Universality, unimpeachably anti-colonial in the 1950s, was thus rendered deeply suspect by the 1970s and 1980s.[87] The enthusiasm with which "Third World" opinion leaders embraced universality in anti-colonial struggles faltered once independence was attained.

What is the public historian to make of these fundamentally contradictory assessments of a key phase in the human rights story? Did the 1970s mark the ascendency of universal human rights or did it in fact mark an era of decline? This question in many ways epitomizes the challenges of conceptualizing and historicizing human rights. It shows that far from being settled history, our understanding of human rights history remains patently a work in progress. Long-standing debates over the meaning, origins, and development of human rights make constructing a "global" public history of human rights an inherently challenging exercise. Apart from the disagreement over which defining episodes constitute the locus of the human rights story, the public historian must also grapple with contentious questions of ordering and prioritizing human rights ideas, events, and personalities. Key questions remain: Does the public historian adopt a simple chronological approach, or a selective thematic approach taking account of the generations of rights schema which has become a canon of human right scholarship? How does the public historian deal with concerns that such ordering privileges a particular ideological and epistemological construct of human rights?

For museum projects, these questions have practical implications. They hold implications for the relative prominence and scope of exhibits and displays; what to emphasize or deemphasize, and what to include or exclude. In the consultations leading to the establishment of the Canadian Museum of Human Rights these questions generated interesting, and sometimes, polarizing public debates. Should the Holocaust exhibits be accorded more prominence than others given its presumed centrality to the origin and development of the contemporary human rights movement? Should Aboriginal rights exhibits take prominence over others given the Canadian historical experience? Do these choices amount to privileging particular human rights narratives? How can gay rights and women's rights material be included in ways that serve an objective human rights agenda rather than an ideological one?[88] My goal here has not been to engage these questions dealing specifically with the public debates concerning the CMHR. The task here has been to explore broader conceptual arguments about meanings and origins, and their implications for constructing a broad public history of human rights.

CONCLUSION

The goal of public history should not simply be to bring academic debates to a wider public. Rather, it should be to inform and engage the public in the very process of historical construction. For museums in particular, the goal should not be to remake them in the image of the academy but to come up with ways to combine the strengths of the history profession in the museum and the academy.[89] Visitors who walk into the halls of a museum of human rights should feel a sense of ownership of and engagement with the histories represented within its walls. A public history of human rights should therefore be able to engage, yet transcend, polemical academic debates about the meaning and origins of human rights. Such histories should be able to draw links between earlier notions of human dignity or distributive justice and modern ideas of "human rights," which are in many ways contextual reinterpretations of age-long notions of defining human worth and value. The concern should be less about placing the "true" origins of human rights than drawing connections between the historical epochs and episodes that have shaped the human rights idea.

The key object of a human rights history, I think, should be to understand and appreciate the varied yet related historical circumstances under which human rights as a normative idea has manifested in different societies. This calls for attention to nuance and context. But given its predilection for structural analysis, contemporary human rights scholarship tends to be driven more by the quest for neat models and precise labels. The messy middle has, for the most part, been left out. Yet, it is the messy middle that reveals the transformative power of the human rights idea. While structural analyses may be useful in systematizing the academic study of human rights, fuller understanding can only come from going beyond these structures to explore the complexities, nuances, and connections that underlie them. This is where the historian's attention to context, change, and continuity becomes relevant. Even if we agree that the UDHR or the universalizing impulses of the 1970s were epoch-making phases in the human rights story, the historian (public or academic) cannot start or stop the story at such break points. It is the historian's task to look for continuities (and discontinuities), for the varied roots of supposedly epoch-making events and how they connect with other historical episodes in the development of the human rights idea. It is inherently more useful to think in terms of a concatenation of defining episodes rather than a compartmentalization of these episodes.

However, in drawing the crucial link between the defining epochs and episodes of human rights, it is important to leave open the possibility that the peoples and societies being studied and represented may not themselves have construed rights in the precise sense and terms of today. Still, a public history of human rights should be able to convey the multiple strands in the evolving human rights story—how the idea of human rights is at once a historical product of the modern age and the outcome of cumulative human experiences; an assertion of individual liberties but also an affirmation of collective entitlements; a means of breaking down the impunity of rulers but also a way of forging relationships; a resource for civil repair but also a transcendental norm of resistance; an effect of power and resistance but also a form of freedom and discipline.[90] The complexity of the human rights idea is that it can play all these roles. A public history of human rights should aspire to capture and reflect these complexities.

NOTES

1. Ronald Dworkin, *A Matter of Principle* (Cambridge, MA: Harvard University Press, 1985).
2. The English jurist and philosopher Jeremy Bentham famously remarked that the very idea of rights is "nonsense on stilts" for there is no right which, when the abolition of it is advantageous to society, should not be abolished. Some contemporary human rights scholars agree. See Jeremy Bentham, *Introduction to the Principles of Morals and Legislation* (London, 1789, n.p.); Roger Scruton, "Nonsense on Stilts," in *International Handbook of Human Rights*, ed. Thomas Cushman (New York: Routledge, 2011), 118–28.
3. Alasdair MacIntyre, "Why Is the Search for the Foundations of Ethics So Frustrating?" *Hastings Center Report*, 9, 4 (1979): 16. Also Jack Donnelly, "In Search of the Unicorn: The Jurisprudence and Politics of the Right to Development," *California Western International Law Journal* 473 (1985).
4. For some exemplary works, see Micheline Ishay, *The History of Human Rights: From the Stone Age to the Globalization Era* (Berkeley, CA.: University of California Press, 2008); Paul Gordon Lauren, *The Evolution of International Human Rights: Visions Seen* (Philadelphia: University of Pennsylvania Press, 2003); John M. Headley, *The Europeanization of the World: On the Origins of Human Rights and Democracy* (Princeton: Princeton University Press, 2007); Lynn Hunt, *Inventing Human Rights: A History* (New York: W.W. Norton, 2007); Elizabeth Borgwardt, *A New Deal for the World: America's Vision for Human Rights* (Cambridge, MA: Belknap Press, 2005).
5. Samuel Moyn, *The Last Utopia: Human Rights in History* (Cambridge, MA: Belknap Press, 2010), 5.
6. Bonny Ibhawoh, *Imperialism and Human Rights: Colonial Discourses of Rights and Liberties in African History* (Albany, State University of New York Press, 2007), 2.
7. Ibid., 3.
8. Moyn, *The Last Utopia*, 5.
9. Ibid., 9.

10. Jenny Martinez, *The Slave Trade and the Origins of International Human Rights Law* (Oxford; New York: Oxford University Press, 2012).

11. Hunt, *Inventing Human Rights*.

12. Alice Conklin, "Colonialism and Human Rights: A Contradiction in Terms? The Case of France and West Africa, 1895–1914," *The American Historical Review* 103, 2 (1998).

13. Ronald Burke, *Decolonization and the Evolution of International Human Rights* (Philadelphia: University of Pennsylvania Press, 2010).

14. Linda K. Kerber, "We Are All Historians of Human Rights," *Perspectives: Newsmagazine of the American Historical Association* 44, no.7 (2006): 3–4.

15. For the notions of domestication or "vernacularization" of rights see Sally Engle-Merry, "Transnational Human Rights and Local Activism: Mapping the Middle" in *American Anthropologist* 108, no. 1 (2006): 38–51; Judy L. Ledger and Kheang Un, "Global Concepts and Local Meaning: Human Rights and Buddhism in Cambodia" in *Journal of Human Rights* 2, no. 4 (2003): 531–49.

16. See for example Ann Curthoys and Paula Hamilton, "What Makes History Public," *Public History Review*, 1 (1993) and Otis Graham, "Editor's Corner," *The Public Historian* 15, no. 1 (1993), 6–7.

17. Jill Liddington, "What is Public History? Publics and their Pasts: Meanings and Practices, *Oral History* 30, no. 1 (2002): 83–93.

18. Graeme Davis, "A Historian in the Museum: The Ethics of Public History," in *The Historian's Conscience: Australian Historians on the Ethics of History*, ed. Stuart Macintyre (Carlton, Vic.: Melbourne Univ. Publ., 2004), 52.

19. Ibid., 52.

20. Thomas A. Woods, "Museums and the Public: Doing History Together," *The Journal of American History* 82, no. 3 (1995): 1112.

21. Museum scholars make a distinction between "human rights museums" and "human rights museology." Human rights museums are museums that explicitly take up the subject of human rights as central to their mission. Human rights museology on the other hand is about a form of practice: "one that proclaims the social vocation of the museum and incorporates practices other than those traditional to the museum: i.e. teaching about citizenship practices and methods of activism." See Jennifer Carteri and Jennifer Orangeii, "Fighting for Equality: Social Change through Human Rights Activism: The Work of Museums: The Implications of a Human Rights Museology," paper presented at Federation of International Human Rights Museums Conference, International Slavery Museum, Liverpool, UK October 10–13, 2011.

22. Carteri and Orangeii, "Fighting for Equality."

23. Many of these museums combine their traditional role of education and commemoration with an activist mandate. For example, the theme of the second international conference of the Federation of International Human Rights Museums in 2011 was "Fighting for Equality: Social Change through Human Rights Activism." www.fihrm.org (accessed January 23, 2012).

24. Museums Act, S.C. 1990 c. 3, as amended, Canadian Museum for Human Rights, http://humanrightsmuseum.ca/about-museum (accessed January 23, 2012).

25. Canadian Museum for Human Rights, http://humanrightsmuseum.ca (accessed January 23, 2012).

26. Ibid.

27. Ibid.

28. Davis, "A Historian in the Museum," 55.

29. Carrierd Avid, *Museum Skepticism: A History of the Display of Art in Public Galleries* (Durham: Duke University Press, 2006).

30. For example, the theme of the second international conference of the Federation of International Human Rights Museums (FIHRM) was: "Fighting for Equality: Social Change through Human Rights Activism."

31. For insight into the public debate surrounding the establishment of the museum see Ira Basen,

"Memory Becomes a Minefield at Canada's Museum for Human Rights," *Globe and Mail*, August 20, 2011.

32. Canadian Museum for Human Rights, http://humanrightsmuseum.ca (accessed January 23, 2012).

33. Basen, "Memory Becomes a Minefield."

34. Stuart Murray, "Goal of Canadian Museum for Human Rights is to Inspire Visitors, Encourage Action," *The Hill Times*, January 24, 2011, http://humanrightsmuseum.ca/about-museum/news/goal-canadian-museum-human-rights-inspire-visitors-encourage-action (accessed January 23, 2012).

35. Marie-Bénédicte Dembour, "What Are Human Rights? Four Schools of Thought," *Human Rights Quarterly* 32, no. 1: 2010.

36. These themes were stressed in Michel Ignatieff's lecture at the Taking Liberties workshop.

37. See, for example, Ishay, *The History of Human Rights*; Lauren, *The Evolution of International Human Rights*.

38. Margaret Macdonald, "Natural Rights," in *Theories of Right*, ed. Jeremy Waldron (London: Oxford University Press, 1984), 27–29.

39. Burns Weston, "Human Rights," *Human Rights Quarterly* 6, no. 3 (1984): 259.

40. The US Declaration of Independence, for instance, states: "all men are created equal, they are endowed by their creator with certain inalienable rights, among these are life, liberty and pursuit of happiness; men are born and remain free and equal in rights."

41. Hunt, *Inventing Human Rights*.

42. Ibid., 20.

43. See for example Robin Blackburn, *The American Crucible: Slavery, Emancipation and Human Rights* (New York: Verso, 2011).

44. Adam Hochschild, *Bury the Chains: Prophets and Rebels in the Fight to Free an Empire's Slaves* (Boston: Houghton Mifflin, 2005), 5.

45. Martinez, *The Slave Trade and the Origins of International Human Rights Law*, 13–14.

46. Ibid., 149.

47. Lamin O Sanneh, *Abolitionists Abroad: American Blacks and the Making of Modern West Africa*. (Cambridge: Harvard University Press), 1999, 10.

48. Ibid., 246.

49. *The Antislavery Examiner* 6 (1838).

50. Sanneh, *Abolitionists Abroad*, 246.

51. For example, Samuel Moyn critiques the notion that human rights is an old idea that finally came into its own as a response to the Holocaust, describing it as a "universally accepted myth" about the origins of human rights. However, he does not question the essential presumption that human rights came to being in the postwar UN system of the 1940s. Moyn, *The Last Utopia*, 6.

52. Orlando Patterson, "Freedom, Slavery, and the Modern Construction of Rights," in *Historical Change and Human Rights: The Oxford Amnesty Lectures 1994*, ed. Olwen Hufton (New York: Basic Books, 1995), 176–77.

53. Article 1 of the Charter of the United Nations.

54. These include the International Covenants on Civil and Political Rights and the International Covenant on Social and Cultural Rights introduced in 1976.

55. The human rights corpus now includes not only United Nations conventions and declarations but also regional instruments and institutions such as the European Convention on the Protection of Human Rights and Fundamental Freedoms. the American Declaration on the Rights and Duties of Man, and the African Charter for Human and People's Rights.

56. Jack Donnelly, "Human Rights and Human Dignity: An Analytic Critique of Non-Western Human Rights Conceptions," *American Political Science Review* 76, no. 2 (1982): 303.

57. Samuel Moyn, "Imperialism, Self-Determination and the Rise of Human Rights," in *The Human Rights Revolution: An International History*, ed. Akira Iriye et al. (New York: Oxford University Press), 162.

58. See Moyn, *The Last Utopia*, 12.
59. Michael Ignatieff, *Human Rights as Politics and Idolatry* (Princeton: Princeton University Press, 2001), 5–7.
60. United Nations Department of Public Information, "A Magna Carta for all Humanity," www.un.org/rights/50/carta.htm (accessed February 6, 2012).
61. Even this point is subject to dispute. At the singing of the UDHR in 1948, many African and Asian countries were still under colonial rule and were not members of the United Nations. They were therefore not party to the drafting of the original document, although most of these nations have since ratified the declaration.
62. Johannes Morsink, *The Universal Declaration of Human Rights: Origins. Drafting and Intent*, Philadelphia: University of Pennsylvania Press, 1999). 12–14.
63. Tiyambe Zeleza and Philip McConnaughay, eds. *Human Rights and Economic Development in Africa: Establishing the Rule of Law* (Philadelphia: University of Pennsylvania Press, 2004), 9.
64. Makau Mutua, *Human Rights: A Political and Cultural Critique* (Philadelphia: University of Pennsylvania Press, 2002), 3.
65. American Anthropological Association, "Statement on Human Rights," *American Anthropologist* 40 (1947), 359–45.
66. Marie Dembour, "Foundations: Critiques" in *International Human Rights Law*, ed. Daniel Moeckli, Sangeeta Shah, and Sandesh Sivakumaran (Oxford: Oxford University Press, 2010), 81; David Slater, "Contesting Occidental Visions of the Global: The Geopolitics of Theory and North-South Relations" in *Beyond Law*, December 1994, 100; Isodore Bonabom, "The Development of a Truth Regime on 'the Human': Human Rights in the Gold Coast 1945–57" (PhD thesis, University of Sussex, 2012), 33.
67. Arguments that Third World actors were not part of the postwar human rights program are contested. Roland Burke has argued that Asian, African, and Arab human-rights specialists played a key role in the evolution of the human-rights program almost from its inception. However, he reaches this conclusion only because he shifts the focus from the story of the creation of the Universal Declaration, which is primarily a Western story, to how its implementation evolved both within the United Nations and in the political interactions between the First and the Third World.
    The essentially West-centric character of the UDHR and developments leading up to its adoption in 1948 remains unchallenged. Ronald Burke, *Decolonization and the Evolution of International Human Rights* (Philadelphia: University of Pennsylvania Press, 2010).
68. Bonny Ibhawoh, "Colonialism: Legacy for Human Rights," in *Encyclopedia of Human Rights*, ed. David P. Forsythe (Oxford: Oxford University Press, 2009), 363.
69. Burke, *Decolonization and the Evolution of International Human Rights*, 37.
70. Bonny Ibhawoh, "Colonialism: Legacy for Human Rights.
71. Moyn, "Imperialism, Self-Determination and the Rise of Human Rights," 164; Moyn, *The Last Utopia*. In particular, Chap. 3: "Why Anti-Colonialism wasn't a Human Rights Movement."
72. A.W. Brian Simpson, *Human Rights and the End of Empire: Britain and the Genesis of the European Convention* (Oxford: Oxford University Press, 2004), 301.
73. Simpson goes on to argue that the real connection between the human rights movement and anti-colonialism lie in a common commitment to the notion of human dignity. Simpson, *Human Rights and the End of Empire*, 301.
74. Petra Goedde, Review of Roland Burke, *Decolonization and the Evolution of International Human Rights*, Human Rights Quarterly, 33 (2011): 564.
75. Hannah Arendt, *The Origins of Totalitarianism* (New York: Harvest Books, 1973), 291.
76. Roger Berkowitz, "Hannah Arendt on Human Rights" in *International Handbook of Human Rights*, ed. Thomas Cushman (New York: Routledge, 2011), 59.
77. Kwame Nkrumah, *The Autobiography of Kwame Nkrumah* (Edinburgh: Thomas Nelson Publishers, 1976), 146.
78. Office of the United Nations Commissioner for Human Rights, hwww2.ohchr.org/english/law/independence.htm (accessed October 17, 2012).

79. Petra Goedde, *Review of Roland Burke, Decolonization and the Evolution of International Human Rights*, 564.

80. Moyn, *The Last Utopia*, 12.

81. Ibid.

82. Bonabom, "The Development of a Truth Regime on 'the Human,'" 30.

83. United Nations Development Program, *Human Development Report: Human Rights and Human Development* (New York: UNDP, 2000), 3.

84. But even here there is disagreement since some scholars argue that pre-UDHR struggles were not human rights struggles.

85. Burke, *Decolonization and the Evolution of International Human*, 95.

86. Ibid., 4.

87. Ibid., 4.

88. One critic described the CMHR as a "Temple of Propaganda," arguing that its supporters have "made a monster of the word tolerance, [have] raped the word gay, and [have] beheaded the term human rights." John Jalsevac, "Winnipeg's Museum for Human Rights: Canada's $300 Million Temple of Ideology," www.lifesitenews.com/news/archive/ldn/2005/jul/050701a (accessed January 25, 2012).

89. Thomas A. Woods, "Museums and the Public: Doing History Together," *The Journal of American History* 82, no. 3 (1995): 1115.

90. Robert Fine, "Cosmopolitanism and Human Rights," in *International Handbook of Human Rights*, 101.

Chapter 3

•◆•

The Rights Revolution in Canada and Australia: International Politics, Social Movements, and Domestic Law

Dominique Clément

Canada was a reluctant human rights advocate by the 1940s. John Humphrey, the Canadian who drafted the Universal Declaration of Human Rights (UDHR), considered his own country's response to the Declaration as "one of the worst contributions" and "a niggardly acceptance . . . the Canadian government did not relish the thought of remaining in the company of those who, by abstaining in the vote, rejected it."[1] According to Humphrey, the "government's attitude toward the Declaration was skeptical; at its extreme, Canada's attitude bordered on hostility."[2] And yet, within a generation, Canada would become a proponent of human rights at home and abroad.

In this article I forward three arguments: First, there is a conceptual distinction between human rights and civil liberties, and in the postwar period Canadians (and Australians) largely defined rights as civil liberties. Second, human rights had a transformative impact on foreign policy, domestic law, and social movements in Canada beginning in the 1970s. Third, to demonstrate the extent of the rights revolution in Canada, I compare Canada and Australia and argue that the rights revolution was more restricted in the latter. Canada's rights revolution represented a profound break with the past. Weak anti-discrimination laws were replaced with expansive human rights codes across the country and, in 1982, the Constitution was amended to include a bill of rights. A social movement dedicated to the principles of the UDHR was born. Finally, as human rights became a cornerstone of international politics, it began to influence Canadian foreign policy.

Meanwhile, in Australia, the transition from a Cold War discourse of civil liberties to human rights was more restricted in scope. Canada and Australia are ideal comparative case studies because of the extensive legal, social, historical, geographical, and political similarities between the two countries. International treaties informed human rights law in both countries and, like Canada, Australia enacted an expansive human rights legal regime. But Australian human rights laws were less sophisticated, and there were no self-professed human rights organizations in Australia. The different historical trajectory of these two countries demonstrates the necessity of understanding how ideas of rights evolve within a particular social context. As E. J. Hobsbawm insisted, rights "are not abstract, universal and unchanging. They exist as parts of particular sets of beliefs in the minds of men and women about the nature of human society and the ordering of relations between human beings within it."[3] The study of human rights must begin locally.

The first part of this article briefly documents instances of gross abuse of state power in Canada and Australia in the 1940s. These events launched national debates that, as we will see, exemplified how the language of civil liberties dominated public discourse surrounding rights. The second part briefly notes how the Cold War stifled human rights progress in international politics, as well as domestically in Canada and Australia. The final part of the article examines the 1970s rights revolutions in Canada and Australia. The rights revolution was transformative, and yet at the same time it was contested and profoundly determined by local conditions.

CIVIL LIBERTIES IN POSTWAR CANADA AND AUSTRALIA

The war was a traumatic event for rights. The Defence of Canada Regulations during the Second World War, according to Ramsay Cook, "represented the most serious restrictions upon the civil liberties of Canadians since Confederation."[4] In particular, the deportation and disenfranchisement of thousands of Japanese Canadians engendered intense debate across the country.[5] Australians accepted similar restrictions on their liberties during the war including censorship, internment camps, limits on due process, and bans on numerous organizations. But it was Canadians who first engaged in a postwar national debate on the vulnerability of civil liberties to state abuse.

Igor Gouzenko, a young Russian cipher clerk, left his embassy in Ottawa one night in September 1945 clutching a handful of classified documents under his coat. He eventually made his way to the RCMP where he declared his intention to defect, and presented the police with evidence of a Soviet spy ring. The federal government's response was, to say the least, excessive: the cabinet used the War Measures Act in peacetime to detain dozens of *suspected* spies, hold them incommunicado, trapped in tiny cells under suicide watch, and subject them to repeated interrogations by the police (who later used the testimony against the accused in court after circumscribing all rights to due process). The event launched a national debate in Canada, and led to the formation of a half-dozen civil liberties associations.

Soon after, the Canadian government received word from San Francisco that the United Nations was drafting a Universal Declaration of Human Rights (UDHR). At the time, Humphrey observed in his diary that "the international promotion of human rights had no priority in Canadian foreign policy."[6] Canada initially abstained when the Third Committee of the General Assembly voted on the proposed UDHR. The Australian government, on the other hand, did not share its Canadian counterpart's reluctance. H.V. Evatt, a key figure in the Australian Labour Party and president of the United Nations General Assembly, embraced his government's enthusiasm for the Declaration.[7] The Australians, who were founding members of the Commission on Human Rights and proponents for an active human rights policy at the United Nations, advocated for the inclusion of social, economic, and cultural rights in the UDHR.[8] In contrast, this issue raised serious concerns in Canada, especially among the Canadian Bar Association and leading members of the federal cabinet.[9] However, Australia did agree with the Canadian position to restrict the scope of the UDHR. Britain, Canada, the United States, and Australia supported South African Prime Minister Jan Smuts's insistence on a domestic jurisdiction clause to prevent the United Nations from intervening in domestic affairs.[10] Pressure from its allies—and the distasteful possibility of voting alongside South Africa, Saudi Arabia, and the communist bloc—ultimately led Canada to support the UDHR in the final vote in 1948. Officially, the federal government insisted that it was concerned about violating provincial jurisdiction.[11] Privately, the acting prime minister, Louis St. Laurent, was far more apprehensive that the UDHR could be used "to provoke contentious even if unfair criticism of the Government."[12]

Australia's Labour Party was defeated a year later and replaced with Robert Menzies's Liberal Party government. Menzies was, at best, lukewarm toward human rights. In fact, fear and hatred of communism led to a national debate in Australia about how far the state should be permitted to restrict rights. The Menzies government attempted twice to ban the Communist Party of Australia, first through legislation in 1950, which was defeated in court, and a year later with a referendum.[13] In each case, the government proposed to declare the party an unlawful association and to dissolve any organizations (including unions) suspected of being communists. The Governor General simply had to declare a person "communist" to suspend them from holding office in a union, the public service, or the military. The onus of proof was placed upon the accused, and the penalty for violating the law was five years in jail. Debates raged in the House of Commons and the media throughout 1950 and 1951. The referendum failed, albeit barely: 50.5 percent voted "no." Rights became prominent public issues in Australia during these debates.[14] As in Canada, Australians responded to these events by forming several civil liberties associations.[15]

What stands out most about postwar debates in Canada and Australia is that the term *human rights* was rarely employed.[16] The Gouzenko affair dominated Canadian newspaper headlines and editorials between February and April 1946. The most common theme was the state's abuse of the suspects' civil liberties. Similarly, Members of Parliament as well as non-governmental organizations framed their concerns using the language of civil liberties. Critics routinely made reference to British tradition. A typical example was one author writing for the *Dalhousie Review* who suggested that the government "created popular sympathy for the accused and erred greatly in not taking scrupulous care that the established practices of British justice were followed."[17] In Australia, rights talk was even more laden with references to British justice. The Australian Council for Civil Liberties (ACCL) published flyers denouncing the dissolution bill on the basis that it was offensive to the "fundamental civil liberties in the British democracies."[18] During the referendum campaign a group of self-declared distinguished citizens published an advertisement urging citizens to vote against the initiative on the basis that the proposal "offends against long-standing British principle."[19] Parliamentarians often made reference to "abandoning British principles" or "inverting the normal processes of British Justice."[20]

The term *human rights* had yet to gain popular currency in either country. Instead, Canadians and Australians were possessed of civil liberties, and popular discourse was often rooted in references to British liberties. The first non-partisan associations dedicated to promoting rights for all citizens were formed in both countries in the 1930s: the ACCL and the Canadian Civil Liberties Union (CCLU). The Gouzenko affair and the Communist Party Dissolution Act spawned similar organizations.[21] There were no self-professed "human rights" associations. The constitutions of the CCLU and the ACCL defined rights as civil liberties, and in particular civil and political rights.[22] Civil liberties organizations campaigned for traditional British liberties as they understood the principles: freedoms of speech, association, assembly, and religion, press; due process; and non-discrimination.

Neither country had a bill of rights or any human rights laws. Saskatchewan passed a provincial Bill of Rights in 1947, which was only the second anti-discrimination law in Canadian history. The statute, however, was narrowly constructed. It recognized freedoms of speech, assembly, religion, and association, and due process, while at the same time prohibiting discrimination solely on the basis of race, religion, and national origin (opinion was divided, however, over whether or not Saskatchewan had the jurisdiction to legislate on fundamental freedoms).[23] Even by the late 1950s there was only a scattering of weak anti-discrimination statutes in Canada. These laws were largely ineffective: they were rarely enforced, few people were aware they existed, and the legislation was poorly drafted.[24] Premier Ernest Manning of Alberta expressed a common belief at the time when he rejected demands for anti-discrimination legislation on the grounds that the "government prefers to rely upon those individual rights and privileges as established by the Common Law of England and the British Commonwealth."[25] Both countries debated a constitutional bill of rights, but to no avail. The Australian Labour Party initiated a referendum in 1944 to add protections for speech and religion to the constitution.[26] In Canada, Parliament formed committees in 1947, 1948, and 1950 to consider a bill of rights. The Australian referendum failed, and the Canadian committees were unable to come to a consensus. Discussions surrounding a bill of rights also focused almost exclusively on civil and political rights.

Moreover, Humphrey was correct when he pointed out that human rights was not a foreign policy priority for Canada. The same was true for Australia. Neither country was dedicated to promoting human rights abroad despite some initial commitments before the war, including participation in the League of Nations and the International Labour Organization (ILO). Australia and Canada had joined the other Western

powers in opposing Japan's attempt to include a section on racial discrimination in the League of Nations's Charter. "The early Canadian attitude toward United Nations involvement with rights," explains Cathal
Nolan, "was clearly apathetic, and even a little smug. Ottawa considered
the US proposal on human rights wrongheaded at best, and at worst as
constituting an invalid interference in the internal affairs of states."[27] The
Menzies government, which governed until 1972, was noticeably hostile to international human rights treaties, if not to the United Nations
itself.[28] Canadian and Australian foreign policy in the 1940s and 1950s
privileged state sovereignty to the detriment of human rights intervention.[29] Canada, for example, opposed intervention over human rights
abuses in South Africa in 1955 and Nigeria in 1968 on the basis of re-
specting state sovereignty.[30]

Inheriting the British tradition of civil liberties had implications
for both countries. Social movements, political leaders, and the media
by the 1950s largely defined rights as civil and political rights. Even the
Australian Labour Party, which supported the inclusion of social and
economic rights in the UDHR, did not seek similar provisions for the
Australian constitution. Another tradition inherited from Britain was
parliamentary supremacy. In justifying his government's decision to
unilaterally suspend the rights of suspected spies, Minister of Justice J.L.
Ilsley claimed that "those principles resulting from Magna Carta, from
the Petition of Rights, the Bill of Settlement and Habeas Corpus Act, are
great and glorious privileges; but they are privileges which can be and
which unfortunately sometimes have to be interfered with by the actions
of Parliament or actions under the authority of Parliament."[31] The Menzies
government routinely appealed to parliamentary supremacy throughout
its campaign to ban the Communist Party of Australia. Paul Hasluck, a
Member of Parliament, insisted that "when changes are expressed by society through a freely elected Parliament, and freely accepted by society
surely there can be no infringement of the democratic principles."[32] A belief in the supremacy of Parliament further contributed to opposition in
both countries to a bill of rights.[33] Stuart Garson, the Canadian minister
of justice in 1950, perfectly captured this sentiment in a memorandum to
the federal cabinet: "If we agree by an international Covenant to submit
to restrictions upon our Parliamentary sovereignty . . . we will have a
rather difficult time arguing within Canada that we are not warranted in
submitting to the restrictions upon our Parliamentary sovereignty which

a bill of rights would involve, for the protection of the civil liberties of our Canadian citizens."[34] Similarly, Menzies rejected the Labour Party's attempt in 1944 to amend the constitution, arguing that "we are British people and we do not need to be reminded that we have inherited these established principles of government from our English ancestors, and that we do not need some solemn piece of writing in a Constitution to make us completely determined that our inherited freedoms will not be taken aware from us by despots or by elected persons."[35]

The United States, Great Britain, and France shared Canada's and Australia's concerns about the UDHR.[36] The major powers did not see human rights as a foreign policy priority.[37] Even the International Labour Organization had never used the language of human rights in its conventions by this time.[38] Human rights simply lacked popular appeal in the postwar period: international lawyers overwhelmingly rejected it as a basis for international law; anti-colonial movements embraced human rights, not to promote individual freedom, but for the purposes of state formation; the United Nations did little to promote human rights; and social movements had yet to embrace human rights as a vision for social change.[39]

COLD WAR HUMAN RIGHTS

The Cold War stifled attempts to promote human rights as a cornerstone of international politics.[40] The United Nations "became a surrogate battlefield for the Cold War, and co-operation between the West and the Soviet bloc deteriorated. The Cold War created ideological arguments over the meaning and determination of which rights deserved entrenchment into the organization's many conventions and treaties."[41] Several recent studies on the history of human rights law and politics have concluded that, until the 1970s, the Cold War had a dampening effect on human rights progress. "The [Great] Powers started to see human rights," insists Mark Mazower, "as a weapon to be deployed against each other."[42] According to Julie Mertus, "the ideological tug and pull of the Cold War impaired human rights enforcement efforts, but human rights standard setting shuffled along in the 1950s and 1960s, emerging as a viable political force in the 1970s and 1980s amid a proliferation of international human rights conferences, treaties, and declarations."[43] The priorities of international politics eroded the moral force of universal human rights as "the expediential demands of the Cold War were used to justify glaring inconsistencies of policy on human rights, democratic practice, arms supplies, trade, aid, and intervention."[44] Human rights, as Kathleen Mahoney argues, were used to advance global strategic interests: "By and large, each side used human rights as a tool for finding fault with and imputing immorality to the other . . . while turning a blind eye to human rights abuses within their own spheres of influence."[45] Cold War politics further undermined opportunities for grassroots mobilization and transnational activism.[46]

The Cold War had a similar impact on human rights in Canada and Australia. The Gouzenko affair, which is often cited as the event that launched the Cold War, and the Communist Party Dissolution Act were clearly part of a global conflict. Only a handful of civil liberties associations were active in Canada and Australia by the 1950s, and yet even these few groups were bitterly divided between communists and social democrats (the latter allied with liberals). During the Gouzenko affair and in response to the Communist Dissolution Act, civil liberties associations were oddly silent given the obvious attack on individual rights. Fears of being associated with communism not only silenced potential critics, but also made co-operation among activists extraordinarily difficult.[47] Civil liberties organizations in both countries became defunct by the 1950s. Australia's ACCL was still active in the 1950s, but it was a shadow of its former self. Ideological divisions undermined attempts to form a national civil liberties association in both countries.[48] Federal and state governments routinely dismissed concerns surrounding human rights abuses, including their own brand of McCarthyism and vicious attacks against trade unionists, by accusing critics of being soft on communism (in Australia, this included purges within the Labour Party, especially in New South Wales).[49] There was no appreciable change in foreign policy, which in both countries was largely dictated by Cold War allegiances. Despite its initial support for the UDHR, Australia shifted "from enthusiastically advocating a range of economic and social rights to attempting to minimise the rights, from insisting on government responsibility in the field to emphasising an individual's correlative duties."[50] In this way a discourse of civil liberties prevailed during the Cold War, and not the more expansive human rights discourse embedded in the UDHR.[51]

But the Cold War began to wane in the 1970s. The first Canadian prime ministerial visits to China, the Soviet Union, and Cuba, as well as several precedent-setting trade agreements, signalled a rapprochement with communist nations. Meanwhile, the Australian Labour Party, dur-ing its brief stint in power between 1972 and 1975, opened diplomatic re-lations with China and East Germany, expanded wheat shipments to the former, and withdrew troops from Vietnam. And the worst excesses of domestic Cold War politics in both countries appear to have dissipated by the 1970s. Communist purges within trade unions and the civil ser-vice were exhausted; several of the most outrageous laws restricting basic rights were eliminated; and political debates no longer drew as heavily on Cold War rhetoric.

Samuel Moyn suggests that human rights came to the forefront of international politics because other utopian ideals, such as commun-ism, had become discredited: "It was, instead, only in the 1970s that a genuine social movement around human rights made its appearance, seizing the foreground by transcending official government institutions, especially international ones."[52] This transformation in international politics took the form of action and rhetoric premised on the belief that citizens and governments had a legitimate interest in the human rights of people in other states. Examples of this transformation abound: the Carter administration's promotion of human rights in American foreign policy; the first US State Department annual human rights reports; the emergence of Amnesty International and Helsinki Watch; international human rights treaties, including the Helsinki Accords; the first postwar international humanitarian effort (in Biafra); the mobilization of trans-national advocacy networks surrounding human rights abuses in South America; the Fraser Committee Congressional hearing on American support for countries responsible for human rights violations; Soviet dissidents and the emergence of human rights movements in Russia; the Ford Foundation's initial forays into human rights promotion abroad; the stirrings of a global campaign against apartheid in South Africa; and the proliferation of human rights policies in individual countries' foreign aid programs. As a result of these and similar developments beginning in the 1970s human rights "reached consensual ('prescriptive') status on the international level."[53] Inevitably, these developments were to have an impact domestically on Canada and Australia, but in dissimilar ways.

CANADA AND AUSTRALIA'S RIGHTS REVOLUTIONS

Canadians began to experiment with anti-discrimination legislation as early as the 1940s, and several provinces introduced legislation in the

1950s banning discrimination on the basis of race, religion, and ethnicity in employment and accommodation. However, it became quickly apparent that the laws were ineffective. Ontario set a new standard in 1962 with its Human Rights Code. The legislation incorporated existing anti-discrimination laws into a single statute and established a commission to enforce the law. It was a landmark achievement, and would never have happened without the efforts of social movement activists. Organizations representing Jews, unionists, African Canadians, churches, and a host of others led the movement for human rights legislation.[54] One of these groups, the Association for Civil Liberties, morphed into the Canadian Civil Liberties Association in 1964. Two similar organizations had been formed in the previous two years: the British Columbia Civil Liberties Association (1962, Vancouver) and the Ligue des droits de l'homme (1963, Montreal). The emergence of these organizations heralded the beginning of a new generation of non-partisan rights associations.

The International Year for Human Rights (1968) was a watershed in Canada. It led to the formation of numerous self-professed "human rights" associations.[55] Unlike *civil liberties* organizations, which restricted their work to civil and political rights, *human rights* organizations embraced the broader principles of the UDHR. The latter's more expansive interpretation of human rights led to bitter debates on prominent issues. For instance, whereas civil liberties groups fought to remove unfair restrictions on citizens who received social assistance (e.g. the prohibition on single women from having male houseguests), human rights groups argued that individuals had a right to economic security, and could not exercise their political and civil rights without proper resources. Such disagreements were evident on numerous issues, such as pornography, immigration, sexual assault laws, and hate speech. These ideological divisions had a tangible impact: for many years the largest national rights association in the country was awkwardly called the Canadian Federation of Civil Liberties and Human Rights Associations. No organization more fully symbolized these divisions than the Ligue des droits de l'homme. The Ligue, which began as a civil liberties association (its original English name was the Quebec Civil Liberties Union), explicitly embraced a human rights platform in 1971. The Ligue's new mandate was to adapt to the changes occurring within Quebec society and to consider the unique problems facing the poor, women, elderly, youth, and ethnic minorities. Instead of concerning themselves with individual rights, the Ligue would achieve equity by improving the social conditions in which those rights were exercised.[56]

An astounding number of social movements had emerged by this time. The student movement and the New Left became a powerful force for social change; the number of women's groups in British Columbia alone increased from two in 1969 to over one hundred in 1974; the first gay rights organizations were formed in Vancouver and Toronto in the 1960s; and the founding of Greenpeace in 1971 symbolized the birth of the modern environmental movement. There were at least four national Aboriginal associations and thirty-three provincial organizations by 1970.[57] These movements employed the language of human rights. Meanwhile, Christian churches shifted toward humanitarian and rights-based work overseas, and formed international NGOs to promote human rights abroad. One project, Ten Days for World Development, was especially successful in generating support within Canada for a rights- and humanitarian-based foreign policy.[58]

The proliferation of social movements was a defining feature in much of the Western world. Although the Australian Council for Civil Liberties was defunct by the 1960s, the gap was filled with several new civil liberties associations beginning with the New South Wales Council for Civil Liberties (1963).[59] There was also an abortive attempt at a national association called the Australia Civil Liberties Council. But there were no human rights associations comparable to the organizations that appeared in Canada. The International Year for Human Rights was a muted affair in Australia.[60] Throughout the 1970s, more than forty civil liberties and human rights associations emerged in Canada, compared to only a handful of civil liberties groups scattered across Australia.[61]

For rights advocates in Canada, a key objective during this period was a constitutional bill of rights. On this issue they had the support of Pierre Elliot Trudeau, who had become prime minister in 1968.[62] The federal government appointed a Special Joint Committee on the Constitution in 1970 to consider, among other things, the viability of a bill of rights. Although the attempt ultimately failed, the hearings symbolized subtle changes in political discourse. Hardly anyone had raised an objection to the 1960 federal statutory Bill of Rights on the basis of restricting parliamentary supremacy, and the Special Joint Committee on the Constitution rejected the principle as an obstacle to a bill of rights: "Parliamentary sovereignty is no more sacrosanct a principle than is the respect for human liberty which is reflected in a Bill of Rights. Legislative sovereignty is already limited legally by the distribution of powers under a federal system and, some would say, by natural law or by the common law Bill of Rights."[63] There was also the beginning of a shift in foreign policy. A 1970 federal White Paper recommended a more vigorous and positive approach to human rights at the United Nations: "There is an expectation that Canada will participate in international efforts in the human rights field on a more extensive and meaningful scale than in the past."[64]

A similar rights revolution was underway in Australia in the 1970s. Whereas every Canadian province had introduced a human rights statute by 1975, the Australia government had only just begun. The federal government used its external affairs power under the constitution to pass the Racial Discrimination Act in 1975. Unlike Canada, where the provinces passed their own legislation, the federal government in Australia imposed legislation on local states.[65] State leaders vigorously objected to the law and accused the federal government of violating state jurisdiction.[66] Still, the Racial Discrimination Act, which survived a court challenge, was only a tentative step. A more expansive bill, the Human Rights Act, was introduced in 1975 but it never became law.

Other countries were also busy enacting human rights legislation.[67] The United Kingdom, for example, established Racial Equality and Equal Opportunities commissions in 1971 and 1975 respectively. Civil rights legislation was also introduced at the state and federal level in the United States. In fact, there was a proliferation of human rights institutions across the globe in the 1970s. Thomas Pegram describes the diffusion of human rights institutions as a "contagion effect"; a process emerging from a "complex domestic, regional, and international interaction of actors, arenas, and modalities of diffusion" that resulted in a "wave phenomenon of varying intensity across regions" beginning in Europe, Australia, and North America.[68]

By 1975 the Canadian government was under intense pressure from international institutions, a domestic human rights movement, and a maturing legal profession to ratify human rights treaties.[69] Canada participated in the negotiations that led to the Helsinki Accords in 1975 with the Soviet Union, which among other things committed each country to a set of human rights principles.[70] In the same year, a federal–provincial Continuing Committee of Officials on Human Rights was created to consult over international treaties.[71] After securing provincial consent, Canada acceded to the International Covenant on Civil and Political Rights, as well as the International Covenant on Economic, Social and Cultural Rights, in 1976.

Canada's new international commitments and activities created a unique opportunity for parliamentarians to become involved in foreign affairs. In the early 1970s, MPs tended to respond to human rights violations in Eastern Europe with vague calls for self-determination or the recognition of rights of minorities. MPs developed a more sophisticated approach, however, as a result of their participation in an Inter-Parliamentary Union conference leading up to the negotiations for the Helsinki Accords and the subsequent Belgrade Review conference. MPs drew on the language contained in the Accords to introduce resolutions in Parliament dealing with family reunification, free movement of people, religious freedom, and other equally precise reforms that demonstrated a far greater understanding of the issues. MPs also participated in increasing numbers in international human rights conferences as part of official Canadian delegations to the United Nations and as members of various monitoring groups abroad. Over time many MPs gained valuable experience and expertise on human rights issues, and they brought this knowledge to Parliament where they continued to pressure the federal government to integrate human rights in foreign policy.[72] A private member's bill was introduced in 1975 to prohibit foreign aid to countries with poor human rights records. The bill drew attention to the human rights component of Canadian foreign policy and forced the government to defend and elaborate its aid policies in public.

Under Menzies and his successors, the Australian federal government had been skeptical about international human rights commitments. Menzies, unlike Evatt and other members of the Labour Party, had never accepted economic and social rights as human rights. Australian foreign policy instead framed human rights as civil and political rights, and routinely denounced communist countries for restricting these rights. Despite being a founding member of the United Nations Human Rights Commission, Australia left the commission in 1956. The Liberal Party recognized the Cambodian regime under Pol Pot, continued to trade with China, and recognized Indonesia's claims over East Timor following the invasion. It was not until 1972 when "Gough Whitlam became prime minister [Labour Party] that Australia became formally integrated into the international human rights regime."[73] The Whitlam government initiated widespread domestic reforms, including the Racial Discrimination Act, and moved quickly to ratify United Nations's human rights treaties as well as several ILO conventions. When the Labour Party returned to power in 1983 it ratified the Convention on the Elimination of All Forms of Discrimination against Women, passed the Sex Discrimination Act, removed most of the previous government's reservations on the International Covenant on Civil and Political Rights, and established a human rights section in the Department of Foreign Affairs and Trade.[74] In this way, as Ann Kent argues, Australia was a latecomer to international human rights politics in that human rights was not integral to Australian bilateral relations until the 1980s.[75] Still, like Canada, there was a relationship between domestic and foreign policy. Domestic reforms promoted changes in foreign policy that in turn provided the impetus for domestic reforms:

> First was the impact of the new politics of the post-Cold War era, wherein human rights assumed greater prominence in line with Australia's greater international visibility. Second was the close interaction between human rights in Australia's domestic policies and foreign policies. By definition, the international human rights regime connects international to domestic policy by affording multilateral human rights monitoring bodies oversight over a state's domestic human rights conditions. Historically, the more confidence Australia has shown in tackling its own domestic human rights problems, the more involved it has been with international bodies and the more accessible it has been to criticism.[76]

As human rights became a cornerstone of international politics, Canada and Australia responded with concrete measures. The Canadian government imposed restrictions on South Africa (banning athletes entering Canada, removing trade commissioners, cancelling export credits, prohibiting arms sales); accepted a higher number of refugees following crises in Chile and Uganda (1973); inserted a section on refugees to the immigration law (1976); withdrew aid from the Amin regime in Uganda; imposed limited economic measures (including bans on exporting food and credits) to Poland and the Soviet Union in 1977; and suspended aid to Chile and Vietnam, and later Guatemala and El Salvador in 1981.[77] The government also accepted for the first time, in principle, that foreign aid should be linked to human rights. Australia was also engaged in using sanctions as a foreign policy tool to promote human rights. The Liberal coalition government of Malcolm Fraser (1975–1983) "abruptly brought an end to the previous [Liberal government] equivocation on the South African question, allying itself squarely behind the 'front-line' African states and in support of Commonwealth initiatives to end apartheid."[78] Australia formally imposed sanctions on South Africa in 1983. Two years earlier, in response to violent abuses under the Pol Pot regime, the Australian government had "de-recognized" the Cambodian regime.[79] True, neither country was above reproach: Canadian foreign aid was re-introduced for Guatemala and El Salvador, and Australia never allowed China's dismal human rights record to affect trade. Even under Gough Whitlam, the Australian government rarely raised concerns surrounding other countries' human rights records.[80] Still, a change was clearly underway.

The most salient illustration of the rights revolution was domestic legal reform. When the federal Human Rights Act came into effect in 1977, comprehensive human rights legislation covered every jurisdiction in Canada.[81] Human rights legislation expanded the scope of pre-existing laws from ethnicity, gender, religion, age, and nationality by incorporating sexual harassment, disability, pregnancy, criminal record, family status, and (over time) sexual orientation. Specially trained human rights officers were hired to investigate complaints and to attempt informal conciliation. When that failed, formal boards of inquiry could impose settlements such as requiring offenders to pay a fine, offer an apology, reinstate an employee, or agree to a negotiated settlement. Human rights commissions, unlike courts, were specialized government agencies that were efficient and accessible, and bore the cost of investigating and resolving complaints. They were also given the resources to pursue vigorous human rights education programs.

The Canadian human rights legal regime was among the most sophisticated in the world. Equality commissions in the United Kingdom and the United States, for example, had far more restrictive mandates and arguably less effective enforcement mechanisms. Despite the proliferation of human rights laws since the 1970s, few of these models incorporated all the strengths of the Canadian system: professional human rights investigators, public education, promoting legal reform, representing complainants before formal inquiries, jurisdiction over public and private sectors, a focus on conciliation over litigation, independence from the government, and an adjudication process as an alternative to the courts.

Legislating prohibitions on employers and merchants from discriminating was simply one more instance of how the rights revolution was contributing to a departure from British tradition.[82] Even the content of these laws represented a more expansive conception of rights. Several jurisdictions prohibited discriminatory hate speech, recognized a mandate to address systemic discrimination, incorporated the concept of equal pay for work of equal value, and imposed a duty to accommodate on employers and service providers. The government of Quebec went so far as to incorporate economic and social rights in its human rights legislation, and to ban discrimination on the basis of social condition. And if the creation of a sophisticated statutory human rights legal regime was not enough to demonstrate the impact of the rights revolution, the entrenchment of a constitutional bill of rights in 1982 constituted an entirely new direction in Canadian law. Moreover, the Charter of Rights and Freedoms recognized gender equality, multiculturalism, Aboriginals, language, and education. Considering the lack of almost any effective statutory or constitutional recognition of human rights before the 1970s, changes in human rights law were truly transformational.[83]

According to Maxwell Yalden, the former chief commissioner of the Canadian Human Rights Commission and a member of the United Nations Commission on Human Rights, the Canadian model had few peers: "It should be noted that it is a particular type of commission that has similar, sister agencies in countries like Australia and New Zealand. But nothing of the sort exists, for example, in France or other European countries."[84] The Australian human rights legal regime, although it took longer to emerge, was akin to its Canadian counterpart. But it was the Australian federal government, using its power to implement treaties and override state jurisdiction, that established a human rights legal regime (although South Australia, New South Wales, and Victoria had passed a few minor anti-discrimination laws in 1975 and 1977).[85] The first federal anti-discrimination statute, the Racial Discrimination Act, was followed by the Human Rights Act (1981) and the Sex Discrimination Act (1984).[86] International treaties provided the framework for these statutes.[87] Individual states later introduced more comprehensive legislation. By the mid-1980s, Australia had become "one of the few western industrialized countries of the world to operate a [national human rights institution] which has powers of monitoring, policy development, education, and complaint handling. Most other institutions, with a notable exception in Canada, have a more narrow range of functions such as consultation and advice, reviewing maladministration in the role of an ombudsman, or conducting education programs."[88]

And yet legal reform in Australia, albeit more advanced than in most other countries, fell short of the Canadian model. The Australian human rights legal system emerged from the federal government whereas the Canadian human rights regime was the result of a sustained grassroots campaign and enjoyed popular support among provincial and federal leaders. The latter also had an established human rights system by the 1970s, whereas Australia's human rights state came to fruition only in the 1980s.[89] Several Australian jurisdictions implemented more restrictive legislation that did not cover key grounds (e.g., religion or sexual orientation), and unlike Canada, human rights legislation in Australia was less uniform. Australian human rights legislation was also poorly enforced: the federal commission had to apply to a court to enforce a remedy.[90] The result was a far more tedious and expensive process, which was precisely why the Canadian system allowed formal inquiries to enforce remedies.[91] And there were other notable differences. Quebec included economic and social rights in its human rights legislation; no similar law existed in Australia. Canadians also entrenched an expansive bill of rights in the Constitution; Australians rejected attempts to entrench rights in their constitution in 1944 and 1988.

CONCLUSION

No two countries offer a better comparison than Australia and Canada in exploring the influence of human rights on law, politics, foreign policy, and social movements. The two nations share a common history as former British colonies. Both countries are federations with parliamentary systems; possess a small population (with a significant immigration base that is multilingual and multicultural) spread out across an enormous land mass; inherited a common law legal system; have a history of conflict with the indigenous population; and have a well-educated, Western, and predominantly English-speaking populace. They are also "middle powers" and have sought to strengthen the United Nations to offset the influence of the great powers.

Each country experienced a rights revolution that came to fruition in the 1970s. They largely abandoned a limited conception of rights as civil liberties and embraced a more expansive human rights ideal.

International human rights treaties had an impact on Canadian and Australian law and political discourse.[92] Both countries endeavoured to address human rights in foreign policy. And yet there were notable differences. There were no self-professed human rights associations in Australia. Human rights laws in Australia were not as comprehensive as the Canadian model. Australia was slower to integrate human rights in foreign policy and domestic law. There was no Australian bill of rights. What accounts for the differential impact of human rights in a local context?

French Canadians played a critical role in the politics of human rights. Quebec's leading rights association, the Ligue des droits de l'homme, was a powerful advocate for collective as well as social, economic, and cultural rights. Normand Caron, the Ligue's executive director in 1975, believed that the Ligue's main contribution to the national movement was to challenge anglophones' definition of human rights as civil and political rights.[93] No other social movement organization played a more central role in drafting the Quebec Charter of Human Rights and Freedoms which, as noted above, was far more expansive than any Australian human rights statute. Finally, the presence of a powerful national minority concerned with culture and language rights helps explain the inclusion of language rights and education in the Charter of Rights and Freedoms.[94] In fact, as some scholars have argued, the Charter itself was created in response to the Quebec separatist movement.[95]

Canadian and Australian federalism, especially in the division of powers, was another distinguishing factor. The Canadian federal government was prohibited from imposing treaty obligations on the provinces. The Australian federal government was not similarly constrained. But local states in Australia fiercely resisted what they perceived to be an invasion of their constitutional jurisdiction, and this may have restricted the federal government's vision for human rights law. Perhaps for this reason Australian human rights laws were never as progressive as their Canadian counterparts. One of the curious distinguishing features in the history of human rights law in the two countries is that such laws had widespread partisan support in Canada: Liberal, New Democratic, Progressive Conservative, and Social Credit Party governments introduced anti-discrimination laws. In Australia, except for the 1977 Victoria Equal Opportunity Act and the federal Human Rights Commission Act (1981), the Labour Party was responsible for passing every human rights law (and instigating referendums in 1944 and 1988) at the state and federal level.[96] In addition, the Canadian federal system did not include a powerful Senate whereas in Australia fierce partisan conflicts between the Senate and the House delayed the introduction of federal human rights legislation. It is also worth noting that the "White Australia" policy continued to inform immigration policy into the 1970s. The conditions that facilitated the White Australia policy may have contributed to opposition (particularly among state leaders) to anti-discrimination legislation in the 1970s.

A few other differences between the two countries are worth noting. Two political parties—one Liberal and the other Conservative—dominated federal politics in each country during this period. However, Conservatives governed almost continually in Australia between 1949 and 1983 whereas Liberals dominated Canadian federal politics between 1935 and 1984. The Australian federal government eschewed multilateralism as well as economic and social rights.[97] In contrast, Liberal governments in Canada, with strong support among French Canadians, favoured multilateralism rather than focusing on ties with the Commonwealth. The Canadian government also provided an unprecedented level of funding for social movements beginning in the late 1960s (which was also partly a reaction to the independence movement in Quebec). Whereas Australian civil liberties associations rarely received state funding, almost every rights association in Canada depended on government grants. Celebrations surrounding the International Year for Human Rights in Canada received generous federal funding. In addition, Canada's divided legal system (French civil law and English common law) facilitated the incorporation of foreign legal precedents into domestic law. And, of course, any amendments to the Australia constitution had to be approved through a referendum, which has proven to be a greater obstacle to a bill of rights than in Canada, where federal and provincial leaders negotiated an agreement. Also, because of its geopolitical situation, there were unique aspects to Canadian foreign policy. The Helsinki negotiations, which did not involve Australia, provided an opportunity for Canadian parliamentarians to place human rights on the agenda for foreign policy.

Finally, although impossible to quantify, American cultural and political influence likely contributed to developments in Canada.[98] The most visible manifestation was the Jewish Labor Committee. The organization, which played a critical role in the campaign for New York's 1945 precedent-setting anti-discrimination law, was the template for a similar organization that was formed in Ontario in 1937. The Canadian Jewish Labour Committee soon had affiliates throughout the country and, more than any other organization, has been credited with leading the campaigns for human rights legislation in Canada many years before Australia.[99]

Although the countries' histories are dissimilar, the rights revolution nonetheless transformed both Canada and Australia. Until the 1970s, the Cold War defined international politics and had a dampening effect within states. Civil liberties organizations fought among themselves, and often fell apart because of internecine ideological conflicts. Governments used the threat of communism to justify human rights abuses at home. Foreign policy priorities, in the context of the Cold War, favoured state sovereignty over human rights. Cold War imperatives, however, do not appear to have had the same influence by the 1970s. Canada and Australia introduced human rights legislation, social movements flourished, politics was changing and support for a constitutional bill of right was growing, and human rights had become a factor in foreign policy. Human rights rhetoric became increasingly pervasive in public debate. Meanwhile, several international human rights treaties were implemented and international institutions became a forum for debating human rights, holding states accountable for human rights violations, and setting new human rights standards for states. What had begun as a debate surrounding a vague declaration of principles in 1948 had become, by the 1970s, a powerful imperative.

NOTES

1.   A.J. Hobbins, "Eleanor Roosevelt, John Humphrey and Canadian Opposition to the Universal Declaration of Human Rights: Looking Back on the 50th Anniversary of the UDHR, "*International Journal* 53, no. 2 (1998): 338.

2.   William A. Schabas, "Canada and the Adoption of the Universal Declaration of Human Rights," *McGill Law Journal* 43, no. 2 (1998): 406.

3.   E.J. Hobsbawm, "Labour and Human Rights," in *Worlds of Labour: Further Studies in the History of Labour*, ed. E.J. Hobsbawm (London: Weidenfeld and Nicolson, 1984), 299.

4.   Ramsay Cook, "Canadian Freedom in Wartime," in *His Own Man: Essays in Honour of A.R.M. Lower*, ed. W.H. Heick and Roger Graham (Montreal: McGill–Queen's University Press, 1974), 38.

5.   For more on these events, see Stephanie Bangarth, *Voices Raised in Protest: Defending North American Citizens of Japanese Ancestry, 1942–49* (Vancouver: UBC Press, 2007).

6.   As quoted in Schabas, "Canada and the Adoption of the Universal Declaration of Human Rights," 424. Schabas also notes: "A 112-paragraph document entitled 'Views of Canada on

Matters Before the United Nations' prepared by External Affairs bureaucrats for the Assembly did not even mention the Declaration."

7.   Jennifer Amos argues that debates surrounding the UDHR were not defined by Cold War allegiences. Australia, for example, advocated for social, economic and cultural rights. Jennifer Amos, "Embracing and Contesting: The Soviet Union and the Universal Declaration of Human Rights, 1948–1958," in *Human Rights in the Twentieth Century*, ed. Stefan-Ludwig Hoffman (Cambridge: Cambridge University Press, 2011), 149. On Australia and the UDHR, see Annemarie Devereux, *Australia and the Birth of the International Bill of Human Rights, 1946–1966* (Sydney: The Federation Press, 2005).

8.   Ann Kent, "Australia and the International Human Rights Regime," in *The National Interest in the Global Era: Australia in World Affairs, 1996–2000*, ed. James Cotton and John Ravenhill (Melbourne: Oxford University Press, 2001), 259.

9.   Canada, Parliament, Senate, *Special Committee on Human Rights and Fundamental Freedoms,* 1950; Hobbins, "Eleanor Roosevelt, John Humphrey and Canadian Opposition to the Universal Declaration of Human Rights."

10.   Mark Mazower, "The Strange Triumph of Human Rights, 1933–1950, " *The Historical Journal* 47, no. 2 (2004): 394–95. On Australia's opposition to interference in domestic affairs, see also Devereux, *Australia and the Birth of the International Bill of Human Rights, 1946–1966*, 204–15.

11.   Robert Bothwell, *Alliance and Illusion: Canada and the World, 1945–1984* (Vancouver: UBC Press, 2007), 21.

12.   Schabas, "Canada and the Adoption of the Universal Declaration of Human Rights," 427.

13.   Frank Cain and Frank Farrell, "Menzies War on the Communist Party, 1949–1951," in *Australia's First Cold War, 1945–1953*, ed. Ann Curthoys and John Merritt (Sydney: George Allen & Unwin, 1984), 131–33.

14.   On the Communist Party Dissolution Bill and the referendum, see Dominique Clément, "'It Is Not the Beliefs but the Crime That Matters:' Post-War Civil Liberties Debates in Canada and Australia," *Labour History (Australia)* May, no. 86 (2004); Cain and Farrell, "Menzies War on the Communist Party, 1949–1951."

15.   National Library of Australia, Brian Fitzpatrick, MS4965, Series 1 (a), f.1/912–1012, correspondence inquiries, letters from Fitzpatrick, 1951; f.1/3299–3347, general correspondence, letters to Fitzpatrick, 1950.

16.   On the Gouzenko Affair, including media coverage, parliamentary debates, and the role of civil liberties associations, see Dominique Clément, "The Royal Commission on Espionage and the Spy Trials of 1946–9: A Case Study in Parliamentary Supremacy," *Journal of the Canadian Historical Association* 11, no. 1 (2000), and "Spies, Lies and a Commission, 1946–8: A Case Study in the Mobilization of the Canadian Civil Liberties Movement," *Left History* 7, no. 2 (2001); www.HistoryOfRights.com.

17.   "Topic of the Day," *Dalhousie Review* 26: 96–98 (April 1946).

18.   Australian Council for Civil Liberties. "The War and Civil Liberties." 1 (December 1940). [A pamphlet published by the ACCL].

19.   "We Oppose these Gravely Disturbing Proposals." *Argus*, September 15, 1951.

20.   One MP went so far as to suggest that it was the most "offensive bill introduced in the English speaking world." Australia, *Hansard Parliamentary Debates*, 1951, vol. 15, 1213–4, 1238, 1266. Mitchell Library. Communist Party of Australia papers, MSS 5021, f. 103 (155), Democratic Rights Council opposed referendum, 1951.

21.   Robin Gollan, *Revolutionaries and Reformists: Communism and the Australian Labour Movement, 1920–1955* (Carleton: Melbourne University Press, 1975), 96–97.

22.   In contrast, the constitution of the Canadian Labour Defence League (a communist-affiliated civil liberties group) incorporated social and economic rights, including the right to work and to a fair wage. The ACCL did not address discrimination against Aborigines. Similarly, the Association for Civil Liberties in Toronto did not campaign for anti-discrimination legislation until the 1950s. J. Petryshyn, "A.E. Smith and the Canadian Labour Defence League" (PhD thesis, University of Western Ontario, 1977), 42; Don Watson, *Brian Fitzpatrick: A Radical*

Life, Sydney (Sydney: Hale & Iremonger, 1979), 92. On the Association for Civil Liberties, see Ross Lambertson, "The Dresden Story: Racism, Human Rights, and the Jewish Labour Committee of Canada," *Labour/Le Travail* Spring, no. 47 (2001). National Library of Australia, Brian Fitzpatrick, MS4965, series 1 (c), Aborigines, correspondence 1936 to 1956, letter from Fitzpatrick to Gordon Birt, May 27, 1946.

23. The statute also made reference to creed and colour. Statutes of Saskatchewan, *An Act to Protect Certain Civil Rights*, 1947, c.35.

24. Dominique Clément, "'I Believe in Human Rights, Not Women's Rights': Women and the Human Rights State, 1969–1984," *Radical History Review* 101 (2008); Walter S. Tarnopolsky, *Discrimination and the Law in Canada* (Don Mills: De Boo, 1982), Chap. 2. For a full account of the history and development of human rights laws, see Ross Lambertson, *Repression and Resistance: Canadian Human Rights Activists, 1930–1960* (Toronto: University of Toronto Press, 2005). Rosanna L. Langer, *Defining Rights and Wrongs: Bureaucracy, Human Rights, and Public Accountability* (Vancouver: UBC Press, 2007), 4; T.M. Eberlee and D.G. Hill, "The Ontario Human Rights Code," *The University of Toronto Law Journal* 15 (1964): 451.

25. Library and Archives Canada, Jewish Labour Committee, MG28 V75, Vol. 36, File 14, letter from Ernest Manning to Michel Gouault (United Council for Human Rights), June 8, 1964. Maureen Riddell, The *Evolution of Human Rights Legislation in Alberta, 1945–1979* (Edmonton: Queen's Printer, 1978–9), 6.

26. National Archives of Australia, A8910, Alteration of Constitution: Federal Referendum, The Case For and Against, by the Chief Electoral Officer of the Commonwealth, April 20, 1944; National Library of Australia, Robert Menzies, MS4936, Series 6, Various Broadcasts 1942–1953, Guarantee Freedom, March 17, 1944.

27. Cathal J. Nolan, "Reluctant Liberal: Canada, Human Rights and the United Nations," *Diplomacy & Statecraft* 2, no. 3 (1990): 287–88.

28. Devereux, *Australia and the Birth of the International Bill of Human Rights, 1946–1966*, 8, 51–57.

29. During the debates surrounding the UDHR, the Canadian delegation was instructed to make every effort to ensure the primacy of state sovereignty over individual rights. Nolan, "Reluctant Liberal," 284–86. See also Paul Gecelovsky and Tom Keating, "Liberal Internationalism for Conservatives: The Good Governance Initiative," in *Diplomatic Departures: The Conservative Era in Canadian Foreign Policy, 1984–1993*, ed. Kim Richard Nossal and Nelson Michaud (Vancouver: UBC Press, 2001), 195.

30. Kim Richard Nossal, "Cabin'd, Cribb'd, Confin'd: Canada's Interests in Human Rights," in *Human Rights in Canadian Foreign Policy*, ed. Robert O. Matthews and Cranford Pratt (Kingston and Montreal: McGill–Queen's University Press, 1988), 50.

31. Canada, *Hansard Parliamentary Debates*, 1947, vol.4, 3214–16.

32. Australia, *Hansard Parliamentary Debates*, 1950, vol. 207, 2280.

33. Library and Archives Canada, Walter S. Tarnopolsky, MG31 E55, vol.31, f.14, speech before the Conference of Human Rights Ministers in Victoria, November 8, 1974.

34. Christopher MacLennan, *Toward the Charter: Canadians and the Demand for a National Bill of Rights, 1929–1960* (Montreal: McGill–Queen's University Press, 2003), 76.

35. National Archives of Australia, Robert Menzies, MS 4936, series 6, Various Broadcasts 1942–53, box 256, speech on the referendum, March 17, 1944.

36. Samuel Moyn, *The Last Utopia: Human Rights in History* (Cambridge, MA: Belknap Press, 2010); Jean H. Quataert, *Advocating Dignity* (Philadelphia: University of Pennsylvania Press, 2009); William Korey, *NGOs and the Universal Declaration of Human Rights: "A Curious Grapevine"* (New York: Palgrave, 1998).

37. Andrew Moravcsik, "The Paradox of U.S. Human Rights Policy," in *American Exceptionalism and Human Rights*, ed. Michael Ignatieff (Princeton: Princeton University Press, 2005).

38. Daniel Roger Maul, "The International Labour Organization and the Globalization of Rights, 1944–1970," in *Human Rights in the Twentieth Century*, ed. Stefan-Ludwig Hoffman (Cambridge: Cambridge University Press, 2011), 305.

39. Moyn, *The Last Utopia*, 225.
40. On human rights and the early Cold War period, see David Forsythe, *Human Rights in International Relations*, 2nd ed. (Cambridge: Cambridge University Press, 2006), 41, 43; Kirsten Sellars, *The Rise and Rise of Human Rights* (Phoenix Mill: Sutton Publishing, 2002); Susan Olzak, *The Global Dynamics of Racial and Ethnic Mobilization* (Stanford: Stanford University Press, 2006); Cynthia Soohoo, "Human Rights and the Transformation of the 'Civil Rights' and 'Civil Liberties' Lawyer," in *Bringing Human Rights Home: A History of Human Rights in the United States*, ed. Cynthia Soohoo, Catherine Albisa, and Martha F. Davis (Westport: Praeger, 2008). See also Stefan-Ludwig Hoffman, ed. *Human Rights in the Twentieth Century* (Cambridge: Cambridge University Press, 2011), 76, 80, 147, 219–20.
41. MacLennan, *Toward the Charter*, 75.
42. Mazower, "The Strange Triumph of Human Rights, 1933–1950," 395.
43. Julie A. Mertus, *Human Rights Matters: Local Politics and National Human Rights Institutions* (Stanford: Stanford University Press, 2008), 5.
44. Nancy Gordon and Bernard Wood, "Canada and the Reshaping of the United Nations," *International Journal* 47, no. 3 (1991): 499.
45. Kathleen Mahoney, "Human Rights in Canadian Foreign Policy," *International Journal* 47, no.3 (1991): 561.
46. Thomas Risse, Stephen C. Ropp, and Kathryn Sikkink, eds., *The Power of Human Rights: International Norms and Domestic Change* (Cambridge: Cambridge University Press, 1999); Margaret E. Keck and Kathryn Sikkink, *Activists Beyond Borders: Advocacy Networks in International Politics* (Ithica: Cornell University Press, 1998).
47. Lambertson, *Repression and Resistance*; Dominique Clément, *Canada's Rights Revolution: Social Movements and Social Change, 1937–1982* (Vancouver: UBC Press, 2008); Watson, *Brian Fitzpatrick*; Clément, "'It Is Not the Beliefs but the Crime That Matters.'"
48. Frank K Clarke, "Debilitating Divisions: The Civil Liberties Movement in Early Cold War Canada, 1946–8," in *Whose National Security? Surveillance and the Creation of Enemies in Canada*, ed. Gary Kinsman (Toronto: Between the Lines, 2000), 177.
49. On human rights and the Cold War in Canada and Australia, see Clarke, "Debilitating Divisions: The Civil Liberties Movement in Early Cold War Canada, 1946–8," 182. Meredith Burgmann, "Dress Rehearsal for the Cold War," in *Australia's First Cold War, 1945–1953*, ed. Ann Curthoys and John Merritt (Sydney: George Allen & Unwin, 1984).
50. Devereux, *Australia and the Birth of the International Bill of Human Rights, 1946–1966*, 51.
51. Mikael Rask Madsen, "Legal Diplomacy: Law, Politics, and the Genesis of Postwar European Human Rights," in *Human Rights in the Twentieth Century*, ed. Stefan-Ludwig Hoffman (Cambridge: Cambridge University Press, 2011).
52. Moyn, *The Last Utopia*, 8.
53. Risse, Ropp, and Sikkink, eds., *The Power of Human Rights*, 266.
54. Ruth Frager and Carmela Patrias, "'This Is Our Country, These Are Our Rights': Minorities and the Origins of Ontario's Human Rights Campaigns," *The Canadian Historical Review* 82, no. 1 (2001).
55. Clément, *Canada's Rights Revolution*, 179–82.
56. Library and Archives Canada, Frank Scott, MG30, D211, vol.47, Bilan de Maurice Champagne, sur ses trois années à la Ligue des Droits à titre de directeur général, présenté à l'occasion de l'assemblée général annuelle des membres, May 28, 1975; Service des archives et de gestion des documents, Université du Québec à Montréal, Ligue des droits de l'homme, 24P6f/4, mémoire au conseil administration sur l'état de la Ligue, April 5, 1984.
57. Howard Ramos, "What Causes Canadian Aboriginal Protest? Examining Resources, Opportunities and Identity, 1951–2000," *Canadian Journal of Sociology* 31, no. 2 (2006), and "Aboriginal Protest," in *Social Movements*, ed. Suzanne Staggenborg (Toronto: Oxford University Press, 2007), 59.
58. Bonnie Greene, ed. *Canadian Churches and Foreign Policy* (Toronto: James Lorimer, 1990); Ruth Compton Brouwer, "When Missions Became Development: Ironies of 'NGOization'

in Mainstream Canadian Churches in the 1960s," *Canadian Historical Review* 91, no. 4 (2010).

59. Clément, "'It Is Not the Beliefs but the Crime That Matters'"; Watson, *Brian Fitzpatrick*; Kenneth Bailey, interview, September 4, 2002; Conor Gearty, *Principles of Human Rights Adjudication* (Oxford: Oxford University Press, 2004).

60. Gearty, *Principles of Human Rights Adjudication*.

61. In 1990, Stephen Cohen compiled a list of advocacy groups in Australia that dealt with a wide range of issues. Among the 465 organizations there was only one self-identified human rights organization: the Human Rights Council of Australia, which was founded in Sydney in 1978. Stephen Cohen, *Australian Civil Liberties Organizations* (Sydney: International Business Communications Directory, 1990).

62. On debates surrounding a Canadian bill of rights, see Clément, *Canada's Rights Revolution*, Chap. 1; MacLennan, *Toward the Charter*.

63. Canada, Parliament, House of Commons and the Senate. *Special Joint Committee on the Constitution of Canada: First Report*, 1972, 18–19. James B. Kelly, *Governing with the Charter: Legislative and Judicial Activism and Framers' Intent* (Vancouver: UBC Press, 2005), 48.

64. Canada, Department of External Affairs. *Foreign Policy for Canadians*, vol. 3 (United Nations, 1970), 26–27.

65. There was one exception: South Australia passed an Anti-Discrimination Act in 1966.

66. Gillian Triggs, "Australia's Ratification of the International Covenant on Civil and Political Rights: Endorsement or Repudiation?," *British Institute of International and Comparative Law* 31, no. 2 (1982): 288.

67. MacLennan, *Toward the Charter*, 234.

68. Thomas Pegram, "Diffusion Across Political Systems: The Global Spread of National Human Rights Institutions," *Human Rights Quarterly* 32, no. 3 (2010); Linda Reif, "Building Democratic Institutions: The Role of National Human Rights Institutions in Good Governance and Human Rights Protection," *Harvard Human Rights Journal* 13, no.1 (2000).

69. Michael Behiels, "Canada and the Implementation of International Instruments of Human Rights: A Federalist Conundrum, 1919–1982," in *Framing Canadian Federalism: Historical Essays in Honour of John T Saywell*, ed. Dimitry Anastakis and P.E. Bryden (Toronto: University of Toronto Press, 2009).

70. Daniel C. Thomas, "Human Rights Ideas, the Demise of Communism, and the End of the Cold War," *Journal of Cold War Studies* 7, no. 2 (2005). Sara Snyder, *Human Rights Activism and the End of the Cold War: A Transnational History of the Helsinki Network* (New York: Cambridge University Press, 2011).

71. Kim Richard Nossal, Stéphane Roussel, and Stéphane Paquin, *International Policy and Politics in Canada* (Toronto: Pearson Canada, 2011), 290.

72. Cathal J. Nolan, "The Influence of Parliament on Human Rights in Canadian Foreign Policy," *Human Rights Quarterly* 7, no. 3 (1985): 387–88.

73. Kent, "Australia and the International Human Rights Regime," 259.

74. Ian Russell, "Australia's Human Rights Policy: From Evatt to Evans," in *Australia's Human Rights Diplomacy*, ed. Ian Russell, Peter Van Ness, and Beng-Huat Chua (Canberra: Australia Foreign Policy Publications Program, 1993), 27.

75. Kent, "Australia and the International Human Rights Regime," 257.

76. Ibid., 258.

77. T.A. Keenleyside and Patricia Taylor, *The Impact of Human Rights Violations on the Conduct of Canadian Bilateral Relations: A Contemporary Dilemma* (Toronto: Canadian Institute of International Affairs, 1984), 5, 244–50. See also Greene, *Canadian Churches and Foreign Policy*. During its brief period as government in 1979, the Conservative Party withheld aid from Vietnam because of gross human rights violations. Nolan, "The Influence of Parliament on Human Rights in Canadian Foreign Policy," 383.

78. Russell, "Australia's Human Rights Policy," 24.

79. Ibid., 27.

80. For a critique of Canadian foreign policy and human rights, see Nossal, "Cabin'd, Cribb'd, Confin'd."; David Gillies, *Between Principle and Practice: Human Rights in North-South Relations* (Montreal and Kingston: McGill–Queen's University Press, 1996).

81. On the impact of international treaties on Canadian human rights legislation, see Shannon Williams, "Human Rights in Theory and Practice: A Sociological Study of Aboriginal Peoples & the New Brunswick Human Rights Commission, 1967–1997" (MA thesis, University of New Brunswick, 1998), 30. Dominique Clément, "Searching for Rights in the Age of Activism: The Newfoundland-Labrador Human Rights Association, 1968–1982," *Newfoundland Studies* 19, no. 2 (2003). Alan D. Reid, "The New Brunswick Human Rights Act," *University of Toronto Law Journal* 18, no. 4 (1968).

82. James Walker, *"Race," Rights and the Law in the Supreme Court of Canada: Historical Case Studies* (Toronto: Wilfrid Laurier University Press, 1997), 175–78.

83. On human rights law in Canada, see Tarnopolsky, *Discrimination and the Law in Canada*; Howe and Johnson, *Restraining Equality*; Dominique Clément, "Human Rights Law and Sexual Discrimination in British Columbia, 1953–1984," in *The West and Beyond*, ed. Sara Carter, Alvin Finkel, and Peter Fortna (Edmonton: Athabasca University Press, 2010), "'Rights without the Sword Are but Mere Words': The Limits of Canada's Rights Revolution," in *A History of Human Rights in Canada*, ed. Janet Miron (Toronto: Canadian Scholars Press, 2009), and "'I Believe in Human Rights, Not Women's Rights.'"

84. Maxwell Yalden, *Transforming Rights: Reflections from the Front Lines* (Toronto: University of Toronto, 2009), 143.

85. The Australian High Court determined that the federal government could impose treaty obligations on states because, unlike Canada, the Australian constitution included an external affairs clause as part of federal jurisdiction. *Attorney-General of Canada v. Attorney-General of Ontario* [1937] 1 Dominion Law Reports 673 [Labour Conventions Case]; *R v. Burgess, Ex parte Henry* [1936] 55 Commonwealth Law Reports 608. On the use of external affairs power to implement human rights legislation in Australia, see Nick O'Neill, Simon Rice, and Roger Douglas, *Retreat from Injustice: Human Rights Law in Australia* (Sydney: The Federation Press, 2004), 29–38. For a detailed discussion of early anti-discrimination laws in Australia, see O'Neil et al, *Retreat from Injustice*, Chap. 18.

86. On Australian human rights legislation, see Louise Chappell, John Chesterman, and Lisa Hill, *The Politics of Human Rights in Australia* (Cambridge: Cambridge University Press, 2009), Chap. 2.

87. "The [Racial Discrimination Act] closely followed the wording of the treaty on which it is based, adopting as the definition of discrimination the same definition used in the [Convention for the Elimination of Racial Discrimination]." O'Neil et al, *Retreat from Injustice*, 478. "It was not until well into the 1970s that the first attempts were made to address the problem of discrimination in [Australia]. . . . The Racial Discrimination Act was largely modeled on the New Zealand Race Relations Act 1971 and the United Kingdom Race Relations Act 1968." Mathews, "Protection of Minorities and Equal Opportunities," 2–3.

88. O'Neill, Rice, and Douglas, *Retreat from Injustice*, 199.

89. There were failed attempts in 1973, 1977, and 1979 to introduce comprehensive federal legislation. The Australian human rights regime also had severe limitations when it first emerged. Peter Bailey and Annemarie Devereux, "The Operation of Anti-Discrimination Laws in Australia," in *Human Rights in Australian Law: Principles, Practice and Potential*, ed. David Kinley (Sydney: Federation Press, 1998); Andrew Byrnes, Hilary Charlesworth, and Gabrielle McKinnon, *Bills of Rights in Australia: History, Politics and Law* (Sydney: UNSW Press, 2009); James Spigelman, *Statutory Interpretation and Human Rights* (Queensland: University of Queensland Press, 2008).

90. State human rights commissions, however, were later empowered to enforce their own remedies. Chappell, Chesterman, and Hill, *The Politics of Human Rights in Australia*, 39.

91. Australian human rights statutes required a judge to preside over a tribunal. The judge had the option of allowing legal representation, and most often lawyers were allowed to participate. In

this way, the Australian system was far more akin to a court, although tribunals have greater flexibility regarding the rules of evidence. In contrast, boards of inquiry in Canada were designed to avoid a courtroom-type approach to human rights adjudication.

92. Dominique Clément, "The Evolution of Human Rights in Canada: From 'Niggardly Acceptance' to Enthusiastic Embrace," *Human Rights Quarterly* 34, no. 3 (2012): 751–78.

93. Service des archives et de gestion des documents, Université du Québec à Montréal, Ligue des droits de l'homme, 24P1/13, minutes of the administrative council, December 5, 1977.

94. Clément, *Canada's Rights Revolution*, Chap. 5.

95. Peter Russell, "The Political Purposes of the Canadian Charter of Rights and Freedoms," *Canadian Bar Review* 61, no. 1 (1983).

96. Mathews, "Protection of Minorities and Equal Opportunities," 4; Howe and Johnson, *Restraining Equality*, 12–13, 91–95.

97. Ann Kent argues that, with regards to Australian foreign policy, "human rights, or more narrowly civil rights, were of consequence in so far as they were abused by Communist states." Ann Kent, "Human Rights," in *Australian Foreign Policy: Into the New Millennium*, ed. F.A. Mediansky (Sydney: Macmillan Education Australia, 1997), 164.

98. On American influences, see Robert Vipond, "The Civil Rights Movements Comes to Winnipeg: American Influence on 'Rights Talk' in Canada, 1968–1971," in *Constitutional Politics in Canada and the United States*, ed. Stephen L. Newman (Albany: State University of New York Press, 2004).

99. On the Jewish Labour Committee, see James Walker, "The 'Jewish Phase' in the Movement for Racial Equality in Canada," *Canadian Ethnic Studies* 34, no. 1 (2002).

Chapter 4

•◆•

"Their Equality Is My Equality":[1] F. Andrew Brewin and Human Rights Activism, 1940s–1970s

Stephanie Bangarth

F. Andrew Brewin was a pioneer in the civil liberties and human rights movements in Canada, using his legal training to defend union members and minority groups, and his Christian compassion as a member of the Anglican Church of Canada to comment on major issues of social justice. His legal career was dominated by human rights work. In the 1940s he acted as legal counsel for the Co-operative Committee on Japanese Canadians and defended Japanese Canadians from expatriation and deportation to Japan in the aftermath of the Second World War. He was also essential in crafting the 1944 Saskatchewan Trade Union Act. In Saskatchewan as elsewhere, the courts nonetheless continued to play a significant role in certain aspects of industrial relations, notably in the case of industrial conflict. It was in this role, the extension of labour rights to workers employed by large industries, that Brewin made a difference in Canadian labour law. In his political life, Brewin spoke out against racial injustice and discrimination in immigration policy. He was a passionate critic of Canada's foreign policy from the 1960s to the late 1970s, and was among the first to bring Canadian attention to the problems of war and famine in Biafra (present-day eastern Nigeria). His concern for human rights continued throughout his political career, and he campaigned in the House of Commons, along with other parliamentarians to develop a foreign policy to deal with difficult situations in Pakistan and Venezuela and Chile.

This chapter seeks to assert the following concepts. First and foremost, it will shed light on the manner in which individual agency shaped the history of human rights norms in Canada, especially since so many movements live or die by the enthusiasm and involvement of key leaders and participants. This study will contribute to an overall understanding of how important issues such as human rights, the social democratic movement, labour reform, and campaigns for a just foreign policy are part of a larger national and transnational historical narrative. Many of these issues have not been linked together in a single study with an empirical connection. Brewin's life as a case study provides a compelling example of someone who campaigned for social justice in a number of contexts and who came to advocate the language of human rights to the end. In this way, his human rights work became a vehicle for activism in Canada from the 1930s to the late 1970s. This chapter will outline the role of the post-Holocaust conscience of the post–Second World War period as having a central effect on activists such as Andrew Brewin, both throughout the 1940s and into the 1970s. Moreover, as a Christian socialist, it is undeniable that the spirit of the social gospel was essential in cultivating Brewin's world view of equality and social justice. The influence of the "modern" Christian activist in Canadian history has only variously been examined and not fully linked to human rights activism. This piece aims to do just that.

Lastly, at a time when works by noted human rights scholars such as Samuel Moyn herald international human rights activism and awareness as a function of the post-1968 period, it is clear that the Canadian model does not fully follow suit.[2] In the pre-1970s period the discussion of the terms *civil rights* and *civil liberties* versus *human rights* in Canada was unclear and perhaps even misleading, as Ross Lambertson has noted elsewhere.[3] It would be better to say that in Canada, *civil rights* has a particular constitutional meaning (and for this one might look at the standard work on our constitution by Peter Hogg),[4] although it is also worth remembering that in the 1940s and 1950s there was some debate as to what this term actually meant. On the other hand, most Canadians frequently used (and still use) the term as if they were Americans—comparable with the concept of civil liberties.

"MY BROTHER'S KEEPER": HUMAN RIGHTS AT HOME

As a Christian socialist, Brewin had a well-developed notion of the state as an instrument of the public good. According to the Rt. Reverend Ted Scott of the Anglican Church of Canada, Brewin believed that "the role of the church was to encourage people to live their Christianity in the world, to develop Christian values and to see how they might be developed in the world. A Christian, in his view, was to live in the world, standing for something, working for something."[5] Indeed, according to Terry Morley, Brewin would eventually join the Co-operative Commonwealth Federation "as a response to what [he] felt as a Christian imperative."[6] Such motivations were not unlike those experienced by his fellow CCFers, J.S. Woodsworth, M.J. Coldwell, and F.R. Scott (the latter two were also Anglicans). Brewin was the son of an Anglican clergyman whose parishioners at St. Simon-the-Apostle Church on Howard Street at Bloor Street East in Toronto were drawn largely from the city's elite, although the parish did reflect the poorer, working-class elements of its surrounding neighbourhoods. Brewin was educated in Britain at Radley College, a public boarding school for boys founded on the principles of the Church of England. Upon his return to Canada, he would go on to study law at Osgoode Hall and articled with J.C. McRuer (father of the Ontario Human Rights Code and later the Chief Justice of Ontario). He spent much of his university and early legal career living in the rectory at St. Simon's where he had an opportunity to observe the deep ravages of the Great Depression on nearby Cabbagetown and East York. It would certainly leave a lasting impression of the degree of inequality in 1930s Toronto.[7] Before he would become one of the central figures in the Ontario CCF in the 1940s he practised law as one of the top lawyers of his generation at his firm of Cameron, Brewin, Weldon, McCallum and Skells in an office at Bay and Richmond Streets in downtown Toronto.

Brewin's early law practice was, in a word, eclectic. As Ian Scott (former Ontario Attorney General and Brewin's second cousin through his mother's Blair relatives) observed, "he took on any case that interested him, so that his practice ranged widely from criminal cases to civil litigation. If he believed in the cause, or in the principle raised by a particular case, he did not even notice if he got paid for his work. In those days there was no formal system of legal aid, but people like Andrew Brewin ensured that cases were heard regardless of finances." Brewin often took on more cases than he could reasonably handle as a result of his commitment to two important principles: that everyone is entitled to legal representation, and that if an important legal principle is involved, it should be defended regardless of the client's finances. [8]

At the same time as he was cultivating his legal practice, Brewin was also engaged in political and civic causes. He joined the CCF in 1935 and in March 1940 became a key member in the Civil Liberties Association of Toronto (CLAT) as a response to the excesses of the wartime Defence of Canada Regulations (DOCR). According to Lambertson, Brewin's membership in CLAT "immeasurably enhanced its image of a respectable organization spanning the ideological spectrum from the moderate right to the moderate left."[9] According to Brewin, CLAT "did useful work" but it "was an elitist organization. It was all chiefs and no Indians."[10] Over the course of the 1940s, CLAT continued to protest the DOCR, along with Ottawa's restrictions on the Communist Party. But these civil libertarian causes would soon be joined by arguments about egalitarian rights, especially as they concerned discrimination against various ethnic and religious minorities. One of the most significant transformations to occur over the course of the Second World War was that Canadians became more rights conscious. Civil liberties groups expanded their areas of concern from libertarian rights (the rights to free speech, to legal counsel, to property ownership) to include concern for violations of egalitarian rights (the right to equal protection of the law). In terms of discourse, the language of rights shifted from an emphasis on "British liberties" to a focus on "human rights." Two issues that dominated much of Brewin's political activism in the 1940s, and that drew upon his legal expertise, included his work crafting labour rights legislation and supporting minority rights.

The 1944 Saskatchewan Trade Union Act was one of Brewin's earliest legal accomplishments in the realm of broad-based workers' rights to self-determination. As Laurel Sefton MacDowell has demonstrated, one of the most dramatic changes to occur over the course of the Second World War was the growth of the organized labour movement. Conflict between labour, industry, and government over wage controls and working conditions, as well as the inadequacy of the existing collective bargaining legislation, resulted in unprecedented levels of industrial conflict.[11] By 1942 the federal CCF had adopted a clear set of priorities for labour. When the CCF under T.C. "Tommy" Douglas won the Saskatchewan provincial election in June 1944, a flurry of new labour legislation was introduced in the assembly that fall, the result of a pre-election promise of a new deal for labour. The CCF introduced the Trade Union Act, which made collective bargaining mandatory and the government extended the rights of civil servants to join unions. The Act was one of the first to grant the central parts of the modern labour relations system—exclusivity, mandatory recognition, bargaining in good faith, and protections against unfair labour practices. An independent Labour Relations Board consisting of members representing employers and employees and a non-aligned chair administered this new system. While there have been some amendments to the Trade Union Act, the

basic structure has remained the same. The Act itself was described by
Walter Reuther, noted American labour leader, as "the most progressive
piece of labour legislation on the continent."[12]

To help facilitate his government's labour program, Douglas brought
in a number of CCF labour specialists, including F.R. Scott, David Lewis
(then-CCF National Secretary) and Brewin who worked with government staff (leading to charges that the bill had been "prepared in
Toronto and fussed up a bit in Regina").[13] Brewin, however, is generally
acknowledged as being responsible for drafting the new Trade Union
Act, referred to in one source as the "Magna Carta for Saskatchewan
labour."[14] One of the main complications, however, was pre-existing
federal legislation order-in-council P.C. 1003 known as the Wartime
Labour Relations Regulations adopted by the Liberal government of
William Lyon Mackenzie King on February 17, 1944. In this case, the
federal government exercised its wartime emergency powers granted
under the War Measures Act to legislate in spheres normally under provincial jurisdiction. Thus, the government of Saskatchewan had to negotiate with the federal government. Brewin had a major role to play in
this, accompanying Saskatchewan Minister of Labour C.C. Williams to
meetings with federal Minister of Labour Humphrey Mitchell in their
discussions on the nature of the province's proposed labour legislation.
Brewin, along with Scott and Lewis, also met with organized labour such
as the Canadian Congress of Labour via its president, Aaron Mosher, a
long-standing supporter of collective bargaining rights.[15]

It was not long before the basic principles of the Trade Union Act
were tested in Saskatchewan. At issue was the dismissal of six employees
from the John East Iron Works in Saskatoon for their involvement in
union activity, which the United Steelworkers of America brought to the
attention of the Labour Relations Board in June 1947. The board ordered
the reinstatement of the affected employees with compensation for lost
wages whereupon the employer decided to appeal to the Saskatchewan
Court of Appeal for, among other concerns, a judicial review of the
board's orders, arguing the board breached constitutional boundaries
and encroached on the authority of the superior courts in the matter.
While the Court of Appeal ultimately ruled that section 5(e) of the Act
was *ultra vires* because it conferred upon the Labour Relations Board
judicial powers in the realm of employee hiring and termination, powers that are exercised by the superior, district, and county courts, it did

regard the issues raised by the case to be of such public importance that it granted the Labour Relations Board appeal to the Judicial Committee of the Privy Council.[16]

Brewin, along with Morris C. Schumiatcher who recently had been invited to join the Saskatchewan Attorney General's office, appeared as counsel for the board. Brewin presented the major arguments which attempted to create "a new statutory regime for collective bargaining, one which rested on different premises and assumptions than those reflected in the law of master and servant."[17] Many of the remedies available to address problems in the master–servant relationship, and certainly the conferring of decision-making power upon a tribunal, would not have occurred to the drafters of the 1867 Constitution Act. Brewin pointed out that the board could not run afoul of section 96 of the Constitution since the federal government had chosen to confer similar powers to labour relations boards and not the courts in other jurisdictions. The Judicial Committee agreed with Brewin and in the judgment written by Lord Simonds reversed the Saskatchewan Court of Appeal, concluding that the board did not overstep its jurisdiction into a court within section 96.[18]

The *John East Iron Works* case would become an important case in the history of Canadian judicial review, but more broadly it now speaks to the issue of collective bargaining as a human right, an idea which was recently reviewed by the Supreme Court of Canada.[19] At the time, the success of the Saskatchewan CCF government with respect to its labour rights agenda spoke clearly to the broader, national CCF vision of "an active role for government" with "human rights legislation and labor legislation encouraging the expansion of unions" as David Goutor has noted.[20] This is not to say that Brewin had in mind the exclusive issue of human rights when drafting his defence of the board, for he saw that success in the Supreme Court would only come on jurisdictional matters. Yet despite the restrictive nature of the legal argument Brewin played a facilitative role both as a member of the CCF, a "left political institution that drew together human rights and labor activists" and as a noted labour rights lawyer in the formation of a connection between the protection of human rights and social and economic rights by the state.[21] When one also takes into account the following two examples, that of his work defending persons of Japanese ancestry from expatriation from Canada and his efforts to bring forward a Canadian bill of rights, it is fair to say that he was central in the building of a body of law concerning human rights in this country, well before the 1970s.

Recent scholarship points to the federal government's policies of incarceration and expatriation of Japanese Canadians as having an impact on the "surge of egalitarian idealism" that took place in postwar Canada.[22] The campaign to obtain justice for persons of Japanese ancestry, especially with respect to the expatriation, represents Canada's earliest and most significant involvement with the discourse of human rights. The attention of advocates and their lobbying strategies moved beyond civil liberties and the call to respect "traditional British liberties" to a rhetoric that included the newly articulated ideals of human rights as expressed in the Atlantic Charter and later in the Charter of the United Nations. While the lack of an American-style Bill of Rights compelled Canadian advocates to look to the international charters to give their arguments meaning and substance, it does not suggest that the Canadian experience heralded something more laudable; indeed, Canadians made a virtue out of necessity.

It is today conventional wisdom that the incarceration policy was a violation of democratic values, but virtually all liberals in 1942 saw it as a necessary evil, justifiable in the context of national security as well as a safeguard against the possibility of anti-Japanese mob violence.[23] But in February of 1945 the federal government provided more details in orders-in-council P.C. 7355, 7356, and 7357 about the future of Japanese Canadians. Unlike the American government, which had recently removed all controls on Japanese Americans, it announced a "voluntary repatriation" program whereby Japanese Canadians could opt either to move east of the Rocky Mountains or be deported/expatriated to Japan. By May over six thousand repatriation forms had been signed, on behalf of over ten thousand men, women, and children, most of them Canadian citizens, and representing over 40 percent of the Japanese Canadian population. It was at this point that the Co-operative Committee on Japanese Canadians (CCJC) stepped into a prominent national role. Formed as a purely philanthropic organization for Japanese Canadian relocatees to Toronto with no political intentions in 1943, by 1946 the CCJC was sufficiently organized to launch a vigorous protest of the government's policy when Andrew Brewin was retained as counsel for the committee.[24]

As Lambertson notes, a majority of CCJC members were representatives of CLAT; these included its president, George Tatham, of the

University of Toronto, Jarvis McCurdy, another University of Toronto academic, journalist Margaret Gould, B.K. Sandwell of *Saturday Night*, and Andrew Brewin.[25] When, despite the public appeal, the orders-in-council authorizing the deportations were announced, the CCJC resolved to take legal action. This decision was a major step for a small executive representing a loosely knit group of organizations. Andrew Brewin was asked to serve as legal counsel for the committee.[26] What began as a writ issued by the CCJC against the attorney general of Canada testing the legality of the orders-in-council was soon referred by cabinet to the Supreme Court. The case, formally titled *In the Matter of a Reference as to the Validity of Orders in Council of the 15th Day of December, 1945 (P.C. 7355, 7356 and 7357) in Relation to Persons of Japanese Race* (1946), hereafter cited as *In the Matter of a Reference*, called on the Supreme Court to consider the limits of power.

In November 1945 a delegation met with the prime minister and several members of his cabinet in Ottawa, where Brewin explained the CCJC position on deportation. To the obvious legal argument against the policy—the emergency wartime situation no longer existed—Brewin added several others that took morality as their common thread: the policy disparaged Canadian citizenship, it discriminated on the basis of race, and it was unjust and inhumane. These arguments were clearly stated in a CCJC leaflet titled *Our Japanese Canadians: Citizens, Not Exiles.* The pamphlet cited the United Nations Charter in support of the CCJC conclusion that the expatriation/deportation policy violated the commitments to human rights made by the Canadian government. It also noted that the orders-in-council would "threaten the security of every minority in Canada, a land of minorities."[27] Following up on this meeting, the CCJC sent a memorandum to all MPs in which it accused the government of employing "the methods of Nazism" for deportation "on racial grounds has been denounced as a crime against humanity, and the war criminals of Germany and Japan are being tried precisely for this offence." In addition to issuing its legal action, the CCJC met with government officials to ask that the case be referred to the Supreme Court. On January 4, a delegation consisting of Sandwell, Tatham, Brewin, and Donalda MacMillan met with the acting minister of justice and his deputy minister. They warned government representatives that numerous organizations across Canada supported CCJC actions and had initiated protests against the orders-in-council. Brewin pointed out that since

Ottawa had the power to deport aliens only, the deportation orders for Canadian citizens were unconstitutional. They asked the two bureaucrats to convey this information to cabinet, with the intention that the matter be submitted to the Supreme Court as a reference case. If their request were not granted, the CCJC threatened to issue thousands of writs of habeas corpus against the government.[28] The argument was heard before the Supreme Court on January 24 and 25.

CCJC counsel Brewin and J.R. Cartwright, a noted constitutional authority who would later be appointed Chief Justice of the Supreme Court, acted on behalf of the CCJC, as did J.A. MacLennan. Brewin also represented the CCF government of Saskatchewan in support of the CCJC; the province of British Columbia supported the attorney general of Canada against the appeal. The question referred to the Supreme Court for hearing and consideration was the following: "Are the Orders-in-Council, dated the 15th day of December, 1945, being P.C. 7355, 7356, and 7357, *ultra vires* of the Governor in Council either in whole or in part and, if so, in what particular or particulars and to what extent?"[29] In making their case to the Supreme Court, the CCJC representatives asserted that the orders-in-council were entirely *ultra vires* of the powers of Parliament. The CCJC sought to prove that the federal government was not granted unlimited powers under the "peace, order and good government" clause of the British North America Act (BNA) and the pursuant War Measures Act.[30]

The CCJC also contested the orders on the basis of race, arguing that the words "Japanese Race" were so vague as to be meaningless, therefore rendering the orders unenforceable. In appealing to humanitarian principles, counsel for the CCJC contended that "there is a presumption that Parliament does not assert or assume jurisdiction which goes beyond the limits established by the common consent of nations" and that deportation of citizens on racial grounds had been declared a "crime against humanity" by the United Nations. Brewin and Cartwright added that, because the orders for deportation and revocation of citizenship threatened the citizenship rights of British subjects, they interfered with British law, namely the British Nationality and Status of Aliens Act, which extended to the Dominion of Canada.[31]

On February 20, 1946, the Supreme Court's decision in *In the Matter of a Reference* satisfied no one, as a majority of the court held that the orders-in-council were partially valid. The justices were unanimous that the deportation of Japanese aliens and naturalized Japanese Canadians was legal. On the dependants of male deportees the court split four to three against deportation. In practical terms this meant that Ottawa could now legally deport the 6,844 adults who had signed requests for repatriation, but their 3,500 dependants could remain in Canada. The court upheld the authority of cabinet as "the sole judge of the necessity or advisability of these measures" and ruled the orders legal simply because the government had power to issue them under the War Measures Act.[32] The CCJC launched an immediate appeal to the Judicial Committee of the Privy Council in London.[33]

For the CCJC and Brewin, the lesson of the Supreme Court judgments was that the courts were concerned only with the legality of the orders, not with the moral justice or injustice of the policy. Considerations of "race" and human rights would have little impact on the lords of the Privy Council. Thus, the material Brewin presented over the four days in session, assisted by two British lawyers, Christopher Shawcross, MP, and Geoffrey Wilson, was confined largely to jurisdictional arguments. The Privy Council handed down its ruling in December 1946. Lord Wright delivered the unanimous judgment that the orders-in-council were *intra vires* under the War Measures Act and valid *in toto* because of the unlimited powers granted to the federal government to do anything it considered necessary for the safety of the country.[34] The sovereignty of Parliament was undisputed. The case made by the CCJC, its affiliates, and coordinating groups would find a more favourable hearing in the court of public opinion and ultimately appealing to this "court" proved to be the more successful tactic.

Alongside the legal preparations the CCJC initiated a series of public meetings. On January 10, 1946, for example, nearly a thousand people attended a meeting held at Jarvis Collegiate in Toronto to hear addresses by Senators Cairine Wilson and Arthur Roebuck, noted human rights supporters. Rabbi Abraham Feinberg of Toronto's Holy Blossom Temple declared his support for rectifying the injustice of the deportation on behalf of "six million Jews who have been slaughtered in Europe for no other reason than that they were Jews." Andrew Brewin spoke about the legal issues at hand. Out of this meeting came two resolutions. One was sent to Prime Minister W.L. Mackenzie King; the other, delivered to Premier George A. Drew of Ontario, challenged the provincial government "to accept the citizenship and residence of Canadians of Japanese origin on a basis of equality with Canadians of other national origins." As a result of the CCJC's continued public education campaign, more letters flowed into the offices of the prime minister, cabinet ministers, and MPs protesting the deportation and demanding the removal of restrictions on Japanese Canadians. [35]

The CCJC was preparing for yet another meeting with the prime minister when on January 24, 1947, the government declared that its deportation policy was "no longer necessary" and repealed the orders-in-council in question. Restrictions on the freedoms and movements of Japanese Canadians would remain until 1949, long after the wartime "emergency" situation. For the CCJC, the Privy Council ruling also underlined the fact that "a nation can never depend upon laws or constitutions to defend its rights" and pointed to the need for a restrictive bill of rights like that of the United States, or some other constitutional limitation of the powers of Parliament or the cabinet.[36] With that, Brewin and the CCJC and the newly formed Japanese Canadian Citizens Association turned their attention to restitution for property losses via the Bird Commission. Brewin and other lawyers affiliated with the CCJC counselled Japanese Canadian claimants but as the issue did not grab the attention of the public, the CCJC quietly wound up its activities by 1950.

Frank Scott once remarked that "constitutionally speaking, the 1950s was predominantly the decade of human rights." Scott was referring to a spate of cases that would become famous for their articulation of a constitutional theory known as the "implied bill of rights."[37] Brewin was a strong advocate throughout his legal and his political career for a bill of rights that would be entrenched in the constitution and played a central role in the articulation of the "implied bill of rights" principle.[38] The Committee for a Bill of Rights (CBR), which followed closely on the heels of the Japanese Canadian campaign and shared many committee members with the CCJC (including Brewin), used the example of the Japanese Canadian issue in connection with the wider issue of the passage of a Canadian bill of rights. In building upon the success of the campaign to end deportations, Canadian advocates began to forward the idea that, in light of events at home and abroad, it was necessary to demonstrate clearly to all Canadians the urgency of a "basic law which recognizes human personality and the right to freedom under the law of every Canadian irrespective of race."[39] The enshrining of a bill of rights in the Constitution was a popular idea among advocates in postwar

Canada and even received serious attention in the House of Commons and in the Senate.

At Brewin's urging, the CBR was created in early 1947 as an adjunct of the Association for Civil Liberties (formed out of CLAT in an attempt to nationalize rights advocacy), specifically to lobby the federal government and to capitalize on growing attention being paid to such a proposal.[40] The group would draw many of the same members as did the CCJC, including Brewin, Sandwell, Irving Himel, a Toronto lawyer and civil rights activist, and Charles Millard, the noted trade union activist. The campaign for a bill of rights would bring together both civil libertarians and egalitarians, and would promote the protection of not only such rights as free speech and freedom of association but also the right not to suffer discrimination on the basis of race, religion, or gender, also reflecting the postwar discourse of human rights in Canada. Groups from both traditions, including the Japanese Canadian Committee for Democracy, the Canadian Jewish Congress, and the nascent Civil Rights Union united with the CBR in the campaign. That said, in many respects it was a "letterhead organization," according to Lambertson, and the ultimate hope for bill of rights advocates turned out to be in the person of John G. Diefenbaker who had long advocated for a version of this bill.[41] In 1948 the committee presented the minister of justice with a petition containing the names of two hundred "respectable" members of the community from across the country calling for a bill of rights, which was also their official submission to the Special Joint Committee of the House of Commons and Senate on Human Rights and Fundamental Freedoms. For the drafting of the brief, the CBR turned to Brewin, who was by this time the president of the Ontario CCF.

Brewin's proposal was for an amendment to the BNA Act [1867] to prohibit the federal and provincial governments from enacting legislation that would infringe upon certain civil rights including freedom of religion, freedom of speech, and the right to lawful assembly, among others. To contextualize the brief's purpose, Brewin provided a historical account of a variety of state-inflicted infringements on civil liberties from the pre-Depression era to the time of the drafting of the brief, and noted that international developments in the realm of human rights merited their protection in Canada. The brief overwhelmingly reflected the emerging discourse of human rights, despite its completion ahead of the 1948 United Nations Declaration on Human Rights in December. Consider the following quote: "It has been officially recognized by the nations of the world that fascism which brought upon the world the most destructive war in history was rooted in contempt for human rights and that, conversely, the peace of the world must rest ultimately upon the universal respect of human rights and fundamental freedoms." He continued by noting that "we in Canada are in a position to give positive adherence to these fundamental international ideals," recognizing the usefulness of UN ideals in forwarding the Canadian agenda of the CBR.[42] Three years later the committee would again pressure the Liberal government of Louis St. Laurent, with a version of the brief even more rooted in international concepts of human rights. But despite the clear hypocrisy of Canada being a signatory to the UNDHR, the federal government refused to move on a constitutionally entrenched bill of rights. As Carmela Patrias has noted, the Liberals of the day were hesitant in supporting a national bill of rights for fear that state action on political rights would lead to state action on social rights and the welfare state.[43]

Diefenbaker's arrival in the prime minister's office in 1957 challenged him with the task of obtaining consent from provincial premiers, such as Quebec's Maurice Duplessis, to achieve a constitutionally entrenched rights guarantee. Without such co-operation he fell back to the defence that a federal parliamentary statute, rather than a constitutional amendment, could provide adequate and effective protection of Canadians' rights. This argument was rejected by constitutional scholars like Frank Scott, Bora Laskin, and Brewin, who correctly anticipated the limited effectiveness of Diefenbaker's Bill of Rights. It represented, as Lambertson has suggested, "half a loaf"; but it also represented the conclusion of a major struggle for the emerging human rights community in Canada.[44] As for Brewin, his activism would finally turn toward Parliament.

"MY BROTHER'S KEEPER": HUMAN RIGHTS ABROAD

Brewin, like others of his generation, entered politics with the aim of advancing his humanitarian activism at a national level. Within the party, he was an eloquent and unrelenting advocate of the party's high regard for the values of equality and the rule of law. Domestically, he continued to argue for a more open and non-discriminatory immigration policy and was a long-time agitator for a separate policy stream for refugees. Taking up "hard luck" immigration cases would comprise a significant portion of his constituency work throughout his entire political career.

When he became well known nationally as a critic of Canadian immigration policy, he received hundreds of appeals from people well outside the geographical boundaries of his riding, Toronto-Greenwood.[45]

It was his sense of social justice that compelled Brewin to do more than just talk about the Nigerian conflict in the House of Commons over the course of 1967–1970. The Nigerian secessionist conflict is not generally well known to Canadians today, and for good reason. Despite the fact that the Canadian public was, for some time, roused to ire over its government's indifferent response, the historical record is nearly silent on the whole affair. This is likely due to the regret that some activists feel today at how Biafran leaders, particularly General Odumegwu Ojukwu, the ersatz Biafran leader, manipulated Western guilt via a sophisticated public relations campaign.[46]

It should be noted that although Nigeria was part of the Commonwealth, its relations with Canada had not been close. As such, the conflict generated little interest in Canada at the outset. The issue of Biafra was first raised in the House of Commons debates in 1967 (twenty-seventh Parliament, January 18, 1966, until April 23, 1968), but the Liberal government under Lester B. Pearson fielded only eight questions. The earliest debate dealt with "internal disorders in Nigeria, Biafran secession and mediation efforts." By the end of the twenty-seventh Parliament, Brewin began to speak heavily on Biafra, as the indexes to the 1968–1969 debates show. A review of Hansard reveals that this conflict and its outcomes were no longer debated after 1970.

As Donald Barry notes, interest groups began their attempts to influence the government's policy by June 1967. In particular, officials of the Presbyterian Church in Canada were knowledgeable of the situation in both Nigeria and Biafra due to their ongoing missionary efforts there. Returned CUSO (Canadian University Service Overseas) volunteers and Biafran students could also count among the early influencers.[47] The Canadian public would begin to pay attention by July 1968, when pictures of starving Biafran children began appearing on television and in newspapers. Criticism of the government's inaction grew, especially when Prime Minister Pierre Trudeau feigned amusement. When asked by a reporter about the possibility of sending Canadian aid to the war's casualties he replied, "You have the funniest questions. We haven't considered this as a government. . . . I think we should send aid to all needy people but we can't send it to everyone and I'd have to see what our priorities are prior to the Biafra people."[48] At a time when African decolonization and liberation were being viewed with high regard by progressives in the West, Trudeau's statements were certainly out of step. The Biafran crisis dominated the Canadian foreign policy landscape throughout 1968.

Among those voices was the Reverend Ted Johnson, Moderator of the Presbyterian Church of Canada. He led a delegation of church leaders to Ottawa to request aid for starving Biafrans, but was refused. As a consequence of that rejection, Canairelief was created through the financial support of Jewish leaders, the Roman Catholic Church, and the major Protestant denominations (mainly the Anglican, Presbyterian, and United churches), along with a partnership with Oxfam. In 670 flights between January 1969 and January 1970, Canairelief delivered to Biafra eleven thousand tons of food and medical supplies.[49] Other countries were sending aid directly, such as France, Portugal, and Israel. Prior to the creation of Canairelief, Johnson and this team had also pursued the political route and had arranged for two MPs—Brewin and United Church minister and Progressive Conservative MP David MacDonald—to fly to Biafra on a fact-finding mission.[50]

While Brewin and MacDonald's fact-finding mission angered Trudeau, it did generate considerable public interest and even more considerable activity in the House of Commons. They arrived in Biafra in October 1968, at a time when the fortunes of secessionist Biafra were at their nadir, on a relief flight in the dead of night. Their official report of their fact-finding mission, *Canada and the Biafran Tragedy*, became a book in 1970 that recommended Canada use its position to prod the United Nations to negotiate a ceasefire, participate in relief operations, push to have Nigerian civil rights violations under the UN Charter enforced, and give money for humanitarian relief.[51] They also wrote evocatively about the starvation they had witnessed, noting that they would not easily forget "the sight of curly red hair and bleached skin" of the children they encountered.[52]

Brewin and MacDonald also hoped to arouse the Canadian Parliament and the Canadian people to action on a double front: exerting pressure for ceasefire and mounting a massive relief campaign to combat the threat of starvation. Their report concluded with a recommendation that an international order be built that can effectively intervene to prevent massive loss of human life and the continuation of wars that threaten large numbers of people, through genocide or otherwise. Ultimately, however, Brewin and MacDonald charged that much of the foot-dragging was largely due to the unwillingness of the Department of External Affairs to change its traditional outlook. They suggested that "the basic reason for Ottawa's refusal to take the Biafran affair to the United Nations has been much more the adherence to a style and attitude in international affairs that has become characteristic of Canada. There is an attitude of caution, and attitude of weighing the views of our allies rather than the merits of the issue."[53]

As David Forsyth notes, as a general historical trend, more attention is now paid toward humanitarianism in world affairs.[54] But until about 1970, the UN system was not utilized to assist in the management of humanitarian disasters. The major relief players (the International Committee of the Red Cross and Joint Church Aid) were left to solve the problems, with the effect that the attempts to operate in a coordinated fashion stymied the efficient distribution of aid. After Biafra, and after changes in other aspects of international relations, the UN General Assembly created the UN Disaster Relief Office in 1971.

Brewin and MacDonald's recommendations in *Canada and the Biafran Tragedy* were clearly forward-thinking, and certainly foreshadowed a trend of increasing internationalism in Canadian foreign policy. Indeed, the historical record indicates that what many Canadians argued for, including Brewin, MacDonald, and Johnson, was a preliminary form of R2P ("responsibility to protect," a United Nations initiative established in 1995). R2P is a norm or set of principles based on the idea that sovereignty is not a privilege, but a responsibility. It focuses on preventing and halting four crimes: genocide, war crimes, crimes against humanity, and ethnic cleansing. While the ineffectiveness of the world community's response to the Rwandan genocide is frequently cited as the genesis of this principle, a close reading of the appeals to Trudeau and External Affairs Minister Mitchell Sharp, and to other Western governments reveals remarkably similar ideologies.[55] Successive governments could no longer avoid the shifting international circumstances brought about in a globalizing world. The Conservative government under Brian Mulroney (1984–1993) would appreciate this, and throughout the 1980s forged closer relationships with Latin America and served as a world leader in its approach to South Africa. Yet, Africa still remains a challenge.

In 1973 over seven thousand Chilean and other Latin American refugees were admitted to Canada after the violent overthrow of Salvador

Allende's democratically elected Socialist–Communist government. Supporters of the Allende regime fled the oppression directed against them by Chile's new military ruler, General Augusto Pinochet. Although Canada took the refugees in, it did so grudgingly—at first. Despite public pressure the government was slow to react, not wanting to antagonize Chile's new military administration nor the United States, which had helped create and then publicly criticized Chile's descent into economic disorder under Allende. When Argentina faced a military coup d'etat in March 1976, an event that marked the beginning of Argentina's now infamous "Dirty Wars" of 1976 to 1983, a second wave of Chilean refugees sought to come to Canada.

In the aftermath of the 1973 coup d'état, members of the Protestant and Catholic churches of Canada called on the Canadian government to denounce the human rights abuses and grant asylum to Chilean refugees located both inside Chile and in neighbouring Argentina. Minister of Immigration Robert Andras and Mitchell Sharp of External Affairs remained reluctant to do so. On the advice of the Canadian ambassador to Chile, Andrew Ross, the Canadian government recognized the Pinochet junta on September 29, 1973, on the ground that it was the only authority in the country. This decision was not well received by refugee advocates, as Andrew Thompson has noted.[56] Many, including the churches, questioned whether the Canadian government was displeased to see the Allende government fall. Andras and Sharp feared that among the refugees were terrorists, communists, and other subversives. Only after a chorus of disapproval from various social justice groups did they reevaluate their position and begin the process by which Canada would take in more than forty-five hundred Chilean refugees by the end of 1976.

But political advocates were also integral the efforts to expand refugee rights. Conversations about a fact-finding mission to Chile began in the spring of 1976. Increasingly disturbing reports regarding imprisonment and exile for political reasons, harassment of refugees, and repression of human rights in Argentina and Uruguay were heard alongside the continuing news of oppression in Chile. The Inter-Church Committee on Chile agreed to sponsor a fact-finding visit by three Members of Parliament to the three countries of the so-called southern cone of Latin America. Several other Canadian organizations, including Amnesty International, Oxfam Canada, and the Canadian Catholic Organization for Development and Peace supported the effort. The purpose of their mission was twofold: to observe and evaluate the situation of refugees and the Canadian response to their needs, and to observe the general situation of human rights in the countries visited.[57]

Each of the three MPs involved in the mission were noted for having taken a special interest throughout their careers in issues of human rights, and in the particular situation in Chile. Brewin, of course, was a member of the NDP and his legal experience, advocacy of civil liberties, and knowledge of immigration policies was well known by this time. Progressive Conservative MP David MacDonald of PEI had an interest in human rights and issues of world development that had led him to undertake several previous fact-finding missions, many together with Brewin.[58] Louis Duclos was a Roman Catholic Liberal MP who represented the Quebec riding of Montmorency. In addition to his years as a civil servant, Duclos spent several years in the Canadian embassy in Bogota, Colombia. The three MPs thus represented the three major Canadian political parties, three diverse geographical backgrounds, and three major Canadian religious denominations. They set out for Santiago on September 27, only to learn that due to a high-level junta decision they would not be permitted to enter Chile. Instead, they arrived in Buenos Aires, Argentina, on September 30 and would spend much of their ten-day visit there and in Montevideo, Uruguay. They arrived back in Canada on October 11, 1976.

As part of their fact-finding mission they examined the Canadian program to assist the refugees. As no refugee policy was specifically in place, selection was done on a group-by-group basis. As of July 1976, the Canadian government pledged to accept six thousand refugees from Chile, with forty-five hundred already in Canada. The main concern that Brewin, MacDonald, and Duclos found with the acceptance of the refugees by Canadian officials was that of delay. The processing of refugee applications from Chile took an average of four weeks, during which time applicants would be in danger of seizure by the Chilean police. No similar delays were encountered in bringing in Hungarian refugees in 1956, the Ugandan Asians in 1972, or the Vietnamese "boat people" in 1975. In fact, the Canadian government was able to grant refugee status to six thousand Ugandan Asians in two months in 1972, yet took eighteen months to admit the first fifteen hundred Chileans after the Allende government fell. The Canadian government also did not do away with prior medical, security, and immigration procedures to speed removal of Latin American refugees, and the RCMP officers in Santiago turned down a high proportion of the initial wave of refugee applications in 1973–1974 on the basis that they posed security threats for Canada. Immigration officers were also found to be treating refugees similarly to ordinary immigrants (such as using identical forms and questions based on the points system) and allowed very few special considerations in view of the emergency situation.[59]

The government painted the Chilean refugees as subversives and dangerous to Canada. This was certainly out of step with the Canadian population, many of whom by way of various organizations were urging the government to accept the refugees, as they had done in the past in other crises. The government was also out of step with the efforts of other nations, including Holland and Sweden, who were treating the Chilean refugees outside the normal flow of immigrants. For their part the three MPs recommended in their report that standards for the definition and admission of refugees be clearly set out in legislation or at least in ex- plicit regulations. Along with their proposal that a separate and suitable application form for refugees be prepared, Brewin, MacDonald, and Duclos recommended that all UN-accredited refugees be considered as refugees for the purposes of Canadian immigration. While Canada accepted the United Nation's definition of a refugee at the time of the report's publication in November 1976, it did not accept the UN deter- mination or assessment of who is a bona fide refugee. Indeed, Canadian immigration officers were known to reject many refugees registered by the UN High Commissioner for Refugees. Brewin would use this infor- mation in recommending numerous amendments to proposed refugee policy being formed at this time. This was done via the Sub-Committee on Immigration of which he was a member and NDP representative throughout the 1970s.[60] 1978, then, marked the first time an Immigration Act included a humanitarian category for refugees needing protection and resettlement. It also established the Private Sponsorship of Refugees Program, which allowed Canadians to be involved in the resettlement of refugees. A noted improvement, reflective of the report written by Brewin, MacDonald, and Duclos, was that they were not required to be outside the country when making their claim.

At the same time as the refugee crisis was being investigated, Brewin, MacDonald, and Duclos also detailed the human rights violations, such as the use of torture and death squads in the search for political adversaries on the left. They even linked the restoration of human rights as a precondition for the granting of loans and capital from Canada, or the rest of the investing international community. In the 1970s, the issue was with Noranda Mines in Chile and Canadian bank loans to that country, which the churches, via the Taskforce on the Churches and Corporate Responsibility, and Amnesty International continued to protest.[61] This led to another outcome of this visit—Brewin's attempt to pass a bill on the issue of fair trade and human rights. In 1978 Bill C-71, a private member's bill, was Brewin's attempt to have principles of human rights recognized in Canadian trade operations. The context of the bill was almost entirely based on the observations he and his colleagues made during their trip to South America in 1976. His effort failed, as the bill died on the floor of the House of Commons, voted down by the majority Liberals. He did, however, follow through on his promise to withdraw all his accounts from the Canadian Imperial Bank of Commerce upon learning of a $210 million loan to the government of Chile.[62]

Activities such as these indicate that Brewin, like many of his contemporaries, believed that people had a moral responsibility to address social ills through active social and ethical leadership. As a committed Anglican, social justice advocate, and believer in the UN and multilateralism, and through his continuous participation in the major foreign policy debates of the 1960s and 1970s, Brewin's voice was chief among those advocating for Canada as a middle power with a human rights conscience.

CONCLUSION

Throughout his political career, Brewin was noted for his commitment to principles of social justice. His efforts to seek a resolution in the Nigerian conflict represented but one of a number of ways that he was dedicated to political principles rather than political expediency. The Biafran issue deeply concerned him, and he felt that the Trudeau government was not doing enough, as he noted in a letter to a concerned Canadian, that "despite Mr. Trudeau's 'swinging' style, he seems to be very conservative when it comes to action."[63] His views on principles of equality stayed remarkably true during the course of his lifetime, as this chapter has demonstrated.

Canadians activists between 1930 and 1980 looked to government positions, believing that work within the political system would provide an effective avenue for reform. At a period when the state was creating and expanding via programs touching many facets of the citizen's life, activism through government employment was an accepted response for those hoping to influence policy deliberations. Thus, this case study has served also to speak to the interconnections between human rights and various areas of activism: labour, foreign policy, religion, and left-wing politics. Individually Brewin, as a lawyer, as a man with deep religious convictions, as an activist, and as a politician was key in the development of a system of human rights protected under law. He was also at the forefront of the CCF/NDP's articulation of human rights principles as its spokesman in the House of Commons on foreign policy for his nearly two decades long political career.

Lastly, can we really say whether or not one period defines human rights success more than another? I think to declare that a single specific period or manifestation of a human rights revolution is more significant than another is problematic. In the Canadian sense, such a claim is not easily sustained. I prefer to subscribe to what Dr. Bonny Ibhawoh has described as the history of human rights by "defining episodes."[64] In this case, then, the universalization agenda of the 1970s is but one of these episodes, alongside the Holocaust and the UDHR epoch that others, including myself, have researched. It might in fact be dangerous and misleading to promote one period over another, for it ahistoricizes recent developments; for example the historic settlement between the federal government and members of the Japanese-Canadian community in 1988 regarding their wartime incarceration cannot be understood without noting the protest movements of the 1940s and the early 1950s. A focus on periodization can also feed into the misguided notions that many Canadians hold—that we are beacons of human rights. It becomes a case of "not us" in the human memory.[65]

Singling out the 1970s for special commendation simply does not hold if one believes that human rights are part of changing cultural values, as James W. St. G. Walker asserts. If the 1970s were a watershed for human rights in Canada, they certainly were not for Aboriginals in Canada, as Dr. Jim Miller's chapter reveals. Brewin's career provides a remarkable case study from which to analyze how human rights became part of changing Canadian cultural values, from labour rights and collective bargaining to the protection of minority group rights, and from devising ways to litigate freedoms to the promotion of Canadian ethics in international trade. When examined from the perspective of an engaged citizen over the course of forty years, it is clear that today's human rights movement could not emerge "seemingly from nowhere." Today's new internationalist "utopia," as Moyn terms it, was fashioned out of a cultural shift that was decades in the making in Canada by way of activists such as Andrew Brewin.

NOTES

1.   R. Gordon L. Fairweather, Chairman, Human Rights Commission, quoted by Andrew Brewin, House of Commons, Ottawa, December 8, 1978.

2.   Samuel Moyn, *The Last Utopia: Human Rights in History* (Cambridge, MA: Belknap Press, 2010).

3.   Ross Lambertson, *Repression and Resistance: Canadian Human Rights Activists, 1930–1960* (Toronto: University of Toronto Press, 2005), 6–8.

4.   Peter W. Hogg, *Constitutional Law of Canada*, 5th ed. (Toronto: Carswell, 2007).

5.   Christian socialism generally refers to those on the Christian left whose politics are both Christian and socialist and who see these two philosophies as being interrelated. While it is true that fellow Anglican Ted Scott has described Brewin as an untraditional socialist in that he did believe in a "mixed economy" and was as comfortable in a business meeting as he was at a trade union meeting, it is fair to say that his commitment to the principles of socialism were very strong throughout his lifetime. See John F. Brewin, "'He Who Would Valiant Be': The Makings of a Canadian Anglican Christian Socialist" (M.Theol. thesis, Vancouver School of Theology April 1999), 75.

6.   J. T. Morley, *Secular Socialists: The CCF/NDP in Ontario, A Biography* (Montreal and Kingston: McGill–Queen's University Press, 1984), 126.

7.   Brewin, "'He Who Would Valiant Be,'" 23–31.

8.   Ian Scott with Neil McCormick, *To Make a Difference: A Memoir* (Toronto: Stoddart, 2001), 27–28. Scott joined Brewin's firm upon graduating from Osgoode Hall. This sentiment is also corroborated in a number of interviews I conducted with the members of the Brewin family and with Brewin's colleagues and contemporaries, including John Brewin, Martha and George Hynna, Mary Lewis, Jane Morley, John Tackaberry, Hon. Bob Rae, and Justice Stephen Goudge.

9.   Lambertson, *Repression and Resistance*, 127. Chapters 1 and 2 of this book gives a detailed and important account of the activities of CLAT and other civil liberties groups in Canada during the Second World War.

10.   Quote from Library and Archives Canada (hereafter LAC), MG32 C26, vol. 69, file 21, letter, Brewin to Don Whiteside, Dec. 22, 1976.

11.   Laurel Sefton MacDowell, "The Formation of the Canadian Industrial Relations System During World War Two," in *Canadian Working Class History: Selected Readings*, ed. Laurel Sefton MacDowell and Ian Radforth (Toronto: Canadian Scholars' Press, 1992), 575–78.

12.   Thomas H. McLeod and Ian McLeod, *Tommy Douglas: The Road to Jerusalem* (Edmonton: Hurtig Publishers, 1987), Chap. 16; Saskatchewan Archives Board (hereafter SAB) R-33.1, file VII 302 (7–8), folder 1 of 3 "Legislation, July 1944–April 1946," Letter, W. K. Bryden, Technical Adviser to the Minister, to L.J. Chase, Provincial Secretary, SK Provincial Command, Canadian Legion, Oct. 28, 1944; MG32 C26, vol. 7, file 27, letter, Brewin to A. D. Cherniak, March 4, 1949.

13.   Quote from Beth Bilson, "*John East Iron Works v. Saskatchewan Labour Relations* Board: a Test for the Infant Administrative State," in *Work on Trial: Canadian Labour Law Struggles*, ed. Judy Fudge and Eric Tucker (Toronto: Irwin Law/Osgoode Society for Canadian Legal History, 2010), 45.

14. McLeod and McLeod, *Tommy Douglas*, 157.
15. It is widely known that the US Wagner Act, passed in 1935 as part of the New Deal legislative program of President Franklin D. Roosevelt, served as the inspiration for the Wartime Labour Relations Regulations. SAB, R-33.1, file VII 302 (7–8), folder 1 of 3 "Legislation, July 1944 – April 1946," letter, C. C. Williams to T. C. Douglas, August 29, 1944.
16. "Labour Board rule argued before P.C.," *Montreal Gazette*, July 20, 1948. For a clear and detailed rendering of the legal facts and importance of this case in Canadian administrative law see Bilson in *Work on Trial*, 43–74. See also SAB, R-1728, File No. 12.2.4, *The Labour Relations Board of Saskatchewan v. John East Iron Works Ltd.,* transcript of proceedings in the Privy Council.
17. Bilson, 54. The master and servant relationship is one where there is no duty to act fairly when deciding to terminate employment
18. Ibid., 54–57.
19. *Health Services and Support—Facilities Subsector Bargaining Assn. v. British Columbia* [2007] SCC 27.
20. David Goutor, "A Different Perspective on the "Labor Rights as Human Rights" Debate: Organized Labor and Human Rights Activism in Canada, 1939–1952," *Labor Studies Journal* 36 (2011): 415.
21. Goutor, "A Different Perspective," 416–17.
22. Note that this author uses the term *incarceration* instead of *internment* to describe the wartime treatment of Japanese Canadians. In fact, only 750 Japanese Canadians and Japanese nationals were interned in the legal sense of the word at a camp near Angler, Ontario. For more on the debate on terminology, see Roger Daniels, "Words Do Matter: A Note on Inappropriate Terminology and the Incarceration of the Japanese Americans," in *Nikkei in the Pacific Northwest: Japanese Americans and Japanese Canadians in the Twentieth Century,* ed. Louis Fiset and Gail M. Nomura, (Seattle and London: University of Washington Press, 2005).
On the "surge of egalitarian idealism," see, for example: Ruth Frager and Carmela Patrias, "'This Is Our Country, These Are Our Rights': Minorities and the Origins of Ontario's Human Rights Campaigns," *Canadian Historical Review*. 82, no. 1 (March 2001); James W. St. G. Walker, *"Race," Rights and the Law in the Supreme Court of Canada: Historical Case Studies* (Waterloo and Toronto: The Osgoode Society for Canadian Legal History and Wilfrid Laurier University Press, 1997); Lambertson, *Repression and Resistance*.
23. This is by way of context only and certainly not an attempt to excuse the reactions of Canadian liberals.
24. More details on the CCJC activities can be found in Stephanie Bangarth, *Voices Raised in Protest: Defending North American Citizens of Japanese Ancestry, 1942–49* (Vancouver: UBC Press, 2008) and Lambertson, *Repression and Resistance,*Chap. 3.
25. Lambertson, Repression and Resistance, 126.
26. McMaster University Ready Archives, CCJC Papers (CCJC-MAC), folder 4, Minutes, November 10, 1945; LAC, MG 28 V1, series, 1, 14, file 1, pt. 2 of 2, Minutes, January 8, 1946.
27. Forrest LaViolette, *Our Japanese Canadians: Citizens, Not Exiles* (April 1946); LAC, MG 28 C 26, vol. 3, file 16; "A Record of the Work of the Cooperative Committee on Japanese Canadians," n.d.
28. "Delegation Asks Ottawa Consider Japs in Canada," *Toronto Daily Star,* January 4, 1946; LAC, MG 32 C 26, vol. 3, CCJC memorandum, "The Concern of the Canadian People for the Christian and Democratic Treatment of Japanese Canadians," January 4, 1946.
29. Saskatchewan was the only province to support the CCJC. In the Matter of a Reference as to the Validity of Orders in Council of the 15th Day of December, 1945 (P.C. 7355, 7356 and 7357), in Relation to Persons of the Japanese Race (1946), S.C.R. 248 [In the Matter of a Reference].
30. LAC, MG 32 C26, vol. 3, "Case for the Appellant, in the matter of a reference as to the validity of Orders-in-Council of the 15th day of December 1945 (P.C. 7355, 7356, 7357) in relation to persons of the Japanese Race, 1946."
31. "Case for the Appellant."

32. In the Matter of a Reference (1946), S. C. R. 248.
33. This would be Brewin's first time arguing a case before the Privy Council. The second time in his career would follow shortly after with *John East Ironworks*, detailed above.
34. *Co-operative Committee on Japanese Canadians et al. v. Attorney-General of Canada et al.* (1947), A. C. 87, 1 DLR.
35. LAC, MG 28, vol. 1, file 1, "Programme," January 10, 1946, and "Permit," Jarvis Collegiate School, 10 January 1946. For letters and petitions protesting the actions of the government, see LAC, RG 25, series G-2, vol. 3554, file 773-B-1–40, pt. 4.
36. CCJC-MAC, folder 13, Brewin, "Memorandum for Co-operative Committee on Japanese Canadians on the Judgment of the Judicial Committee of the Privy Council," December 22, 1946.
37. Frank R. Scott, "Expanding Concepts of Human Rights," in *Essays on the Constitution: Aspects of Canadian Law and Politics* (Toronto: University of Toronto Press, 1977), 353.
38. Eric Adams asserts that Brewin was the first to use this phrase in his *Switzman* case comment: F. Andrew Brewin Case Comment on *Switzman v. Elbling* (1957), *Canadian Bar Review* 35, no. 5 (May 1957): 557. Eric Adams, "Building a Law of Human Rights: *Roncarelli v. Duplessis* in Canadian Constitutional Culture," *McGill Law Journal* 55, no. 3 (2010): 440.
39. Quoted from a 27 January 1947 speech delivered by Brewin to the Civil Liberties Association of Toronto, enclosed in a letter, Brewin to Roger Baldwin (ACLU president), February 3, 1947, Princeton University, Mudd Library, ACLU Papers, box 1055, folder 6.
40. LAC, MG30 D211, vol. 10, reel H-1222, file "Civil Liberties, National Council 1946–1951"; Brewin to Scott, March 24, 1947; "A Bill of Rights for Canada," *Toronto Star*, January 31, 1947.
41. Lambertson, *Repression and Resistance*, Chap. 8, "The Bill of Rights."
42. "Submission of Committee for a Bill of Rights in Support of Statement for a Bill of Rights to the Special Joint Committee of the Senate and the House of Commons on Human Rights and Fundamental Freedoms," Special Joint Committee on Human Rights and Fundamental Freedoms (1947, 1948), vol. 51.
43. Carmela Patrias, "Socialists, Jews, and the 1947 Saskatchewan Bill of Rights," *Canadian Historical Review* 87, no. 2 (June 2006): 269.
44. For more on the political movement to obtain a constitutionally entrenched Bill of Rights, see Christopher MacLennan, *Toward the Charter: Canadians and the Demand for a National Bill of Rights, 1929–1960* (Montreal and Kingston: McGill–Queen's University Press, 2003); Lambertson, *Repression and Resistance*, 370.
45. Interview with John Tackaberry; interview with Dr. Tozun Bahcheli. See also the Brewin Papers, LAC, MG 32 C26, vols. 20–40 (this represents a full twenty archival boxes of strictly immigration files). Tackaberry was Brewin's executive assistant in the late 1970s.
46. Many people I have interviewed expressed as much to me, including Gerry Caplan and Stephen Lewis.
47. Donald Barry, "Interest Groups and the Foreign Policy Process: The Case of Biafra," in *Pressure Group Behaviour in Canadian Politics*, ed. A. Paul Pross (Toronto: McGraw-Hill Ryerson, 1975).
48. James Eayrs, *Montreal Star*, September 16, 1968.
49. Hugh McCallum, "Remembering the Nightmare of Biafra," *Presbyterian Record* (September 2004), 2.
50. Interview, Stephanie Bangarth with Rev. Walter McLean, January 5, 2012. Waterloo, ON. When he was first elected to Parliament in 1979 (Waterloo) McLean was the only member who had lived anywhere in the developing world, becoming the ranking member of the parliamentary foreign affairs committee.
51. Andrew Brewin and David MacDonald, *Canada and the Biafran Tragedy* (Toronto: James Lorimer, 1970); see also Stephen Lewis, *Journey to Biafra* (Don Mills, ON: Thistle Printing, 1968).
52. Brewin and MacDonald, *Canada and the Biafran Tragedy*, 11. This description is evidence of *kwashiorkor*, a disease produced by lack of protein resulting in permanent brain injury and

death. Direct news reports also came from Charles Taylor of *The Globe and Mail*, who accompanied Brewin and MacDonald on their trip, and also from Stephen Lewis, an Ontario MPP, who had his reports published in the *Toronto Daily Star*, which were later published in a single booklet. Charles Taylor's reports appeared in *The Globe and Mail* on the following days in 1968: October 5, 7, 9–12, and 14. Stephen Lewis's reports appeared in the *Toronto Daily Star* on October 9–12 and 14, 1968.

53. Brewin and MacDonald, *Canada and the Biafran Tragedy*, 135.

54. David Forsyth, "International Humanitarianism in the Contemporary World: Forms and Issues," in *Multilateralism Under Challenge: Power, International Order and Structural Change*, ed. Edward Neuman, Ramesh Thakur, and John Tirman (Washington: Brookings Institution Press, 2006), 237–38.

55. Rev. McLean, John Brewin, and David MacDonald expressed as much during their interviews with me.

56. Andrew S. Thompson, *In Defense of Principles: NGOs and Human Rights in Canada* (Vancouver: University of British Columbia Press, 2010), 22.

57. Andrew Brewin, Louis Duclos, and David MacDonald, *One Gigantic Prison: The Report of the Fact-Finding Mission to Chile, Argentina and Uruguay* (Toronto: Inter-Church Committee on Chile, 1976).

58. Interview with David MacDonald.

59. *One Gigantic Prison*, 12–15.

60. Ibid.

61. LAC, MG 32 C 28, vol. 42, files 2 & 3.

62. LAC, MG 32 C 26, vol. 78, file 5. Letter, Brewin to Martin Dufresne, CIBC, May 10, 1978.

63. LAC, MG 32 C 26, vol. 74, file 16. Letter, Brewin to Mrs. J.V. Hill, December 18, 1968.

64. Bonny Ibhawoh, "Where do we Begin? Human Rights, Public History and the Challenge of Conceptualization," paper presented at the Taking Liberties conference, McMaster University, March 2, 2012.

65. With this last sentence I am channeling the remarks that Dominque Marshall made as panel commentator at the Taking Liberties conference, McMaster University, March 2, 2012.

Chapter 5

•◆•

Transnational Links and Citizens' Rights: Canadian Jewish Human Rights Activists and Their American Allies in the 1940s and 1950s

Ruth A. Frager and Carmela Patrias

"We are tolerant of ethnic and cultural diversity" and "we are different from Americans": these are two key attributes habitually and often somewhat smugly invoked in the seemingly perpetual quest to define Canadian national identity. Many Canadians would undoubtedly be surprised, therefore, to learn that Canada's turn toward tolerance of diversity during the twentieth century owes a great deal to ideas and practices imported from the United States. A growing body of studies on the history of human rights in Canada reveals the significance of American influences, and points to the key roles that minority groups such as African Canadians, Japanese Canadians, and Jews played in transmitting American ideas and practices to Canada during the 1940s and 1950s.[1] Yet the nature and extent of American influence needs to be emphasized further. To date, there has been no systematic study of how American ideas about human rights penetrated Canadian human rights campaigns, nor about the way in which these American ideas shaped Canadian campaigns against racist and religious prejudice and discrimination. The purpose of our study is to begin this process by investigating the central role of Canadian Jews in importing American ideas and techniques for fighting prejudice and discrimination in postwar Canada and in adapting them to Canadian circumstances.

Canadian Jews assumed a leading role in fighting prejudice and discrimination during and after the Second World War for three main reasons. First, by then, their ranks included not only English-speaking, educated professionals, but also a large number of organized workers, social democrats, and communists, some of whom were willing and able to lead such a fight, at times even to the point of overcoming class and ideological divisions. Second, Jews had the most developed organizational base for fighting discrimination: by the 1940s two different Jewish bodies were dedicated to fighting racist ideas and actions. In response to the intensification of anti-Semitism in Canada and abroad in the late 1930s, the Public Relations Committee of the Canadian Jewish Congress (CJC) and the Anti-Defamation League of B'nai Brith came together to form the Joint Public Relations Committee (JPRC). "Public relations" in the organization's name stood for combatting anti-Semitism. The JPRC was joined by the end of the war by the Jewish Labour Committee (JLC), a branch of an American organization by the same name, established in 1936 to aid Jews and socialists in Nazi-dominated Europe. After the Second World War, this organization also focused on fighting prejudice and discrimination at home. In 1947 the two organizations formally joined forces, with the JLC becoming the main body to carry out such work in the labour movement. Together these organizations could rely on an extensive communications network, because while most Jews lived in larger urban areas, some Jews, primarily small business owners, could be found through much of Canada. Many small-town Jews belonged to the Canadian Jewish Congress and undertook to promote its campaigns in their communities. Third, Jewish activists in Canada received guidance and support from American Jewish organizations with more experience in fighting discrimination and promoting intergroup harmony. In fact, links within the Jewish diaspora extended beyond North America. In the field of human rights, however, the connection between Jews in the United States and Canada was the most important.[2]

Whereas historians of Canada's Jews have commonly stressed the distinctiveness of this country's Jewish communities,[3] the myriad cross-border ties among Jews have been under-emphasized. Although it is true that Canada's Jewish communities were not simply small-scale replicas or extensions of American Jewish settlements, there were strong Canadian-American religious and cultural links as well as crucial political and trade-union links. In Canada's Jewish labour movement, for example, the key unions (most notably the International Ladies' Garment Workers' Union and the Amalgamated Clothing Workers) originated in the United States and remained headquartered there. The North American centre of Reform Judaism was also in the United States (first Cincinnati and then New York City), and, in fact, the two Reform rabbis who played important roles in Ontario's human rights campaigns were both American-born and had been ordained in the United States well before moving to Canada.[4] More broadly, Canada's Jews frequently read

American Jewish newspapers and literature, while also generating their own Canadian Jewish newspaper editors, poets, novelists, and thinkers. Many Jewish extended families had relatives on both sides of the border.

One important reason that Canadian Jewish human rights activists in particular turned to the United States for guidance was that American Jewish organizations were more established and had greater resources than Canadian ones, in large part because of the difference in the scale and timing of mass immigration to the two countries. In the 1800s, Jewish immigrants from Western Europe had arrived in the United States in greater numbers than in Canada. More importantly, mass migration from the peripheries of Europe began much earlier to the United States than to Canada, and East European Jewish immigrants flocked to the United States. By the interwar years a growing number of the descendants of these "new immigrants," who faced discrimination in the United States, were involved in promoting greater tolerance. The American Jewish Committee (AJC), the oldest of the Jewish organizations, was the most conservative. Led by German-Jewish notables, it employed informal means to fight discrimination. The Anti-Defamation League of B'nai Brith (ADL) emerged in 1913 to fight against anti-Semitism in the United States. It focused on combatting negative stereotypes of the Jews in the media. The American Jewish Congress, established in 1918, represented Jews of Eastern European descent and more modest socio-economic standing. Finally, the Jewish Labor Committee was founded in 1934 and while it continued to help survivors after the war, it turned mainly to fighting prejudice and discrimination among American workers.[5] Escalation of anti-Semitism in the 1930s led the AJC and the ADL to mount a joint campaign of education to eradicate negative views of Jews which they saw as rooted in ignorance.[6]

The restriction of immigration to the United States in the 1920s turned attention to the problem of integrating minorities living in that country.[7] Various bodies were involved in the work of immigrant and minority integration, but Jews collaborated with most of them, first and foremost in order to publicize and obtain greater legitimacy for the fight against anti-Semitism. For example, the National Conference of Christians and Jews was established at this time to counter anti-Semitic and anti-Catholic agitation. It initially encouraged meetings among clergy from different denominations and by the 1930s involved broader groups in Brotherhood Day observations which promoted religious toleration. The conference also sponsored research on the roots of prejudice in general and on methods of countering it.[8] The American Jewish Committee helped the Foreign Language Information Service, an agency that translated and disseminated government reports to the foreign-language press.[9] The AJC also financed intercultural education experiments in New York public schools in the 1930s and funded other projects of the Service Bureau for Intercultural Education.

The escalation of racism at home and anti-Semitism abroad intensified Jewish involvement in such campaigns and led Jewish organizations to study and later fund research by academics on the causes of racist and religious prejudice.[10] The most influential result of such collaboration was the five-volume *Studies in Prejudice Series* by the German-Jewish émigrés of the Frankfurt School.[11] This research suggested that prejudice against Jews was correlated with prejudice against other minority groups.[12] Indeed, by the eve of the Second World War, activists redefined Jewish interests in universal terms.[13] Consequently, the ADL, for example, established a nominally independent agency, the Institute for Democratic Education, to disseminate materials against prejudice through newspapers, magazines, books, pamphlets, radio, and film. Some of the scholars who collaborated with Jewish activists, especially Kurt Lewin, became advocates of "action research programs." These programs looked for the roots of anti-Semitism, rather than its manifestations. They also studied the forces that exacerbated or mitigated anti-Semitism.[14] They concluded that the impersonal, mass appeals against anti-Semitism through the press, radio, and pamphlets had not proven very effective. Instead, they advocated fighting prejudice through more intimate groups such as labour, business, women's, and other voluntary organizations. Moreover, since these scholars believed that the roots of prejudice in general, and anti-Semitism in particular, were psychological, they concluded that efforts to fight against it should address the emotions rather than the intellect.[15]

By the 1930s, moreover, American Jews were well integrated into the labour movement in both the American Federation of Labor and the Congress of Industrial Organizations. A number of important union leaders, such as David Dubinsky of the International Ladies' Garment Workers' Union (ILGWU) and Sidney Hillman of the Amalgamated Clothing Workers (ACW), were Jewish. These Jewish unionists owed their influence, especially in industrial unions, to the presence of men and women of Eastern and Southern European descent in these unions in the United States.[16] The recognition of the right to collective bargaining as part of President Roosevelt's New Deal—well before similar rights were enacted in Canada—also contributed to greater union strength and therefore increased labour's potential for anti-discrimination activism in the United States.

The Second World War witnessed a great intensification of the fight against prejudice and discrimination. In the context of unprecedented state involvement in all aspects of life, minority groups recognized that the discrepancy between the stated war aims, on the one hand, and discrimination at home, on the other hand, provided an exceptional opportunity for mobilization against racist views and actions. The attainment of tolerance seemed especially urgent because the large wave of migration by African Americans to industrial centres in the Northern and Western United States unleashed hate strikes against integration in the workplace and riots against the integration of working-class neighbourhoods.[17] The Jewish Labor Committee was particularly active in the fight against such racism.[18] To promote civil rights activities within the labour movement, it established joint AFL and CIO local labour committees in New York, Philadelphia, Detroit, Pittsburgh, Chicago, Los Angeles, and San Francisco. JLC local representatives, as executive secretaries of the committees, were their "moving spirits." The JLC's New York Office published and distributed much of the educational material on which the committees relied. Most important was its monthly newsletter *Labor Reports*. Cartoons and articles from the newsletter were frequently reproduced in the newsletters of key American unions.[19]

The JLC, the American Jewish Congress (headed by Canadian-born David Petegorsky), the American Jewish Committee, the ADL, and local community relations councils were particularly active in the legal battle against discrimination. Jews provided a significant part of the money, staff, research, and legal expertise for the enactment of state and local fair practices laws in the United States. New York state led the way with the Ives-Quinn Bill of 1945 for fair employment practices, and in the midst of the Cold War, seventeen states adopted similar laws by 1960.[20]

From the 1930s Canadian Jews followed developments in the United States and adopted many of the strategies of their American counterparts. Taking their cue from American religious leaders, Canadian Jews and Protestants, under the leadership of Chicago-born Rabbi Maurice

N. Eisendrath and Reverend Edwin Silcox of the United Church, established the Committee on Jewish–Gentile Relationships in Toronto in 1934. Modelled after the American National Conference of Christians and Jews, the committee invited Christian and Jewish leaders to participate in seminars to improve relations between the two groups. It also distributed a series of pamphlets intended to dispel myths about the Jews and to fight anti-Semitism. In 1940 the committee was revitalized as the Canadian Conference of Christians and Jews under the directorship of Reverend Silcox. The conference's main goal was to foster harmonious relations among Canada's different religious groups.[21] Its publication, *Fellowship,* appeared every six weeks and copies were sent to thousands of clerics and influential laypersons. Among other actions to fight discrimination, it publicized campaigns for the introduction of anti-discrimination bills during the war. Most of the funding for the conference came from the CJC.

In 1947, the Canadian Council of Christians and Jews (CCCJ) was reorganized under the leadership of Rev. Richard Jones, who came up from New Jersey, with the intention to move beyond the clergy to lay groups, especially Roman Catholic ones, who had not previously taken part in the organization. Jones succeeded "in winning the confidence and active participation of both lay and clerical elements of the Catholic Church." By 1952, the CCCJ received funds from all three faiths and focused on educational work, especially by promoting an annual Brotherhood Week.[22]

Yet the American parent organization continued to be important in Canada. When an anti-Semitic article appeared in the *Canadian Messenger of the Sacred Heart* (the anglophone magazine of Canada's Jesuit order) in 1953, the JPRC pondered how to respond. One of its members suggested that the committee turn to the Catholic Department of the National Conference of Christians and Jews in the United States in order to obtain "suitable material" to help prepare a rebuttal to be submitted to the *Canadian Messenger.*[23]

One of the most innovative American anti-discrimination programs that Canadian Jews introduced to Canada, the Springfield Plan, was initiated and funded by the American National Council of Christians and Jews. Designed by a committee comprised of social scientists and educators, the plan was introduced in the schools in Springfield, Massachusetts, in 1939. It provided students with citizenship education while fighting racial prejudice. Children were taught about the contributions of minority groups to their community and about the music and arts of different groups. They celebrated holidays such as Christmas and Hanukkah together. The plan not only revised school curricula to foster appreciation of ethnocultural diversity and fight prejudice, but it required hiring teachers who would represent the multiethnic composition of the population of Springfield. The goal was to educate through experience. Pupils had a measure of control over school life through collaborating with teacher and parent committees. The schools also attempted to ensure equal access to employment for their pupils. Springfield schools refused to disclose the racial, ethnic, religious, and national background of pupils applying for jobs. The educators reasoned that employers would thus be unable to discriminate in hiring.[24]

The CJC first discussed plans for "intercultural education" with Ontario's deputy minister of education as early as 1940, but it continued to publicize the Springfield Plan specifically throughout the war.[25] In 1945 Warner Brothers approached the JPRC in Toronto to publicize *It Happened in Springfield*, its film about the plan. The Jewish agency responded by notifying Jewish and non-Jewish groups throughout the province.[26] The plan was introduced after the war in Teck Township (Kirkland Lake) and Welland.[27]

When the national office of the JPRC initiated plans to establish a committee to deal with employment discrimination in 1939, it contacted Jewish organizations with the same goals in New York, Chicago, Cleveland, Cincinnati, Detroit, and Washington.[28] Two years later, H.M. Caiserman, director of the JPRC, travelled to New York to learn about the anti-discrimination programs of the American Jewish Committee, the American Jewish Congress, and the Anti-Defamation League of B'nai Brith. In addition to studying the structures and strategies of these organizations, Caiserman requested that they supply the CJC with material "suitable for distribution in Canada." Not surprisingly, therefore, both the character and the content of the CJC's activities against discrimination closely resembled those of its American counterparts. Research to uncover the nature and extent of employment discrimination in Canada provided the foundation for its programs. Simultaneously, it promoted materials and discussions about human rights through radio, newspapers, magazines, films, books, and speakers. To carry out these programs it collaborated with various non-Jewish business, labour, patriotic, women's, church, youth, and foreign-language groups. The CJC both sponsored goodwill meetings and initiated campaigns for anti-discrimination legislation.[29]

When Canadian Jewish unionists decided to fight against discrimination within and through the labour movement, they also turned to American precedents.[30] At the urging of the New York JLC and Bernard Shane (who had been sent to Canada by the ILGWU in 1934), the JLC supporters in Canada prevailed on the leaders of the Trades and Labour Congress of Canada to establish a Standing Committee on Racial Discrimination during the 1944 convention of the Congress.[31] Shane persuaded Kalmen Kaplansky, a Jewish printer from Poland, appointed to head the JLC in Canada, to go to New York to study American approaches to fighting discrimination. Upon Kaplansky's return to Canada, the JLC adopted the organizational structures of its American counterpart, fostering the establishment of joint labour committees that brought together AFL and CIO affiliates in key communities across Canada. Meanwhile, the Canadian JLC's approach to Catholic unionists on this side of the border had been facilitated by American connections. In 1946, New York's Catholic Interracial Council had contacted "the Catholic leadership of Canada" on the JLC's behalf, and the JLC optimistically reported that it was "assured of the active cooperation of the [Catholic] hierarchy in conducting its work among" Catholic unionists in this country.[32]

Canada's Jewish activists continued to adhere to the American Jewish practice of working behind the scenes because they feared that more open human rights leadership by Jews could inadvertently fuel anti-Semitic propaganda about world Jewry's alleged plot to dominate the globe. The Canadian public was, therefore, not aware of the extent of their involvement in these campaigns.

As American Jewish organizations did in their own country, the JPRC and the JLC played key roles in Canadian campaigns for the adoption of anti-discrimination legislation. Guided by the advice of Jewish lawyers and activists across Canada about the feasibility and likelihood of the introduction of such legislation, the JPRC launched a successful campaign for the introduction of Ontario's 1944 Racial Discrimination Act, which prohibited the publication or display of signs, notices, or symbols expressing racist or religious discrimination. The Act was built on resource materials and drafts prepared by the JPRC.[33] Its most outspoken proponent was Jewish communist MPP Joe Salsberg. Saskatchewan launched the first bill of rights in Canada in 1947 largely thanks to the efforts of Morris Shumiatcher, who relied on the research of American Jewish organizations when he drafted the bill.[34]

The Canadian JLC also played a decisive role in the decision by Canadian labour and CCF activists that provincial Fair Practices Acts were more effective in combatting discrimination than were bills modelled on Saskatchewan's 1947 Bill of Rights Act. Since very few cases were tried under the Act, JLC activists decided that it would be more effective to follow the American practice of targeting specific areas of discrimination (such as employment or accommodation) and establishing enforcement machinery in the form of commissions to investigate infringements. Not only would commissions be staffed by "experts" in the field, but ideally their responsibility, like that of their American counterparts, would extend to the development of educational programs to increase public awareness of the existence of prejudice and discrimination and the need and means to overcome them. Moreover, since appeals would be free and far less complicated than prosecution through the courts, commissions would deal efficiently with many more cases, at least in theory. These cases, in turn, would heighten public awareness and act as deterrents.[35]

The close collaboration between American Jewish organizations and academics was another reason that Canadian Jews looked to their American counterparts. Although some Canadian academics participated in campaigns against discrimination and prejudice in Canada by the 1940s, most of them found their way into these campaigns not through the academy but through participation in civic-minded voluntary organizations. Canadian scholars were not yet involved in research on the origins of racism. Aware of the collaboration between American scholars and Jewish agencies, the CJC sent JPRC member Manfred Saalheimer to New York in 1944 to study this research as well as prospects for social action. Saalheimer spoke to such leading social scientists in this field as Max Horkheimer, director of the Institute of Social Research, Columbia University, and research consultant for the American Jewish Committee; Kurt Lewin, MIT professor of psychology; Dr. H.H. Giles, director of the Bureau of Intercultural Education; and M.A. Davis, Yale professor of sociology. Saalheimer and Horkheimer agreed to apply the new approach of appealing to the emotions rather than the intellect and working with small labour, business, women's, and other voluntary organizations in

Canada. More specifically, they decided to examine the impact of the American cultural anthropologist Hortense Powdermaker's *Probing Our Prejudices* on several YMCA and YWCA clubs in Montreal. Such collaboration continued after the war. In 1947, Saalheimer arranged for the American anti-discrimination film *Don't Be a Sucker* to be circulated in rural Canada by the National Film Board, accompanied by questionnaires developed by the research department of the American Jewish Committee to test audience reactions.[36]

Saalheimer's support for the American approach and its subsequent adoption by the CJC[37] marked the introduction of a conservative, depoliticized strand in the Jewish community's anti-discrimination campaign. However, human rights campaigns on both sides of the border were quite pragmatic and continued to pursue broadly based strategies against racism. As Saalheimer reported to the CJC's Saul Hayes, American social psychologist Goodwin Watson (whose book on group relations was commissioned by the AJC) believed that fighting discrimination through "all forces of social control," such as the ballot box, the courts, the legislature, and mass petitions, was far more effective than fighting prejudice through brotherhood weeks and public relations programs. The AJC's Petegorsky believed that educational campaigns designed to promote tolerance were doomed if they failed to consider the role of social, economic, and political inequality in the development of prejudice and discrimination.[38]

A willingness to emphasize the cross-class appeal and conciliatory methods characterized some steps taken by American and Canadian activists alike. In 1939, when Canadian unions had not yet obtained the right to collective bargaining, the JPRC in Toronto, whose ranks included Jewish employers, cited developments in the United States to urge all Jewish employers to foster the growth of labour unions, because unions officially opposed employment discrimination.[39] By the end of the war, despite its strong labour and socialist traditions, the JLC entered into discussions with the Canadian Council of Christians and Jews "with a view to holding labor-management conferences on human relations, at local plant levels." This move was modelled on American precedents: The National Conference of Christians and Jews in the United States had held a number of these conferences in such firms as General Cable Corp, General Electric, X/Ray Co., and Revere Copper and Brass Company. These programs enjoyed the support of both the AFL and the CIO. Canadian activists planned to start a pilot labour-management conference on human relations in Toronto with the help of their more experienced American counterparts. The CJC made plans to invite businessman Charles Luckman, president of Lever Brothers, to come to Canada.[40] The JLC and the JPRC collaborated in such plans despite the fact that JPRC members did not share the JLC's faith in social democracy and even though labour activists such as Kaplansky were distrustful of CJC members who engaged in union-busting activities.[41]

While these cross-class initiatives took place on both sides of the border, by the late 1940s anti-union ideologues in the United States started to use the language of rights to try to secure the "right to work" for anti-union employees. Such conservative rights-based discourse was far less salient in Canada in this period.[42]

The JPRC emphasized "the man [who] is emotionally and morally subverted by being refused the right to earn his daily bread solely because of his religion, race, or national origin." But the organization's members also sought to promote the idea that fair employment practices would benefit employers, too, as well as benefiting society more broadly. Thus a 1951 JPRC report declared that "society plunders its own treasures by denying itself skills and know-how solely because the owners of that skill and know-how have the 'wrong' religion, race, or birthplace."[43]

Because fair practices acts had been operating in parts of the United States for some time when Canadians undertook to introduce them in Canada, the example of the United States could be used to assuage common fears against such legislation. The Canadian Association of Adult Education published a pamphlet about such legislation in 1948 to supplement a CBC broadcast on the subject. The pamphlet stated: "None of the dire predictions of those who opposed [New York's] Ives-Quinn Bill have been fulfilled. It has not so far been necessary to hold a formal hearing. Company officers have not been subjected to a succession of appearances before the commission, or in the courts. The contention of the sponsors of the Act that most employers would readily co-operate in carrying out the letter and the spirit of the new law seems to have been realized. Industries have not left the state of New York in protest against the Act, and there have been only an insignificant number of resignations among employees in the majority group. Nor has the predicted loss of customer goodwill materialized."[44]

Such willingness to collaborate with employers by activists on both sides of the border may seem to lend support to the arguments of labour historians that the adoption of a rights-based approach in the labour movement signified the abandonment of unions' claims to class-based collective interests and rights, a turning away from social and economic rights to individual rights. In the 1940s and 1950s, however, activists who campaigned for human rights legislation saw no contradiction between such legislation, on the one hand, and collective working-class interests and labour's social and economic goals, on the other hand. Members of the JLC in particular believed that "the effort of organized labour to achieve security and improve economic condition," would make "an important contribution towards the elimination of prejudice and hostility among the many racial and religious groups in Canada."[45] In their eyes anti-discrimination legislation marked a dramatic new approach to defending the rights of minority workers because it involved state intervention in privately owned businesses. As Kalmen Kaplansky explained, such legislation was justified, "even if it meant some further control over the individual employer, because it would guarantee equality of economic opportunity regardless of racial or religious origin."[46]

At the same time, Kaplansky had difficulty convincing some immigrant Jewish socialists to prioritize anti-discrimination activities. After all, they commonly highlighted class oppression, as well as anti-Semitism, and believed that only socialism would bring about true equality. They were not satisfied by a vision of a society that had eliminated racist and religious discrimination while maintaining dramatic economic inequalities.[47] Commenting on the Jewish labour movement's struggles against both Jewish and non-Jewish employers in Toronto's clothing industry, for example, one Jewish leftist had declared rhetorically: "Why should I feel better if I am exploited by a Jew?"[48] But in the absence of an immediate socialist revolution, the stings of anti-Semitism motivated some to agree with Kaplansky. Besides, as one leftist Jewish clothing worker explained: "Just because we had a hard life to make a living, we wanted our children should have it better. So no matter how poor a cloakmaker was, he wanted his son to be a doctor, a lawyer."[49] At a time when Jewish access to law schools, medical schools, and hospital internships was limited, struggles against racist and religious discrimination made sense. Kaplansky himself had little patience with the argument that piecemeal reforms were not important because socialists should focus on bringing about the revolution.[50]

Moreover, for Jewish socialists, the struggle against racism was not just a matter of moderate reforms—even if they had to frame their concerns in this way when lobbying government leaders for anti-discrimination legislation. As the JLC's 1957 Report declared in Yiddish, "our [anti-discrimination] work is built on a larger idea of freedom, on all our socialist beliefs."[51] These Jewish activists believed that racism worked hand in hand with economic exploitation.[52] Racism was not the product of individual pathology but was intrinsic to the capitalist system; employers stirred up these animosities to divide the working class, thereby enriching themselves while various groups of workers quarreled with one another over the crumbs. From this point of view, the fight against discrimination was also necessarily a fight for major changes in society.

Emphasis on fair practices legislation was not the product of a naive belief that discrimination would be contained and eventually eliminated by dealing with individual cases. Indeed, Kaplansky viewed racist and religious discrimination as deeply embedded in Canada, but he believed it important to highlight certain individual cases in order to educate people—especially Anglo-Canadians—about the impact of discrimination, because "you can't fight abstractions."[53] In the aftermath of the Holocaust, few of Canada's Jews would have believed that anti-Semitism resulted simply from the occasional acts of aberrant individuals. Indeed, like their American counterparts, they likened prejudice to an infectious disease which threatened to spread rapidly unless North Americans, especially children, were immunized against it.[54] The importance of such immunization was demonstrated by the persistence of racism in the United States even after fair practices acts were introduced. Legislation was ineffective when the courts and the public continued to adhere to racist ideas. The fate of the Saskatchewan Bill of Rights also showed the limits of legislation in and of itself as a remedy for prejudice and discrimination. Initiated by the state, that bill had been introduced without being accompanied by public education.[55]

When comparing anti-discrimination legislation to the "good will" practices that earlier dominated intergroup relations, mid-twentieth-century activists on both sides of the border saw anti-discrimination legislation as the more promising approach. Rabbi Abraham Feinberg of the Holy Blossom Synagogue in Toronto, for example, believed that legislation against discrimination would be far more effective than "good will" approaches to non-Jews. He informed a conference of American Reform rabbis that "despite brave and sometimes effective ventures into progressive project-teaching methods, visual education and inter-cultural group experiments, such as the Springfield Plan . . . techniques of good-will are in the main hortatory. Rabbis know the futility of preachment!" American Jewish Committee activist Samuel Flowerman favoured a similar approach: "When we ask people to love their brothers, we have not really defined for them what they are to do. But when we ask them to vote for FEPA [i.e. the Fair Employment Practices Act], we at least define the goal and the method to achieve it."[56]

Sid Blum, a New Yorker who replaced Kalmen Kaplansky as head of Canada's JLC in the mid-1950s, argued that, unfortunately, one of the main "US imports was 'the ceremony.'" He charged that these "ceremoni-als" did not allow for a frank exchange of ideas and experiences because people were on their good behaviour and pulled back from dealing hon-estly with the difficult issues. Blum strongly supported focusing on fair employment legislation instead. He declared that

> prejudice and discrimination are also frequently confused with each other. Prejudice is the feeling, discrimination is the act. Acts of dis-crimination, which after all concern the denial of the necessities of life (employment, housing, etc.) to the minority group member, are more important to combat than prejudices. . . . The lip service given to the evils of prejudice is not half as convincing as a job obtained by a quali-fied member of a minority group in an area where entry was previ-ously denied. He also stressed that anti-discrimination laws educated the public.[57]

Even Saalheimer emphasized the importance of legislation. Writing in 1949, he rebutted the common argument that "you cannot do away with prejudice by laws; it will yield only to a long, slow process of educa-tion." This argument was built on the "basic fallacy that prejudice and discrimination are synonymous." "It is quite true that prejudice cannot be eliminated by legislation against it," Saalheimer explained. "Some go so far as to concede that a man has a right to his individual prejudices. Nevertheless discrimination as the overt manifestation of prejudice is no man's right, since discrimination . . . infringes upon another man's rights and liberties." He declared that "recent social research has shown us that the attack on discrimination promises better and more immediate re-sults than the attack on prejudice and, therefore, should precede it." For him, it was not a matter of either anti-discrimination laws or education, but "education *through* legislation," for "ninety percent of our population are fair and law-abiding citizens. . . . Thus, if the law indicates that public policy is opposed to hiring procedures based on race, religion, colour or national origin, the bulk of the people will not only conform but will recognize the fair practices as the only right ones."[58]

Canadian activists were quite conscious, however, that although they had much to learn from their American counterparts and some of the materials developed by the Americans could be usefully employed in Canada, circumstances in Canada were not the same as in the United States. At the simplest level, materials produced in the United States had to be "Canadianized" to be distributed at home. A good example is the CJC's promotion of the radio series *The American Dream*. This award-winning series of radio programs, starring Helen Hayes, Fredric March, Paul Lukas, Sam Levene, and Canada Lee, "conveyed 'a message of human brotherhood and intergroup understanding.'" The series originally consisted of fourteen dramatized stories that attempted to show how "ordinary people" (e.g., a housewife, a schoolteacher, a cab driver, a storekeeper, and a professor) succeed in overcoming prejudice and discrimination in their communities. The CJC had access to the series because it had been sponsored by the American Jewish Committee.[59] When the CJC convinced the CBC to broadcast it in Canada, the CBC chose nine of the stories that were the most relevant to the Canadian situation and changed the name of the series to *The Dream*.[60]

Canadian reliance on anti-racist American material was pronounced in the 1940s when the Canadian Jewish activists were struggling to establish a more solid foundation.[61] But while the Canadians often adapted American radio programs, films, posters, and pamphlets for use here, their American counterparts also benefited from Canadian input, especially in the 1950s. In 1951, for example, one of New York's JLC leaders wrote to Kaplansky asking for copies of the French edition of the booklet, *Discrimination Costs You Money*, for distribution to French Canadian textile workers in New England.[62] Six years later, when Sid Blum had devised a special series of worksheets to be used at educational workshops on fair employment practices, he sent copies to a JLC official in New York, along with very detailed—and much appreciated—advice about how to use these worksheets and how to adapt them to the American situation.[63]

The most important cross-border connections were between Jewish activists in Montreal (the location of the JLC's head office in Canada) and Toronto, on the one hand, and New York City, on the other hand, not only because of geographical proximity but also because these two Canadian cities contained the country's largest concentrations of Jews. In 1946, when JLC activists set out to develop a branch of the organization in Winnipeg (the location of Canada's third largest Jewish community), leaders from New York and Montreal travelled there to help out.[64]

The greatest difference confronted by Canadian human rights activists was that, owing to the large number of African Americans, racial discrimination in the United States was a highly visible and identifiable problem, whereas in Canada a myth of "racelessness" prevailed. Here African Canadians constituted a small part of the population, most Canadians of Asian descent were concentrated in British Columbia, and even groups of Eastern and Southern European descent, considered "non-preferred" in interwar Canada, comprised a smaller proportion of urban populations than in the United States. The JLC's Sid Blum stressed not only that "Canada did not have a large minority, deprived of its rights by tradition and law" but also that "Canadians had . . . the tradition of British politeness which made less obvious the big gap between the actual treatment of minority groups and democratic principles." This meant that in Canada it was harder to be "arousing public interest in problems of the rights of minority groups. While vacation resorts in Ontario and Quebec featured signs saying 'No Jews or Negroes Allowed' or 'Gentiles Only'; and employment ads restricted applicants to a special religion, people said, 'This is Canada, not the United States, we don't have discrimination here.'"[65]

Rabbi Feinberg was struck by Canadian hypocrisy. Canadians were shocked by racism against people of African heritage in the United States and South Africa, but many Toronto "churchgoers [seemed] convinced that Jesus [was] a segregationist on Sunday mornings." Having moved to Canada in 1943, the rabbi was appalled by the internment of Japanese Canadians, by Canadian immigration policies that discriminated against people from China and the Caribbean, by "the exclusion of Negroes from Toronto apartment houses," by "bank managers who honour[ed] Jewish cheques but never hire[d] Jewish clerks," by real estate agents who rejected "the client [who] prays in a synagogue," and by "otherwise keen-witted Jewish social climbers who can't discern that snobbery toward the Negro makes them brother to the Nazi." In his memoirs, published in 1964, Feinberg also explained that because he focused on discrimination against African Americans and African

Canadians, he "was tardy in apprehending that Canada's [thousands of] Indians are a forgotten minority, a moral blot concealed by common consent of the Canadian people."[66]

Feinberg was also insistent that the struggles against anti-Semitism and the struggles against other forms of racism were "indivisible." He recalled that some Jews declared: "Our job is Jews. What have we to do with the Negro problem!" In response, he asserted that "the plight of one persecuted group [is] the fight of all," and he clearly saw this as a moral issue. He added that "there was a shabby practical rejoinder too: the appetite for someone to hate grows by what it feeds on; a Negro-hater 'graduates' to Jew-baiter."[67]

According to Kalmen Kaplansky, the belief that there was no racism in Canada meant that activists had to convince even their allies and friends that racism was a serious problem. He recalled that in 1946, in conversation with Winnipeg trade union leaders, he discovered "ignorance of, or insensitivity to, the issue of racial, ethnic or religious discrimination." "I believe that this ignorance arose basically from failure to perceive that persistent and continuing non-violent discriminatory acts, such as denial of equal access to economic opportunities, educational institutions, or recreational and social facilities, could have long-range negative impact on the victims as pogroms and lynchings," Kaplansky explained. "What's more," he added, "my contacts in Winnipeg, many of whom were steeped in Independent Labour Party and CCF tradition, people of genuine compassion, were familiar with the Japanese problem in B.C., or the excesses of the Orange Order, or certain Catholic clergy in Quebec, but were totally blind to discrimination in Winnipeg or Manitoba."[68]

Although as Kaplansky explained, the myth of racelessness affected even Anglo-Canadian social democrats, CCF support was crucial for the success of anti-discrimination campaigns. In fact, the importance of the CCF in Canada stands in marked contrast to the absence of a social democratic party in the United States. Unlike the CCF, Canada's mainstream parties resisted the idea of extending state intervention in the private sector. During the unusual circumstances of the war, Jewish Communist MPP Joe Salsberg could play a key role in the introduction of Ontario's first anti-discrimination bill. As the Cold War intensified, however, any connection to the communists served to discredit human right campaigns. That is why Jewish involvement in the CCF was so

important. Support for anti-discrimination legislation from other European minority groups had been linked primarily to the Communist
Party of Canada. By the 1950s, the voices of such advocates fell silent.
The CCF, however, enjoyed sufficient support during the Cold War to
remain active and influential in the fight for human rights. And while Joe
Salsberg retained a following among Ontario Jews, other Jewish activists
succeeded in dissuading him from pursuing a communist campaign for
anti-discrimination legislation at a time when that political connection
would have discredited the campaign altogether.

Whereas the acceleration of the Cold War led to the intense anti-
communism of McCarthyism in the United States, Canadian anti-
communism was not as severe. Consequently, some of the American-
produced anti-discrimination materials, such as *Brotherhood of Man* (a
film produced by the United Auto Workers), which were discredited in
the United States for allegedly being pro-communist, continued to be
useful in Canada.[69]

In addition, the absence of the kind of black–white polarization
that existed in the United States made the task of fighting discrimination somewhat easier in Canada. As American labour historians have
shown, even while the official policy of CIO unions in particular became
non-discriminatory starting in the 1930s, union locals which became inclusive of all workers of European descent and offered them economic
security not only tolerated colour bars but even took action against the
integration of African Americans in the workplace.[70] The initiative for
human rights in the Canadian labour movement also came from the
leadership, but their campaigns did not encounter the same resistance
from the rank and file. By excluding people of colour, Canada's racist immigration policies minimized American-style deep divisions among the
most marginalized Canadian workers. Consequently, the labour movement's human rights campaigns increased the movement's appeal to
these workers. Men and women of Eastern and Southern European descent played an important role in obtaining collective bargaining rights
for Canadian workers.

The limitations of human rights campaigns undertaken by American
United Automobile Workers (UAW) officials in Canada illustrate the
difference in circumstances between Canada and the United States and
highlight the different strategies required to battle discrimination north
of the border. Bill Macdonald, the union's education officer in Canada,

for example, saw no need to supply the Oshawa local of the UAW with anti-discrimination literature since, in the absence of a notable number of people of colour there, he assumed that Oshawa unionists did not practise or experience racist discrimination. Yet members of Eastern European descent in Local 222 had faced discrimination. Originally from the United States, Macdonald was well aware of discrimination against people of African descent. He did not need to be told that discrimination existed in Windsor, where he was stationed, for Windsor had a sizeable African-Canadian population. But the presence of even larger numbers of Eastern and Southern Europeans in the city evidently did not alert him to important forms of discrimination directed against these immigrant workers in Canada.[71]

Another important difference between the American and Canadian human rights campaigns was the constitutionally enshrined dual English–French character of Canada. Dualism created special problems for Jews in Quebec because the division of control over the public sector between Catholics and Protestants left little room for non-Christians. In the field of education, for example, although various accommodations were made periodically to allow Jewish children to attend schools within the Protestant system, as late as 1951 the Hampstead Protestant School Board refused to admit Jewish children to its schools.[72] The policy of allocating a set number of such public sector positions as municipal tax assessors to Catholics and Protestants also excluded Jews.[73]

At the same time, some French Canadians perceived the universalism of fair practices acts by which Jewish activists and their allies proposed to remedy such discrimination as endangering the distinctive identity of francophone, Roman Catholic institutions. *Le Travail*, the official organ of the Canadian Catholic Confederation of Labour (CCCL), for example, opposed the introduction of a federal fair employment practices act on the grounds that some interpretations of such a law would lead to the negation of the principles that inspired its members—"the social doctrine of the church" and "combatting communism"—presumably by requiring that all be admitted regardless of religious and ideological affiliations.[74] Other influential members of the CCCL, such as its secretary, Jean Marchand, were willing to embrace the JLC's human rights campaigns, perhaps because they were no longer committed to the confessional character of the labour organization. Even under their influence, however, the CCCL merely collaborated with the secular Montreal Labour

Committee Against Racial Intolerance rather than affiliating with it as did the other two Canadian labour federations.

During the reign of Premier Maurice Duplessis, the political climate of Quebec was hostile to human rights and civil liberties. His notorious Padlock Law provided ammunition for the suppression of activists who were red-baited. Thus Quebec did not introduce human rights legislation until the end of the Duplessis era.

Meanwhile, English–French dualism, along with their belief that anti-Semitism was particularly intense in Quebec, led Jewish human rights activists to believe that prejudice and discrimination in Quebec could be tackled only on a piecemeal basis, by approaching "bottom leadership, through the French-language press, lower level clergy, academics and the like." The JLC relied primarily on Canada's two main labour federations for carrying out its work in the province. In 1945 Adolph Held, chair of the American JLC, outlined plans to combat intolerance in order to provide security for minorities; the Quebec Federation of Labour (AFL) and the Montreal Labour Council (including the CIO) endorsed his proposals. Both labour organizations passed resolutions against Jew-baiting and in support of admitting Jewish refugees to Canada.[75] The JLC's monthly bulletin, *Canadian Labor Reports*, appeared in both English and French. The organization's executive secretary made a point of showing anti-discrimination films to CCCL workers engaged in various strikes. By 1953 the JLC had succeeded in convincing the CCCL itself to use a variety of its anti-discrimination materials. The willingness of Jewish human rights activists to note discrimination against French Canadians helps to explain their ability to transcend linguistic and religious differences at times. Uncovering and publicizing such discrimination, they believed, would be essential to the success of human rights campaigns in central Canada.[76]

French–English dualism was also responsible for the fact that Canada, unlike the United States, did not subscribe to the key liberal precept of the separation of church and state. Constitutional guarantees of publicly funded Roman Catholic schools dated back to the time of Confederation. Since that time, however, different provincial governments sought both to eliminate such funding, as in the case of Manitoba, and to introduce religious instruction to public schools, as in the case of Ontario's introduction of nominally "undenominational" religious instruction to public schools during the Second World War. Since Jews were the largest non-Christian group in Ontario's public schools, it is not surprising that protest against this move came chiefly from their ranks. They framed their protest in classical liberal terms of individual rights.

Ohio-born Rabbi Abraham Feinberg, chair of the JPRC, was the principal author of a brief to the Royal Commission on Education in 1945, which explained the reasons for Jewish objections to this program. Such instruction—which conflicted with the right to freedom of belief and worship—would foster intolerance and thereby undermine the principles of democracy for which Canada had fought during the Second World War. By drawing attention to religious differences, religious education in the public schools would "fan the flames of intolerance in every community where a religious minority exists." The fact that minority pupils would be excused from the classroom during religious instruction did not diminish the potentially damaging effects of the proposed plan, for these children should not have to "endure the spot-light of being 'different.'" The requirement that classroom teachers provide religious instruction also opened the door to employment discrimination against teachers. Ironically, to avoid the disruptive consequences of such education to the bonds of "Canadianism," the CJC brief recommended the introduction of the American Springfield Plan to Canadian schools.[77]

Feinberg was more explicit about his objections to religious instruction when he addressed the Central Conference of American Rabbis in Montreal in 1947. "To my objections on principle," he explained, "the answer was given that 'this is a Christian country.'"[78] Feinberg believed that such a departure from the separation between church and state was a serious matter. Religious instruction in state-funded schooling undermined the central credo of Reform Judaism, namely, liberalism, "the ineradicable conviction that human beings are potential citizens of a world governed by intelligence, consecrated by fellowship and illuminated by a sense of everyman's inviolable sanctity."[79] But neither the CJC brief nor Feinberg's paper mentioned that publicly funded Roman Catholic schools in Ontario could not be reconciled with the separation of church and state. Moreover, "the more pacific element in [Ontario's] Jewish communal leadership" objected to Feinberg's course of action and informed him that "our position here is not strong enough for your American brand of militancy." But Feinberg stood his ground.[80]

Although no religious minority enjoyed access to publicly funded education at this time in the United States, American Jews were also concerned about a proposal to allow public school pupils to leave school early so that they could receive religious instruction. American Jewish activists, including Canadian-born David Petegorsky, believed this move to be antithetical to the separation of church and State. He saw it as an opening wedge to introduce religious instruction in public schools.[81] According to the officers of the JPRC, the Ontario brief served "as a basis for similar submissions in many parts of the United States."[82]

Another distinctly Canadian Jewish initiative was the JLC campaign to promote support for the admission of displaced persons (DPs) to Canada and to help integrate them into the Canadian labour movement. As Kalmen Kaplansky pointed out in 1950, resentment of DPs really stood for a growing anti-immigrant feeling in the labour movement.[83] The advocacy for a greater acceptance of DPs signalled a campaign for greater acceptance of Canada's postwar immigration policy. Although the United States also made an exception to its anti-immigration policy by admitting some DPs after the war, proportionally far more of them were admitted to Canada. Moreover, south of the border strict limits to immigration remained firmly in place until the mid-1960s.[84]

In fact, the JLC's support for DPs served a number of purposes. First, it would help the admission of Holocaust survivors from Europe. Second, it provided an opportunity for denouncing racist attitudes toward immigration which continued within the labour movement. Third, it provided ammunition in the JLC's ideological battle against the communists. The Canadian Communist Party supported the Soviet Union's position that DPs should be required to return to their countries of origin, which now formed part of the Soviet bloc. Apart from Holocaust victims, Canadian communists tended to label immigrant DPs as anti-union fascists. CCF MPP Eamon Park and Communist MPP Joe Salsberg clashed on this matter in the Ontario legislature in February 1950. In the context of a long speech on the problems of unemployment, Park asserted that "there are those who are interested in using the naturally disturbed feelings of the people about the unemployment situation to exploit it on . . . national and racial grounds. A great many workers have been told that the whole problem is on account of the displaced persons coming to Canada. It has been a common line shoved at the labour movement in this country by the Communist Party." In response, Salsberg declared that this accusation was "an absolute lie."[85] Although Salsberg had published an editorial in the Canadian communist newspaper a month earlier where he explained that unemployment was caused by the capitalist system, not by immigration per se, he had also charged that "with but minor exceptions the government pursued a most reactionary, anti-labour, cold-war immigration policy": "big business was permitted to select its own 'work-gangs' in the DP camps. . . . The industry representatives picked the most reactionary-minded, anti-union types they could find. . . . The government also favored the DP's who refused to return to their native lands because they served the Hitler invaders. . . . Our government brought them [to Canada] as political allies and with the purpose of keeping them as storm-troop groupings to be used against labor at home and as mercenaries for an anti-Soviet war."[86]

JLC activists were deeply concerned that growing unemployment in the 1950s threatened to intensify hostility toward immigrants. The JLC's publications emphasized immigrants became part of Canada's population "on the way to full citizenship" from the moment they landed in Canada. Growing unemployment in the country was not caused by these immigrants but by deeply rooted problems in the economic system. Unless organized workers were careful, however, employers would use anti-DP and anti-immigrant sentiments to sow discord within unions in the hope of breaking them. Kalmen Kaplansky believed that many DPs joined unions because the labour movement stood up for them.[87]

The extensive reliance of Canadian human rights activists on their American counterparts offers a hitherto unexplored example of the importance of transnational approaches to the study of immigrants and minorities. This study supplements the emphasis of existing transnational studies in this field on the need to consider immigrant and minority groups in relation to both their regions of origin and of settlement. It emphasizes the importance of transnational ties between minority groups in different countries of settlement. As the case of the Jews illustrates, studying such links sheds new light not only on the history of minority groups but also on their contributions to the transformation of host societies. By acting as conduits for the ideas and practices of American human rights activists and by reshaping this material to fit Canadian circumstances, Canadian Jewish activists helped make Canada's institutions more responsive to, and more reflective of, the diversity of Canada's people.

Canadian historians have often emphasized Canada's distinctiveness from the United States while minimizing or even neglecting cross-border ties, for it is only very recently that transnational history has become fashionable. In this country, anti-Americanism surged during the mid-to-late 1960s and early 1970s, especially as the United States became mired in the war in Vietnam, but it is important that historians do not simply assume that the same dynamics existed in the 1940s and 1950s. In more recent times, Canadian nationalists have often stressed the idea that—in contrast to the United States—we have had a kinder, gentler, multicultural nation, with better welfare provisions. Yet Canada's Jewish human rights activists believed that they had a lot to gain from close ties to their American counterparts, even as they adapted American anti-discrimination campaigns to Canadian circumstances.

NOTES

1. James Walker, "*Race,*" *Rights and the Law in the Supreme Court of Canada* (Waterloo: Wilfrid Laurier University Press, 1997) and "The 'Jewish Phase' in the Movement for Racial Equality in Canada," *Canadian Ethnic Studies* 34, no. 1 (2002): 1–24; Ross Lambertson, "The Dresden Story: Racism, Human Rights, and the Jewish Labour Committee of Canada," *Labour/Le Travail* 47 (Spring 2001): 755–76; Carmela Patrias and Ruth Frager, "'This Is Our Country, These Are Our Rights': Minorities and the Origins of Ontario's Human Rights Campaigns," *Canadian Historical Review* 82, no. 1 (March 2001): 1–34; Ross Lambertson, *Repression and Resistance: Canadian Human Rights Activists 1930–1960* (Toronto: University of Toronto Press, 2005); Carmela Patrias, "Socialists, Jews, and the 1947 Saskatchewan Bill of Rights," *Canadian Historical Review* 87, no. 2 (2006): 265–92; Stephanie Bangarth, *Voices Raised in Protest: Defending North American Citizens of Japanese Ancestry, 1942–1949* (Vancouver: University of British Columbia Press, 2008); Dominique Clément, *Canada's Rights Revolution* (Vancouver: University of British Columbia Press, 2008); Sarah-Jane Mathieu, *North of the Color Line: Migration and Black Resistance in Canada, 1870–1955* (Chapel Hill: University of North Carolina Press, 2010); David Goutor, "A Different Perspective on the 'Labor Rights as Human Rights' Debate: Organized Labor and Human Rights Activism in Canada," *Labor Studies Journal* 36, no. 3 (2011): 408–27.

2. See for example, Canadian Jewish Congress Charities Committee National Archives (CJCCCNA), CJC Organizational Records, Chronological File Series (CJCCF), ZA 1943, box 2, file 13, Minutes of meeting of Bureau of Social and Economic Research of Canadian Jewish Congress, September 20, 1943, on connection to the Board of Jewish Deputies in London.

3. See, for example, Gerald Tulchinsky, *Canada's Jews* (Toronto: University of Toronto Press, 2008).

4. Both Reform rabbis eventually moved back to the United States where Eisendrath became especially active in the civil rights movement. See urj.org/about/union/history/eisendrath/ (Union for Reform Judaism's website) (accessed January 21, 2012); archive.jta.org/article/ 1973/11/12/2966741/rabbi-maurice-n-eisendrath-uach-president (Jewish News Archives' website) (accessed January 21, 2012); & Biographic Sketch of Rabbi Feinberg, Finding Aid to the Abraham L. Feinberg Papers, American Jewish Archives, americanjewisharchives.org/aja/ findingaids/feinberg.htm (accessed 21 January 2012).

5. "The Jewish Labor Committee Story," supplement to *70th Anniversary Commemorative Journal of the Jewish Labor Committee* (1934–2004).

6. Stuart Svonkin, *Jews Against Prejudice: American Jews and the Fight for Civil Liberties* (New York: Columbia University Press, 1997), 15.

7. David Roediger, *Working Toward Whiteness: How America's Immigrants Became White* (Cambridge, MA: Basic Books, 2005), 149.
8. Richard Steele, "The War on Intolerance: The Reformulation of American Nationalism, 1939–1941," *Journal of American Ethnic History* 9, no. 1 (Fall 1989): 17–18.
9. Nicholas V. Montalto, *A History of the Intercultural Education Movement, 1924–1941* (New York: Garland, 1982), 31.
10. Montalto, *Intercultural Education Movement*, 212 ff.
11. Svonkin, *Jews Against Prejudice*, 32–33.
12. Ibid., 214.
13. Ibid., 17.
14. CJCCCNA, CJCCF, ZA 1944, box 5, file 97, CJC Dominion Council Memorandum by M. Saalheimer, Interview with Dr. H.H. Giles, Director, Bureau of Inter-Cultural Education, December 8, 1944.
15. CJCCCNA, CJCCF, ZA 1944, box 5, file 97, CJC Dominion Council, Memorandum by M. Saalheimer, "Research Committee of the American Jewish Committee," December 7, 1944; M. Saalheimer to Saul Hayes, Commission on Community Inter-Relations of the American Jewish Congress, December 7, 1944; Interview with Professor M.A. Davie, December 8, 1944.
16. Roediger, *Working Toward Whiteness*, 200.
17. Kevin Boyle, "'There Are No Union Sorrows that the Union Can't Heal': The Struggle for Racial Equality in the United Automobile Workers, 1940–1960," *Labor History* 36, no. 1 (Winter 1995): 5–23; Nelson Lichtenstein, *The Most Dangerous Man in Detroit* (New York: Basic Books, 1995), 207–8; Philip Gleason, "Americans All: World War II and the Shaping of American Identity," *The Review of Politics* 43, no. 4 (October 1981): 501.
18. Jewishlabor.org/JLC_Basic_History (accessed October 2, 2012).
19. Library and Archives Canada (LAC), Kalmen Kaplansky Records (KK), vol. 20, file 3, 1946–47, 13.
20. Svonkin, *Jews Against Prejudice*, Chap. 4; Anthony S. Chen, "'The Hitlerian Rule of Quotas': Racial Conservatism and the Politics of Fair Employment Practices in New York State, 1941–1945," *The Journal of American History* 92, no. 4 (March 2006): 1238–64; and Nathan Glazer and Reed Ueda, "Prejudice and Discrimination, Policy Against" in *Harvard Encyclopedia of American Ethnic Groups*, ed. Stephan Thernstrom (Cambridge, MA: Harvard University Press, 1980): 854.
21. CJCCCNA, CJCCF, ZA 1943 and 1944, box 4, file 85.
22. Jewish Archives of Ontario (JAO), JPRC Collection, MG8 S, Box 5, file 12 (Memos, Reports, 1952), unlabelled JPRC report, 2.
23. JPRC Collection, Box 5, file 2, JPRC Minutes, June 25, 1953.
24. Steele, "The War on Intolerance," 9–35; and Clarence I. Chatto and Alice L. Halligan, *The Story of the Springfield Plan* (New York: Barnes & Noble, 1945).
25. JAO, JCRC Collection, file 160.6, International Relationships, Oscar Cohen to Rabbi Eisendrath, Resume of the Conference between Dr. Silcox, O. Cohen and Dr. McArthur, Deputy Minister of Education, April 8, 1940.
26. ZA 1945, box 2, file 19, Minutes of JPRC, Toronto, July 25, 1945.
27. Archives of Ontario (AO), Annual Report of the Minister of Education, Province of Ontario, 1946, 12, and 1947, 15.
28. ZA 1939, box 2, file 15, Employment and Economics, Report of the Meeting of the Committee on Economic Problems, February 21, 1939.
29. CJCCNA, DA 1, Box 8, file 1, H. M. Caiserman to Samuel Bronfman, May 28, 1941; and DA 1, Box 8, File 17, National plan for the public relations work in the Dominion to be carried on by the JPRC, Suggested by H.M. Caiserman, Director, n.d.
30. On the importance of the international unions in this context, see, for example, LAC, Jewish Labour Committee Collection, MG28 V75, vol. 49, file 49–12, Sid Blum to Jacob Pat, February 10, 1960.

31. KK, vol. 20, file 7, 91.
32. JLC Collection, vol. 50, file 50–21, 1946 JLC Report, 26.
33. See Carmela Patrias, *Jobs and Justice: Fighting Discrimination in Wartime Canada* (Toronto: University of Toronto Press, 2011), 62.
34. ZA 1945, Box 2, File 22, Morris Shumiatcher to Samuel Bronfman, October 6, 1945; Saul Hayes to Morris Shumiatcher, October 11, 1945; and M. Saalheimer to Commission on Law and Legislation, American Jewish Congress, October 16, 1945.
35. Patrias, "Socialists, Jews and the Saskatchewan Bill of Rights," 265–92.
36. ZA 1943, Box 2, File 13, M. Saalheimer to Saul Hayes re Interview with Dr. H.H. Giles, Director, Bureau of Inter-Cultural Education.
37. JAO, JPRC, Memo from Saul Hayes to Members of the National Executive Committee, Canadian Jewish Congress, Joint Public Relations Committee of the Canadian Jewish Congress and B'nai B'rith, January 20, 1946.
38. Svonkin, *Jews Against Prejudice*, 85.
39. ZA 1939, Box 2, File 15, Minutes of the Executive Committee on Economic Problems, June 1, 1939.
40. KK, Vol. 22, File 12, 1951; and JAO, JPRC, File: Ben Kayfetz, Schedule of Activities Arising from meeting between Ben Kayfetz and Ben Lappin, November 15, 1949.
41. KK, 31.
42. Goutor, "A Different Perspective," 420–22.
43. JAO, JPRC Collection, Box 5, file 10, "Report, National Joint Public Relations Committee, October 1951," 2.
44. KK, vol. 20, file 5, Reports of Activities for Improved Human Relations, 1948.
45. KK, vol. 20, file 20–12, Reports of Activities for Improved Human Relations, 1951.
46. KK, vol. 20, file 5, Reports of Activities for Improved Human Relations, 1948, 70.
47. Interviews with Kalmen Kaplansky (June 30, 1995) and Ben Kayfetz (April 29, 1997).
48. Interview with Sadie Hoffman, 1985.
49. Interview with Bessie Kramer, 1984.
50. Interview with Kalmen Kaplansky, June 30, 1995.
51. LAC, JLC, vol. 50, file 50–23, 1957 JLC Report,Yiddish section, n.p.
52. JLC, vol. 9, file 12, Correspondence, Michael Rubinstein, JLC Montreal, 1959, Address to the CCL 7th Convention by Michael Rubinstein, National Chairman, JLC.
53. Interview with Kalmen Kaplansky, June 30, 1995. Concerning the anti-discrimination measures that were enacted in Canada in this period, the Jewish human rights activists had to settle for the best they could get, especially given the political clout of the Conservative and Liberal parties.
54. Svonkin, *Jews Against Prejudice*, 30.
55. Patrias, "Socialists, Jews and the Saskatchewan Bill of Rights."
56. Robert E. Wagner Labor Archives, New York University, Jewish Labor Committee fonds, box 30, file 15, Abraham Feinberg, "A Re-evaluation of the Good-Will Movement," Paper delivered at Central Conference of American Rabbis, June 25, 1947, 8–9.
57. Sid Blum, "Making People Like Each Other," *Food for Thought* 18 (April 1958): 331–36. (Reprinted by Canadian Labour Reports as a pamphlet entitled "Education, Equality and Brotherhood.") On Blum's background, see Lambertson, *Repression and Resistance*, 292–94.
58. Manfred Saalheimer, "Laws Also Educate," *Food for Thought* 10, no. 1 (Oct. 1949), 39–43.
59. KK, vol. 20, file 12, "Reports of Activities for Improved Human Relations," 1951.
60. JAO, JPRC Collection, File: 1948–49, Minutes of Legal Subcommittee, March 14 ,1949.
61. See, for example, JLC, vol. 50, file 50–19, Kalmen Kaplansky to Ann Terech, Sept. 14, 1946.
62. JLC, vol. 49, file: 49–18, George Silver to Kalmen Kaplansky, July 13, 1951.
63. JLC Collection, vol. 49, file 49–14, Sid Blum to Jacob Schlitt, May 29, 1957; Schlitt to Blum, July 3, 1957; and Blum to Schlitt, July 12, 1957.
64. JLC, vol. 50, file 50–21, 1946 JLC Report, 57–58 (in the Yiddish section).
65. Blum, "Making People Like Each Other," 331.

66. Abraham L. Feinberg, *Storm the Gates of Jericho* (Toronto: McClelland and Stewart, 1964), 65–67.
67. Ibid., 71.
68. LAC, Kalmen Kaplansky Fonds, Notes on reports of activities for improved human relations, 1946-47, vol. 20, file 2, 18–19, 84–6, 152–3.
69. See Svonkin, *Jews Against Prejudice*, 52–53.
70. Roediger, *Working Toward Whiteness*, 211; Lichtenstein, *The Most Dangerous Man in Detroit*, 206–11.
71. LAC, Ontario Labour Committee for Human Rights, vol.3, file 14, Correspondence General, July-Dec. 1950, William C. Macdonald to Gordon Milling, September 13, 1950; and JLC, vol.43, file 21: Correspondence Windsor Joint Committee for Human Rights, June-December 1953, Report for the month of October 1953.
72. JLC vol. 34, file 6.
73. JLC vol. 8, file 6, M. Saalheimer to S.D. Cohen, February 23, 1955.
74. JLC vol. 8, file 6, April 24, 1953.
75. KK, 1950, 31–32.
76. JAO, JPRC, File 23A "Fair Employment Practices," Murray Shiff to Ben Kayfetz, November 16, 1950.
77. AO, Royal Commission on Education in Ontario, brief presented by Rabbi Abraham L. Feinberg, September 19, 1945, on behalf of the Canadian Jewish Congress, Central Division.
78. Wagner Labor Archives, Jewish Labour Committee fonds, Box 30, Folder 15, "A Re-Evaluation of the Good-Will Movement," by Rabbi Abraham L. Feinberg, Holy Blossom Temple, Toronto, June 25, 1947. The paper was sent to Adolph Held, JLC Chair, by Feinberg.
79. Ibid.
80. Feinberg, *Storm the Gates*, 289.
81. JLC, vol. 20, file 3, Memorandum on NCRAC Meeting, M. Saalheimer to Saul Hayes, March 21, 1947.
82. JLC, vol. 20, file 6, Progress Report of the JPRC, Central Region.
83. KK, 1950, 32.
84. KK, 1946–47, 234.
85. Proceedings of the Second Session of the Twenty-Third Legislature of the Province of Ontario, March 2, 1950, C-7 through C-9.
86. J.B. Salsberg, "Unemployment, DP's and the Unions," *Canadian Tribune*, January 23, 1950.
87. KK, 1952, 47.

Chapter 6

•◆•

A Limited Vision: Canadian Participation in the Adoption of the International Covenants on Human Rights

Jennifer Tunnicliffe

In 1947, members of the United Nations (UN) drafted the International Bill of Rights, articulating for the first time a proposed set of inalienable and universal human rights to be codified in international law. The debates that ensued led ultimately to the adoption of the Universal Declaration of Human Rights (UDHR) in 1948 and two related covenants on human rights in 1966. While the International Bill of Rights offered a new framework for ideas of liberty and equality, and created a new rights-based language that could be used to define and shape understandings of individual and collective rights, its principles were deeply contested. Societies around the world held their own particular interpretations of liberty, rights, and freedoms, and it is worth considering how these conflicted with, shaped, and were reformulated by the international human rights regime that developed in the postwar era.

Canada's policy approach toward the International Bill of Rights provides an interesting example of how domestic understandings of rights intersected with the universalist discourse of the United Nations beginning in the late 1940s. The concept of rights that emerged from UN discussions challenged customary understandings of how civil liberties could best be protected within Canada's federal parliamentary system. For this reason, the Canadian government attempted to delay the adoption of the UDHR in 1948, and actively resisted efforts to draft legally binding covenants on human rights throughout the 1950s. This history has been largely ignored, however, as government officials worked to promote a vision of Canada as a long-standing advocate for international human rights. The website for Foreign Affairs and International Trade Canada proclaimed in 2013 that, "Canada has been a consistently strong voice for the protection of human rights and the advancement of democratic values, from our central role in the drafting of the Universal Declaration of Human Rights in 1947/1948 to our work at the United

Nations today."[1] This rhetoric ignores the extent to which concepts of universal rights were opposed within the Canadian government and efforts at the United Nations to introduce an international bill of rights resisted by Canadian policy-makers.

To address this gap, scholars such as William Schabas and Michael Behiels have begun to take a more critical look at Canada's historical approach to international human rights.[2] Building upon their work, this paper considers how traditional understandings and practices surrounding rights and freedoms in Canada influenced the government's participation at the United Nations in debates over the International Covenants on Human Rights from 1949 to 1966. I argue these covenants embodied a much broader interpretation of rights than Canadian officials were willing to accept and, uneasy about the effect a binding international treaty on human rights could have on Canadian policy, the government resisted any positive participation in their development. When Canada did finally take steps to support the covenants, it did so only in response to new pressures from within the UN and mounting support for human rights at home. Contrary to what the government would have Canadians believe, Canada's role in the development of early international human rights law was neither central nor consistent.

In 1941, Franklin D. Roosevelt defined freedom as "the supremacy of human rights everywhere."[3] Yet, when representatives met at Dumbarton Oaks in 1944 to lay the groundwork for the United Nations, human rights were hardly mentioned. It took pressure from non-governmental organizations and smaller nation-states to convince the United States, Britain, and the Soviet Union to include human rights obligations as a central aspect of the organization.[4] Canadian officials expressed only marginal interest in human rights provisions, sharing the concern of larger states that because these rights could fall within domestic jurisdiction, their inclusion could threaten national sovereignty.[5] The addition of a domestic jurisdiction clause alleviated these concerns. Consequently, the 1945 Charter of the United Nations referenced human rights seven times, calling upon member states to promote "universal respect for, and observance of, human rights and fundamental freedoms."[6]

The Economic and Social Council of the United Nations (ECOSOC) established a Commission on Human Rights in 1946 to draft the instruments and machinery required to promote the rights and freedoms outlined in the Charter. The commission consisted of representatives from eighteen member states, and was chaired by Eleanor Roosevelt.[7] Canada was not a member, although a Canadian, John P. Humphrey, was the first Director of the UN Division of Human Rights and did sit on the commission. As a member of the UN Secretariat, however, Humphrey did not represent the Canadian government or its interests.[8] By December 1947, the commission had completed a draft international bill of rights, which included three parts: a declaration of rights that would act as a broad statement of principle, a single covenant of rights that would be legally binding on all signatory states, and a document outlining the measures for implementation. Eager to adopt a human rights instrument quickly, and recognizing the challenge of reaching a consensus over a binding covenant, the commission chose to move forward first with the declaration.[9]

The Canadian government was cautious to support the International Bill of Rights. A Special Joint Parliamentary Committee on Human Rights and Fundamental Freedoms was established in 1947 to consider how the human rights obligations set out in the UN Charter could be implemented. An Interdepartmental Committee on Human Rights was also created to help determine the Canadian position. The government asked these committees to examine the draft Declaration and report to cabinet in the spring of 1948. In their subsequent reports, both committees suggested the Declaration could be more concise and redrafted to be more effective, but endorsed it in principle.[10] Both reports also mentioned possible constitutional constraints for the federal government, given that property and civil rights fell within provincial jurisdiction under the BNA Act. The committees noted, however, that, as a quasi-legal instrument, a declaration would have the force of a recommendation only and would therefore not bind the federal government to legislative changes that could be challenged.[11]

Throughout the fall of 1948, the draft Declaration was debated first at ECOSOC and then within the General Assembly. Canada pushed to delay a final vote on adoption until 1949, with no success.[12] Correspondence between the government and the Canadian delegation focused increasingly on possible constitutional constraints, and External Affairs and cabinet considered the possibility of abstaining at the final vote.[13] Sensing the negative diplomatic implications of this, Secretary of State for External Affairs Lester Pearson suggested a different tactic. Pearson wrote to his department, "by abstaining we might find ourselves in a rather undesirable minority—including principally the Soviet bloc and South Africa."[14] Instead, the Canadian delegation abstained in the vote in the Third Committee to make its point, but changed its final vote to support the Declaration in the plenary session to avoid international embarrassment.[15]

Historian Michael Behiels attributes Canadian resistance to the UDHR to the decentralist nature of Canadian federalism. He argues that the government was influenced by a 1937 British Privy Council decision that found it unconstitutional for the federal government to legislate, in compliance with international agreements, in areas that belonged to the provinces under the BNA Act.[16] Yet, according to William Schabas, officials were being disingenuous when they raised the issue of jurisdiction as, in his view, the matter had been settled at the Joint Parliamentary Committee when it was made clear a declaration would hold no legal weight.[17] Ultimately, Schabas blames Canada's sometimes hostile and often indifferent attitude toward the UDHR on serious misgivings within cabinet and a lack of a "human rights culture" within the Department of External Affairs.[18] Alternatively, George Egerton argues there was a rights culture within government, but one so firmly rooted in Christian values that officials were cautious to commit to the Declaration because it did not explicitly recognize the primacy of God.[19]

The process to develop and adopt the International Covenants on Human Rights provides further opportunity to test these arguments. Whereas the UDHR was a statement of principle, the Covenants would be submitted to member states for ratification once they were adopted by the United Nations and would impose legally binding obligations upon signatory states. Fully aware of the implications of a covenant, members of the UN debated the content and form of these documents for the better part of two decades. Canada's role in, and reaction to, these debates can shed light on how Canadian policy-makers understood the concepts of rights and freedoms in the postwar period, and help to explain why the government continued to resist the development of international human rights instruments.

After the adoption of the UDHR, the United Nations turned its attention to the draft Covenant on Human Rights. A covenant would act as a clearer articulation of both the specific rights outlined in the Declaration, and their limitations. The Commission on Human Rights released its first draft to member states in 1949. To encourage a speedy adoption, this draft excluded the most controversial articles from the UDHR, those relating to economic and social rights. By 1950, however, the desirability of including these rights in the same covenant as the civil and political rights became a clear issue for debate.[20] In response to a proposal by the United States, the General Assembly voted to instruct the Commission on Human Rights to draft two separate instruments.[21] The resulting International Covenant on Civil and Political Rights, and International Covenant on Economic, Social and Cultural Rights, received first reading in the General Assembly in 1954. They were both adopted and opened for signature and ratification in December 1966. In total, it took seventeen years for the UN to reach an agreement on the Covenants, highlighting deep divisions over questions of human rights. These divisions caused some member states that had originally been enthusiastic about a covenant, such as the United States, to withdraw their support.[22] The Canadian government worked in reverse, as officials initially resisted the idea of a legally binding human rights instrument but reluctantly came to support the Covenants by 1966.

The Department of External Affairs was largely responsible for determining Canadian policy toward the Covenants, subject to the approval of cabinet and the prime minister. The Interdepartmental Committee on Human Rights was resurrected in 1950 to provide support, and included representatives from the Privy Council and the Department of Justice.[23] Other departments expressed only limited interest.[24] Within the House of Commons, the UDHR and the Covenants were rarely discussed and when Members of Parliament did talk about rights, they focused on domestic issues.[25] There was also no consultation between federal and provincial governments regarding the Covenants prior to their adoption.[26] With such little attention on human rights developments at the UN, officials within External Affairs had a great deal of autonomy in setting policy.

Even within External Affairs, however, there was little interest in international human rights. In the larger context of Canadian foreign policy in the 1950s, human rights issues remained low on the agenda. Many of the departmental documents relating to the sessions of the United Nations held in this period did not even mention human rights.[27] A 1953 internal memo explained the department's lack of enthusiasm on "skepticism as to the value of the international instruments to protect rights."[28]

Within the department there was a sense that Canadian citizens did not need international human rights protection because they did not experience the same problems with discrimination as other nations. In 1948, Canadian delegate Ralph Maybank confidently told members of the UN that the problems minorities experienced elsewhere simply did not exist in Canada.[29] Two years later, Justice Minister Stuart Garson argued that Canadian law already provided most of the provisions of the draft Covenant, and so it could only have been designed to improve conditions in *other* countries.[30] Gordon Robertson, a prominent bureaucrat from 1945 until the late 1970s, declared in 1957 that he felt no one in the Canadian government believed the UDHR or the Covenants promoted any greater protection of human rights in Canada.[31] Refusing to acknowledge the shortcomings of Canadian law and society to prevent the many violations of human rights that did occur in Canada, these federal officials saw an international covenant as unnecessary.

When the draft Covenant was made available for comment in 1949, External Affairs prepared a statement of Canadian views to be sent to delegates at the UN.[32] This statement became the basis for Canadian criticisms of both international covenants on human rights. In addition to listing concerns over format, language, and content, the government argued that a federal state clause was required in order for Canada to support any covenant on human rights. This clause would allow states to become party to a covenant without being bound by international law to carry out obligations that would be under the jurisdiction of its provincial governments. According to Michael Behiels, federal officials were constrained by Canada's "federalist conundrum," whereby treaty-making powers were under the jurisdiction of the federal government, but powers of implementation belonged to the provinces.[33] The Canadian government simply did not have the authority to implement international human rights treaties in the pre-Charter era, and the government was fearful of challenging the provinces in this area. This caused Canada to appear ambivalent toward the Covenants when, in fact, it was simply powerless.[34]

One of the problems with this argument, however, is that it leads the reader to believe that, jurisdictional issues aside, the federal government supported a covenant on human rights, both in principle and in content. Yet a detailed examination of debates among federal officials, and communications between the Department of External Affairs and Canadian delegates at the United Nations, suggests policy-makers also resisted the International Covenants on Human Rights because the concept of universal human rights articulated in these instruments conflicted with their own limited vision of rights. This vision was limited in its conceptualization of what could legitimately be considered a human right, in how these rights could best be protected under international law, and in how an international covenant on human rights could interact with domestic policies. Consequently, federal officials could not, and would not, understand the need for an international treaty that included such an expansive interpretation of human rights.

In the 1940s and 1950s, Canadians held a very narrow definition of rights. The terms *civil liberties* or *civil rights* were commonly used to discuss issues of rights and freedoms, and these referred to the basic rights of free speech, religion, assembly, association, property ownership, and legal counsel.[35] The term *human rights* was less frequently used and had a much broader meaning, including rights that were not commonly reflected in Canadian law, such as economic and social rights.[36] Within the Canadian legal tradition, government played a minimal role in the protection of civil liberties. This conflicted with the concept of universalism coming out of the UN, in which states were obliged not only to protect political and civil rights, but also to promote the economic, social, and cultural well-being of all. In evaluating the draft Covenant in 1950, civil servants within the Departments of Justice and External Affairs noted that certain articles called for greater government interference than was the tradition in Canada. Jules Léger claimed this degree of interference was incompatible with Canada's form of parliamentary democracy.[37] The Interdepartmental Committee had expressed this same concern during the process to adopt the Universal Declaration, stating that some of the articles were "based on the premise that the State should be paternalistic" and that this may not be acceptable to the Canadian government, whose thinking was "laissez-faire."[38] The quasi-legal nature of the Declaration had soothed these concerns somewhat, but the draft Covenant caused them to resurface.

The Canadian government also argued that only individual rights should be included in a covenant. Canada opposed any articles it believed articulated collective rights on the basis that they were neither rights nor principles under international law. This included Article 1 of each covenant, the articles on self-determination.[39] While the Canadian delegation assured other member states that it was sympathetic to the problem of self-determination, Canada could not support its inclusion in the Covenants because it saw the issue as "more of a goal than a right" and "a collective matter rather than an individual human right."[40]

Economic and social rights provided the greatest challenge for Canadian officials. The Canadian delegation was told to support any attempt to exclude these rights from the Covenants and, if the majority of states supported inclusion, to avoid participating in the debate and abstain on all votes.[41] The Canadian position was that civil and political rights were fundamentally different from economic and social rights. The former were "safeguards against the abuse of power by Parliaments and Governments" whereas the latter were "essentially matters of detailed social legislation and economic and financial policy on both the national and international scale."[42] According to this argument, economic and social rights, such as the right to work or to education, could not be achieved by simply declaring them in a covenant. They required the application of legislation, and for this reason were not considered legitimate rights by Canadian policy-makers.[43] At the United Nations, the Canadian delegation argued that economic and social rights could not be protected in the same manner as civil and political ones, largely because there was no way to create practical and enforceable legal remedies in the case of their violation."[44] In 1953, the deputy attorney general of Canada commented on economic, social, and cultural rights by saying, "I am somewhat dubious about the effect of numerous articles which 'recognize the right' to certain things, but I presume that these have a certain value as an enunciation of idealistic objectives."[45] Other delegates were far less supportive, such as L.A.D. Stephens, who claimed that the Latin American and Asian countries that advocated for economic and social rights were looking to create a "welfare world."[46] Canada continued to oppose the inclusion of economic and social rights even after the separation into two covenants. Delegates repeated the Canadian objections at each session of the General Assembly as member states debated the Covenants article by article. In final votes, the Canadian delegation abstained on eight of the ten articles within the International Covenant on Economic, Social and Cultural Rights that listed the rights themselves.[47]

Opposition to the inclusion of economic and social rights in the Covenants was not limited to bureaucrats within the Departments of External Affairs and Justice. It reflected a dominant understanding of rights within the Liberal Party in this period. Many party members were suspicious of economic and social rights, believing these rights to be a threat to the traditional values of individual freedom, the rule of law, and freedom in the marketplace.[48] Advocacy for social and economic rights was believed to be the domain of the CCF, not the Liberal or Conservative parties.[49] Throughout the 1940s, the Liberal government had opposed calls for a domestic bill of rights in part due to concerns over the inclusion of economic and social rights.[50] Even rights activists themselves most often prioritized legal and political rights over social rights prior to the 1970s.[51] Many organizations active in Canada from the 1940s to the mid-1960s took what Dominque Clément has termed a "minimalist approach to human rights," equating human rights with political and legal rights.[52] In this context, there was little pressure on the government to expand its definition to include economic and social rights.

Part of the difficulty Canadian policy-makers had in defining which rights should be included in the Covenants related to the government's second major area of concern, a general discomfort with the codification of rights. In 1946, when the United Nations began its work to draft an international bill of rights, Canada had virtually no domestic legislation to explicitly protect human rights or prevent discrimination. Historical notions of liberty and equality were inherited from British common law, and Canada had nothing resembling a national codified bill of rights. Instead, the Canadian system was based on the dual principles of parliamentary supremacy and the rule of law; statutes passed by Parliament acted as the highest and final source of law and all citizens were subject to, and technically had equal protection under, this law. Canadian lawmakers believed the most effective way to protect civil liberties was to rely upon the unwritten powers implicit in British constitutionalism rather than having a formally written bill of rights.[53] Throughout the 1950s, several jurisdictions in Canada adopted forms of anti-discrimination or fair practices legislation, but the first federal bill of rights was not enacted until 1960. Therefore, the codification of rights that characterized the UN's efforts was a significant departure from the traditional methods of the Canadian government for protecting its citizens, and policy-makers remained unconvinced a written covenant was the most effective way to defend rights.

The Canadian government also had difficulty reconciling the obligations inherent in a covenant with their desire to maintain national sovereignty. Having already supported a declaration on human rights, officials were unsure as to the need for another instrument, particularly one that would bind signatory states. In its initial response to the draft Covenant, the Department of External Affairs indicated it felt that the way in which rights and freedoms were promoted and protected in individual states was a matter of decision for that state, in accordance with its own constitution and traditions.[54] Minister of Justice Stuart Garson worried that a covenant on human rights might "commit the Canadian Parliament, if not to a legislative programme, at least to an undertaking not to derogate from existing rights granted by legislation."[55] The government examined how the universality of the rights outlined in the draft Covenants would impact domestic policy and identified a number of provincial and federal statutes that would have to be altered or repealed to meet its standards. Deputy Minister of Citizenship and Immigration Laval Fortier wrote a letter to External Affairs in defence of Canada's selective immigration policy, stating he was unwilling to enter into an international debate over the appropriateness of that policy.[56] Louis St. Laurent and Stuart Garson also questioned how the adoption of the Declaration and the Covenants would limit Canada's ability to pursue less formal policies, such as preventing the spread of communism.[57] The government even expressed concern that support for an international bill of rights would promote the idea of a national bill of rights. David Mundell, a Justice representative in the Interdepartmental Committee, suggested the United Nations should go no further than the Universal Declaration in its attempts to legislate international human rights. He argued it was "hopeless" to expect a covenant could ever be implemented because those states in need of such a convention would never follow it, while states for which it was unnecessary, like Canada, would only be opening themselves up to propaganda attacks through the use of the new machinery of the international human rights regime.[58] Civil servants within the Department of External Affairs shared the views of Garson and Mundell.[59]

Canadian policy-makers therefore objected to the International Covenants on Human Rights due in large part to their anxieties over definitions of rights and fears of the implications of what they saw as an unnecessary treaty on domestic legislation. The difficulty was that the government did not want to appear to oppose the principles of universal human rights. From the beginning of the process, there was a sense among officials that opposition to any part of the International Bill of Rights may be seen as an admission that "our house not being in order, we refuse to clean it up."[60] Rather than admitting Canada had fundamental issues with the way in which the Covenants articulated and would implement universal human rights, delegates highlighted other concerns, principally the need for a federal state clause.

Officials were not being insincere, however, when they brought forward constitutional issues. There were legitimate concerns over the ability of the federal government to implement international treaties dealing with areas under provincial authority, and it was in the best interest of the federal government to show respect for Canadian federalism when working at the United Nations. Yet, in the case of the Covenants this respect for federalism was also used to mask the government of Canada's desire for inaction in the area of international human rights. For all the concern expressed over provincial opposition to the federal government negotiating international human rights treaties, the Canadian government made no effort to determine or test provincial attitudes.[61] Even in 1965, when it was clear the Covenants were near adoption, the Department of External Affairs had no immediate plans to invite the provinces to a meeting to consider ratification.[62] The federal government did nothing to persuade provincial officials, or Canadians more generally, of the urgency of adopting international agreements protecting universal human rights. If the government was strongly in support of the Covenants but fearful of how the provinces would interpret this support, there could have been some level of federal–provincial dialogue. Jurisdictional concerns alone seem insufficient to explain Canada's policy approach toward the Covenants. Representatives from other states such as the United Kingdom speculated that, by linking its support of the Covenants to a federal clause, Canada was actively taking steps to provide a future justification for failing to ratify the Covenants.[63] In 1954, External Affairs did consider the possibility of ceasing its calls for the inclusion of a federal clause for this very purpose.[64]

Canada's opposition to the Covenants was reflected in its lack of contribution to negotiations at the United Nations. From 1951 to 1956, Canada's approach wavered between either a desire that the Covenants would be abandoned altogether, a hope that if they were completed their content would be such that Canada could easily oppose them, and a fear that if they emerged in a form Canada felt obliged to sign, they would contain articles that would be problematic.[65] The government worried that any active participation in the debates would be interpreted as a sign that Canada was committed to the Covenants, and so in 1950 the Department of External Affairs instructed the Canadian delegates in Paris to "take no action that might be construed as giving support."[66] Officials urged Canadian delegates to stay on the periphery of the debates. The Canadian delegation was advised to refrain from participating in the discussions over articles it opposed and to abstain from voting on many proposals and amendments. Uncertain of the status of a federal clause, the Canadian delegation was also instructed not to participate in discussions in any areas deemed to be outside federal jurisdiction. Even relating to articles it supported, the delegation was told to avoid specific statements of support or enthusiasm. The most modest expressions of support could potentially be awkward. In 1951, members of External Affairs became upset when a Canadian delegate referred to the Covenant on Civil and Political Rights as "admirable project" and a "positive achievement."[67] Escott Reid worried how this wording would misrepresent a government that, in his own words, "considers that the project is far from admirable and sincerely hopes that it will be stillborn."[68] Reid and A.D.P. Heeney contacted the head of the Canadian delegation in Paris and requested that, from that point forward, Stuart Garson do all of the speaking.[69] Canada also avoided sitting as a representative on the UN Commission on Human Rights out of fear that such active participation would be interpreted as support for the Covenants. When Canada was approached to join this commission in 1953, acting Under-Secretary of State S. Morley Scott argued that, as its attitude toward the Covenants had been so "lukewarm," the government would gain little from a seat.[70]

The contributions Canada did make to negotiations over the Covenants were largely critical. Policy-makers took a very legalistic approach to the documents because a covenant was a binding agreement. This led to two seemingly contradictory criticisms. First, officials, particularly in the Department of Justice, claimed the language used in the draft was too imprecise to be effective, pointing to the use of vague terms such as *democracy*, *peoples*, and *nations*, and ambiguous statements like "within a reasonable time."[71] External Affairs told Prime Minister John Diefenbaker in 1957 that some of the articles suffered from such excessive generality as to be rendered meaningless.[72] Yet officials also criticized attempts to make the Covenants more specific through the inclusion of lists of restrictions and limitations. Stuart Garson warned that such lists could have the effect of overriding the basic rights outlined in the

Covenant.[73] The challenge was in drafting a covenant that was consistent, precise, and definite *without* listing limitations and exceptions within each article. The Canadian government seemed disinclined to help work toward this goal, however, and Canada proposed few amendments to improve the details of the Covenants. Instead, delegates were instructed to support only the text for articles that included a clear statement of principle but did not include any details about how the article would be implemented or any comprehensive definition of the right. In all other cases, the delegates were to refrain from participating in the discussions and abstain in all votes.[74] This approach was not appreciated by the majority of member states, and the Canadian delegates in Paris reported in 1956 that they were feeling increasingly isolated in the debates.[75]

Canada was able to take the position it did toward the Covenants largely because the government felt little pressure to do otherwise. Human rights activism within Canada in the 1950s was primarily focused on campaigns for domestic legislation, not activities at the UN.[76] This included federal and provincial campaigns for fair practices legislation and the push for a federal bill of rights. In 1951, on the eve of the third anniversary of the UDHR, the Toronto Civil Rights Union wrote to the Privy Council Office urging the government to mark the anniversary by committing to protect basic civil rights in Canada and testing the constitutionality of Quebec's controversial Padlock Law. The Covenants were not even mentioned.[77] At a conference organized to commemorate the tenth anniversary of the adoption of the UDHR, the panel that received the most attention was a roundtable discussing the proposed federal bill of rights.[78] Kathleen Bowlby of the United Nations Association in Canada claimed there simply was little interest in Canada for international human rights.[79] Having no desire to fuel this interest, the government worked to downplay its commitment to the Covenants in its domestic publicity and educational campaigns for the UN. When External Affairs was listing non-governmental organizations that may be interested in UNESCO publicity about the UDHR, bureaucrat G.C. McInnes warned against appearing too supportive of international human rights instruments in the cover letter sent to organizations. He wrote, "the Canadian Government is by no means sold on the idea of an international covenant on human rights." McInnes argued it would put the government in a difficult position if organizations in Canada became too enthusiastic and petitioned the government for action.[80] Action was what officials hoped to avoid.

Canada also experienced less pressure from its allies at the UN to support the Covenants than it had experienced with the UDHR. Initially, Canadian bureaucrats worried that opposition to a covenant on human rights would once again place Canada in the company of "undesirable bedfellows" such as the Soviet Union.[81] This was because Canada's most important allies, the United States and Britain, were originally committed to supporting the draft Covenant. In 1953, however, the United States announced that, due to an unfavourable climate at home, it would not ratify the Covenants. The American government instructed its delegates to withdraw from active participation in the debates.[82] The British government took its own critical approach to the Covenants beginning in the early 1950s, including opposition to the inclusion of social rights and disappointment over the exclusion of a colonial clause. By 1957, the Department of External Affairs reported that "friendly" states such as the United States, the United Kingdom, Australia and, to a lesser extent, New Zealand, were all "unsympathetic" toward the Covenants.[83] This relieved some of the pressure on Canada to support the instruments.

By the late 1950s, however, various Canadian delegates to the UN began calling on the federal government to change its policy approach to the Covenants. Canada had repeated the same reservations and criticisms at every session of the UN, and delegates were anxious to take a more active role. The delegation complained to External Affairs that their instructions limited the delegates' ability to participate in discussions and often put them in the uncomfortable position of constantly abstaining or opposing amendments in a minority position.[84] Delegates argued that Canada supported articles "of such a weak and declamatory nature that the majority of the committee was not disposed to pay much attention to what the Delegation said."[85] The department's instructions tended to criticize the Covenants without providing any constructive advice for how to modify or improve the text, and other member states were becoming increasingly upset with Canada's position.[86] In January 1957, tired of reiterating the constitutional argument, the Canadian delegation asked if they could assume that a federal clause would be included in the Covenants, so as to allow them to participate in the debates with "the possibility of making a positive and helpful contribution toward the drafting of a less unreasonable covenant."[87] The frustration of the Canadian delegates did not directly change the government's policies, but it did cause officials within External Affairs to be more sensitive to the question of how Canada's participation was perceived by other member states of the United Nations. This became relevant as membership in the organization continued to expand throughout the 1950s and 1960s.

When the draft Covenant was introduced in 1949, there were fifty-nine member states in the United Nations. Ten years later there were eighty-two members, and when the Covenants on Human Rights were adopted in 1966, there were 122 members.[88] This growth was fuelled by the addition of new states from Asia, Africa, and Latin America. These states were largely supportive of the idea of a covenant on human rights and openly criticized the position of what they characterized as the "Western colonial states."[89] Canadian officials became convinced that, with the support of these new member states, the Covenants would eventually be adopted in some form or the other and noted that other Western states were changing their policies accordingly. In 1959, an External Affairs memo to the minister reported, "during the past few sessions certain countries have tended to consider these covenants not as legal documents but as ideals and principles to serve as a guide for national legislation."[90] This shift allowed these countries to be less anxious about the legal implications of a covenant on human rights and provide greater support for its principles, as they had with the UDHR. The Department of External Affairs suggested two explanations for this: first, that realizing the Covenants would eventually be adopted, some member states were working to improve the text of the articles they were unable to accept in order to make them more palatable; and second, that other states, such as the United States, no longer had any intention of ratifying the Covenants and so ceased to argue legal points.[91]

In response, the Department of External Affairs and the Interdepartmental Committee on Human Rights had an extended discussion on whether or not the Canadian government should continue to approach the Covenants from a legal standpoint or to give more weight to political considerations.[92] The government felt strongly that there was still a good argument for taking a hard line against the Covenants based on legal arguments, but recognized this would leave Canada in a minority position once again. Reminiscent of Pearson's memo before the vote on the UDHR in 1948, a 1962 departmental memo stated, "given the present inclination of some of the Western countries, we might find ourselves isolated with a few countries such as South Africa, Portugal and China. Abstention in such circumstances is likely to be misunderstood not only by the non-aligned countries but perhaps even within Canada itself."[93] This time, the government was feeling the pressure not from its allies, but from other states. While the vision of Canadian policy-makers in regards to human rights may not have changed significantly, the government realized the political implications of choosing to oppose the Covenants.

Pressures at home in Canada were changing as well. While there was still little attention paid to the Covenants themselves, there was a growing support for Canada's participation in UN programs.[94] UNESCO-sponsored education programs and UN-supported commemorations of the anniversary of the adoption of the UDHR created greater public awareness of human rights initiatives at the UN.[95] Domestic campaigns resulting in new federal and provincial human rights legislation also led to a greater acceptance of human rights law generally. In 1957, John Diefenbaker's Conservatives defeated the Liberals in a federal election, and a year later Diefenbaker introduced a national bill of rights to Parliament. Politicians and members of the public debated the merits of this legislation for two years, and in 1960 the Canadian Bill of Rights became law. This legislation, and Diefenbaker's commitment to and understanding of human rights, have been criticized, but the experience of adopting its own national bill of rights did influence Canada's approach to the Covenants.[96] International human rights continued to remain on the periphery of foreign policy considerations under the Conservatives, but Canadians had their own example of a bill of rights to provide perspective to the International Bill of Rights.[97] Within the Department of External Affairs, there was a sense that the public would strongly support the principles of the Covenants. If, as officials now believed, these instruments would ultimately be adopted, the government did not want to be criticized at home for opposing them. With this in mind, several Canadian officials urged the Canadian government to work to influence the form and content of the Covenants as much as possible. Marcel Cadieux wrote that it was time for Canada to "get off the fence" regarding the Covenants.[98] Even Stuart Garson, the justice minister who so opposed the first draft, encouraged Canada to "make the best of a bad job" by working to improve the Covenants.[99]

Canada's position did become less rigid in the 1960s. External Affairs continued to instruct delegates to abstain from articles the government could absolutely not accept, but otherwise delegates were instructed to aim for the broadest interpretation of individual articles. They were also encouraged to try to improve the texts wherever possible.[100] This was a reversal in approach from the government's original concern over the lack of precision and clarity in the first-draft Covenant. Yet the government could hardly be considered enthusiastic. When the Greek delegation put forward a resolution to speed up the process of adoption, Canada opposed this resolution, stating, "slow discussion of the Covenants [is] not particularly bad since these Covenants are to stand for all time and another ten or fifteen years in their drafting would not unduly delay the advent of the era of Human Rights when viewed in the long prospect of world history."[101]

The shift in Canada's position was most evident in 1963, when delegates learned there would be no federal clause to alleviate jurisdictional concerns. Despite years of insisting that, without this clause, Canada would not be able to support a covenant on human rights, the government continued to participate in negotiations at the UN.[102] External Affairs identified twelve out of a total of eighty-four articles in the Covenants that would require consultation with provincial governments, but opted to support the instruments nevertheless.[103] This was not the result of a new federal–provincial understanding on jurisdiction. Instead, the Canadian government no longer felt comfortable using constitutional concerns as justification to hold back its support. As a result, Canada voted in favour of both covenants when they came before the plenary session for adoption in December 1966.

It took Canada another ten years to ratify the Covenants. In 1967, Prime Minister Lester Pearson sent a letter to the provincial premiers asking them to study the instruments and indicate their willingness to enact any legislation that might be necessary for implementation; dialogue with the provinces was slow. In the first few years after Pierre Trudeau became prime minister, the government focused on constitutional reform, and international human rights were not a priority.[104] There remained little awareness of the Covenants within the public and, even from within activist communities, little specific pressure for ratification. In 1971, the League for Human Rights of B'nai Brith initiated a petition campaign to educate the public about the Covenants, and to encourage Ottawa to speed up the ratification process.[105] Trudeau responded and, by 1974, nine of the ten provinces had confirmed their support for Canada's accession. The government of Quebec, while supportive of the Covenants themselves, continued to have issues with the protocols surrounding provincial involvement in the reporting and accountability system established by the instruments.[106] Federal–provincial meetings were scheduled for 1975, resulting in a tentative agreement. Yet it was international factors that once again motivated the Canadian government to move forward quickly. On December 23, 1975, Czechoslovakia became the thirty-fifth state to ratify the Covenant on Civil and Political Rights. As a result, the Covenant would officially enter into force three months later and the new Human Rights Committee of the United Nations would come into existence in six months. In order to be eligible to have a representative sit on this committee, member states would have to ratify the Covenant on Civil and Political Rights by May 19, 1976.[107] Eager to nominate a Canadian, the Trudeau government worked to secure Quebec's support and was able to successfully file the instruments of accession one day before the deadline. Almost thirty years after the introduction of the International Bill of Rights at the UN, Canada became party to both International Covenants on Human Rights.

What is perhaps most interesting in all of this is how the Canadian government remade the story of Canada's participation in the development of the International Bill of Rights. Within one year of the adoption of the Covenants, Glen S. Shortliffe of External Affairs wrote that a quick ratification of the covenants in Canada would be "consistent" with Canada's early support of international human rights, particularly "in light of the contributions which Canada made over the years to the drafting of the Covenants."[108] Ten years later, in a report on the influence of international human rights on Canadian foreign policy, the government claimed, "Canada has been at the forefront of multilateral human rights initiatives designed to promote human rights."[109] Within only a decade, Canada's reluctance to support the International Bill of Rights was forgotten.

Roger Normand and Sarah Zaidi argue that the debates over universal human rights which took place within the United Nations in the postwar period were important because, "it mattered to governments whether or not their ideological visions and legal systems—or those of their enemies—were validated in international law."[110] In negotiating the form and the content of the International Covenants on Human Rights, states exposed the diversity in how individual societies understood and practised human rights. For the Canadian government, a limited understanding of civil liberties, rights, and freedoms shaped participation in the drafting of the Declaration and the Covenants. Aware of the limits to federal authority to implement an international treaty on human rights, policymakers abdicated their responsibility by focusing on jurisdictional issues rather than admitting they had serious reservations over both the need for a covenant on human rights and the content of the draft provided by the UN. The dilemma Canada faced was in how to publicly support the UN's work in the field of human rights without committing itself to an international human rights regime that conflicted with the government's own ideas about rights. John Holmes, a permanent delegate to the UN when the draft Covenant was introduced, characterized this dilemma as "what to do in the face of a majority which has not accepted the Canadian way."[111] Canada's initial solution was to limit its participation in the hope a covenant on human rights would never develop. When it became obvious this would not be the case, the government took the advice of Stuart Garson and worked to make "the best of a bad job." Neither of these approaches measures up to the image of Canada as a long-standing advocate for the development of international human rights. Certainly, Canada had not been the "consistently strong voice for the protection of human rights" the government would have us believe.

NOTES

1.   "Canada's International Human Rights Policy," Government of Canada, Foreign Affairs and International Trade, last modified March 9, 2012, accessed January 22, 2013, www.international.gc.ca/rights-droits/policy-politique.asp.

2.   William A. Schabas, "Canada and the Adoption of the Universal Declaration of Human Rights," *McGill Law Journal* 43, no. 2 (1998): 403–41; Michael Behiels, "Canada and the Implementation of International Instruments of Human Rights: A Federalist Conundrum, 1919–1982," in *Framing Canadian Federalism: Historical Essays in Honour of John T Saywell*, ed. Dimitry Anastakis and P.E. Bryden (Toronto: University of Toronto Press, 2009), 151–84. See also George Egerton, "Entering the Age of Human Rights: Religion, Politics and Canadian Liberalism, 1945–50," *Canadian Historical Review* 85, no. 3 (2004): 451–79; A.J. Hobbins, "Eleanor Roosevelt, John Humphrey and Canadian Opposition to the Universal Declaration of Human Rights," *International Journal* 53, no. 2 (1998: Spring): 325–42; and Christopher MacLennan, *Toward the Charter: Canadians and the Demand for a National Bill of Rights, 1929–1960* (Montreal and Kingston: McGill–Queen's University Press, 2003), 65–75.

3.   Franklin D. Roosevelt, "Annual Message to Congress," January 6, 1941.

4.   Mark Mazower, "The Strange Triumph of Human Rights, 1933–1950," *Historical Journal* 47, no. 2 (2004): 391; Samuel Moyn, *The Last Utopia: Human Rights in History* (Cambridge, MA: Belknap Press, 2010), 62; Roger Normand and Sarah Zaidi, *Human Rights at the UN: The Political History of Universal Justice* (Bloomington and Indianapolis: Indiana University Press, 2008), 113–20.

5. Kim Richard Nossal, "Cabin'd, Cribb'd, Confin'd?: Canada's Interests in Human Rights," in *Human Rights in Canadian Foreign Policy*, ed. Robert O. Matthews and Cranford Pratt (Kingston and Montreal: McGill–Queen's University Press, 1988), 49–50; John W. Holmes, ed., *The Shaping of Peace: Canada and the Search for World Order, Vol. II* (Toronto: University of Toronto Press, 1979), 44.

6. Normand and Zaidi, *Human Rights at the UN*, 133. See also Louis B. Sohn, "A Short History of United Nations Documents on Human Rights," *The United Nations and Human Rights*, 18th report (New York: Commission to Study the Organization of Peace, 1968): 39–186.

7. Member states were: Australia, Belgium, Byelorussian SSR, Chile, China, Egypt, France, India, Iran, Lebanon, Panama, Philippine Republic, Ukrainian SSR, United Kingdom, United States, USSR, Uruguay, and Yugoslavia.

8. Humphrey wrote the the first draft of the UDHR. John P. Humphrey, *Human Rights & the United Nations: A Great Adventure* (New York: Transnational Publishers, 1984).

9. Humphrey, *Human Rights & the United Nations*, 26.

10. Canada, Parliament, Special Joint Committee on Human Rights and Fundamental Freedoms, *Proceedings, 20th Parliament, 3rd and 4th Sessions*, 1947–8; and Library and Archives Canada (hereafter LAC), RG25, Vol. 6281, File 5475-W-2-40, Part 1.1, "Report on the Draft International Declaration on Human Rights by Inter-Departmental Committee on Human Rights," 1948. Both committees opposed the inclusion of economic and social rights. The parliamentary committee urged explicit recognition of God. The interdepartmental committee was more concerned with the implication of specific articles on existing legislation.

11. Ibid.

12. Throughout October and November, Canada repeatedly proposed that the Declaration be sent to an external international legal body for review, but found little support.

13. For example, see LAC, RG25, Vol. 3701, File 5475-DG-2-40, Canadian Delegation to Lester B. Pearson, October 4, 1948.

14. Ibid., Canadian Delegation to Lester B. Pearson, November 23, 1948.

15. The General Assembly adopted the UDHR by a vote of forty-eight in favour, zero opposed, and seven abstentions.

16. Behiels, "Canada and the Implementation of International Instruments of Human Rights," 154. Behiels refers to the 1937 *Labour Conventions* case in which the provinces challenged laws passed by the federal government to give domestic effect to three conventions of the International Labour Organization.

17. Schabas, "Canada and the Adoption of the Universal Declaration of Human Rights," 441.

18. Ibid.

19. Egerton, "Entering the Age of Human Rights," 451–79.

20. Normand and Zaidi, *Human Rights at the UN*, 200–12.

21. The American delegation proposed the split, recognizing it was in the minority in its opposition to the inclusion of economic, social, and cultural rights, and preferring to keep these rights separate from the more traditional civil and political rights. Canada supported the split for the same reason. The result of the final vote, held in 1952, was twenty-seven in favour, twenty opposed, and three abstentions. LAC, RG25, Vol. 6409, File 5475-W-40, Part 5.2, "Report on the Sixth Session of the General Assembly, Human Rights," February 26, 1952.

22. In 1953 the United States announced it would not ratify the Covenants.

23. LAC, RG25, Vol. 6408, File 5475-W-40, Part 2.2, A.J. Pick to Under-Secretary of State for External Affairs, July 10, 1950.

24. Ibid. Initially, the interest of other departments was limited to one or two articles. For example, Citizenship and Immigration was only interested in Article 8 of the draft Covenant, on freedom of movement.

25. Two private members resolutions were submitted to have Parliament ratify the UDHR, but in each case the Government disposed of the issue by explaining the UDHR did not require

ratification. Canada, *House of Commons Debates*, May 21, 1951, February 28, 1952, and December 7, 1953.

26. In 1956, External Affairs reported that, to date, there had been no communication with the provinces over the UDHR or Covenants. LAC, RG25, Vol. 6927, File 5475-W-15–40, Part 5.2, E.G. Lee to File, November 20, 1956.

27. Schabas, "Canada and the Adoption of the Universal Declaration of Human Rights," 415.

28. LAC, RG25, Vol. 6409, File 5475-W-40–9, Department of External Affairs to Heads of Canadian Posts Abroad, December 31, 1953.

29. LAC, RG25, Vol. 3700, File 5475-DM-1–40, "Statement on Minorities and Minority Rights by Mr. Ralph Maybank in Committee Three," November 27, 1948.

30. LAC, RG25, Vol. 6408, File 5475-W-40, Part 2.2, Stuart Garson to Lester Pearson, June 30, 1950.

31. Ibid., R.G. Robertson to Jules Léger, March 12, 1957.

32. LAC, RG25, Vol. 6407, File 5475-W-40, Part 2.1, "Draft Statement of Canadian Views on International Covenant on Human Rights," April 19, 1950.

33. Behiels, "Canada and the Implementation of International Instruments of Human Rights," 151–84.

34. Ibid., 151. See also: MacLennan, *Toward the Charter*, 63–64.

35. Walter S. Tarnopolsky, *The Canadian Bill of Rights*, 2nd ed. (Toronto: Oxford University Press, 1964), 13.

36. For a discussion of conceptual differences between human rights and civil liberties, see Dominique Clément, *Canada's Rights Revolution: Social Movements and Social Change, 1937–1982* (Vancouver: UBC Press, 2008), particularly 5–10; Ross Lambertson, *Repression and Resistance: Canadian Human Rights Activists, 1930–1960* (Toronto: University of Toronto Press, 2005); and MacLennan, *Toward the Charter*.

37. LAC, RG25, Vol. 6425, File 5475-DP-40, Part 2.1, Jules Léger to the Minister, August 29, 1957.

38. LAC, RG25, Vol. 6281, File 5475-W-2–40, Part 1.1, "Report of the Interdepartmental Committee on Human Rights," April 1948.

39. LAC, RG25, Vol. 6923, File 5475-W-40, Part 12, "Final Report on Item No. 28: Draft International Covenants on Human Rights," 1955.

40. Ibid.

41. LAC, RG25, Vol. 8126, File 5475-DS-18, Part 1.1, "Memorandum to Cabinet: General Instructions to the Canadian Delegation to the Thirteenth Session of ECOSOC," July 23, 1951.

42. LAC, RG25, Vol. 8118, File 5475-W-8–40, Statement by L. Mayrand to the Senate Committee on Human Rights and Fundamental Freedoms, May 3, 1950.

43. LAC, RG25, Vol. 8126, File 5475-DS-18–40, Part 1.1, "Memorandum to Cabinet: General Instructions to the Canadian Delegation to the Thirteenth Session of ECOSOC," July 23, 1951.

44. Ibid., Part 1.3, Lester Pearson to Canadian Delegation to the Thirteenth Session of ECOSOC, August 24, 1951.

45. LAC, RG25, Vol. 6927, File 5475-W-15–40, Part 5.1, N.E. Curie, Department of External Affairs Memo, October 22, 1956.

46. LAC, RG25, Vol. 6409, File 5475-W-40, Part 6, "Canada and the United Nations 1951–52, Section II—Economic and Social," L.A.D. Stephens, United Nations Division, Department of External Affairs, June 14, 1952.

47. Canada abstained in the Third Committee from Articles 6, 7, 8, 9, 10, 11, 12, 14, and 15.

48. R. Brian Howe, "The Evolution of Human Rights Policy in Ontario," *Canadian Journal of Political Science* 24, no. 4 (December 1991): 786.

49. Carmela Patrias, "Socialists, Jews, and the 1947 Saskatchewan Bill of Rights," *The Canadian Historical Review* 87, no. 2 (June 2006): 265–92.

50. Ibid.

51. Howe, 786. See also Clément, *Canada's Rights Revolution*.

52. Clément, *Canada's Rights Revolution*, 12. See also Lambertson, *Repression and Resistance*.

53. Liberal MPs expressed this view throughout the 1940s and early 1950s in debates over a

domestic bill of rights. See, for example Canada, *House of Commons Debates*, May 7, 1946 (Paul Martin), 1311.

54. LAC, RG25, Vol. 6408, File 5475-W-40, Part 2.2, "Observations by Mr. Garson on First Draft of International Covenant on Human Rights," June 27, 1950.

55. Ibid.

56. LAC, RG26, Vol. 81, File 1–24–27, Part 1, Laval Fortier to Under-Secretary of State for External Affairs, February 22, 1955.

57. "Observations by Mr. Garson on First Draft of International Covenant on Human Rights," June 27, 1950; and LAC, RG25, Vol. 3701, File 5475-DP-40, Louis St. Laurent to Canadian Delegation, October 1948.

58. LAC, RG25, Vol. 6408, File 5475-W-40, Part 2.2, "Minutes and Comments of the First Meeting of the Interdepartmental Committee," July 26–27, 1950.

59. Ibid., A.D.P. Heeney to the Chairman of the Canadian Delegation to the United Nations, July 13, 1950.

60. LAC, RG25, Vol. 6281, File 5475-W-2-40, Part 1.1, "Report on the Draft International Declaration on Human Rights by Inter-Departmental Committee on Human Rights," 1948.

61. LAC, RG25, Vol. 6927, File 5475-W-15-40, Part 5.2, E.G. Lee to File, November 20, 1956.

62. LAC, RG6, Vol. 146, File 17–2–4, Part 1, W.H. Barton to Jean H. Lagassé, Department of Citizenship and Immigration, November 15, 1965.

63. LAC, RG25, Vol. 6927, File 5475-W-15-40, Part 5.1, M. Cadieux to Legal Divison, Department of External Affairs, October 17, 1956.

64. Ibid.

65. This indecisive approach to the Covenants was noted in a 1956 internal memo of the Department of External Affairs. LAC, RG25, Vol. 6927, File 5475-W-15-40, Part 5.1, Memo by M. Cadieux, October 23, 1956.

66. LAC, RG25, Vol. 6408, File 5475-W-40, Part 2.2, A.D.P. Heeney to the Chairman of the Canadian Delegation to the United Nations, July 13, 1950.

67. LAC, RG25, Vol. 6409, File 5475-W-40, Part 6, File 5.2, "Statement by Delegate of Canada, Mrs. R.J. Marshall, In the Third Committee of the Sixth Session of the General Assembly on the Draft International Covenant on Human Rights," 1951.

68. Ibid., Escott Reid to A.D.P. Heeney, January 3, 1952.

69. Ibid., A.D.P. Heeney to David M. Johnston, Permanent Delegate of Canada to the UN, January 4, 1952.

70. LAC, RG25, Vol. 6409, File 5475-W-40, "Report on work of Sixteenth Session of ECOSOC," S. Morley Scott, 1952. Canada did not sit on the Commission on Human Rights until 1963.

71. LAC, RG25, Vol. 6927, File 5475-W-15-40, Part 5.1, A.J. Pick to Escott Reid, April 19, 1950.

72. LAC, RG25, Vol. 6425, File 5475-DP-40, Part 2.1, Jules Léger to Secretary of State for External Affairs, August 29, 1957.

73. LAC, RG25, Vol. 6407, File 5475-W-40, Part 2.1, "Draft Statement of Canadian Views on International Covenant on Human Rights," April 19, 1950; and A.J. Pick to Escott Reid, April 19, 1950.

74. These instructions came as early as July 1950. LAC, RG25, Vol. 6408, File 5475-W-40, Part 2.2, Memo from A.D.P. Heeney to the Chairman of the Canadian Delegation to the United Nations, July 13, 1950. They were reiterated when the General Assembly began its article-by-article examination of the Covenants in 1956. LAC, RG26, Vol. 82, File 1–24–27, Part 2, "Report of the Eleventh Session of the Third Committee," 1956.

75. "Report on the Eleventh Session of the General Assembly," 1956.

76. Studies of early Canadian human rights activism focus almost exclusively on the push for domestic legislation. See, for example Lambertson, *Repression and Resistance*; MacLennan, *Toward the Charter*; and Clément, *Canada's Rights Revolution*.

77. LAC, RG2, Vol. 206, File U-41-H-3, Toronto Civil Rights Union to the Privy Council Office, December 9, 1951.

78. LAC, RG25, Vol. 6950, File 5475-DP-1-40 Part 3, Publicity for the UN Declaration of Human Rights.
79. LAC, RG25, Vol. 6950, File 5475-DP-3-40, Part 1.1, Memo to file noting a phone conversation between P. McDougall of External Affairs and Kathleen Bowlby of the UN Association of Canada, September 26, 1957.
80. LAC, RG25, Vol. 8125, File 5475-DM-1-40, Part 2.1, G.C. McInnes to Mr. Thibault, April 13, 1951.
81. LAC, RG25, Vol. 6408, File 5475-W-40, Part 3.1, Memo to Cabinet from the Department of External Affairs, September 8, 1950.
82. The American member of the Commission on Human Rights (Mrs. O.B. Lord) made this announcement on On April 8, 1953.
83. LAC, RG25, Vol. 6425, File 5475-DP-40, Part 2.1, Jules Léger to John Diefenbaker, August 29, 1957.
84. LAC, RG26, Vol. 82, File 1-24-27, "Report of the Eleventh Session of the Third Committee, Department of External Affairs," 1956.
85. Ibid.
86. LAC, RG25, Vol. 6928, File 5475-W-15-40, Part 8, "Report of the Fourteenth Session of the Third Committee of the General Assembly," 1959.
87. LAC, RG25, Vol. 6927, File 5475-W-15-40, Part 6.1, Telegram from the Canadian Delegation to the Department of External Affairs, January 10, 1957.
88. "Growth in United Nations Membership, 1945–present," United Nations Organization, http://www.un.org/en/members/growth.shtml, accessed June 17, 2012.
89. See Normand and Zaidi, *Human Rights at the UN*. In 1957, the Department of External Affairs reported that increasingly debates over the Covenants were reduced to "acrimonious debate" between anti-colonial and so-called colonial countries. Jules Léger to John Diefenbaker, August 29, 1957.
90. LAC, RG25, Vol. 6928, File 5475-W-15-40, Part 8, Memo to Minister, September 2, 1959.
91. LAC, RG25, Vol. 5118, File 5475-W-15-40, Part 9, UN Division to Legal Division, DEA, "Canadian Position on Draft Internatioanl Covenants on Human Rights," Department of External Affairs, January 25, 1962. When the United States announced that it would not be ratifying the Covenants, Canada lost its greatest ally in the quest for a Federal Clause.
92. LAC, RG25, Vol. 6928, File 5475-W-15-40, Part 8, "Report of the Fourteenth Session of the Third Committee of the General Assembly," 1959.
93. Ibid.
94. Adam Chapnick, *The Middle Power Project: Canada and the Founding of the United Nations* (Vancouver: University of British Columbia Press, 2005), 147–48.
95. The adoption of the UDHR was celebrated every year. The fifth, tenth, and fifteenth anniversaries saw more extensive commemoration programs in Canada. See LAC, RG25, Vol. 6950 and Vol. 8125.
96. For an overview of the development of the Canadian Bill of Rights and Diefenbaker's role, see MacLennan, *Toward the Charter*, especially Chap. 6.
97. Diefenbaker himself, while certainly passionate about a Canadian Bill of Rights, took little personal interest in the adoption of the International Covenants on Human Rights.
98. LAC, RG25, Vol. 6927, File 5475-W-15-40, Part 5.1, M. Cadieux to Legal Division (DEA), October 23, 1956.
99. LAC, RG25, Vol. 6409, File 5475-W-40, Part 5.2, Memo from F.M Tovell, United Nations Divison, to M. Scott, re: Human Rights—Mr. Garson's Views, March 10, 1952.
100. LAC, RG25, Vol. 5118, File 5475-W-15-40, Part 9, Memo to Legal Division from UN Division, "Canadian Position on Draft International Covenants on Human Rights (Civil and Political Rights)," January 25, 1962.
101. LAC, RG25, Vol. 6928, File 5475-W-15-40, Part 7.2, "Final Report on the Thirteenth Session, Third Committee of the General Assembly," January 8, 1959.

102. LAC, RG25, Vol. 13112, File 45–13–2–3, Part 1, M.H. Wershof to Head of the UN Division of External Affairs, December 17, 1963.
103. In the article-by-article votes within the General Assembly, Canada abstained on most of the articles within provincial jurisdiction. Ibid., E.G. Lee to G.S. Murray, Department of External Affairs, January 20, 1964.
104. Behiels, "Canada and International Instruments of Human Rights," 170–77.
105. LAC, MG31, Vol. 19, Files 12–14, LHR Human Rights Covenants Campaign: correspondence.
106. LAC, RG25, Vol. 13650, File 45–13–2–3, Part 10, "Briefing Book Entry: Canada's Proposed Accession to the International Human Rights Instruments."
107. LAC, RG25, Vol. 13650, File 45–13–2–3, Part 10, Internal memo from J.S. Stanford, Director of the Legal Advisory Division, April 12, 1976.
108. LAC, RG25, Vol. 14947, File 45-CDA-13-1-1, A.S. Shortliffe to W.H. Barton, February 8, 1967.
109. LAC, RG25, Vol. 15901 File 45-CDA-13-1-1, Part 2, "The Impact of Human Rights on Canadian Foreign Policy," V.M. Edelstein, United Nations Division, Department of External Affairs, May 18, 1979.
110. Normand and Zaidi, *Human Rights at the UN*, 200.
111. Holmes, *The Shaping of Peace*, 292.

Chapter 7

•◆•

Children's Rights from Below: Canadian and Transnational Actions, Beliefs, and Discourses, 1900–1989[1]

Dominique Marshall

INTRODUCTION

Who uses the language of children's rights, and in which circumstances? Who in the past has defined the notion and fought for its recognition, and which traditions did they rely on? How have this rhetoric and the related legal instruments influenced social practices and representations? How does this history relate to the general history of human rights? Ninety years after the adoption of the first universal Declaration of the Rights of the Child by the League of Nations, and twenty-five years after the Convention on the Rights of the Child of the United Nations, historians can help in understanding the roles and meanings of universal entitlements for the young. Based on close examinations of social movements, personal engagements, and institutions, this paper attempts to show what social forces have, on occasion, led children's rights to play a significant role in public life, in Canada and abroad. It analyzes the elements of the ready popularity of the rights of the child, and its timing, to see how, why, and by whom such notion has been evoked. It also pays attention to the scale of the politics of children's rights to show how complex the entanglements of those invoking them have been with local, regional, national, and international institutions.[2]

THE DECLARATION OF THE RIGHTS OF THE CHILD OF THE LEAGUE OF NATIONS, 1924

In 1910, the Commercial and Sanitary Department of the British Foreign Office received an invitation from Belgium to participate in an international gathering on the health of the newborn. In the margin of the correspondence, an official asked his colleagues why the Foreign Office, of all places, should "take these infants in charge?"[3] After a few more letters of this kind, British diplomats started to take these exchanges about the welfare and the status of children seriously. Fourteen years later in Geneva, on September 26, 1924, the British delegation to the General Assembly of the League of Nations championed the adoption of the Declaration of the Rights of the Child (DRC), "the first international declaration of rights in world history."[4] Moreover, the British would dominate the work of the Child Welfare Committee of the League of Nations, created the same month.

What had happened in between? And why were children the first objects of an international declaration of human rights? The social movements that carried claims to children's rights across borders had been widespread and growing, and they had become too important to ignore. At home in Britain, many constituencies had alerted the Foreign Office to the transnational nature of children's lives and to the importance of childhood in the diplomacy of war and peace. Abroad, the Belgians were centralizing the interests of many national movements for child welfare, and gathering an authority which London set to challenge. The Save the Children International Union (SCIU) was the main author of the Declaration of the Rights of the Child. An examination of the nature and motivations of the SCIU leadership and alliances of the movements they represented helps understand what these activists tried to accomplish and how they had come to think of children's rights as the best way to do it.[5]

In the short term, the SCIU initiative came from the First World War, when the amount of popular support for international child saving surprised even its early proponents, and focused their actions. The ingredients of this public support were many. At a time when the international treaties on war protected only soldiers and prisoners,[6] the rights of children presented a way to address the vulnerability of all. The Declaration's author and future founder of the Save the Children International Union, Eglantyne Jebb, wrote explicitly to the head of the International Prisoner-of-War Agency of the Red Cross, Adolphe Ferrière, that she wanted to do for children what the Red Cross had done for soldiers.[7] During the war, Eglantyne and her sister Dorothy had translated German news to try to maintain among the British public a sense that the Germans, adults and children alike, were not all the enemies depicted by the propaganda. After the Armistice, they had lobbied the British government to stop the blockade imposed on the vanquished. Putting their principles to work, they launched a collection of money to feed the starving children of Vienna. They used the latest techniques of information and publicity, and the levy mobilized an unprecedented amount of public support, from many classes, creeds, and soon other countries.[8] The International Committee of the Red Cross redirected the efforts of its International Prisoner-of-War Agency toward the activity of the SCIU, and Pope Benedict XV endorsed the new organization's campaigns, bringing to its treasury the donations of thousands of Catholics.[9] All the while, SCIU founders insisted on the rational and international aspect of their project of saving children; such emphasis on universal principles represents an essential ingredient in the history of human rights.[10]

Public campaigns for the children of Central and Eastern Europe followed, as well as a massive fundraising operation in favour of Russian children struck by famine. But only a few years after the SCIU creation, the popular enthusiasm for the help of children of former enemies waned. In order to keep its practical work of relief going, the SCIU lowered its critique of European diplomacy; within the Union, the ideas of justice and reason that had informed the campaign against the blockade receded before the work of those who emphasized emotions of compassion.[11] International child saviours watched their supporters' efforts and donations shift toward exclusive domestic concerns, mainly for the construction and reconstruction of national institutions of child welfare. In this context, those who wanted to salvage the transnational co-operation of wartime thought that their best chance was to commit national governments to a common declaration of the rights of children.

The theme of childhood also figured prominently among those who thought that only a democratization of international relations would help prevent wars. They conceived of the League of Nations as a "model of rational participation,"[12] which would convey the wishes of world public opinion. As Hans-Martin Jaeger suggests, the theme of childhood had been central to those who argued that the formation of an international public was possible: to them, the very fact that people readily saw dependent children as wards entrusted to the community was the best proof of the existence of a world public opinion.[13] Many internationalist and pacifist movements arrived at childhood as the last possible theme of mobilization for the construction of world public opinion. More pragmatically, they counted on the rights of the child as a theme that would help them keep their relevance in the larger public, raise funds, and muster a new generation of supporters.[14]

The Declaration of 1924 was also the outcome of pressures toward entitlements for children across borders, which had been present in northern democracies long before 1914. They had come from groups of women,[15] workers, and middle-class philanthropists, who placed children first in their domestic demands for justice, reform, or social control. International exchanges had played many roles in the respective histories of these movements from the mid-nineteenth century onwards: shared information helped establish the nature of the problems they were fighting—as a result, an appreciation of the transnational scale of some of these problems alerted them to the need for universal standards; shared methods and alliances strengthened their respective leverage at home; common work demonstrated the worth and potential of an international community. Children themselves helped place children's rights on the international agenda. Historians have only begun to research their political struggles. For instance, many children who received relief from the Commission for the Relief Belgium of Herbert Hoover during the war considered this material help to be an entitlement rather than a gift.[16] More forcefully, the growth of youth movements in the interwar years and the ability of communist and fascist movements to attract youth, turned many politicians' attention to the demands of the young.[17]

The text of the Declaration of the Rights of the Child of the League of Nations represented the recognition "by all men and women of all nations" that "mankind owes to the Child the best that it has to give." It listed five entitlements for children, which were as many duties for mankind: material and spiritual development; aid to hungry, sick, backward, delinquent, orphaned, and erring children; priority relief in time of emergency; preparation for work and protection from exploitation; and preparation for "the service of fellow men." But there was no official mechanism in place at the League of Nations to monitor the progress of the new principles of the Declaration of the Rights of the Child. So what became of these rights after 1924? Who referred to the Declaration? How did it influence politics? While it is difficult to follow and gauge the general impact of the Declaration on the status of the world's children, we can gather some significant elements of answers from the work of historians.

One hope of the authors of the Declaration was that its principles would become well known worldwide, and that this knowledge would bring the five principles to life. The very simplicity of the text made it easy to remember, even by the children it was meant to protect. Accordingly, much publicity followed the unanimous adoption by the General Assembly of the League of Nations in the fall of 1924, from radio programs to reprints, articles in newspapers, posters, and poetic adaptations. The League of Nations' Child Welfare Committee, professional associations of social workers, and the SCIU all contributed to this transnational work of diffusion. In France, a copy had to be hung in every school.[18] When the Christmas issue of the bulletin of the Social Service Council of Canada reproduced the text on its front page, a schoolteacher of Alberta proceeded to assess the lives of children in her district against the five principles. She sent the resulting document to the bulletin, and the Save the Children International Union reprinted it in its quarterly publication, as an example of the influence of the Declaration. Offprints of the Canadian report circulated widely, until the Canadian officials of External Affairs judged that this represented an undue intrusion in domestic matters. They alerted League of Nations officials, who instructed SCIU leaders to stop circulating the report, which they did.[19]

A more direct way to promote the rights of the child would be the activities of the Child Welfare Committee of the League. One related hope was that common work on international projects dear to all nations would assuage international animosities and prepare for the harder work of solving territorial conflicts. The membership of the Child Welfare Committee was a mix of national representatives chosen by their respective governments, assessors appointed by non-governmental organizations such as the SCIU and the Girls Guides, and international civil servants of the International Labour Organization and the Health Committee of the League of Nations, supported by two employees of the social section of the League's Secretariat. At a time when there was no mechanism for the official recognition of the consultative status of NGOs by the League, the very selection of the assessors depended on a diplomacy dominated by the British and the Americans. The influence of the humanitarian assessors invited to the table was to be independent from national governments, but they lost their voting power in the mid-1930s. A diminutive budget and only occasional grants from private agencies further limited the committee's ability to accomplish its mandate of investigation and setting of standards.[20]

We know of several important failures of the League of Nations' work on behalf of children: the agencies responsible for the Declaration of 1924 were denied the League's material support to continue to work for the relief of children in the postwar world, in defiance of the second and the third principles; similarly, projects for a convention relative to the protection of foreign minors never overcame national governments' fear of having to pay for the welfare of their parents.[21] In all of these instances, entrusting the promotion of human rights to the member states of the League of Nations curtailed the formation of world public opinion envisaged by many promoters of the Declaration of the Rights of the Child of 1924. Still, the League and the committee are remembered for their pioneering reports on child placement and orphanages, nutrition, the treatment of young offenders and foreign minors, and international adoption and traffic; for the collection and publication of national statistics on child welfare; and for the vast operation of rescue of Armenian children.[22]

The impact of the League of Nations' Declaration of the Rights of the Child on national legislation was not insignificant: a close examination of the politics of childhood in the province of Quebec shows that in 1944, Geneva's standards for the placement of children in families legitimized the claims of the commission intent on breaking the monopoly of the Catholic Church on orphanages;[23] and that, in return, the work of Quebec's clinics against tuberculosis became an example of good practice for the Child Welfare Committee's members. As a result, the League of Nations' work on behalf of children remained its most popular aspect among Canadians during the interwar years. In fact, it was the one kind of international collaboration which received the most interest among the Canadian groups supporting the League, such as the League of Nations Associations, the Women's Christian Temperance Union, and the Canadian Red Cross Society.[24]

In the United States in 1922 and 1928, a Bill of Rights for Children, which also originated in humanitarian work on behalf of children hurt by the war in Europe, had an important and long-lasting effect. It was written by Herbert Hoover to inform the work of the American Child Health Association (ACHA), based on the Declaration of the League, where many American reformers collaborated in the work of the Child Welfare Committee. The Bill successfully galvanized the energies of child welfare, and an updated version acted as a focus for the work of the White House Conference of 1931. The text was disseminated, celebrated, widely mentioned in the press, and invoked by activists. Again, measuring the

general impact of the Bill is difficult, but the history of the rights of children to birth registration is instructive. Leaders of the ACHA judged that
birth registration was a precondition to all other rights of children, and
it embarked on a campaign for uniform state laws and strong systems of
implementation. In doing so, they invited American parents to claim such
reform in the name of the rights of their children. The campaigns were a
success. Only where the population was otherwise disenfranchised was the
progress of the child registration bureaucracy slowed down: where there
existed large concentrations of Native and Afro-American families. In this
case, the voluntary sector was the main force behind the promotions of
the rights of the child, in accordance with conservative ideals of public life.

Meanwhile in Geneva, the authors of the Declaration of the Rights
of the Child undertook to promote children's rights on their own, in
addition to the work of their representative with the Child Welfare
Committee of the League of Nations. First, they compiled a world survey,
in order to make children's problems widely known; they organized summer schools to teach technical means to lift the standards of children's
lives throughout the world, and published an international child welfare
review. Again, the effect of this work is not easy to gauge. But we know
that sending to Geneva statistics of their progress in this area became a
means for new states to make their mark among nations, and that the
incentive encouraged many of them to accelerate the creation of their
child welfare apparatus.[25]

In the meantime, SCIU leaders believed that the best way to keep
the spirit of the Declaration alive was to extend its reach to non-Euro-
pean countries. Making sure that the rights of the child existed "above
all considerations of race, nationality or creed" as the preamble of the
Declaration stated, would be the true test of its universality; for some,
it was even the most important aspect of the rights of children.[26] Such
gestures toward racial equality came from the wider critique of Western
civilization, which had not only motivated the movement against the
blockade of Europe during the First World War, but included a critique
of imperialism.[27]

SCIU leaders embarked on a campaign for the rights of African children, beginning with a widespread inquiry in 1928 and a conference in
1931.[28] Mindful of not imposing European standards, they wished to
encourage children to contribute to their civilization by being aware of
their heritage and of what others had to propose. For this reason, they

insisted that Africans should be included.[29] But their invitations were carefully crafted to avoid conflicts, and limited finances prevented many from accepting. In the end a dozen of people of African descent registered among the 200 participants. East African nationalist leader Jomo Kenyatta, for instance, figured among the list of participants mainly because he was helped by a British reformist patron who paid for his passage. In this context, it is not surprising that the large majority of attendees would be European missionaries. They adopted the language of children's rights with ease, used as they were to consider the spiritual equality of natives and to think of African adults as children in need of the compassionate guidance of Western instructors.[30]

THE RIGHTS OF THE AFRICAN CHILD, 1928–1939

In 1931, the Afro-American communist and future vice-presidential candidate James W. Ford made a spectacular speech on the rights of African children in Geneva. An uninvited guest at the SCIU Conference of the African Child, he surprised the participants, two hundred or so missionaries, League of Nations officials, colonial administrators, doctors, humanitarians, and a handful of African delegates, by arguing that the notion of the rights of the child as it was articulated in the Declaration of the Rights of the Child of 1924 was a way for colonial powers to deny the political rights of adults; saving children was a "hypocritical gesture invented because you fear that the African population that produces huge profits may die out and endanger the income of imperialist coupon clippers."[31] Even when it concerned the young, the project of universal rights of children ignored the profound economic reforms required for a true promotion of their well-being. Ford advocated more radical social and economic rights—free hospitals, free and universal schools and colleges for everybody, unemployment insurance—and the range of political rights which had been discarded by the authors of the Covenant of the League of Nations: freedom to organize unions, the restitution of lands to local populations, the right to self-determination, and the right of colonial people to refuse to serve in metropolitan armies.[32] Ford was on his way back from Moscow where, as a guest of the Soviet government, he had discussed the politics of race and communism. He had also stopped by Amsterdam for the international congress of African workers. But for the delegation of the International Labour Office, headed at the time by a socialist, the Europeans present shunned his speech.

More importantly, the dozen of African delegates did not share his outrage. Why did they come? And what use did they have for the language of the rights of the African child? We know that on the day of the adoption of the Declaration of the Rights of the Child by the General Assembly seven years earlier, the delegate from Japan, whose country had championed in vain the principle of racial equality during the drafting of the Covenant of the League of Nations, had declared that the text was the proof of nations' commitment to racial equality.[33] Like Japan, most participants at the Conference of the African Child saw in the apparently benign language of universal entitlements for children an opportunity to address questions that were pressing in their own societies, in the context of harsh inequality in front of which the Covenant had proved to be useful.

One debate, however, pitted the African delegates against European humanitarians: female circumcision. It opposed the East African Jomo Kenyatta and the British Duchess of Atholl, representing women's unions. To Kenyatta and the Kikuyu Central Association he represented, this was a matter of national prerogatives, and humanitarian standards could not trump national customs. But even in this case, he argued that Europeans and Africans needed to work with "sympathy and mutual understanding . . . to go back to the real causes of these customs, which had received the religious or political sanction of people."[34] It is in this spirit that the African representatives sanctioned Kenyatta's position.

What happened to the conference's resolutions? The first outcome was research education and advocacy, in the best tradition of the Save the Children movement, and a Child Protection Committee (CPC), led from London and Geneva, would be responsible for the work. It set to document the extent and nature of infant mortality. Like Hoover at the same time in the United States, volunteer doctors and SCIU officials focused on birth registration as the fundamental reform to ensure children's health. But the corresponding means in the civil society were lacking: no tight network of African doctors and of volunteers as in the United States, a situation similar to that of the residual pockets of Afro-Americans and Natives of the country. Moreover, there was no enfranchised citizenry of parents able to carry the claims of a child's right to registration. Only from the 1960s onward would African experts in public health statistics be organized enough to promote such data collection. And only much later in the 1990s would some humanitarian groups such as Plan

International and UNICEF be able to promote the right of children to birth registration (now enshrined in the 1989 Convention of the Rights of the Child) by educating and organizing citizens. The SCIU also made representations to the Child Welfare Committee regarding child labour in European colonies, with no immediate consequence.

Conference participants had great hopes for future fieldwork. Such ambitions were quickly curtailed by the lack of funds and the reluctance of European powers to let humanitarians enter their jurisdictions. One of the Africans who had not made it to the conference in Geneva for lack of means, H. Quarmina Hesse, a Gold Coast student of the School of Medicine at Durham University in Newcastle upon Tyne, observed rightly that universal ideals for African children were compromised the minute they were entrusted to colonial states: "I was not surprised to hear that the main issues were studiously avoided. No doubt that the body that organized the conference sincerely sought to arrive at the truth of the matter, but they made the first move toward defeating that object when they invited delegates from the Governments."[35]

The exceptional circumstances of the Ethiopian war broke this deadlock. Called in by Haile Selassie, Emperor of Ethiopia, to help civilians suffering from the war, the SCIU delegate, Frédérique Small, dealt directly with an autonomous African government over the protestation of Britain. The Emperor welcomed her field intervention, in the name of the urgency of war, for a child welfare centre for children of soldiers to be located in the capital. It was a first in the history of humanitarianism. The SCIU was able to raise public funds by evoking the emergency of the conflict, and the embryonic Ethiopian Red Cross provided the welcoming structure and the parameter of the work.[36] In a hierarchical society, their only volunteers came from the aristocratic class. Six months after her arrival in the fall of 1936, Frédérique Small returned to Europe. This was as long as the Emperor has promised; the funds quickly dried up, as the attention of the European public shifted toward the Spanish civil war.[37] The Emperor's own ability to invoke human rights would be long curtailed, as the history of the UN refusal to include Ethiopia in the War Crimes Commissions shows.[38]

For a decade, the CPC became a meeting ground for African internationalists present in London such as Una Marson, Harold Moody, and Stella Thomas. As in the more general history of the interwar years, under the umbrella of a transnational NGO, the language of human rights could offer a tool to criticize oppressive governments.[39] Nationalist leaders had invested many hopes in the creation of the League of Nations and in the League's commitment toward the self-determination of peoples. Historians have shown how the principles often proved to be "diplomatic platitudes." But they have also shown that in mandated territories, the Leagues' principles served as a beacon for nationalist struggles for justice. For many of these members of the African elite and of the diaspora, the conference acted at once as an important point in their reflection about the politics of childhood and as a legitimation of their own positions in their respective societies. In a later period, their encounter with the SCIU would help bring to life public institutions of child welfare and education. In this way, the conference can be considered as a brief moment of experimentation where some Western and African elites debated themes of world peace, self-determination, and the place of human rights in constitutions.[40]

THE UNITED NATIONS DECLARATION OF THE RIGHTS OF THE CHILD OF 1959

In 1948, John Humphrey, the Canadian lawyer who was Secretary of the Commission of Human Rights of the United Nations, received an official demand from the SCIU that the UN update the League of Nations Declaration of the Rights of the Child to acknowledge the evolution of standards of the protection of children. To SCIU officials, who had asked for such an update since the beginning of the UN, Humphrey objected that the UN Charter and UDHR, by addressing the rights of all, made the DRC obsolete.[41] Ten years later, the UN General Assembly adopted its own Declaration of the Rights of the Child. Far from being obsolete, the Declaration now represented a list of the "special safeguards for the child, by reason of his physical and mental immaturity" which the UDHR had called for. Why had Humphrey changed his mind?

The UN Declaration of 1959 was the first document of its kind after the UDHR, the only one the HR Commission could agree upon in the context of the Cold War.[42] It added five new principles to the League of Nations' document of 1924: a stronger responsibility for national governments; an explicit mention of the importance of voluntary organizations; more specific entitlements to social and economic rights; and play, love, and happiness as the entitlement of the young. Eastern countries' objections to binding international laws concerning civic and political rights for adults, which brought the work of the Human Rights Commission to a standstill, could accommodate the civic and political rights promised to children: a name, a nationality, and the means to prepare for their "energy and talents [to] be devoted to the service of . . . fellow men." Conversely, Western members of the Human Rights Commission, reluctant to promise social security and education to all, welcomed engagements toward welfare and instruction more easily when they concerned future generations. Moreover, with India present at the table, another kind of consideration helped push the cause of the rights of children from the developing world: international entitlements would help governments of countries where malnutrition and poverty were widespread to call on the resources of the developed world.[43]

Behind such diplomatic manoeuvrings, the UN was answering demands from below. In this case, the history of the Canadian political culture of the 1940s offers some examples from the Western bloc. The rhetoric of the rights of the child played an important role in public life in at least two significant instances. First, the launch of the program of universal family allowances in 1945 was presented by the federal government to the public as a "Children's Charter," a law that would ensure Canadian youngsters' rights to education and welfare. Second, on the external face of the state, Canadian diplomats on their way to New York in 1947 to oppose the creation of a permanent UNICEF changed their minds when they understood how much the Canadian public was investing in the new processes which led to the adoption of the UDHR.[44] The universal rights of the child had come to represent a powerful theme of popular mobilization and legitimacy. Why, and to what effect?

Of all the promises of universal equality made by the Canadian government to its soldiers and the home front during the Second World War, family allowances became the first to be fulfilled and, in some ways, the last. By promising them on the eve of the general election of 1944, Prime Minister Mackenzie King was responding to general pressures from the electorate and specific claims from trade unions, soldiers, and mothers, and attempting to resolve problems of national unity.[45] The family allowances program, the first universal welfare measure in the history of Canada, catered to the immediate demands of people employed in war work for wages that would allow them to raise a family. It also offered to working mothers of the home front a material acknowledgement of their domestic responsibilities. In addition, it referred to an older rhetoric of self-help and household respectability.[46] The precedent of the soldiers' dependents' allowances of 1939 helped much: a fully state-sponsored program that had shown that families acted responsibly with public allowances and had broken to some degree the stigma attached to welfare payments, to give them the prestige of a wage for mothers. Family allowances stood as the first, and the symbol, of many of the reforms toward a comprehensive program of social security, which had been long in the making during the last years of the Depression. If such a reduction from the promises for all citizens to programs for children was easily accomplished, it is partly because the government of Mackenzie King was not denying the promises of equality made to all, but only delaying them to the next generation. At the symbolic level, the tradition of speaking of social policies in the language of kin was familiar to the populations of Western countries,[47] and made family allowances an easier program to enact.

If the use of the rights of the child by governing powers can be seen as a reluctant commitment to the welfare of all, the fact that the strategy worked is not insignificant. They referred to a long tradition of the promotion of children's rights from below. In Quebec, trade unions were fighting for children's rights to compulsory schooling; to those who objected that the obligation to send one's children to school represented an infringement of parental rights, the editors of the newspaper *Le Monde ouvrier* answered that it was an obligation they were ready to fulfill. In this way, "human rights were viewed by both sides as a reliable means of anchoring their position on the moral high ground."[48] And the new public role imparted to children and women during the war had added to their sense of entitlement. The program called for an unprecedented operation of identification of the population under sixteen years old. The systematic and centralized review of the provincial systems of birth registration established more firmly citizens' public identity and belonging.[49]

Another explanation from below for the timing and the content of Declaration of the Rights of the Child of 1959 comes from the history of humanitarian aid to children during the Second World War. Conventions on the treatment of civilians in wartime were still a fact of the future and, again, the rights of children often stood for those of all non-combatants. This movement from below took a different form than the mobilization of the First World War. Groups such as the SCIU, now the International Union of Child Welfare, continued to help,[50] but the bulk of aid to enemy children belonged to the United Nations

Relief and Rehabilitation Administration (UNRRA). In a context of total war, Allied forces decided to give aid only to civilians once liberated. What was devised instead was that for those who joined the Atlantic alliance, the promises of the Atlantic Charter of 1941, the international document listing the universal social entitlements for individuals in the Allied countries, would be honoured.[51] This made for more systematic aid organized by governments. UNRRA included a special branch devoted to children only, and it enjoyed a popularity similar to that of the Save the Children Fund two decades earlier. The extraordinary fate of the film *Seeds of Destiny* illustrates this well, which raised $200 million for UNRRA and won an Academy Award, by showing to Western audiences how the starved children of today would become the Hitlers of tomorrow.[52] The folding of UNRRA at the end of the war followed the familiar pattern of the previous war. In the face of such disengagement, the same constituencies argued for the continuation of child welfare work, at least temporarily. Sudden withdrawal from occupied territories would plant the seed of war, and the better way to counter these dark forces was to fulfill the entitlements due to children. UNICEF was intended to last a few years longer, until the budget of UNRRA was spent. When humanitarians argued for the continuation of UNICEF, the Canadian diplomats of the Liberal government of Louis St. Laurent disagreed, mindful of the financial commitment this would entail. But, as we have seen earlier, they had to change their position in the light of the support human rights was gathering at home.

Uses of the rhetoric of children's rights seem to have receded after 1959, first because newly independent countries in the developing world broke the deadlock at the Human Rights Commission of the United Nations, a role foreshadowed by India in 1959. The new collaboration led in 1966 to the two Covenants pertaining to civil and political rights and to economic, social, and cultural rights. These binding documents included rights that were specific to children, such as the entitlement to registration at birth, but that were part of a list that pertained to all. Second, as contemporary humanitarians acknowledged, there seem to have been a diminished interest from below for international instruments of justice.[53] Recent historians of human rights argue that it is only in the 1970s that organizations like Amnesty International finally channelled energies from below to constitute a global public strong enough to counter the power of nation-states over international organizations. The history of former campaigns in favour of children's rights, and a closer look at the origins of Amnesty, suggest that it was not the first organization to focus on human rights in the hope of mobilizing an otherwise disillusioned and apathetic public.[54]

The movement toward children's rights per se became vocal again around 1979, on the occasion of the twentieth anniversary of the Declaration, when UNICEF coordinated an International Year of the Child (IYC) around the principles of 1959.[55] Those who initiated the celebrations hoped that a campaign in the name of children would gather more energies than contemporary international campaigns of a more general nature. They ensured that the organization of the IYC would be decentralized to avoid what they called the politicization of the issue. A remarkable number of NGOs and states, from both the North and the South, received the invitation enthusiastically and initiated local inquiries, legislative reviews, and programs, in a fashion that recalls the large movement of compassion of 1919. As a result, private contributions to UNICEF increased.

This round of campaigning in favour of children distinguished itself from former movement for the rights of the child by its inclusion of claims for political entitlements of children as children; the Convention on the Rights of the Child of 1989, which crowned the campaign started in 1979, included an important series of articles empowering children far beyond the promises of being raised to be responsible citizens of the former Declarations. The radical expression of this movement was that of child liberationists who demanded full citizenship for the young.[56] In Canada, a milder form of children's influence came from the Canadian Commission for the International Year of the Child, which toured the country to listen to children of all classes. Its chairperson, Landon Pearson, remembers how surprised she was to hear about the recurring difficulty of young people to be respected in public places, and the suspicion which they encountered. Her attitude was directly informed by her own experience as a child during the Second World War, when she had been trusted by many institutions of the home front, and shows how dangerous it is to assume a linear progression toward a better situation.[57]

One of the most memorable instances of support from below for the International Year of the Child came from South Africa, where the apartheid government had avoided the IYC because its potential effect of publicizing the conditions of black children in the country.

But anti-apartheid groups seized the opportunity offered by the UN to document and publicize the living conditions in the Bantustans and reserves. According to Monica Patterson, the historian of this campaign, the Year of the Child met many needs at once: since there was a large proportion of young people among those fighting against apartheid, the language of the Declaration of the Rights of the Child of the United Nations of 1959 gave a universal resonance to the movement, and added to its legitimacy.

At the initiative of its women's secretariat, the African National Congress (ANC) of South Africa published a pamphlet entitled "Our Children," which highlighted the effect of apartheid on children; it could reach a larger international public, more receptive to the language of humanitarianism. Finally, activities conducted in the name of children, with their apparent innocence, could provide a cloak to more politically challenging causes.[58]

Patterson also shows how, in other circumstances, the ANC's appropriation of the campaigns for the rights of children represented a way to control the youth associated with the movement against apartheid. Such defence of national authority by the leaders of movement of liberation—which recalls Kenyatta's position on female circumcision fifty years previously—helps explain why the optional protocols for the rights of child soldiers enacted later were so uneven: tolerated by armies of rebels, children soldiers are often vilified by the same groups once they are in power.[59]

THE CONVENTION OF THE RIGHTS OF THE CHILD, 1989

Canadian Prime Minister Brian Mulroney became the co-chair of the eleventh UN Summit on the Convention of the Rights of the Child of 1990. In the meantime, at home, he presided over the abolition of universal family allowances, despite the overwhelming support for the measure demonstrated at the parliamentary committee on family allowances, launching instead a program of tax credits and a war against child poverty which did little to diminish inequalities. Seen this way, the rights of children seem to stand for the retreat from the guarantee of the rights of all. The story becomes more complicated when we consider that Mulroney also championed the rights of black people in South Africa and led the boycott movement among Commonwealth nations, much of which was conducted in the name of ending the misery of black children. But this use of the rights of the child, as critics have pointed out, represents a kind of imperialism.[60] It recalls the conservative participants of the conference of 1931, who were keen on "civilizing" the parental habits of colonial peoples while they accepted large measures of injustice at home and abroad. How could such a position be maintained?

During the International Year of the Child, many used the UN Declaration of the Rights of the Child of 1959 as tool for education, ensuring not only the publicity of the notion but also a widespread realization of the weakness of the instrument and the discussion of new subjects— street children and disabled children in particular—and new approaches. The history of the Convention from below remains to be researched, but we know that NGOs played an exceptional role in its drafting and its subsequent monitoring.[61] The Canadian part of the story shows that a rising interest among citizens, as well as a remarkable preference for charities working on behalf of children of the global South, informed the actions of Conservative Prime Minister Brian Mulroney. Like his British predecessors of the 1910s, there was more than international positioning in his diplomacy of child welfare.[62]

Now that legally binding principles were at stake, the demand for precision accounted for much of the document, and delegates from the global South, significantly present for the first time for the drafting of a universal list of children's rights, were the most insistent. This largely explains the length of the document of fifty-four articles, ten times more than in 1924, when a child could remember the list of her entitlements. In 1990, the Organisation of African Unity also adopted its own African Charter on the Rights and Welfare of the Child. This regional and complementary document owes its existence to the wish to express African cultural values.[63] Observers have shown how the thorough mechanism of implementation can be viable only if it receives the support of a strong and informed public. For this task, they call on the efforts of public opinion, in a way which recalls the efforts of the promoters of the League of Nations Declaration of the Rights of the Child in Africa in the 1930s. But the political culture of the 1990s had changed: the examination of the fate of one of the provisions of the Convention, the rights of children to registration at birth, shows that the campaigns for birth registrations in Africa of the last two decades resemble the American campaigns of the 1930s: the NGOs and UN agencies rely on the education of citizens to muster the public support necessary for the promotion and the implementation of the entitlement.[64]

CONCLUSION

Historians have helped in better understanding what causes sudden and widespread movements of sympathy toward children, and what legal entitlements for children can lead to. This review of a century of uses of children's rights from below shows, to use the words of the historian of the rescue of Armenian children in the 1920s, the "contingent and circumscribed nature of allegedly universal human rights conceptions at the moment."[65] Children's rights can offer specific kinds of leverage, specific ways to muster public opinions, and an idiom for discussions on the democratization of public life. There are also ways by which children's universal rights have been used to limit people's citizenship; in such instances, they represented, to use this time Mark Mazower's expression, a "way of doing nothing and avoiding commitment."[66] Contradictory and varied traditions of actions, beliefs, and discourses have accompanied the making of the rights of children over the last century; and today's claims bear the marks of this history.

NOTES

1. Acknowledgements: I thank the audience and organizers of the conference on the new history of the League of Nations in Geneva, August 2011, for their generous comments on a preliminary version of this text. My current work is made possible by the financial support of a SSHRC institutional grant.

2. On the need to "measure the claims of human rights against other political claims and projects," see Jay Winter's "Review Essay on Samuel Moyn. *The Last Utopia* ... and Michael Barnett, *Empire of Humanity* ... ," H-Diplo, April 20, 2012, http://h-net.msu.edu/cgi-bin/logbrowse. pl?trx=vx&list=H-Diplo&month=1204&week=c&msg=CpaFZDDnzrjgYN4jddwkEQ&user =&pw= (accessed March 2012). On the importance of understanding the complex agendas leading to the current "international human rights regime," and of reflecting on the specific role of children's rights in this constellation, see this books' editors' "Research Brief," which prompted the writing of this article. Research Workshop on the Impact of the Universalism of Human Rights in the 20th Century in the English-speaking World," March 1–2, 2012, McMaster University, Hamilton.

3. UK National Archives, Foreign Office, FO, Commercial and Sanitary Department: General Correspondence from 1906, 368, 386 1910, 11458. Manuscript comment in the margin.

4. Samuel Moyn, *The Last Utopia: Human Rights in History* (Cambridge, MA: Belknap Press, 2010), 257, n.39; this is the only allusion to the rights of children in the book. Paul Gordon Lauren, *Visions Seen: The Evolution of International Human Rights* (Philadelphia: University of Pennsylvania Press, 1998); "Geneva Declaration of the Rights of the Child, Adopted 26 September, 1924, League of Nations", Preamble and article 5, www.un-documents.net/ gdrc1924.htm (accessed September, 2012).

5. This story has been told many times, but the recent and best-documented account comes from Emily Baughan, "'Every Citizen of Empire Implored to Save the Children!' Empire,

Internationalism and the Save the Children Fund in Interwar Britain," *Historical Research* 86, no. 231 (February 2013) doi: 10.1111/j.1468–2281.2012.00608.x. See also Linda Mahood, *Feminism and Voluntary Action: Eglantyne Jebb and Save the Children, 1876–1928* (New York: Palgrave Macmillan, 2009), and my article, "The Formation of Childhood as an Object of International Relations: The Child Welfare Committee and the Declaration of Children's Rights of the League of Nations," *International Journal of Children's Rights* 7, no. 2 (1999), 103–47.

6. Annette Becker, "The Dilemmas of Protecting Civilians in Occupied Territory: The Precursor of World War," *International Review of the Red Cross* 94, no. 885 (Spring 2012): 117–32.

7. For Jebb's own acknowledgement of Ferrière's influence, see Archives of the Save the Children Fund, SF/22, letter to Ferrière, June 27, 1924. It is significant that Jebb founded the SCIU in the hall where the Red Cross had started; Francesca M. Wilson, *Rebel Daughter of a Country House* (London: George Allen and Unwin, 1967): 180. The relation between the humanitarian waves of sympathy which lead to the international conventions for the amelioration of the conditions of the wounded and sick in armies in the field (1864 and 1907) and the rise of democracies, mass media, and armies of citizens has also been studied from below; Jonathan Marwil, "Photography at War," *History Today* 50, no. 6 (June 2000); and "The New York Times Goes to War," *History Today* 55, 6 (June 2005).

8. Emily Baughan, "Every Citizen of Empire;" two decades earlier, several of them had fought the internment of Boer civilians by the British army in South Africa and organized a similar movement to feed the children of the enemy.

9. In both cases such sponsorship was unprecedented. Reggie Norton, "Benedict XV and the Save the Children Fund," *The Month*, July 1995, 281–83.

10. The "idea that the behavior of states towards their citizens should be governed by enforceable codes of conduct" is central for "the emergence of human rights as a 'hegemonic political discourse;'" Tom Buchanan, "Human Rights," in *The Palgrave Dictionary of Transnational History*, ed. Akira Iriye and Pierre-Yves Saunier (Basingstoke: Palgrave, 2009); Buchanan cites Jack Donnelly, *Universal Human Rights in Theory and Practice* (Ithaca: Cornell University Press, 2001), 38.

11. Baughan, "Every Citizen of Empire." Samuel Moyn speaks similarly of the public appeal of the theme of the "spectacular causes of violence" being greater than the "structural causes of violence;" Moyn, "Spectacular Wrongs." Patricia Sellick argues that the history of the British Save the Children Fund, by far the strongest constituency of the SCIU, followed a cycle of distance from and proximity with national governments; "Responding to Children Affected by Armed Conflicts: A Case Study of the Save the Children Fund (1919–1999)" (PhD thesis in peace studies, Bradford University, 2001).

12. Helen McCarthy, "Democratizing British Foreign Policy: Rethinking the Peace Ballot, 1934–1935," *Journal of British Studies* 49, no.2 (April 2010): 358–87.

13. Hans-Martin Jaeger, "'World Opinion' and the Turn to Post-sovereign International Governance," in *Observing International Relations: Niklas Luhmann and World Politics*, ed. Mathias Albert and Lena Hilkermeier (London and New York: Routledge, 2004), 142–56. On discussions over the fate of war orphans, see also Emily Baughan, "Building a 'True League of Nations' Collaboration between the League of Nations and the British Save the Children Fund in Relief for Russian Refugees and Famine Victims, c. 1920–1930," paper presented at the conference "Towards a New History of the League of Nations," Geneva, 2011.

14. Maybe the bearer of the "moral authority" of the League, that given to it by the "bearer of hopes"; Michael Ignatieff, "The Confessions of Kofi Annan," *NYRB*, December 6, 2012.

15. On women's groups, expectations for the League of Nations, see Ellen Carol Dubois, "Women and Women's Rights at the League Of Nations", conference "Towards a New History of the League of Nations," Geneva, 2011. Carol Miller, "Lobbying the League: Women's International Organizations and the League of Nations" (D.Phil. thesis, Oxford University, 1992).

16. Dominique Marshall, "Children's Rights and Children's Actions in International Relief and Domestic Welfare: the Work of Herbert Hoover Between 1914 and 1950," *Journal of the History*

of Children and Youth 1, no.3 (Fall 2008): 351–88; Barbara Bennett Woodhouse, *Hidden in Plain Sight: The Tragedy of Children's Rights from Ben Franklin to Lionel Tate* (Princeton: Princeton University Press, 2008).

17. Joelle Droux, "Les projects de conventions sur l'assistance aux mineurs étrangers (1890–1939): enjeux et impasses sur l'internationalisation des politiques sociales (1890–1939)," presented at the conference "Towards a New History of the League of Nations", Geneva, 2011.

18. Kathleen Freeman, *If Any Man Build: The History of the Save the Children Fund* (London: Hodder and Stoughton, 1965), 42.

19. A. Josephine Dobbs, "The Children's Charter (Declaration of Geneva: An Alberta Teacher's Reaction,"*Social Welfare* (May 1924): 15–155; Procès-verbal du Conseil exécutif de l'Union internationale de secours aux enfants, 124e séance, August 5, 1924, Archives de l'Association internationale de protection de l'enfance, Archives d'Etat de Genève.

20. V.-Y. Ghébali, *La Société des nations et la réforme Bruce: 1939–1940* (Geneva: Centre Européen de la Dotation Carnegie Genève, 1970).

21. Baughan, "Building a 'True League of Nations'" and Droux, "Les projects de conventions." Because of such national jealousies, the League's direct humanitarian actions to rescue thousands of Armenian and Greek children from Turkey to Syria and Greece could only take place in mandated territories, where the absence of sovereignty allowed a freer hand, and could not be translated into international legal principles; Keith David Watenpaugh, "The League of Nations' Rescue of Armenian Genocide Survivors and the Making of Modern Humanitarianism, 1920–1927," *American Historical Review* 115, no. 5 (December 2010), 1315–39.

22. Watenpaugh, "The League of Nations' Rescue," 1334.

23. *Premier Rapport de la Commission Garneau d'Assurance-Maladie de Québec Sur le problème des garderies et de la Protection de l'Enfance* (Quebec, King's Printer: 1944), 7.

24. D. Marshall, "The Transnational Movements for Children's Rights and the Canadian Political Culture: A History," in *The History of Human Rights in Post-Confederation Canada*, ed. Janet Miron (Canadian Scholars' Press, 2009), 168.

25. D. Marshall, "The Rise of Coordinated Action for Children in War and Peace: Experts at the League of Nations, 1924–1945," in *Shaping the Transnational Sphere: Transnational Networks of Experts and Organizations (C. 1850–1930)*, ed. D. Rodogno, B. Struck, J. Vogel (Oxford: Berghan Books: 2013).

26. Aloïs Hentsch, "Le Conseil général de l'UISE", typed manuscript of ten pages, not dated, 9, Archives of the International Labour Office (AILO), "UISE. General Council to be held in Geneva, 22–23 February 1923", D600/406/4. Edward Fuller, *The Right of the Child: A Chapter in Social History* (London: The Beacon Press, 1951), 50–71.

27. M. Adas, "Contested Hegemony: The Great War and the Afro-Asian Assault on the Civilizing Mission" in *Making World After Empire: The Bandung Moment and its Political Afterlives*, ed. C. Lee (Athens: Ohio University Press, 2010): 69–106.

28. Dominique Marshall, "Children's Right and Imperial Political Cultures: Missionary and Humanitarian Contributions to the Conference on the African Child of 1931," *International Journal of Children's Rights* 12 (2004): 273–318.

29. *If Any Man Build*, 46.

30. Nicholas Thomas, "Colonial Conversions: Difference, Hierarchy, and History in Early Twentieth-Century Evangelical Propaganda," in *Cultures of Empire: Colonizers in Britain and the Empire in the Nineteenth and Twentieth Centuries: A Reader*, ed. Catherine Hall (Manchester: Manchester University Press, 2000): 298–328. John Darwin, Book Review of Mark Manzower, *No Enchanted Palace: The End of Empire and the Ideological Origins of the United Nations*, in *the American Historical Review* 116, no.1 (February 2011): 153–54. See also Baughan, "Every Citizen of Empire." Thomas argues that the language and images of family relations, which presented at once a hierarchy between members in the present and an equality in the future, offered an idiom to talk about the asymmetries of the "civilizing mission" and "trusteeship" harboured in the interwar years by most colonial governments. For a similar

sense among American progressives, that the world would benefit from their guidance, see Jennifer Polks, "Constructive Efforts: The American Red Cross and YMCA in Revolutionary and Civil War Russia, 1917–24"(PhD thesis in history, University of Toronto, 2012). More generally, Moyn argues that "humanitarianism established in the imagination powerful relationships between the compassionate and the suffering, and worked in tandem with imperial and market expansion;" "Spectacular Wrongs," Book review of *Freedom's Battle: The Origins of Humanitarian Intervention*, by Gary J. Bass, *The Nation*, October 13, 2008: 30–36.

31. The text of his speech was later reprinted: "Imperialism Destroys the People of Africa (A Speech delivered by James W. Ford at the International "Save the Children of Africa Conference, at Geneva, Switzerland, July, 1931)," in James W. Ford, *The Communist and the Struggle for Negro Liberation* (New York: Harlem Division of the Communist Party, 1936): 34–40.

32. J.W. Ford (Geneva), "The International Conference on African Children," *International Press Correspondence*, no. 39 (July 23, 1931), 736–37.

33. On the "global disillusion" of 1919 about racial equality, see Marilyn Lake and Henry Reynolds, *Drawing the Global Colour Line: White Men's Countries and the International Challenge to Racial Equality* (Cambridge: Cambridge University Press, 2008), 305–9; Erez Manela, *The Wilsonian Moment. Self-determination and the International Origins of Anticolonial Nationalism* (Oxford: Oxford University Press, 2007). Thanks to Danielle Kinsey for these references.

34. Save the Children International Union, *Proceedings of the International Conference on African Children* (Geneva, 1931), 26.

35. Hesse to Graves, July 14, 1932, in Anna Melissa Graves, Graves, ed., *Benvenuto Cellini Had No Prejudice Against Bronze: Letters From West Africans* (Baltimore: Waverley Press, 1942), 1, 4–5.

36. See my article "The Rights of African Children, the Save the Children Fund and Public Opinion in Europe and Ethiopia: The Centre of Child Welfare of Addis Ababa, Spring 1936," in Siegbert Uhlig. ed. *Proceedings of the International Conference of Ethiopian Studies* (Wiesbaden: Harrassowitz Verlag, 2006): 296–306.

37. On the success of humanitarians' use of mass communications, Célia Keren, "Autobiographies of Spanish Refugee Children at the Quaker Home in La Rouvière (France, 1940): Humanitarian Communication and Children's Writings," *Les Cahiers de Framespa* [En ligne], 5 (2010), http://framespa.revues.org/268.

38. Richard Pankhurst, *Sylvia Pankhurst: Counsel for Ethiopia* (Hollywood: Tsehai Publishers, 2003).

39. Meredith Terretta, "'We Had Been Fooled into Thinking that the UN Watches over the Entire World.' Human Rights, UN Trust Territories and Africa's Decolonization," *Human Rights Quarterly* 34, no. 2 (May 2012), 329–360.

40. Lee, *Making World After Empire*, 15. J. Go, "Modeling States and Sovereignty: Postcolonial Constitutions in Asian and Africa," in Lee, *Making World after Empire*, 124–28. This stance is critical of the more pessimistic interpretations of self-determination presented by authors such as Marika Sherwood, "'Diplomatic Platitudes': The Atlantic Charter, the United Nations and Colonial Independence," *Immigrants and Minorities* 15, no.2 (1996), 135–50.

41. The UDHR even mentioned children specifically. The IAPC was among the many NGOs present in San Francisco pressing for a Charter. In front of the various and large amount of demands made upon them, the authors reached a compromise. The specialized declarations can be seen as a perpetuation of the process of San Francisco. D. Marshall, "Canada and Children's Rights at the United Nations, 1945–1959", in *Canada and the Early Cold War. 1943–1957*, ed. Greg Donaghy (Ottawa: Department of Foreign Affairs and International Trade, 1998): 205, note 16.

42. Marshall, "Canada and Children's Rights at the United Nations."

43. Several historians, and internationalists such as Amartya Sen, comment on the ways by which tales of human rights told from above underestimate the efforts that local populations affected by war, disasters, or hardship place in their own campaigns to help their children first, long before they call for outside help for the sake of the children.

44. Dominique Marshall, "Reconstruction Politics, the Canadian Welfare State and the Ambiguity of Children's Rights, 1940–1950," in *Uncertain Horizons: Canadians and their World in 1945*, ed. Greg Donaghy (Ottawa, 1996), 261–83.

45. Quebec and the future province of Newfoundland were specifically targeted. See my *The Social Origins of the Welfare State: Québec Families, Compulsory Education, and Family Allowances, 1940–1955*, trans. Nicole Doone Danby (Waterloo: Wilfrid Laurier University Press, 2006). Since then, Maghda Fahrni has documented further uses of notions of entitlements among Montreal citizens of all classes. *Household Politics: Montreal Families and Postwar Reconstruction* (Toronto: University of Toronto Press, 2005).

46. Mike Di Francesco, "We Walked Around With Holes in Our Sole and Souls": Men and Masculinity During The Great Depression in Canada" (MA thesis in history, Carleton University, 2010). S. Pennybaker, in this collection, has insisted the most on the importance of the history of socio-economic rights and the attending history of communism.

47. "Governmentality," in *The Foucault Effect: Studies in Governmentality*, ed. Graham Burchell, Colin Gordon, and Peter Miller (Chicago, IL: University of Chicago Press, 1991): 87–104. W. Norton Grubb, Marvin Lazerson, *Broken Promises: How Americans Fail their Children* (New York: Basic Books, 1982).

48. Daniel Maul, *Human Rights, Development and Decolonization: The International Labour Organization, 1940–70* (Houndsmill: Palgrave Macmillan and International Labour Office), 294.

49. On this question, see Keith Breckenridge and Simon Szreter, eds., *Registration: The Infrastructure of Legal Personhood in Historical Perspective* (Oxford: Oxford University Press, 2013).

50. Freeman, *If Any Man Build.*

51. Marshall, *The Social Origins of the Welfare State.*

52. I.K. Atkins, "Seeds of Destiny: A Case History", *Film and History* 2 (1981): 25–33.

53. McCarthy suggests that hopes for the formation of a world public opinion were largely recuperated by "'scientific' polling techniques, ethnographic investigations . . . and governments' . . . assertive approach to the presentation and communication of their foreign policy aims." McCarthy, "Democratizing British Foreign Policy," 362; see also Jaeger, "'World Opinion.'" On the eroding support of labour organization for universal entitlements in the postwar years, see Peter McInnis, *Harnessing Labour Confrontation: Shaping The Postwar Settlement In Canada* (Toronto: University of Toronto Press, 2002).

54. Tom Buchanan, "'The Truth Will Set You Free': The Making of Amnesty International," *Journal of Contemporary History* 37, no. 4 (2002): 575–97.

55. Michael Jupp, "The International Year of the Child 10 Years Later," *Proceedings of the Academy of Political Science* 37, no. 2 (1989): 31–44 (Caring for America's Children); Maggie Black, *The Children and the Nations: Growing Up Together in the Post War World* (New York: UNICEF and Macmillan, 1987): 228–42.

56. In her famous column in *The Independent* on the occasion of the adoption of the Convention on the Rights of the Child of 1989, Australian feminist Germaine Greer argued that the document had no significance: UN officials did not really wish to answer their public demands. Children when asked what they wanted would call for a permanent supply of candies, she joked, but more seriously, what would the world community make of their recurring concern for their parents to stay together, and for the end of wars that killed and dispersed their family members? "Home Thoughts: Germaine Greer on the Folly of 'Children's Rights,'" *The Independent Magazine*, January 20, 1990. For a considered examination of this argument, set against the 1970s movement for child liberation, see Laura Purdy, "Why Children Shouldn't Have Equal Rights," *International Journal of Children's Rights* 2 (1994): 223–41.

57. Landon Pearson, "From Strength to Strength: The Intersection of Children's and Women's Rights over the Life Cycle," Florence Bird Lecture, March 8th, 2012, Carleton University, www.youtube.com/watch?v=TgHGOo7yvwQ&feature=youtu.be (accessed September 4, 2012).

58. Monica Eileen Patterson, "Constructions of Childhood in Apartheid's Last Decades" (PhD dissertation, University of Michigan, 2009).

59. David Rosen, "Child Soldiers, International Humanitarian Law, and the Globalization of Childhood," *American Anthropologist* 109, no.2 (2007): 296–306; for the protocols, see www.unicef.ca/en/discover/the-optional-protocols-to-the-convention (accessed January 2013).

60. Vanessa Pupavac, "Misanthropy Without Borders: The International Children's Rights Regime," *Disasters* 25, no.2 (2001): 95–112.

61. Michal Longford, "NGOs and the Rights of the Child," in *The Conscience of the World": The Influence of Non-Governmental Organizations on the UN System*, ed. Peter Willet (Washington, DC: Brookings Institute, 1996), 216. For the text of the Convention, www.unicef-irc.org/portfolios/crc.html (accessed September, 2012).

62. Stephen J. Toope. "The Convention on the Rights of the Child: Implications for Canada," in *Children's Rights: A Comparative Perspective*, ed. Michael Freeman (Aldershot: Dartmouth Publishing, 1996): 33–35. For the text of the Convention, www.unicef-irc.org/portfolios/crc.html (consulted in January, 2013).

63. Dejo Olowu, "Protecting Children's Rights in Africa: A Critique of the African Charter on the Rights and Welfare of the Child," *International Journal of Children's Rights*, 10 (2002): 126–36.

64. In Jon Rohde, "Completing Jim Grant's 'Agenda for the World's Children,'" in *Jim Grant, UNICEF Visionary*, Carol Bellamy (New York: UNICEF, nd): 148–56.

65. Watenpaugh, "The League of Nations' Rescue," 1334.

66. Mark Mazower, *No Enchanted Palace* (Princeton: Princeton University Press, 2009), 8.

Chapter 8

•◆•

Social Movements and Human Rights: Gender, Sexuality, and the Charter in English-Speaking Canada

Miriam Smith

This paper explores the dynamics of social movement organizing around sexuality and gender in English-speaking Canada. These forms of organizing—second-wave feminism, lesbian feminism, the gay liberation movement, the lesbian and gay movement[1]—were important to the development of a broad conception of human rights and citizenship. What were the roots of these movements in Canada and how were they influenced by domestic legal and political factors? How did these movements contribute to the transition from a formal to a substantive conception of human rights? Did these movements contribute to a progressive agenda in which the sphere of human rights was continuously expanded, or were there unintended consequences of the seemingly progressive social movement activism?

I argue that, although these social movements were influenced by transnational and international influences, the form of their activism was shaped by domestic factors including the shifting structure of Canadian political institutions and the legal legacies encoded in the Canadian constitutional structure that encouraged the formulation of state-focused political demands for citizenship and inclusion. I draw on theories of historical institutionalism from political science to illustrate how gender-based social movements contributed to the shaping of human rights discussion in Canada and how the movements themselves were shaped by the legal and political context. While these social movements achieved important legal and political changes, the pursuit of liberal human rights agendas through human rights commissions and through the Charter has been difficult to reconcile with the complexities of an increasingly diverse society. With the rise of the neo-liberal political project, legally focused definitions of human rights reinforced individualism and were ill-suited to challenge social and economic inequality.

In the first section of the paper, I provide a brief overview of the origins of human rights engagement by the women's movement and the lesbian and gay movement. I will then describe historical institutionalism and its relevance for the study of social movements and human rights, especially in terms of debates over the entrenchment of the Charter. The entrenchment of the Charter had important effects not only on the substance of human rights protections, especially for the lesbian and gay movement, but also on social movement politics itself, as outlined in the third section of the paper. By privileging discrimination claims defined in terms of specific grounds of discrimination, the post-Charter human rights regime encouraged social movements to make claims centred on particular axes of discrimination, while excluding other forms of inequality (for example, people with multiple identities). The paper concludes by considering the relationship between human rights and neo-liberalism.

ORIGIN OF SEXUALITY AND GENDER MOVEMENTS OF THE 1970S AND 1980S

The politicization of sexuality and gender during the 1970s and 1980s played an important role in the development in human rights in Canada. Second-wave feminism undermined the divide between public and private by arguing that the "personal is political." While first-wave feminism had argued for the right to vote and participate in the public sphere, it had very largely left the gendered division of labour, traditional sex roles, and heterosexual dominance unquestioned. In contrast, second-wave feminism opened up demands for women's control of their own bodies, their right to be free of sexual assault and violence, their right to participate equally in education and the labour force, and their right to question family roles. The discussion of gender among second-wave feminists was critically important in creating space for lesbian feminism, for valorizing women who broke with traditional gender roles, and for the public legitimation and celebration of same-sex sexual and romantic relationships among women. While the relationship between lesbians and the women's movement was fraught and contradictory in Canada, as elsewhere, many lesbians found their first political home in the women's movement and, in some cases, after critiquing hetero-dominated feminist movements, turned to building lesbian social and political institutions in the 1970s and 1980s. Others chose to participate directly in the gay liberation movement.[2]

Although sexuality and gender movements are often discussed separately, in fact, they are inextricably and intimately linked. Feminism was a movement that questioned and politicized gender roles. At the same time, the gay liberation movement of the 1970s and the emerging "lesbian and gay" and queer movements of the 1980s were concerned with the public recognition of same-sex behaviour, including the legitimation and celebration of non-normative gender roles. The cultural lexicon of the queer communities included drag queens, fairies, trans people, dykes, femmes, two-spirit people and many others who operated outside traditional gender roles. Same-sex sexual behaviour was only part of the equation and, in some cases, such as for some trans people or two-spirit people, identification with particular gender choices was more important to political and social identity than sexual behaviour or romantic attachment. As male activists acknowledged, the gay liberation movement of the 1970s, which focused in part on same-sex human rights demands, was indebted to second-wave feminism for problematizing traditional gender roles and contesting the public–private divide.[3]

The emergence of these movements in the 1970s and 1980s occurred in the context of broad sociological changes that affected Canada, as other Western societies. The advent of the baby boom generation and the increased participation of women in the labour force were important background factors to the emergence of new social movements around gender and sexuality. The international context was also important; feminists in English-speaking Canada were influenced by feminist theory and practice from the United States and Britain. In English-speaking Canada, queer activists drew on American examples and models, which were disseminated through an extensive network of gay media that grew exponentially during the 1970s and 1980s. While, in the 1950s and 1960s, Canadian gay men and lesbians were aware of publications of early homophile groups such as the Mattachine Society in the United States or the Daughters of Bilitis, based in California, by the 1970s, Toronto's *Body Politic* magazine was a leading gay liberation newspaper that was disseminated throughout the English-speaking world, regularly reporting on queer political events in Canada, Britain, the United States, and continental Europe.[4] American publications such as the *Advocate* were widely read in Canada, and political events such as Stonewall were well known to gay activists in English-speaking Canada. Recent historical work by David Churchill has documented the extent to which the homophile movements in Canada and the United States were linked, especially through the consumption of media.[5] Therefore, gender and sexuality movements in Canada emerged in tandem with similar movements in other societies of the global North.[6]

As gender and sexuality movements arose in the 1970s, they encountered a particular set of legal and political institutions which encoded particular understandings of human rights. While gender and sexuality movements throughout the developed capitalist democracies of this period shared some common political stances on issues such as abortion, legalization of homosexuality, and the need for anti-discrimination protections in the workplace, the education system, housing, and other spheres, the domestic circumstances of each particular movement also shaped their trajectory and impact.

In the Canadian case, second-wave feminism and gay liberation arose at a historical moment in which Canadian political institutions were undergoing constitutional change and at a historical moment in which the human rights machinery itself was in the process of expansion with the advent of the Canadian Charter of Rights and Freedoms. These social movements contributed to the development of the Charter and to the development of new human rights institutions in Canada; at the same time, they were also shaped by their encounter with existing political and legal institutions. In order to understand this interaction, the next section outlines a historical institutionalist approach to the relationship between social movements and the development of human rights.

SOCIAL MOVEMENTS AND HUMAN RIGHTS: A THEORETICAL APPROACH

Historical institutionalism, developed by political scientists, offers a useful approach for understanding the interaction between the rise of social movements and the development of state policies, including policies on human rights. Perhaps in part because of its US origin, it proceeds without reference to the transnational or international context; its aim is to explain the evolution of law and public policy at the domestic level. Nonetheless, it offers fruitful avenues for understanding the evolution of social movements and human rights within a particular country and for comparative work on similar systems such as the United States, Britain, and Canada.[7]

Historical institutionalism focuses the role of political institutions and public policies in shaping the process of political mobilization for civil society actors such as social movements. Historical institutionalists start with state structures, with the field of political institutions and the legacies of previous policies, to explain policy outcomes, treating the state in the Weberian tradition as an independent player and not simply as the passive reflection of the play of social forces, however conceived.[8] The legacies of previous policies play a key role in shaping current political battles. Political institutions create openings and obstacles for social movements seeking political and legal change that determine their success or failure. For historical institutionalists, the evolution of law and public policy must be considered over time, and institutionalists have developed concepts such as policy feedback and path dependency which purport to explain how existing policies are reinforced over time as particular policy pathways incur sunk costs and cannot be reversed.[9] My comparative work on the lesbian and gay movements in the United States and Canada adopts this framework in explaining how extensive public policies to recognize lesbian and gay rights were established relatively quickly in Canada in the 1980s–2000s, while the United States has made only halting and partial progress toward the recognition of lesbian and gay rights claims in key areas such as the passage of anti-discrimination laws, the legalization of homosexuality, and the recognition of same-sex relationships.[10] In other words, as scholars of public policy have long noted, policies make politics.[11]

Historical institutionalists initially tended to view state structures in instrumental and mechanical terms. For example, in my work, I emphasize the ways in which federalism creates obstacles for the political mobilization of the lesbian and gay movement in the United States because of the fact that many of the key policy issues for the movement fall under state, rather than federal, jurisdiction. In areas such as changes to criminal law (i.e. legalization of homosexuality or the elimination of sodomy laws) or the recognition of same-sex marriage, states have jurisdiction, in contrast to Canada, where these policy areas fall under the jurisdictional purview of the federal government. Therefore, I suggest that policy change would be easier in Canada than in the United States simply because policy and legal change only needed to occur in one jurisdiction— the federal jurisdiction—rather than across each of the fifty states, as in the United States.[12]

Similarly, some analyses of women's political mobilization have emphasized the role of institutional factors in facilitating or impeding policy development around issues such as abortion and child care. In particular, Haussman argues that, in the case of abortion, institutional differences, especially the impact of federalism, affect the availability and legality of abortion in Canada, the United States, and Mexico. State jurisdiction over criminal law and other matters combined with the fragmentation of the division of powers system in the United States compared to Canada creates multiple obstacles to political change and increases the cost of political mobilization for women seeking safe and legal access to abortion.[13] Vickers's recent analysis of women's activism and federalism in the United States and Canada stresses the diverse conclusions of the literature on gender and political institutions.[14] Some scholars emphasize that institutional factors have impeded progressive political change while others view federalism as a potential advantage for women's political mobilization because it provides additional opportunities for change through both the provincial and federal levels.[15] Recent scholarship on gender and political institutions also calls attention to the ways in which institutional differences and policy legacies differ across policy sectors.[16]

Feminist institutionalists have paid particular attention to the role of discourse and ideas in policy-making, a strand that has always co-existed uneasily with other aspects of historical institutionalism. While historical institutionalism has emphasized the structural limits of institutional and policy legacies, ideas and discourse have sometimes been used to explain policy change or treated as the medium through which policy legacies operate.[17] For example, in an early study, Weir emphasized how pre-existing policies set limits on policy debates by foreclosing options that were deemed overly expensive or not feasible in light of existing administrative and policy structures.[18] Policy ideas were treated as sealed off from institutions and actors and as tools that could be picked up or not in policy debate and conflict. More recent forms of feminist and discursive institutionalism have built on the earlier institutionalist consideration of the role of ideas in policy-making by conceptualizing institutions and policies themselves as embodied in discourse. In this way, recent scholarship on the evolution of state–social movement interactions has moved beyond the structural limits of traditional historical institutionalist approaches and into a more constructivist, poststructuralist or even Foucauldian form of policy analysis.[19]

While historical institutionalism's theoretical emphasis on exploring policy development over time, considering the impact of existing policies on policy debate, and comparing the impact of political institutional structures are all useful for understanding the development of human rights policies, the recent discursive and ideational turn in institutional analysis is less useful in its conflation of political action into discourse. From a theoretical perspective, it is important to ensure that policy or legal ideas are not divorced from political and economic power.[20] If particular policy ideas take hold at a given time, we must explore the sources of these ideas and the social and political conditions that give rise to them. We cannot undertake this exploration if we view the institutions and political actors as themselves existing in a discursive field. Political institutions do provide pathways that favour some policy ideas over others, and political actors also take up and put down various policy stances, ideologies, and policy ideas. This process is of critical importance to understanding the trajectory of human rights protections. How did the ideas of legal, political, and civil rights for disenfranchised groups become a credible policy option? How were human rights linked to other popular political debates of the period and with what effects? The next section approaches these issues by drawing on a historical institutionalist approach to understand gender and sexuality movements in the Canadian case.

THE WOMEN'S MOVEMENT, THE LESBIAN AND GAY MOVEMENT, AND DOMESTIC HUMAN RIGHTS PROTECTIONS

The women's movement and the LGBT movement played a key role in the development of domestic human rights in Canada during the 1970s and 1980s. The women's movement's demands in Canada were quite similar to those of other advanced capitalist democracies, emphasizing workplace equality and reproductive rights while the gay liberation movement of the 1970s in Canada—like the gay liberation movement in the United States and elsewhere—called for human rights for lesbian and gay citizens, including protection from discrimination in housing and employment, among other issues. Yet, both movements were influenced by what historical institutionalists would call policy legacies, that is, the policies on human rights that were in place at the time that the movements arose. These included the human rights commission model across provincial jurisdictions as well as the Canadian Bill of Rights. Moreover, as second-wave feminism entered its second decade in the 1970s and as gay liberation began to emerge in Canada, beginning in 1971, the federal government undertook constitutional and institutional modernization, including the establishment of the Canadian Human Rights Commission in 1977 and the constitutional patriation of 1982, including the Canadian Charter of Rights and Freedoms. These initiatives fundamentally altered the external political institutional environment for social movement politics, greatly enhancing the pull of legal mobilization.[21]

While the constitutional debate had nothing directly to do with the rise of second-wave feminism or gay liberation, it was a reaction to the Quiet Revolution in Quebec, which, itself, was fuelled by and complemented by the social movement fervour of the period. Therefore, like the development of human rights legislation and human rights commissions, political institutional developments were not divorced from social movement politics. The federal government's response to the rise of this new form of state-focused and progressive nationalism in Quebec was to undertake initiatives to enhance language equality through the passage of official bilingualism and to undertake political changes to modernize the Canadian Constitution. In doing so, the federal government drew on ideas of human rights that were circulating internationally and transnationally. Nonetheless, the specific institutional conundrums of the Canadian Constitution provided the context and opportunity for the empowerment of the judiciary and the entrenchment of a revamped bill of rights. The prospect of foundational political institutional change opened up specific opportunities for the women's movement and the LGBT movement to influence constitutional equality rights. Social movement mobilization was shaped by these institutional changes and new political opportunities as the women's movement and the LGBT movement were drawn into discussions of human rights.[22]

Recent scholarship in history and political science has pointed to the role of social movements in relation to constitutional change, although none of it has directly engaged with theoretical approaches such as historical institutionalism. The "new human rights history," a flourishing field of Canadian history, has documented the civil society organizations that pushed for the establishment of human rights legislation and for the entrenchment of human rights in the Constitution. This work documents the growth of civil rights groups, many of which drew on international sources and sought to strengthen civil rights in Canada through the implementation of a Canadian Bill of Rights. This new historical scholarship emphasizes the societal roots of domestic human rights protections in Canada and shifts the focus from the "top-down" interpretation of the Bill of Rights and the Charter as the brainchild of political leaders (John Diefenbaker in the first case, Pierre Trudeau in the second case) or as the product of elite accommodation and negotiation.[23]

Most importantly, this scholarship shows the ways in which human rights legislation emerged in the provinces in part as the result of mobilization of groups representing ethnic and racialized minorities such as Jewish and Italian Canadians. Although the women's movement was dormant in the 1940s and 1950s, the legacy of first-wave feminism's focus on protective legislation for women was picked up in early legislation such as Ontario equal pay law of 1951. Starting with the Saskatchewan Bill of Rights of 1947, passed by the Tommy Douglas CCF government of the time, human rights legislation prohibited discrimination on the grounds of race, ethnicity, and religion, discrimination that was rampant in the law and practice of the time, such as racial quotas for university admission, segregation in public services and housing, restrictive racial covenants on property, and open discrimination in employment, which had been upheld by the Supreme Court of Canada.[24]

Similarly, many political scientists have emphasized the process through which the Charter was altered through the intervention of civil society actors who took the federal government's text and worked hard to ensure that the document's wording would strengthen their group's position. In this way, human rights in law are seen as having important domestic social roots. In the constitutional debate of the early 1980s, these civil society actors included First Nations, the women's movement and ethnocultural communities. The resulting Constitution Act 1982 (including the Charter) contains section 35 on Aboriginal rights, section 27 affirming the multicultural heritage of Canada, section 28 reaffirming equality rights for women and section 15 on equality rights, which were shaped through the parliamentary committee hearings and by the political mobilization of stakeholder groups who sought to influence the government and public opinion throughout the process of constitution-building.[25]

In doing so, these groups drew on their experience with the Canadian Bill of Rights, the anaemic legislation that had been passed by the Diefenbaker government in 1960. This limited document, which only applied in federal jurisdiction, was the object of criticism by legal scholars and by some civil society groups in particular because of the way it was interpreted by judges. In an infamous case on women's rights (*Bliss*) and another on Aboriginal women's rights (*Lavell*), the courts interpreted the Bill of Rights in terms of negative rights rather than substantive equality. In the case of *Bliss*, the Supreme Court upheld rules governing unemployment insurance that denied benefits to pregnant women on the grounds that discrimination based on pregnancy was not sex discrimination. In the case of *Lavell*, the Supreme Court ruled that depriving Aboriginal women of their Indian status when they married those without status was procedurally fair as all married women were treated in the same way.[26] These cases (and others) formed what historical institutionalists would term policy legacies that shaped debates over human rights in the Charter. Those contending over the wording of the proposed Charter made frequent reference to the Bill of Rights and argued for recognition of substantive and inclusive equality rights.

The women's movement focused on two specific clauses of the proposed Charter, section 15 on equality rights and section 28 which further affirmed women's equality. With respect to section 15, the women's movement pushed for specific wording in the equality rights section to ensure that positive action to ensure equality for women (and all other groups protected by section 15)—affirmative action in the wording of section 15—was explicitly permitted under the section's equality guarantee. Drawing on the experience of the US women's movement, the Canadian women's movement also pushed hard for expansive wording in section 15, which states that "Every individual is equal before and under the law and has the right to the equal protection and equal benefit of the law without discrimination" (Constitution Act 1982, s. 15. (1)). By including "before and under the law," the section overcame the limitations of *Lavell*, one of the key defeats for women's equality under the Canadian Bill of Rights, in which one of the justices ruled that equality before the law refers only to procedural sameness in the way individuals are treated and not substantive equality of outcome. The wording "under the law" as well as what was viewed at the time as the import of American "equal protection" wording were added to ensure that the door would be open to legal interpretations of substantive, rather than purely formal, equality. In US terms, by naming the grounds of discrimination and leaving the list open-ended, section 15 states that all of the named grounds form the basis for strict scrutiny or, in other words, that they formed suspect classes, in US terms.[27] The open-ended list of grounds permitted courts to add analogous grounds and, indeed, in the parliamentary committee hearings on the proposed Charter under questioning from Svend Robinson, then Justice Minister Jean Chrétien conceded that the courts might add sexual orientation to section 15 of the Charter by reading it in as an analogous ground of discrimination.[28]

Furthermore, the women's movement also pushed hard to add section 28 to the Charter. This section states that "notwithstanding anything in this Charter, the rights and freedoms referred to in it are guaranteed equally to male and female persons" (1982 Constitution Act, s. 28). The women's movement argued for the insertion of this additional clause to reiterate the equal application of Charter rights to men and women given that the federal or provincial governments could override section 15 of the Charter for a period of five years. This override clause, which was added to propitiate the provinces who were concerned about the effect of judicial activism on provincial powers, potentially undermined section 15 equality rights and, because of the design of the override and its application to section 15, the women's movement (as well as First Nations and ethnocultural groups) sought additional protections in clauses that were outside and beyond the scope of the override (e.g. section 27 affirming the multicultural heritage of Canadians).

After the entrenchment of the Charter, the women's movement was a key player—arguably the most important player—in early constitutional litigation on section 15. While the women's movement was part of a network of section 15 stakeholders, it was the most consistently proactive in litigating and intervening in cases on constitutional equality with the deliberate intent of influencing the interpretation of section 15, in order to avoid *Bliss*-like judgments. The movement put forth what it termed "substantive equality" and drew a sharp distinction between formal and substantive equality in its interventions. In the first section 15 case in 1989, *Andrews*, the Women's Legal and Education Action Fund (LEAF) intervened and is viewed as having influenced the broad interpretation that was given to section 15 in the decision.[29] Further, LEAF intervened in a raft of other cases, sometimes successfully, sometimes unsuccessfully; however, LEAF's role consistently brought feminist arguments to bear on gender equality issues.

Has the women's movement been drawn into legal mobilization? While the women's movement was skeptical about the deployment of law in the pursuit of equality, there is evidence that women's equality in English-speaking Canada has increasingly defined its political strategies in Charter terms. First, in terms of women's organization, groups at the pan-Canadian (federal) and provincial level have declined with the exception of LEAF, which undertakes Charter challenges. Although the women's movement has been recently reinvigorated in reaction to the Harper government's anti-feminist politics, LEAF was certainly one of the few pan-Canadian organizations remaining after the demise of the National Action Committee on the Status of Women in the late 1990s and 2000s. This would suggest that, over the long term, the women's movement in English-speaking Canada was drawn into the process of Charter-based legal mobilization around human rights claims.[30] Second, substantive equality under the Charter has been resistant to intersectional feminist claims, especially those centred on racialization, ethnicity, religion, and national origin.[31] As Lépinard has recently argued in her exploration of the sharia arbitration debate in Ontario, the engagement of second-wave feminism with the human rights template of the Charter has solidified and encouraged attachment to specific jurisprudential conceptions of equality that make it difficult to consider intersectional human rights.[32] Third, the equality-seeking of the Charter has failed to challenge the rise of neo-liberalism. The template of human rights and equality-seeking in Canada excludes reference to social rights and, as many feminists have pointed out, it is very difficult to litigate issues of women's economic equality under the Charter. Canadian courts have proved resistant to claims of this type. Perhaps most famously, in the Newfoundland and Labrador Association of Public and Private Employees case of 2004, the Supreme Court permitted the Newfoundland government to set aside a pay equity settlement for women workers in the para-public sector on the grounds of fiscal constraint. Despite the fact that equality rights were involved, the Court deferred to the provincial government in framing the issue as a question of fiscal probity rather than a question of equality for historically low-paid women workers.[33]

Therefore, the women's movement in English-speaking Canada has shaped the process of constitution-making, even while its political thinking and organizing has been influenced by the empowerment of the judiciary in the wake of the Charter. On the one hand, as many scholars have demonstrated, the women's movement's political mobilization shaped the constitutional settlement of 1982 and, in particular, clauses 15 and 28 of the Charter. In the years since the Charter's enactment, the women's movement has been drawn into litigation, even as other forms of political mobilization have been relatively weakened. The movement's engagement with a domestic human rights regime that lacks protections for economic or social rights and that is characterized by a judiciary unwilling to challenge the economic and fiscal decisions of government means that the legalized women's movement lacks the political resources to challenge neo-liberalism. Further, the strict boxes of grounds of discrimination in Charter litigation have reinforced a unitary conception of women's interests and identities that has become increasingly divorced from the multiracial reality of Canadian society. In this way, political institutions and public policy have been shaped by women's social movement mobilization even as, over time, newly empowered political institutions such as the judiciary, armed with the Charter, have in turn shaped social movements. Perhaps more importantly, the policy and legal framing of human rights has influenced the women's movement, privileging litigation strategies and highlighting a political discourse based on a particular conception of equality rights.

The relationship between political institutions, social movements and policy legacies has also played out in complex ways in the LGBT movement. The lesbian and gay movement was a relative latecomer to the field of human rights activism, arising slowly through the homophile movement of the 1960s and emerging into the open with birth of the gay liberation movement, which is usually dated to 1971. The early movement deliberately undertook legal challenges to the exclusion of lesbians and gay men from protections in provincial and federal human rights legislation as well as specific cases which were undertaken as a means of community-building and consciousness-raising, aimed both at closeted gay men and lesbians as well as at the wider community.

The LGBT movement was very weak in the late 1970s and early 1980s and did not play a role in debates over the Charter. The Canadian Lesbian and Gay Rights Coalition, which had brought together gay liberation groups in a pan-Canadian coalition in the 1970s, had exhausted itself and disbanded by 1980. Ottawa's gay liberation group, Gays of Ottawa, played some role in following debates over the Charter and occasionally writing briefs on human rights issues. However, in general,

LGBT activism focused on the urban level. The human rights agenda of the 1970s, in which gay liberation groups had often deliberately undertaken human rights challenges in order to call attention to gay and lesbian marginalization, had dissipated in the face of the AIDS epidemic, which began to take off in 1981. Therefore, the movement did not have the resources to undertake a political campaign, such as that undertaken by the women's movement. Furthermore, given that the gay liberation movement had been defeated in every human rights case it had brought forward in the 1970s and given that only one province (Quebec) had amended its human rights code to include sexual orientation, it seemed unlikely that a Charter-based human rights lobbying effort would succeed in securing the inclusion of sexual orientation as a named ground of discrimination in section 15 of the Charter. Thus, unlike the women's movement, the LGBT movement did not play a role in Charter enactment and its use of human rights claims in the 1970s was mainly focused on human rights commissions, which were exploited strategically to draw attention to the lesbian and gay issue, rather than with the expectation that actual policy change would result from lesbian and gay legal and political mobilization.[34]

Yet the entrenchment of the Charter galvanized new forms of organizing in the LGBT community. Just as elite women and legal professionals had spearheaded the women's movements campaigns around the entrenchment of the Charter, so too lawyers played a key role in pushing lesbian and gay rights to the forefront in the wake of the Charter, and these new forms of organizing, based in Ottawa, were often disconnected urban organizing. Instead of gay liberation, the new movement organizations and networks, such as Égale (founded in 1986), drew on legal expertise to mount a sustained challenge to the legal edifice of inequality. While LGBT organizing has traditionally focused on the urban level, pan-Canadian organizing around an LGBT human rights agenda began to emerge in the mid-1980s and, by the 1990s had developed into a full-blown legal network that litigated on LGBT human rights issues, especially discrimination and relationship recognition.

The framing of LGBT demands was also shaped by engagement with the Charter in similar ways to the experience of the women's movement. Just as the women's movement was boxed in by the category of gender as an undifferentiated ground of discrimination under the Charter, so too the LGBT movement found it difficult to escape the unitary subject—the

LGBT individual or the same-sex couple—and the homogenizing impact of Charter categories such as sexual orientation. The drive for marriage equality was embedded in the logic of equality claims for same-sex couples and, aside from decisions made by legal activists in the LGBT movement, it was a demand that was pushed to the fore by plaintiff couples, some of whom filed cases that were outside the control of social movement organizations. Plaintiff couples who wanted to get married provided a grassroots dimension to same-sex marriage organizing. While many in the queer community criticized the drive for same-sex marriage as entailing the integration and even assimilation of distinctively queer cultures into normative middle-class lifestyles,[35] others within the community have also criticized the movement for its relative whiteness, both in terms of activist leaders and in terms of the framing of the same-sex marriage issue.[36] Class was also centrally important to the same-sex marriage debate, as some argued that the creation of the legally privileged and married same-sex couple was a human rights gain that would be purchased at the expense of single queers and same-sex couples on social assistance that would be policed through spouse-in-the-house rules. Further, same-sex marriage would encode same-sex couples as responsible for their economic and social fate, reinforcing the dynamics of neoliberal consumerism and individualization at the expense of collective social and economic provision.[37]

In scholarly terms, new theoretical work in the United States by scholars such as Jasbir Puar has argued that the queer subject in US politics is highly racialized and implicated in US nationalist projects such as the so-called "War on Terror."[38] As yet, these perspectives have not been extensively applied in LGBT scholarship in Canada; however, it may be expected that the critique of the dominant human rights–oriented strain of queer politics will strengthen as both activists and scholars consider how to navigate the complex intersectionalities of racialization, gender, gender identity, and sexual orientation. A historical institutionalist perspective suggests that LGBT activists have not chosen particular framings of human rights; to some extent, in the Charter era, these framings are shaped by the structure of legal and political institutions and the legacies of previous policies that create incentives for particular types of human rights claims. While social movement organizations can play a role in litigation, the same-sex marriage example shows that organizations cannot control plaintiffs who put forward equality rights claims.[39] It is the

Charter that creates the legal and political opportunity for such individual claims; therefore, activist leaders' strategies are in part a product of these institutional and policy structures. In this sense, engagement with state-based human rights is not a project that undermines the power relations of settler societies or that permits the articulation of complex positions on race, gender, and sexuality. Theoretical approaches such as historical institutionalism suggest that, right or wrong and regardless of our personal views, the institutional and legal structure is a heavy object that weights on the social movement activists of any particular historical period, limiting their agency and influencing their framing of the issues. At the same time, critical junctures such as the period around the Charter's entrenchment can also create openings for social movement agency. The women's movement successfully exploited the political opportunities of the early 1980s constitutional debate to strengthen the liberal rights guarantees of the Charter for women. While the LGBT movement was unable to mobilize at the time of the Charter's entrenchment, the legal opportunity for the movement, which was provided by the Charter, and by the extent of pre-existing legal inequality for same-sex couples and for lesbian and gay citizens, generated a dynamic of Charter-based political mobilization. This mobilization was a human rights success in incorporating LGBT people as formal legal citizens. However, as in the case of the women's movement, this success set into motion a dynamic that marginalized other forms of difference within queer communities, especially around class and race.

CONCLUSION

This paper has considered the domestic roots of human rights in Canada in the most recent period, the 1970s through the 2000s, focusing in particular on the emergence of the women's movement and the lesbian and gay movement and the role of these movements in shaping human rights' practices in English-speaking Canada. Both movements made important contributions in moving Canadian human rights policies away from the relatively weak Bill of Rights–era protections, centred on restricted ideas of formal equality, and toward a substantive definition of equality rights. The second-wave feminist movement shaped the substantive content of gender rights in the Charter as well the ways in which equality was framed and conceptualized in the post-Charter period. Although the lesbian and gay movement was not successful in the 1970s in using human rights claims to secure greater recognition from governments or human rights commissions, the movement's very existence raised completely new issues of sexual and gender identity that eventually emerged into the full light of the political mainstream in the 1990s and 2000s. Further, in the post-Charter period, the lesbian and gay movement, as well as a raft of individual plaintiffs, took up Charter litigation to expand the citizenship rights of LGBT Canadians. This resulted in rapid and far-reaching policy and legal change, culminating in the legalization of same-sex marriage in 2005.

I have argued that historical institutionalist theory provides a lens through which we can view the interaction of political and legal institutions with social movement agency. Although historical institutionalism focuses on domestic political and legal factors, it calls attention to the structural forces that shape the agency, choices, and legal framings of social movement ideas. Institutional features of the domestic state, such as the jurisdictions of federalism or the process of judicial empowerment, as occurred in Canada in the wake of the Charter, exert a foundational influence on social movement politics. At the same time, at critical junctures in the evolution of the domestic human rights regime, the political and legal mobilization of social movements has also shaped the institutional and legal context.

The Charter-focused template of human rights protections that has evolved in Canada over the last thirty years has yielded some victories for the women's movement and for the LGBT movement. Yet, as a number of scholars have highlighted, the legal and policy legacies of section 15 equality rights marginalize considerations of the ways in which gender, sexuality, race, and multiculturalism intersect. At the same time, the expansion of certain forms of legal citizenship, such as the recognition of same-sex couples in Canadian law, is congruent with neo-liberal principles of individual responsibility and consumerism. Despite its sometimes progressive edge, Charter litigation does not challenge neo-liberalism. As the case of pay equity shows, the lack of social and economic rights in the Charter, as well as the reticence of Canadian judges to challenge governments' budgetary decisions, undercut legal challenges to social inequity. In this sense, the expansion of human rights in Canada in the post-Charter period has been an ambiguous project with a decidedly mixed legacy.

NOTES

1. Lesbian feminism, especially in the 1970s, operated autonomously from the male-dominated gay liberation movement and was often explicitly referred to as the "autonomous lesbian movement." The term *gay movement* was often used during the 1970s to refer to gay liberation. Starting in the 1980s, the term *lesbian and gay movement* was used to denote state-directed social movement politics. The term *bisexual* was added in the 1990s and the term *transgendered* and then *transgender* in the 2000s. Although the term *queer* was used from the 1980s with the advent of Queer Nation groups as well as *queer theory* in the humanities, *queer* is often used today as an umbrella term to denote the LGBT communities. I mention this range of movements in order to emphasize the importance of the internal diversity in these communities.

2. Sharon Dale Stone, "Lesbian Mothers Organizing," in *Lesbians in Canada*, ed. Sharon Dale Stone (Toronto: Between the Lines, 1990), 198–208; Sharon Dale Stone, "Lesbians Against the Right," in *Women and Social Change: Feminist Activism in Canada*, ed. Jeri Wine and Janice Ristock (Toronto: James Lorimer, 1991), 236–51; Jill Vickers et al. *Politics as If Women Mattered: A Political Analysis of the National Action Committee on the Status of Women* (Toronto: University of Toronto Press, 1993), 263–5; Becki Ross, *The House That Jill Built: A Lesbian Nation in Formation* (Toronto: University of Toronto Press, 1995), 24–56; Miriam Smith, *Lesbian and Gay Rights in Canada: Social Movements and Equality-Seeking, 1971–1995* (Toronto: University of Toronto Press, 1999), 26–36.

3. Tom Warner, *Never Going Back: A History of Queer Activism in Canada* (Toronto: University of Toronto Press, 2002), 61ff; Smith, *Lesbian and Gay Rights*, 36–38.

4. Ed Jackson and Stan Persky, eds. *Flaunting It! A Decade of Gay Journalism from The Body Politic* (Vancouver: New Star Books, 1982).

5. David S. Churchill, "Transnationalism and Homophile Political Culture in the Postwar Decades," *GLQ: A Journal of Lesbian and Gay Studies* 15: 1 (2009): 31–66.

6. For an overview, see Barry D. Adam, *The Rise of a Gay and Lesbian Movement*, rev. ed. (New York: Twayne Publishers, 1997).

7. On other social movements, see Dominique Clément, *Canada's Rights Revolution: Social Movements and Social Change, 1937–1982* (Vancouver: University of British Columbia Press, 2008) and Suzanne Staggenborg, *Social Movements*, 2nd ed. (New York: Oxford University Press, 2011).

8. Theda Skocpol, "Bringing the State Back In: Strategies of Analysis in Current Research," in *Bringing the State Back In*, ed. Peter B. Evans, Dietrich Rueschemeyer, and Theda Skocpol (Cambridge: Cambridge University Press, 1985), 3–37. See also Peter Graefe, "Political Economy and Canadian Public Policy," in *Critical Policy Studies*, ed. Michael Orsini and Miriam Smith (Vancouver: University of British Columbia Press, 2007), 19–40.

9. Paul Pierson and Theda Skocpol, "Historical Institutionalism in Contemporary Political Science," in *The State of the Discipline*, ed. Ira Katznelson and Helen Milner (New York: Norton, 2002), 693–721.

10. Miriam Smith, *Political Institutions and Lesbian and Gay Rights in the United States and Canada* (New York: Routledge, 2008).

11. Paul Pierson, "Public Policies as Institutions," in *Rethinking Political Institutions: The Art of the State*, ed. Ian Shapiro et al. (New York: New York University Press, 2006) 114–31.

12. Smith, *Political Institutions*, 2–30.

13. Melissa Haussman, *Abortion Politics in North America* (Boulder, CO: Lynne Rienner, 2005), 1–12.

14. Jill Vickers, "A Two-Way Street: Federalism and Women's Politics in Canada and the United States." *Publius* 40: 3 (2010): 419–20.

15. Sylvia Bashevkin, *Women on the Defensive: Living Through Conservative Times* (Toronto: University of Toronto Press, 1998), 9–10; 132–33.

16. Vickers, 412–20.

17. Daniel Béland, "Ideas, Institutions, and Policy Change," *Journal of European Public Policy* 16: 5(2009): 701–18.
18. Margaret Weir, "The Federal Government and Unemployment: The Foundation of Policy Innovation from the New Deal to the Great Society," in *Politics and Social Policy in the United States*, ed. Margaret Weir, Ann Shola Orloff, and Theda Skocpol (Princeton: Princeton University Press, 1988), 149–90.
19. Vivien A. Schmidt, "Discursive Institutionalism: The Explanatory Power of Ideas and Discourse," *Annual Review of Political Science* 11: 1 (2008): 303
20. See the discussion in Andreas Gofas and Colin Hay, "Varieties of Ideational Explanation," in *The Role of Ideas in Political Analysis: A Portrait of Contemporary Debates*, ed. Andreas Gofas and Colin Hay (London and New York: Routledge, 2010), 13–55.
21. For an overview of constitutional developments, Peter H. Russell, *Constitutional Odyssey: Can Canadians Become a Sovereign People?* 3rd ed. (Toronto: University of Toronto Press, 2004).
22. Alexandra Dobrowolsky, *The Politics of Pragmatism: Women, Representation and Constitutionalism in Canada* (Toronto: Oxford University Press, 2000); Matt James, *Misrecognized Materialists: Social Movements in Canadian Constitutional Politics*. (Vancouver: University of British Columbia Press, 2006).
23. Examples of the new human rights history are: Clément, *Rights Revolution*; Ross Lambertson, *Repression and Resistance: Canadian Human Rights Activists 1930-1960* (Toronto: University of Toronto Press, 2005); Christopher MacLennan, *Toward the Charter: Canadians the Demand for a National Bill of Rights, 1929-1960* (Montreal and Kingston: McGill–Queen's University Press, 2003); Carmela Patrias and Ruth A. Frager, "'This Is Our Country, These Are Our Rights'; Minorities and the Origins of Ontario's Human Rights Campaigns," *Canadian Historical Review* 82: 1 (March 2001): 1–35. For examples of the top-down approach, see Russell, *Constitutional Odyssey* and Kenneth McRoberts, *Misconceiving Canada: The Struggle for National Unity* (Toronto: Oxford University Press, 1997).
24. James W. St. G. Walker, *"Race", Rights and Law in the Supreme Court of Canada: Historical Case Studies* (Waterloo: Wilfred Laurier Press, 1997); Robert B. Howe and David Johnson, *Restraining Equality: Human Rights Commissions in Canada* (Toronto: University of Toronto Press, 2000).
25. Alan C. Cairns, *Charter versus Federalism: The Dilemmas of Constitutional Reform* (Montreal and Kingston: McGill–Queen's University Press, 1992).
26. Sharon McIvor, "Aboriginal Women Unmasked," *Canadian Journal of Women and the Law* 16 (2004): 107–36.
27. Walter S. Tarnopolsky, "The Historical and Constitutional Context of the Proposed Canadian Charter of Rights and Freedoms." *Law and Contemporary Problems* 44: 3 (Summer 1981): 188–89; Penney Kome, *The Taking of Twenty-Eight: Women Challenge the Constitution* (Toronto: The Women's Press, 1983); Dobrowolsky, *Politics of Pragmatism*, 39–74.
28. Smith, *Lesbian and Gay Rights*, 66–67.
29. For example, Emily Grabham, "Law v. Canada: New Directions for Equality Under the Canadian Charter?" *Oxford Journal of Legal Studies* 22: 4 (2002): 641–61; see also Manfredi 2004: 50ff.
30. On LEAF, see Christopher P. Manfredi, *Feminist Activism in the Supreme Court : Legal Mobilization and the Women's Legal Education and Action Fund* (Vancouver: University of British Columbia Press, 2004), 43–49; Dobrowolsky, *Politics of Pragmatism*, 39–74.
31. Nitya Iyer, "Disappearing Women: Racial Minority Women in Human Rights Cases," *Canadian Journal of Women and the Law* 6: 1 (1993): 25
32. Eléanore Lépinard, "In the Name of Equality? The Missing Intersection in Canadian Feminists' Legal Mobilization Against Multiculturalism," *American Behavioral Scientist* 53: 12 (2010): 1763–87.
33. Melanie Randall, "Equality Rights and the Charter: Reconceptualizing State Responsibility for Ending Domestic Violence," in *Making Equality Rights Real: Securing Substantive Equality Under the Charter*, ed. Fay Faraday et al. (Toronto: Irwin Law, 2006), 287–89.

34. Smith, *Lesbian and Gay Rights*, 60–65; See also Valerie J. Korinek, "'The Most Openly Gay Person for at Least a Thousand Miles': Doug Wilson and the Politicization of a Province, 1975–1983." *Canadian Historical Review* 84: 4 (2003): 517–50.

35. John D'Emilio, "Will the Courts Set Us Free?: Reflections on the Campaign for Same-Sex Marriage," in *The Politics of Same-Sex Marriage*, ed. Craig A. Rimmerman and Clyde Wilcox (Chicago and London: University of Chicago Press, 2007), 39–64; Suzanne J. Lenon, "Marrying Citizens! Raced Subjects? Re-thinking the Terrain of Equal Marriage Discourse," *Canadian Journal of Women and the Law* 17: 2 (2005): 405–21.

36. Iyer, 25–30; Lenon, 406–10.

37. Susan Boyd and Claire F. L. Young, "From Same-Sex to No Sex? Trends towards Recognition of Same-Sex Relationships in Canada," *Seattle Journal of Social Justice* 3 (2003): 757–93.

38. Jasbir K. Puar, *Terrorist Assemblages: Homonationalism in Queer Times* (Durham and London: Duke University Press, 2007).

39. Thomas Keck, "Beyond Backlash: Assessing the Impact of Judicial Decisions on LGBT Rights," *Law and Society Review* 43: 1 (March 2009): 175–77.

Chapter 9

•◆•

Human Rights for Some: First Nations Rights in Twentieth-Century Canada[1]

J.R. Miller

In the 1946–48 period, when Canadian John Peters Humphreys was working with the likes of Eleanor Roosevelt and Jacques Maritain on what became the UN Declaration of Human Rights, in Ottawa a parliamentary committee was toiling partially in the same spirit of advancing rights on a far different document. In the Canadian capital, a Joint Parliamentary Committee on the Indian Act was reviewing the statute with a view to its overhaul. Although the 1876 consolidation of legislation affecting First Nations people, or "Indians," differed dramatically from the incipient UN Declaration, those at work in New York and Ottawa shared a desire to advance human rights in their respective jurisdictions. In the federal capital, one of the effects of Canada's heavy participation in the Second World War, which was portrayed as a struggle of democracies against totalitarians and racists, was an awakening of both awareness and concern about the ideological bases of legislation dealing with First Nations. Not only had Canada's commitment of approximately a million servicemen and servicewomen piqued the country's interest in international issues, but the disproportionately high rate of volunteering by First Nations men had attracted favourable attention. During the war public attitudes toward Indians shifted from predominantly indifferent or negative to positive and concerned. Immediately at war's end, public officials detected a heightened desire in the general public to reward First Nations people for their contributions by advancing their rights.[2] That was one of the factors that led to the creation of the joint committee on the Indian Act. As an Alberta member of that joint committee said, "the Canadian people as a whole are interested in the problem of the Indians; they have become aware that the country has been negligent in the matter of looking after the Indians and they are anxious to remedy our shortcomings. Parliament and the country is [*sic*] 'human rights' conscious."[3]

Certainly the "shortcomings" in Indian policy were many and deep-rooted by the 1940s. Although Canada's denial of the rights of First

Nations was based on an 1876 statute, the underpinnings of the policies went much deeper. The Indian Act that Parliament passed in 1876 was merely a consolidation of legislation, much of it developed in the colonial forerunners of Ontario, that regulated the relations between the colonial state and First Nations. Given the origins of Canadian Indian policy in the colonial relationship, the mistreatment of First Nations and their rights through legislation is, perhaps, not surprising. What is astounding, though, is that that legislation's main elements—including its gross violations of human rights—would persist until late in the twentieth century. Although Aboriginal peoples used different mechanisms to protect rights in their communities, meaning the conventional human rights framework does not fit them well, understanding their experience does help us understand the failures of Canadian government policy to live up the state's claimed principles.

The basic point about the Indian Act is that it assumed that First Nations peoples were not adults. It structured the relationship between the federal government and First Nations as that of a trustee and ward, or parent and child. That the federal government framed the relationship in this manner formally from 1876 onward was a particular affront to western First Nations, but, more generally, First Nations throughout the country found that it contravened their understanding of their relationship to the Crown. In the particular case of western First Nations, they had only recently signed treaties—indeed, two of the seven numbered treaties were concluded after passage of the Act—that they assumed formalized a different relationship between themselves and the Queen and her people. Operating from their own cultural values and customs, they understood the recent treaties as mechanisms for creating kinship between First Nations and the Queen's people. They thought that they and the Queen's people were siblings—brothers and sisters—whose relationship was established by treaty and renewed annually by the payment of annuities promised in the treaties. Indeed, one Plains chief in 1881 addressed Lord Lorne, Governor General and son-in-law of Queen Victoria, as "brother."[4] They had the same fictive mother or actual mother-in-law, after all. For such leaders, the coerced shift to a ward–trustee relationship founded on the Indian Act was a source of first confusion, and then a sense of betrayal, and finally bitterness.

First Nations' enforced legal infantilism took many forms, including political rights such as voting in federal, provincial, or territorial elections.

As legal children, First Nations people did not possess the franchise outside their own reserves. They did, however, have access to enfranchisement of a different sort. Since 1857, when the Province of Canada (forerunner of Southern Ontario) passed the Gradual Civilization Act, adult First Nation males who applied and could convince a board of examiners that they were literate, debt-free, and of good moral character could surrender their status as "Indians" and become full British Canadian citizens, with all attendant rights, including the vote, after a three-year probationary period in which they would demonstrate further their fitness to join the general citizenry. (Status was determined by ancestry—descent from a status parent—community acceptance, the imprimatur of the government department responsible for Indian affairs; and the overriding consideration, infrequently enforced, that a person be of at least one-quarter Indian blood.) Moreover, they would acquire a twenty-hectare share of their former reserve land as a freehold tenure. The statute's reach was considerable: an enfranchised male's wife and children would also become enfranchised and lose Indian status, as would all their descendants forever. The reaction of First Nations to the measure was overwhelmingly negative. A chief from Kahnawake, the Mohawk reserve on the south shore of the St. Lawrence River opposite Montreal, charged that "there is nothing in it to be for their benefit, only to break them to pieces." Collectively, First Nations responded with passive resistance. Between 1857 and 1876 only one man was granted enfranchisement. His band responded by refusing to surrender twenty hectares of land for his individual allotment, and after much argument and delay he had to settle for cash compensation.[5]

Undeterred, the government of Canada kept enfranchisement on the books for over a century. The 1857 measure was continued in the 1869 Gradual Enfranchisement Act, and then embodied in the 1876 Indian Act. The codifying statute added a new twist: involuntary enfranchisement for a limited group of men. Male members of the liberal professions—law, medicine, religion—or any man who obtained a university degree "shall *ipso facto* become and be enfranchised."[6] Within four years the government recognized the folly of involuntary enfranchisement for select males. By the amendment of the Indian Act in 1880, which also created a Department of Indians Affairs (DIA), it was now the case that male professionals and degree-holders "upon petition to the Superintendent General [the Minister of Indian Affairs], *ipso facto* become and be enfranchised under this Act."[7] Henceforth, educated males could be enfranchised without undergoing examination and a probationary period, but only if they applied to be. Between 1880 and 1920 enfranchisement remained unchanged in its fundamentals, although minor tinkering was performed to make qualifying for enfranchisement easier in some cases.[8]

But in 1920 a drastic change was introduced at the behest of a deputy minister of Indian Affairs who expressed his and his department's frustration at First Nations' slow adoption of DIA policies. Duncan Campbell Scott explained:

> I want to get rid of the Indian problem. I do not think as a matter of fact, that this country ought to continuously protect a class of people who are able to stand alone. That is my whole point . . . That has been the whole purpose of Indian education and advancement since the earliest times. One of the very earliest enactments was to provide for the enfranchisement of the Indian. So it is written in our law that the Indian was eventually to become enfranchised.- . . . Our object is to continue until there is not a single Indian in Canada that has not been absorbed into the body politic and there is no Indian question, and no Indian Department.[9]

The Indian Act was amended to make it possible for the minister of Indian affairs to enfranchise a male whether the individual wished it or not, but the change lasted only from 1920 to 1922, when a new Liberal government under Mackenzie King repealed the involuntary provision. Involuntary enfranchisement for males returned in modified and diluted form in 1933 and lasted in the Act until 1951.[10] There is no evidence that any Indian male was involuntarily enfranchised after 1920.

First Nations women did not fare nearly as well with enfranchisement. Beginning with the 1869 Gradual Enfranchisement Act, Canadian legislation instituted a regime of gender discrimination that led to tens of thousands of First Nations women losing their "Indian status" through marriage. The 1869 provision, which was incorporated into the Indian Act in 1876, said that any Indian woman who married a non-Indian man would lose her Indian status, and all her descendants would similarly be non-Indians. On the other hand, Indian men who married non-Indian women conferred their status on their spouses, and on the children of their unions. Theoretically, it was possible for an Indian woman who was regarded as having status by the government to marry a man who was culturally Indian but who was not recognized as having status by Ottawa, to lose her Indian status. Similarly, a woman with status who married a Métis man lost her status through marriage. This gender discrimination was motivated, in part, by a desire to protect Indian land holdings, because the prevailing view in government was that non-Indian males could usurp reserve lands by marrying into a band, a process that had caused problems in some localities. The effect of the legislation, however, was not protective but damaging: many First Nations women and their offspring lost status and the right to reside on their reserves. This gender discrimination would persist in the Indian Act for over a century.

Both First Nations women and men also found their property rights circumscribed in a number of ways under the Indian Act. First, and most fundamental, was the legal status of land holdings on reserves. Reserve occupants did not own their land outright in freehold tenure, whether individually or collectively. Rather, their lands were held in trust by the Crown—that is, the government—and they operated in fact as mere occupants and users of the land. As the twentieth century advanced, this limited territorial right would cause First Nations individuals and bands problems. For example, because they did not own their land, Indian farmers could not get lending agencies to grant mortgages to purchase land or buy capital equipment or operating supplies. The status of individual holdings on reserve thus proved an impediment to economic development. From time to time Indian Affairs and other interested parties initiated steps to encourage subdivision of reserves into individual holdings, but these efforts never made much headway. A push by the Department of Indian Affairs in the 1880s to get bands to agree to subdivide their reserves and allow reserve farmers to hold their plots in severalty—or individual control—was met by passive resistance and defeated by First Nations communities.[11] In the twenty-first century the government of Canada is once more championing individual reserve land ownership, though now explicitly on a voluntary basis.

The nature of their land tenure was by no means the only limitation on the property rights of reserve people. Most telling was a clause of the Indian Act that required them to get a permit signed by the Indian agent or reserve farming instructor to be able to take their harvest or other products of reserve enterprise to non-Native communities for sale.[12] Again, officially, the motive underlying this restriction was to protect reserve farmers from exploitation at the hands of non-Native businesspeople, but the provision also enhanced the agent's and department's ability to control the movement and discipline the behaviour of reserve residents. The necessity to obtain an official's signed permission at a minimum caused considerable inconvenience and inefficiency, as it might take the farmer hours or even days to locate the agent to ask for a permit. The requirement also enabled DIA officials to "police" behaviour, perhaps even withholding permission to sell goods off reserve as a form of punishment. Indian Affairs officials never seemed to recognize that such a restriction undermined the department's agricultural policies. The federal government claimed that its aim was to promote the adoption of Euro-Canadian economic practices and values, but its permit policy discouraged the practice of market-oriented behaviour. Another example of how the Indian Act interfered with First Nations people's private property was the clause that stipulated that no will of an Indian person was valid without the approval of the minister of Indian affairs. Again, such tutelage was a deterrent to adoption of more individualistic and materialistic approaches.[13]

Other, related policies that the Department sought to enforce at various times had a similar ironic effect. The pass system, for example, which was instituted in the Prairie West in 1885, was anything but an inducement to behave like an active entrepreneur. Initially a response to the military emergency caused by the Métis insurrection in the spring of 1885, the requirement that a reserve resident have a pass signed by the agent to be lawfully off the reserve, persisted for many years. Even when, in 1892, the Mounted Police informed Indian Affairs that they did not want to enforce the pass system any longer because it had no legal basis—it was not based on any provision of the Indian Act or federal order-in-council, and it contravened promises of mobility that had been made during treaty negotiations—and made maintaining good relations with the bands more difficult, Indian Affairs still thought that the police should carry on because the pass system was a matter of policy favoured by the DIA.[14] It is not known with any certainty or precision how long or effectively the pass system remained in force. But there were still passes being issued during the first third of the twentieth century, although it is not clear how widespread the practice was. Whatever its duration, it clearly violated First Nations' rights.

For an eight-year period near the end of the nineteenth century the department also interfered with reserve occupants' property rights in an even more bizarre manner. Between 1889 and 1897, thanks largely to the convictions and efforts of a single official, Indian Affairs foisted what has come to be known as its "peasant farming" policy on farmers on western reserves.[15] Hayter Reed, initially commissioner of Indian affairs in the prairies and then in 1893 deputy minister, subscribed to the latest social scientific theories concerning indigenous peoples. Nineteenth-century social science held an evolutionary view of social development, a schema in which peoples advanced from a state of savagery to one of barbarism, and then finally to "civilization."[16] The last stage was distinguished by different forms of economic organization in agriculture. Early in the "civilized" phase, people followed subsistence agriculture, with minimal holdings worked principally with hand implements and limited animal assistance. Later they evolved toward larger scale farming geared toward the production of surplus crops for the market. They had to go through these successive stages; any path other than learning farming first in peasant style would doom them. Therefore, under Reed the department tried to compel farmers to use only hand tools, focus on just a few hectares of arable land, and rely principally on root crops for their own consumption. That all around western reserves non-Native farmers were forming co-operatives and buying the newfangled steam-powered equipment that was becoming available in the United States, mattered not at all to Indian Affairs under Hayter Reed. The result of this ill-conceived policy was the retardation of reserve agriculture, the frustration of many Indian farmers who were trying to become successful agriculturalists in an age when they no longer had bison to sustain them, and not a few frustrated DIA employees who had to try to enforce the hare-brained scheme. Mercifully, in 1896 a change of government led to the sacking of deputy minister Reed the following year. But while the "peasant" farming policy was in force it caused enormous damage and seriously curtailed reserve farmers' freedom of economic action.

Freedom of political action was another area in which Indian Act policies severely infringed the rights of First Nations from the latter part of the nineteenth century onward. Beginning in 1869 with the Gradual Enfranchisement Act, Parliament both limited the scope of decisions that bands could take and attempted to reshape their general approach to governance. The 1869 measure specified a limited range of powers for bands, a restriction that was maintained by the Indian Act when it was adopted in 1876. As the municipal-style mandate was phrased, chiefs and bands could legislate on "care of public health, the observance of order and decorum at assemblies of the Indians . . . the repression of intemperance and profligacy, the prevention of trespass by cattle, the maintenance of roads, bridges, ditches, and fences . . . ," although any resolution that a council might pass was "subject to confirmation by the Governor in Council," or federal cabinet.[17] Compounding the problem was the reality that the agent usually convened band council meetings, presided over deliberations, kept the minutes, and sent them to Ottawa for "confirmation." Band council powers were expanded somewhat in the 1884 Indian Advancement Act, which was available only to First Nations in Eastern Canada, but that gain was obtained at the price of having to elect councils annually instead of triennially.[18] And, finally, the federal government reserved the right to depose chiefs and councillors of whom they did not approve. Originally, in the 1869 Gradual Enfranchisement Act, deposition was contemplated for "dishonesty, intemperance, or immorality," and the lack of detail implied that it would be Ottawa that would decide which leaders were dishonest, intemperate, or immoral. In the Indian Act seven years later, the grounds for possible deposition were broadened to "dishonesty, intemperance, immorality, or incompetency." The potential for abuse in the capacious term "incompetency" was great.

The other major area of political interference involved the type of governance. Along with a profound belief in the virtue and efficacy of private property ownership, the federal government has held to elections as an *idée fixe* since soon after Confederation. The 1869 legislation offered bands the blessings of British Canadian government in the form of triennial elections, albeit with the proviso that bands that had "life chiefs" could continue with that form of government during at least the lifetimes of their traditional chiefs: "all life Chiefs now living shall continue as such until death or resignation, or until their removal by the Governor." An 1880 amendment to the Indian Act authorized the federal government to order the use of elections by selected bands, and now specified that in such situations life chiefs lost their authority once elections were held. (And, as noted, the Indian Advancement Act of 1884 offered annual elections to some bands.) On the other hand, Prime Minister and Superintendent General of Indian Affairs John A. Macdonald insisted that the Electoral Franchise Act adopted in 1885 include the right to vote in federal elections for adult male Indians residing east of Manitoba who met the minimum property qualification. That provision was soon enough deleted in 1898 by a Parliament now led by the Liberal government of Sir Wilfrid Laurier.

As these various developments concerning band council jurisdiction and elections suggested, Indian Act policy tended to become more coercive over time. The underlying reason for the government's increasing resort to compulsion was frustration. Ottawa found that bands did not take to land-holding in severalty or electing leaders or becoming enfranchised. The federal government, particularly after 1885, resorted increasingly to coercion to secure adoption of policies that clearly did not commend themselves to First Nations. Two of the areas in which Indian Affairs attempted to impose its will were deposing leaders that it regarded as recalcitrant and attempting to impose the elective system on bands. In the prairie region in the late nineteenth century, for example, chiefs like Piapot in the Qu'Appelle Valley and White Bear in Southeastern Saskatchewan were deposed for their opposition. Piapot's offence was to contravene the prohibition on summer ceremonials,[19] while White Bear's transgression was broader and more challenging. He and a majority of his band refused to buy into the policies that promoted agriculture, Euro-Canadian schooling, and Christian missions. His band followed an alternative strategy of maintaining a mixed economy consisting of some gardening, cattle-raising, commercial fishing, and the manufacture and sale of handicrafts to local settlers. In both cases, the heavy hand of Ottawa was defeated, as the DIA had to recommend that the chief be restored to office in order to get any co-operation from a band dominated by his followers.[20]

Federal efforts to promote the electoral system fell with particular force on bands in Eastern Canada, where, the DIA thought, Indians were more acculturated and ready to participate in Euro-Canadian institutions. The difficulty was that a number of bands were not interested in doing so. A particular thorn in the government's side were the Mohawk, who traditionally governed with a council of sachems chosen by clan mothers. In 1898, when Ottawa attempted to impose elections on Akwesasne, the Mohawk reserve near Cornwall, Ontario, the clan mothers sent a polite reply saying that they had chosen their life chiefs and would not need elections. Matters came to a head the next year. When federal officials attempted to hold elections at Akwesasne, violence broke out that resulted in the death of Jake Ice, brother of one of the traditional chiefs. Tension persisted, with Akwesasne residents indicating in 1904 that they favoured traditional governance two to one, but by 1908 an elective system was in operation.[21]

Although the situation was more complicated on the Six Nations Reserve near Brantford, Ontario, the central dynamic of the dispute that developed there was similar to the confrontation at Akwesasne. The similarity was the federal government's determination after the Great War to try to impose elective government on the band, which appears to have had a majority who favoured traditional, non-elected governance. The differences that complicated the scene on the Grand River were found in two features of the reserve. First was the Six Nations' long-standing view that they were allies, not subjects of the Crown, and that they were not bound by the policies and will of Ottawa. As well, within the band a modernizing group—known usually as the Dehorners because they wished to knock the horns or symbols of office from the heads of traditional leaders—had emerged in the late nineteenth century and by the 1920s were challenging the authority of traditional leaders. The assertion of sovereign status caused the Six Nations to pursue international recognition at the League of Nations, while the presence of the Dehorners emboldened the Department of Indian Affairs. In 1924 federal police invaded the reserve, and an elective council was established at Oshweken, the reserve's central town.[22] Disputes over governance have bedevilled Six Nations—as has been the case at sister reserves at Tyendinaga, near Belleville, Akwesasne, Kahnawake, and Kahnesatake—as traditionalists and pro-election factions contended through the twentieth century. The salient point of the sad affair is that the government presumed to dictate governance to people over whom they could not demonstrate they had sovereignty, not having conquered or made a treaty with them.

The related areas of culture and religion, traditionally human rights of communities, did not escape the interfering tendencies of Indian Affairs. By the late nineteenth century, both government officials and missionaries recognized that the persistence of cultural institutions such as the potlatch of the Northwest Coast were forces for social cohesion that stood in the way of the government's assimilative program. The sharing and feasting ceremony was a form of governance, too, because it was the mechanism by which these First Nations regulated conflict within the group and between communities. Indeed, potlatching was known as "warring with property." It also contradicted many of the individualistic, acquisitive qualities of Euro-Canadian society that bureaucrats and missionaries believed First Nations should come to love. As a result, an amendment of the Indian Act in 1884 outlawed participation in "the

Indian festival known as the 'Potlach' or in the Indian dance known as the 'tamanawas'" and authorized the courts to levy fines for breaches of the Act.[23] Unfortunately for the assimilators, the first time the law was applied, the judge threw the measure out as too vague and indeterminate to be enforced. In due course, in 1895, Parliament returned to the issue, this time not banning named cultural institutions, but instead specifying the actions that were forbidden. Participation "in any Indian festival, dance or other ceremony of which the giving away or paying or giving back of money, goods or articles of any sort forms a part . . . [or] any celebration or dance of which the wounding or mutilation of the dead or living body of any human being or animal forms a part or is a feature, is guilty of an indictable offence and is liable to imprisonment" for two to six months.[24] Although the statute appeared to narrow the prohibition by targeting it more specifically, in fact it broadened the Act's application. The prohibition on giving away and mutilation brought prairie summer ceremonials such as the Sun Dance and Thirst Dance into the zone of prohibition. Both these cultural practices included giving presents to those who attended, and the Sun Dance also sometimes involved young males piercing their breasts or shoulders in a symbolic act of sacrifice.[25] Although the clause was enforced unevenly, it did cause problems while it remained on the books.

The attack on First Nations' cultural institutions such as the potlatch and the promotion of residential schooling were rooted in the same ideology. There was even a causal link between the cultural ban and residential schools, because the desire to prevent parents from taking their children out of school for up to two weeks in June was one of the arguments used to justify the assault on the Sun Dance in 1895. And if there was any denial of human rights greater than interference with cultural and spiritual observances it was the attempt to remake a community's children's identity and way of life. But that is precisely what the residential schools that the federal government began to sponsor systematically in the 1880s aimed to do. Indian Affairs bureaucrats and most Christian missionaries believed at the time that it was necessary to refashion First Nations society through education and the cultural transformation of the children. And because policy planners recognized that attendance at day schools would not achieve that objective, in part because it would allow the continuity of parental influence, they preferred custodial educational institutions that would allow teachers and missionaries to provide a concentrated version of instruction while minimizing the parental and community influence that usually worked against assimilation. Consequently, after 1883 the federal government promoted custodial schools, especially in the West and North where it was believed the need for rapid acculturation was greatest, for First Nations and later Inuit. Beginning in 1920, mandatory attendance provisions were inserted into the Indian Act,[26] but it was never the case that children had to attend a residential school. Compulsory attendance merely meant that the young had to be in some sort of school, and it remained true throughout the existence of these institutions that only a minority of status Indian children attended residential school. Many more went to day schools, or often to no school at all.

Although the reach of the residential school might have been limited, its impact was great. This was the case because even those who did not attend a residential school could be affected by the attitudes and behaviour of those who had. Moreover, when younger generations ceased to be sent to residential schools, they still had to contend with the intergenerational effects of the challenges their parents and grandparents had faced. The problems that the schools created had to do, not just with the severe physical and sexual abuse that has captured most of the media and political attention since the 1990s, but the undermining of the students' identity as Aboriginal people and the erosion of their sense of worth and belonging. Because the religious and secular instruction that staff imparted frequently emphasized the negative about indigenous society and its spiritual practices, students often emerged not knowing their cultural identity or their language, and not believing they had a secure lodging anywhere. Abuse at the hands of some staff had a similarly devastating effect, as the young victims, already barraged with messages that denigrated their parents' spiritual beliefs and ways of living, too often assumed that they were somehow to blame for the evils that had befallen them. Tens of thousands of them emerged from residential schooling damaged, confused, unattached to a community, and sometimes bitter and angry at what had happened. By the time both government and the missionary bodies that ran the schools day to day woke up to the reality that the schools did not succeed pedagogically or religiously, while they inflicted enormous damage on their students and students' families, tens of thousands had been damaged. The schools were phased out, beginning in 1969, but their legacy continues to haunt Canada, not to mention survivors who deal with the symptoms of residential school attendance all the time.[27]

How to categorize the harm that residential schooling represented in the century after the early 1880s has proven a controversial matter. The residential schooling experiment is sometimes described, particularly by those engaged in political campaigns, as an engine of genocide, while others prefer the softer appellation *cultural genocide*. There are problems with these labels. Neither the federal government nor Christian churches that operated the schools intended to eliminate Aboriginal peoples physically, though they clearly wished to transform them culturally, making them over into brown-skinned Euro-Canadians. It is sometimes argued that residential schooling amounted to genocide because it worked to transfer the children of a society from one group to another, one of the manifestations of genocide explicitly mentioned in the UN Convention on Genocide. But the problem with this argument is twofold. First, the school promoters did not wish to transform the indigenous societies into Euro-Canadian ones, but rather to alter their beliefs and practices to ones that were more compatible with Euro-Canadian norms and practices. Moreover, since only a minority of even status Indian children ever attended a residential school—and a smaller proportion of Inuit, and only a very small fraction of Métis—the actual experience of residential schooling does not make a persuasive case for inclusion in the genocide category. It should also be remembered, especially in light of the many provisions of the Indian Act to encourage enfranchisement, that there were large numbers of non-status Indians in Canada at least until the very late years of the twentieth century. Those afflicted by residential schools constituted a small proportion of the total Aboriginal population of Canada. A more convincing case can be made for referring to residential schools as an initiative that aimed at cultural genocide. One might also, more simply, refer to the corrosive processes at work in residential schools as coercive assimilation.

The government's administration of Indian Act policies became more coercive and punitive over time. The clauses dealing with governance, which were present in the Act from its earliest days but were implemented from the 1890s to the 1920s, constitute one example. Another is the 1884 and 1895 attempts to ban cultural and spiritual practices. With these there was an uptick in enforcement at the end of the Great War, although the prohibition always remained only partially applied. Enfranchisement shows the same pattern of the government moving from encouraging voluntary enfranchisement, at least in the case of males. Resort to involuntary enfranchisement of males occurred at the beginning, from 1876 to 1880, for males with high educational or professional attainments, but not again until 1920. The timing of the movement toward greater interference and coercion indicates increasing disappointment on the part of policy-makers with the failure of their policies. The notorious outburst of the deputy minister, D.C. Scott—"I want to get rid of the Indian problem"—clearly demonstrated the frustration felt over failed policies. In a situation of government dominance over indigenous minorities the oppressor blamed the oppressed for its failure, and countered with more coercion.[28] The frustration, bitterness, and determination that Scott demonstrated in 1920 continued through the interwar period. In 1927, at the behest of Indian Affairs, Parliament amended the Indian Act to outlaw Indians from soliciting or giving funds for "the prosecution of any claim [by] the tribe or band of Indians to which such Indian belongs."[29] This extraordinary measure, which effectively thwarted First Nations' use of lawyers and large-scale efforts to organize politically, was Scott's and the government's response to the campaign by First Nations in British Columbia, particularly the Nisga'a, for recognition of their Aboriginal title claims to lands where no treaties had been made. That approach would persist for decades more.

If the frustration D.C. Scott expressed in 1920 was symptomatic of official exasperation, the prevailing political and popular mood by 1945 was noticeably different. The Second World War dented, but did not destroy, the deeply entrenched racism that underlay many of Canada's discriminatory policies, including those directed toward First Nations. Until 1943 the Royal Canadian Navy would accept only servicepeople who were "of Pure European Descent and of the White Race," and the Royal Canadian Air Force, while it had its own racial exclusion practices, accepted First Nations.[30] The army had admitted First Nations men since at least the Great War. However equivocal the Canadian military's commitment to equality, it was hard to deny in the midst of a war against Germany and Japan especially that racially based policies were characteristics of the foe. It was also difficult to fight discrimination abroad without noticing the racism of Canadian policies, including the Indian

Act. Employing the rhetoric of right and justice to promote the war effort helped to bring about changes in attitudes toward some minority groups generally and First Nations specifically. In 1944, a Member of Parliament declaimed "we are not fighting to-day merely to defeat Germany and Japan; we are fighting in defence of definite principles. We are fighting for a peace based on justice, and justice must be granted to minorities as well as majorities."[31] In the same year, the *Globe and Mail* quoted a parent as saying, "We who have our sons and daughters in the fight and who pray and work from dawn to dusk, that honor and right shall prevail in this struggle are not going to permit our own officials to act like Huns towards the Indians right under our noses."[32] Clearly, as a result of the war, attitudes had changed. As an MP would put it a few years later, by war's end "the Canadian people as a whole are interested in the problem of the Indians."[33]

As events would show, Canadians' approach to First Nations was self-interested. The enthusiasm for "human rights" at war's end obscured the reality that there were many interpretations of human rights, and that non-Native Canadians would prove uncomprehending of the fact that First Nations often defined rights differently. One example of the underlying difference in attitude was found in the fact that the wartime shift in public attitudes toward Indians had been from a perception of Indians as outsiders and deviants to a view of them as "potential citizens."[34] The problem with that transition, however, was that many First Nations did not consider themselves citizens, potential or actual. Rather, in many cases they thought of themselves as simply Cree or Haida, or generally First Nations. A very few, such as the Six Nations and some Mohawk communities in Ontario and Quebec, saw themselves as sovereign peoples, not subjects or fellow citizens. Many of these differences in perception and aspiration played out in the hearings and deliberations of the Special Joint Committee on the Indian Act between 1946 and 1948. While First Nations representatives stated clearly in written briefs and in appearances before the parliamentarians that they opposed the assimilationist policies of the Indian Affairs Branch, they usually did not express a desire to become and be treated as citizens like any of the other Canadians who had acquired Canadian citizenship—as distinct from being British subjects—with the coming into force of the Citizenship Act in 1947.

The self-interested approach that the Canadian majority had toward the rights of minorities goes far to explain the bizarre outcome of the labours of the Special Joint Committee on the Indian Act. Although the country was reportedly "human rights conscious" as the process of review began, the changes that culminated in a major revision of the Indian Act in 1951 were far less than people would have expected. For example, with residential schooling, which attracted more attention than those who set up the committee expected, custodial schools persisted under denominational operation in spite of all the criticism they had attracted. The explanation for this outcome could be found in the lobbying that Roman Catholic leaders, and the missionary order of Oblates in particular, mounted to dissuade the St. Laurent government from making wholesale changes to the schools.[35] In other areas there were significant reforms of some of the policies of attempted control and assimilation embedded in the Indian Act. The 1927 prohibition on soliciting or giving money for pursuit of an Indian claim was repealed. Similarly, the 1933 re-introduction of involuntary enfranchisement of male Indians at the discretion of the government—a return to the draconian measure of 1920–22 with protection for treaty rights—was stripped from the legislation. The involuntary loss of Indian status that legislation had inflicted on women since 1869, however, remained in the Act. And the attack on the potlatch and prairie summer ceremonies that had been introduced in 1884 and 1895 was retired. But the underlying drive and purpose of the measure to bring about cultural change in First Nations persisted. As a leading scholar of Indian policy put it, what had happened was that the 1951 amendment "returned to the philosophy of the original Indian Act: civilization was to be encouraged but not directed or forced on the Indian people. Assimilation for all Indians was a goal that should be striven for without an abundance of tests or the compulsory aspects of the preceding Indian Acts."[36]

The Canadian government's "human rights consciousness" in relation to First Nations continued for another generation to ignore First Nations' views. Two of the most glaring examples of this tendency in the quarter-century after the Second World War were found in residential schools and voting rights. Although the 1951 amendment of the Indian Act had left residential schooling largely undisturbed, Indian Affairs bureaucrats wished to reduce the government's reliance on schools for both ideological and financial reasons. First, given the background of the war and the Special Joint Committee, maintaining racially segregated schools for First Nations children was, at a minimum, awkward.

Second, given the rapidly escalating birthrate among Indians that was noticeable by the war years, continuing to depend on residential schools meant heavy capital costs for the many new institutions that would have to be built to meet the burgeoning population. Indian Affairs instead adopted a policy of integrated schooling, in which it contracted with local public school boards to accommodate First Nations students alongside non-Native children. The operating costs that the tuition agreements negotiated with school boards were less onerous than the capital costs of constructing more schools, and they had the added convenience of flexibility. The problem with this arrangement, one that some of the missionaries involved with residential schooling futilely predicted, was that First Nations students found the adjustment to public schools difficult, and non-Native classmates and their parents in most cases were anything but welcoming. In spite of the problems that quickly emerged and persisted through the 1950s and early 1960s, Indian Affairs did not begin to move away from the integration policy until a revolt by some First Nations parents and new ideological leadership at the highest levels caused a revolution in the late 1960s.[37] Until then, Indian Affairs carried on with a policy that met its, rather than First Nations', needs.

The same attitude toward First Nations interests was obvious in the area of voting rights. Of course, as "legal children" First Nations were usually denied the right to vote in elections other than those at the band level that officialdom favoured. (The exception was a period between passage of the Electoral Franchise Act in 1885 and repeal of the clause that permitted some adult male Indians east of Manitoba to vote in 1898.) In fact, the various "enfranchisement" acts that had been on the legislative books since 1857 required First Nations to give up their status in order to gain the rights of citizens, including the right to vote in municipal, provincial, and federal elections. Indeed, the long history of excluding First Nations from the franchise created a situation in which being Indian and citizenship, with its right to vote, developed into something of an antithesis. Exclusion evolved *de facto* into a badge of Indian identity.[38] In the case of most Mohawk those feelings were strengthened by their belief that they were allies, not subjects, of the Crown. When the right to vote came to First Nations, therefore, it was not always welcomed or used. Granting the right to vote in federal elections was the unilateral act of a Conservative prime minister, John Diefenbaker, who simply believed that it was the right thing to do. Provincial governments were no better than their federal counterpart. Ontario had actually legislated "to remove doubts" that some Indians might have the right to vote by stating explicitly in its 1876 Elections Act that on-reserve Indians could not vote. Quebec and Prince Edward Island ruled out Indians when they implemented manhood suffrage. Initially, only New Brunswick did not exclude First Nations. Following the Great War, a number of provinces (PEI, Ontario, and Manitoba) followed federal example and allowed Indians who had served in the war to vote. Similar provisions were made by some provinces for veterans of the Second World War and Korean War. New Brunswick, British Columbia, and Saskatchewan extended the vote to Indians living off reserve. Full provincial enfranchisement followed in BC (1949), Manitoba (1952), Ontario (1954), Saskatchewan (1960), New Brunswick and PEI (1963) and Quebec (1969). In Saskatchewan's case, Premier T.C. Douglas had to break his word to chiefs not to implement voting until they approved.[39]

It is not surprising, then, that First Nations have not exercised the franchise they were granted with much enthusiasm or frequency. And in some circumstances, of which the 1992 referendum on the Charlottetown Accord is the clearest example, numerous First Nations have expressed their opposition to participating in the rite of citizenship by barring Elections Canada from their reserves. The most germane aspect of the tale, though, is that yet again non-Native politicians legislated in an area of rights to satisfy their own, rather than First Nations', desires.

When Canada went through its own rights revolution at the behest of Prime Minister Pierre Elliott Trudeau between 1968 and 1982, the same pattern of self-interested behaviour by the majority was prevalent. The failure to act in concert with First Nations when purporting to legislate in their interest was most glaring in 1969, on the first anniversary of the election of the Trudeau government. On that auspicious day Indian Affairs Minister Jean Chrétien rose in the Commons to introduce the government's policy proposal for First Nations, a document that has become notorious as the White Paper on Indian policy. The missive was presented as the result of lengthy consultations with First Nations leaders, but in fact was largely the distillation by bureaucrats in the prime minister's office of Trudeau's political philosophy as applied to matters such as Indian status, treaties, reserves, and federal jurisdiction over First Nations. Briefly, the White Paper was an emphatic statement of individualist thinking, decrying treaties between groups within the same society, for example, and promising to "wind up" the Department of Indian Affairs and have First Nations obtain government services previously obtained through the DIA from the provinces, like other Canadians.[40] Although the ensuing uproar took the Trudeau cabinet unawares, the reaction of First Nations leaders was hardly surprising. Trudeau had to suspend the White Paper proposals within a year, but the episode left bitterness and provided another illustration of the casualness with which Canadian governments regarded and treated First Nations' long-held rights.

The same syndrome was obvious in the behaviour of federal governments a decade later when they stumbled toward renewing the Constitution in an effort to respond to the emergence of Quebec sovereignism. The election of a Parti Québécois (PQ) government in November 1976 provoked a frenzy of federal–provincial consultations, and one of the results of the campaign to defeat the PQ's proposal for sovereignty-association in a 1980 provincial plebiscite was a flurry of negotiations in 1981–82. Neither the government of Joe Clark that was in office in the late 1970s nor that of Pierre Trudeau that was re-established early in 1980 showed any interest in hearing the views of First Nations leaders, even though the interests of the communities they led were often being discussed. Inclusion of a clause providing constitutional protection for some aspect of Aboriginal rights was actually on the table for discussion in the autumn of 1981, but was pushed off as Trudeau made concessions in an effort to win support from western premiers. It was only after the package of constitutional changes was agreed to in November 1981, and only by ferocious lobbying, that First Nations, Inuit, and Métis leaders were able to get section 35, which recognized and affirmed both Aboriginal and treaty rights, back into the constitutional reform package. When First Nations leaders went to London, to the Westminster Parliament that had to pass anything that would change the Canadian Constitution, to lobby against federal action, both the Clark and Trudeau governments at different times had counselled the United Kingdom government to ignore their protests.

The closing chapters of the constitutional drama were equally revealing. The discussions at Meech Lake in 1987 that were intended to negotiate a package of constitutional reforms that would allow Quebec to sign the 1982 agreement with, in Prime Minister Brian Mulroney's words, "honour and enthusiasm" studiously ignored the issues that Aboriginal people had been raising for years. In a series of four First Ministers' Conferences between 1983 and 1987 the Native leaders had pressed for agreement on a definition of "Aboriginal and treaty rights" that had been recognized and affirmed. During the most recent effort in 1987 they had urged the first ministers to agree in principle that Aboriginal self-government was one of those rights, only to be told that the concept was too vague for the premiers, especially those from the West, to agree. Yet, a short time later, the same leaders had no problem agreeing that Quebec constituted a "distinct society" and that its provincial legislature had the right and duty to promote that distinctiveness. What did that language mean? Clearly, no one knew. The Aboriginal leaders could only fume impotently until the spring of 1990, when Mulroney's high-risk tactics to secure ratification and the determination of a lone First Nations member of the Manitoba legislative assembly combined to kill the Accord by preventing its approval in time to meet the three-year deadline. Even then the prime minister could not give First Nations their due. Instead, Mulroney blamed the collapse of the Meech Lake Accord on the obstinacy of Premier Clyde Wells of Newfoundland rather than acknowledge that First Nations had done it in.

In the run-up to the Charlottetown Accord in 1992 non-Native leaders finally indicated that they now "got it" so far as First Nations were concerned. In these talks Aboriginal political leaders participated, and the Charlottetown Accord included some woolly language about Aboriginal self-government. The politicians' perceptiveness turned out to be too little, too late. In the referendum in the autumn of 1992, the Charlottetown Accord was turned down emphatically, including by most of those First Nations communities that chose to participate in the voting. Through the constitutional struggles that followed the Quebec provincial election of 1976, Canada's non-Native leaders had acted in a manner that indicated that, while a variety of rights were important, those of First Nations and other Aboriginal peoples generally were not.

The 1982 settlement had lingering effects on First Nations. The package so painfully assembled, in fact, was a good news–bad news proposition so far as Aboriginal groups were concerned. Section 35's recognition and affirmation of Aboriginal and treaty rights effectively placed two broad categories of rights beyond the reach of provincial legislatures or

Parliament, unless the legislators chose to invoke the "notwithstanding" clause in the agreement that shielded legislation.[41] It was the Charter of Rights and Freedoms (CORAF) that was both support and menace for Aboriginal peoples. Section 25 declared that none of the Charter's guarantees could "be construed so as to abrogate or derogate from any aboriginal, treaty or other rights or freedoms that pertain to the aboriginal peoples of Canada including . . . the Royal Proclamation of October 7, 1763; and any rights or freedoms that now exist by way of land claims agreements or may be so acquired." The Charter also contained an equality rights clause that would prove more problematic for First Nations. Section 15 stated: "Every individual is equal before and under the law and has the right to the equal protection and equal benefit of the law without discrimination and, in particular, without discrimination based on race, national or ethnic origin, colour, religion, sex, age or mental or physical disability."[42] It was obvious that the long-standing gender discrimination in the Indian Act contravened section 15 and would have to be corrected. Since the agreement on constitutional change in 1982 included "delayed justiciability" (a delay of three years before rights could be litigated under the Charter) in relation to equality rights, it was also apparent that the government and Parliament of Canada had only three years to deal with the issue before aggrieved women who had lost status by "marrying out" would go to court.

Bill C-31, Parliament's mechanism for responding to the gender discrimination in the Indian Act, resolved some difficulties, but created others in both the short and the long term. The positive contribution of the 1985 amendment was the elimination of the practice of enfranchisement, meaning giving up Indian status, which had been on the books for a century and a quarter. In dealing with the issue of gender discrimination, Indian Affairs faced substantial opposition from mostly male First Nations leaders who were concerned that restoring status for those who had lost it through marriage would create large numbers of restored "Indians" who would want to move back to the reserves and gain access to services. They asked the government to provide additional funds to deal with the anticipated influx of new residents. Ottawa would not do that, but it did suggest a means by which women who had regained status as a result of the legislation could still be denied band services. This was done by distinguishing between *Indian status* and *band membership*. The former could be obtained under Bill C-31, but the latter was only possible if returning women met the criteria in the membership codes that the federal government encouraged bands to establish. Needless to say, many bands drew up the most restrictive codes they could devise and Indian Affairs would accept. The result of distinguishing between status and band membership has been the creation of a group of women in limbo, women who have had their Indian status restored under the terms of C-31, but who cannot live on what they consider their home reserve or access services such as housing, education, and welfare there.[43]

The difficulties with Bill C-31 did not end with the status–membership divide: although the legislation was designed to eliminate gender inequality, it perpetuated it. Under the complex rules of C-31, "women who lost status through marrying out before 1985 can pass Indian status on to their children but not to their children's children. However, their brothers, who may also have married out before 1985, can pass on status to their children for at least one more generation, even though the children of the sister and the brother all have one status Indian parent and one non-Indian parent."[44] And under the rules of C-31, it is possible—probably likely—that tens of thousands of restored status Indians will see their grandchildren lose their status through marriage. The reason for this is that the child of a person who regained status under C-31 must marry a person with status, and their children must marry people with status for the grandchildren to retain Indian status. Given the high rate of movement off reserve and the tendency of urban Indians to marry partners of different backgrounds more frequently than on-reserve Indians, Bill C-31 thus constitutes a time bomb so far as the status Indian community is concerned.[45] As one authority describes the problem, "rather than repealing the patriarchal assumptions" of the Indian Act, "Bill C-31 only displaces them by two generations."[46] The long-term problem is even greater: Bill C-31's rules could eventually bring about an absolute decline in the numbers of status Indians. One demographic projection has found that the number of people who will be ineligible for registration as "Indians" will surpass those who will be eligible in about 2080.[47] Unchanged, could Bill C-31 ultimately satisfy the desire D.C. Scott expressed in 1920 and bring about the complete disappearance of status Indians?

Another effect of Bill C-31 has been that it has set up a confrontation between some First Nations and women who identify as members of those bands and are seeking reinstatement under C-31. It has also provoked controversy between non-Native women's groups and some First Nations. This clash is a direct consequence of the distinction between Indian status, which is government-controlled, and band membership, which is largely determined by the First Nations. A few oil-rich bands in Alberta have sought to establish in law their right to absolute control of their membership, having been provoked to do so by fears that their populations will be overwhelmed by large numbers of returning "Indians" who have no knowledge of the community or its culture and who are suspected of wanting membership restored to gain access to band resources. In an effort to establish that right, the Sawridge First Nation in Northern Alberta, supported by two other First Nations in the province, went to the Federal Court, to this point without success. While being stymied by the courts was difficult enough, Sawridge's leaders were even more angered by the behaviour of the federal government and some women's rights organizations. A number of such groups, all funded by the federal government, obtained status as intervenors in the action, thereby complicating the litigation and making carrying it on much more expensive for Sawridge, which, of course, was not assisted financially by Ottawa.[48]

Finally, even when Canada moved to address and protect human rights explicitly through legislation, it ended up discriminating against First Nations. When Parliament in 1977 passed the Human Rights Act (CHRA) and established a Canadian Human Rights Commission (CHRC), First Nations people were not given full protection. Section 67 of the Act specified, "Nothing in this Act affects any provision of the Indian Act or any provision made under or pursuant to that Act," and it "also precludes complaints against the Government of Canada alleging that provisions of the Indian Act itself are discriminatory."[49] Responding to the government's argument that Indians should be left out "because the government had made a commitment to First Nation representatives that there would be no modification to the Indian Act except after full consultations" and government argued that "applying the proposed human rights regime to matters falling under the Indian Act could, in substance, result in changing the Indian Act," the CHRA omitted the right of appeal. But, the CHRC was later to note, section 67 shielding the federal government from complaints "was to be a temporary measure, a short-term expedient."[50]

As with so many temporary expedients in Ottawa, the short term proved extraordinarily durable. When the original bill had been under consideration in 1977, Justice Minister Ron Basford had spoken against deleting the exclusion of First Nations appeals by arguing that there were ongoing consultations with the National Indian Brotherhood, the status Indian organization, looking toward thorough amendment of the Indian Act. "I do not think we should jeopardize that machinery and that relationship"; any defects in the CHRA "should be corrected in the context of the consultations going on." Conservative MP Gordon Fairweather responded sarcastically but accurately, "the discussions are ongoing; I guess it is perhaps 15 years. But ongoing is an elastic word here."[51] Later, as human rights commissioner, Fairweather would be able to do something about the problem. His commission began, first, pointing out and, then, complaining about the ongoing discrimination against First Nations from the 1980s on,[52] but it was not until 2008 that the offending section 67 was repealed. Even then, repeal did not come fully into effect until the spring of 2011.[53]

Canada's sorry record on extending human rights to First Nations reminds one of what Pierre Trudeau once wrote about democracy in Quebec. "Historically," he observed in 1958, "French Canadians have not really believed in democracy for themselves; and English Canadians have not really wanted it for others."[54] It was not so much that First Nations did not subscribe to human rights. Rather, they did not accept non-Natives' approach to protecting human rights because it was culturally inappropriate for their societies. In their communities, rights were recognized and respected by an elaborate system of kin and clan requirements, and individual rights were subordinate to those of the collectivity. One owed obligations to kinfolk, including fellow clan members and those who were kin by marriage or ascription, that constrained one from acting in ways that violated the kinfolk or clan person's rights or interests. An individual's or family's "rights" were protected by kinfolk who acted because of a shared sense of kinship obligations. In other words, protecting rights was a matter of kinship obligation, not state action. Euro-Canadians, on the other hand, exalted the individual, and the protections of human rights that were constructed in their society placed a premium on the rights of the individual, usually elevating the solitary person's rights above those of the community. That clash underlaid the difference between Sawridge Cree Nation and the women's rights groups who faced off in Federal Court. On the other hand, the history of Canadian Indian policy illustrates clearly that non-Native Canadians have subordinated both the rights and the interests of Aboriginal peoples to their own. It is that reality that explains the systematic, continuous, and enduring refusal to recognize First Nations' human rights in Canada.

How could a parliamentary democracy that prides itself on the tranquillity that marks social relations within the country perpetrate such long-standing wrongs? Canadians have deluded themselves that they are superior to others, especially their American neighbours, in how they treat minorities. Although the evidence that historically Canadians have been more tolerant than Americans is, at best mixed, Canadians subscribe to a myth of moral superiority so far as treatment of indigenous minorities is concerned.[55] Among the most familiar themes of this mythology is the contrast between treaty-making in the Canadian West and war-mongering in the States in the 1870s, or the sharp difference between the Mounted Police and the American "long knives" (sabre-wielding cavalry). And since Confederation the government department responsible for administering Indian policy has assiduously promoted an exaggeratedly favourable view of Native–government relations.[56] Canadians have pursued a policy of human rights for some in relation to Indians because they mistakenly believe, thanks in part to the efforts of the Department of Indian Affairs over the years, that they have always and do now treat First Nations well.

NOTES

1. I wish to thank the Social Sciences and Humanities Research Council of Canada, whose Standard Research and Gold Medal Grants supported research for this paper; Ms. Carling Beninger, who conducted some of the research on which it is based; and my colleague Bill Waiser, who read an earlier draft. As well, the essay has benefited from a number of comments at the McMaster Symposium in March 2012.

2. R. Scott Sheffield, *The Red Man's on the Warpath: The Image of the "Indian" and the Second World War* (Vancouver: University of British Columbia Press, 2004), espec. Chaps. 2–5. See also Ronald Haycock, *The Image of the Indian: The Canadian as a Subject and a Concept in a Sampling of the Popular National Magazines Read in Canada 1900 to 1970* (Waterloo, ON: Waterloo Lutheran University, 1971).

3. J.H. Blackmore, Canada, Special Joint Committee of the Senate and the House of Commons [on] the Indian Act, *Minutes of Proceedings and Evidence* 2 (1947): 1673, June 10, 1947.

4. Library and Archives Canada [LAC], RG 10, Records of the Department of Indian Affairs [RG 10], vol. 3768, file 33,642, reel C-10122. Notes of Councils at Fort Qu'Appelle and Battleford, 1881.

5. RG 10, vol. 245, part 1, 145510–11, Minutes of Great Council, September 20–29, 1858. The Gradual Civilization Act and its aftermath are covered in J.R. Miller, *Skyscrapers Hide the Heavens: A History of Indian-White Relations in Canada*, 3rd ed. (Toronto: University of Toronto Press, 2000), 141–44.

6. Statutes of Canada [SC] 1876, c. 18, sec. 86 (1).

7. SC 1880, c. 28, sec. 99(1).

8. J.R. Miller, "Aboriginal Enfranchisement," in *Oxford Companion to Canadian History*, ed. Gerald A. Hallowell (Oxford University Press, 2004), *Oxford Reference Online*, www.oxford reference.com/views/ENTRY.html?subview=Main&entry=t148.35, accessed January 26, 2012; Robin Jarvis Brownlie, "'A Better Citizen Than Lots of White Men': First Nations Enfranchisement—an Ontario Case Study, 1918–1940," *Canadian Historical Review* 87, no. 1 (March 2006): 33–34.

9. RG 10, vol. 6810, file 470–2–3, pt. 7, reel C-8533, evidence of D.C. Scott before special parliamentary committee on compulsory enfranchisement amendment to Indian Act, 1920.

10. For a brief summary of these experiments in involuntary enfranchisement, see J.R. Miller, *Lethal Legacy: Current Native Controversies in Canada* (Toronto: McClelland & Stewart, 2004), 35–37.

11. Sarah Carter, *Lost Harvests: Prairie Indian Reserve Farmers and Government Policy* (Montreal and Kingston: McGill–Queen's University Press, 1990), 193–209.

12. What evolved into the "permit system" began in the original Act's prohibition on disposing without permission of "any trees, timber or hay . . . of . . . any of the stone, soil, minerals, metals, or other valuables therefrom for sale . . ." and evolved into wider coverage. See SC 1876, c. 18, sec 17, and Carter, *Lost Harvests*, 156–58.

13. Don Purich, *Our Land: Native Rights in Canada* (Toronto: Lorimer, 1986). Noted Purich in 1986, "This law remains in force."

14. Miller, *Skyscrapers*, 258–60; and "Owen Glendower, Hotspur, and Canadian Indian Policy," *Ethnohistory* 37, no. 4 (fall 1990): 390–91.

15. Carter, *Lost Harvests*, 209–36.

16. Carter, "Two Acres and a Cow: 'Peasant' Farming for the Indians of the Northwest, 1889–97," *Canadian Historical Review* 70, no. 1 (March 1989): 27–52, espec. 34–35.

17. SC 1876, c. 18, sec. 63.

18. SC 1884, c. 28.

19. John L. Tobias, "Payipwat," *Dictionary of Canadian Biography online*, accessed January 16, 2012.

20. Miller, *Lethal Legacy*, 71–73.

21. Ibid., 74.

22. Ibid., 74–76; E. Brian Titley, *A Narrow Vision: Duncan Campbell Scott and the Administration of Indian Affairs in Canada* (Vancouver: University of British Columbia Press, 1986), Chap. 7, espec. 124–26.

23. SC 1884, c. 27, sec. 3

24. SC 1895, c. 35 , sec. 6.

25. K. Pettipas, *Severing the Ties that Bind: Government Repression of Indigenous Religious Ceremonies on the Prairies* (Winnipeg: University of Manitoba Press, 1984), 58–59.

26. . . . 1919–20, c. 50., sec. 1.

27. On residential schools and their impacts see J.R. Miller, *Shingwauk's Vision: Native Residential Schools in Canada* (Toronto: University of Toronto Press, 1996); and John S. Milloy, *A National Crime: The Canadian Government and the Residential School System, 1879 to 1986* (Winnipeg: University of Manitoba Press, 1999).

28. Anthropologist Noel Dyck refers to this sort of relationship as "coercive tutelage." *What is the Indian 'Problem'? Tutelage and Resistance in Canadian Indian Administration* (St. John's, NF: ISER Books, 1991), 3, 31.

29. SC 1928, c. 32, sec. 6.

30. Sheffield, *The Red Man's on the Warpath*, 45. Sheffield notes that a small number of Aboriginal men had enlisted in the navy prior to the lifting of the ban.

31. Quoted in Sheffield, 99.

32. Quoted in Sheffield, 99–100. Wallace Havelock Robb, "Indian Leaders Encouraged to Press Claims for Justice," *Globe and Mail*, June 7, 1944 [LAC RG 10, vol. 8585, file 1/1/-2–17].

33. J.H. Blackmore, MP, *Minutes of Proceedings and Evidence* 2 (1947): 1673, June 10, 1947.
34. This is the principal conclusion of Scott Sheffield, *The Red Man's on the Warpath*, 167–69.
35. Jayme K. Benson, "Different Visions: The Government Response to Native and Non-Native Submissions on Education Presented to the 1946–48 Special Joint Committee of the Senate and the House of Commons," (MA mémoire in history, University of Ottawa, 1991); Miller, *Shingwauk's Vision*, 377–82 and 389–90.
36. J.L. Tobias, "Protection, Civilization, Assimilation: An Outline History of the Indian Act,"in *Sweet Promises: A Reader on Indian-White Relations*, ed J.R. Miller (Toronto: University of Toronto Press, 1991), 140.
37. See Miller, *Shingwauk's Vision*, 381–83 and 402.
38. Alan Cairns, "Citizenship and Indian Peoples: The Ambiguous Legacy of Internal Colonialism," in *Handbook of Citizenship Studies*, ed. Engin F. Isin and Bryan S. Turner (Thousand Oaks, CA: Sage Publications, 2002), 209–30, espec. 224–27. I am grateful to Professor Cairns for providing me with a copy of this article.
39. Richard H. Bartlett, "Citizens Minus: Indians and the Right to Vote," *Saskatchewan Law Review* 44, no. 2 (1979–80): 163–93; espec. 168, 183, 185, 189, 192, and 193. James M. Pitsula, "The Saskatchewan CCF Government and Treaty Indians, 1944–64," *Canadian Historical Review* 75, no. 1 (March 1994) 32–37.
40. Sally M. Weaver, *Making Canadian Indian Policy: The Hidden Agenda 1968–1970* (Toronto: University of Toronto Press, 1981).
41. The notwithstanding clause, section 33 of the 1982 constitutional amendments, said that legislatures and Parliament could pass legislation that violated the fundamental freedoms clause (section 2) or sections 7–15 (legal and equality rights) of the Charter by inserting in it a statement that it was valid "notwithstanding" what the Charter said. In other words, the notwithstanding clause was a mechanism for overriding rights. Such an override could be in effect for up to five years, and could be renewed by Parliament or a legislature.
42. Constitution Act 1982. Part I, containing the first twenty-five clauses, constitutes the Charter of Rights and Freedoms. Section 35 is located in Part II, which details the "Rights of the Aboriginal peoples of Canada."
43. For a useful summary of the issues see Royal Commission on Aboriginal Peoples, *Final Report* (5 vols) (Ottawa: RCAP, 1996), vol. 4, 33–53; and Miller, *Lethal Legacy*, 42–46.
44. RCAP, *Final Report*, vol. 4, 37.
45. Ibid., 39–42.
46. C. Lesley Biggs, Susan Gingell, and Pamela J. Downe, *Gendered Intersections: An Introduction to Women's & Gender Studies* (Halifax: Fernwood, 2011), 448.
47. Stewart Clatworthy, Mary Jane Norris, and Eric Guimond, "A New Open Model Approach to Projecting Aboriginal Populations," in *Aboriginal Policy Research* vol. IV: *Moving Forward, Making a Difference*, ed. Jerry P. White, Susan Wingert, Dan Beavon, and Paul Maxim (Toronto: Thompson Educational Publishing, 2007), 243–62, espec. Figure 15.4, 255. See also Clatworthy's analysis of the specific impact of one particular factor, failure to register paternity at birth, in the case of the offspring of C-31 parents. Stewart Clatworthy, "Unstated Paternity: Estimates and Contributing Factors," in *Aboriginal Policy Research*. Vol. II: *Setting the Agenda for Change*, ed. Jerry P. White, Paul Maxim, and Dan Beavon (Toronto: Thompson Educational Publishing, 2004), 225–43.
48. In the interests of full disclosure I must explain that I was one of the academic experts retained by Sawridge and prepared a report for the action. The information in this paragraph comes from contacts made while working on that report and from my own experience.
49. Canadian Human Rights Commission, *A Matter of Rights: A Special Report of the Canadian Human Rights Commission on the Repeal of Section 67 of the Canadian Human Rights Act* (Ottawa, Oct. 2005), 2 and 4.
50. *A Matter of Rights*, "Introduction" and 5–6.
51. Minutes of the Standing Committee on Justice and Legal Affairs, May 25, 1977, 15:44 (Ron Basford) and 15:46 (Gordon Fairweather)

52. See CHRC, *A Matter of Rights: A Special Report of the Canadian Human Rights Commission on the Repeal of Section 67 of the Canadian Human Rights Act*, October 2005, www.chrc-ccdp.ca/pdf/Report_A_Matter_of_Rights_en.pdf (accessed January 7, 2012).

53. *Globe and Mail*, June 20, 2011, A11

54. P.E. Trudeau, "Some Obstacles to Democracy in Quebec," *Federalism and the French Canadians* (Toronto: Macmillan, 1968), 103. The article first appeared in the *Canadian Journal of Economics and Political Science* in 1958.

55. Russel Lawrence Barsh, "Aboriginal Peoples and Canada's Conscience," in *Hidden in Plain Sight: Contributions of Aboriginal Peoples to Canadian Identity and Culture*, ed. David R. Newhouse, Cora J. Voyageur, and Dan Beavon (Toronto: University of Toronto Press, 2005), 281–82; Paulette Regan, *Unsettling the Settler Within: Indian Residential Schools, Truth Telling, and Reconciliation in Canada* (Vancouver: University of British Columbia Press, 2010), espec. Chap. 3, "Deconstructing Canada's Peacemaker Myth."

56. J.R. Miller, "Cultural Insecurity in the Peaceable Kingdom: Assimilatlon Policy and Government Propaganda," unpublished paper, British Association of Canadian Studies, University of Birmingham, April 6, 2011.

Afterword

• ◆ •

Rights, History, and Turning Points

William Schabas

Three hundred years ago, the Peace of Utrecht began the transfer of the northern part of North America from France to Britain. Article 14 of the Peace and Friendship Treaty of Utrecht between France and Great Britain of 1713 ensured certain fundamental rights to the subjects of the King of France who were "willing to remain there, and to be subject to the kingdom of Great Britain, and to enjoy the free exercise of their religion, according to the usage of the church of Rome, as far as the laws of Great Britain do allow the same."[1] Half a century later, in article 4 of the Treaty of Paris of 1763, the King of Great Britain agreed " . . . to grant to the inhabitants of Canada the freedom of the Catholic religion: consequently [he] will give the most precise and most effectual order, that his new Roman Catholic subjects may profess the worship of religion according to the rites of the Romish church, as far as the laws of Great Britain permit." These are among the earliest treaty provisions anywhere to address the protection of individual rights—some of the so-called "capitulations" in treaties between Christian European powers and the Ottoman Empire come a bit earlier—that are recognized and cherished to this day.

The movement against slavery is another early manifestation of human rights, as Bonny Ibhawoh explains in his chapter in this book. The first Canadian measures on the subject are contained a statute enacted by the initial legislative assembly of the province of Upper Canada: An Act to Prevent the further introduction of slaves and to limit the term of Contracts for Servitude within this Province.[2] The legislation confirmed that it was legal to own slaves but said that the children of slaves, upon reaching the age of twenty-five years, would be liberated.

By the twentieth century, like most modern democracies, Canada was engaged with human rights issues at both the domestic and international levels. In national law, the absence until 1982 of genuine constitutional protections does not seem to have helped, although perhaps this explains why other legal mechanisms, including human rights codes and commissions, took on such importance in the country. International human rights law, whose genesis can be traced to the post–First World War period, has provided opportunities both to activists within the country and to the government itself. Indigenous peoples were the first to recognize the possibilities, exploiting the new forum of the League of Nations to advance their claims against the federal government, as J.R. Miller explains. In the 1930s, the federal government invoked conventions on the rights of labour in its attempt to defend the constitutionality of the Canadian "new deal."

The crucible for the development of modern human rights was the period immediately following the Second World War. The major legal instruments that govern the modern world order and that set its tone were adopted at this time: the Charter of the United Nations, the Charter of the International Military Tribunal, and the Universal Declaration of Human Rights. The significance of the postwar law-making is now contested by revisionist historians like Samuel Moyn and Mark Mazower. In his influential new study, Professor Moyn points to the dark ages of the 1950s (what Dominique Clément calls "Cold War human rights") as evidence to gainsay the achievements of the 1940s. The real defining moment for human rights was the late 1970s and not the late 1940s, he contends. There is certainly a big kernel of truth in this analysis, to the extent that Professor Moyn recognizes the springtime of human rights in the 1970s. But bulbs only flower in the spring when they are planted months earlier. That is what happened with human rights in the 1940s.

A similarly negative assessment might be made of the legacy of the Nuremberg trial. Until the 1980s, it appeared as a curious and unique experiment, unlikely to be repeated. From the perspective of the postwar decades, Nuremberg, and international criminal justice more generally, was a dead letter, only punctuated by isolated bursts of activity like the Eichmann trial. Then, driven by several factors including the dynamism of international human rights, with its new focus on accountability and impunity, and the new political environment accompanying the end of the Cold War, international criminal justice quickly became a huge component of the contemporary world order. The seeds planted at Nuremberg had finally sprouted.

One of the great skills of talented historians is an ability to recognize seemingly small or insignificant developments that mark the start of great transformations, a bit like spotting the butterfly whose flapping wings start the chain of events resulting in a major hurricane or a heat wave. Mark Mazower is especially good at this, pointing for example to the establishment of the Institut de droit international in 1873 as a landmark in attempts at governing the world.[3] Some brilliant individuals actually understand the changes when they are taking place. These perceptive people stake their careers on ambitious, innovative projects, ignoring well-meaning advice that they are wasting their time.

This was surely the case in the post–Second World War context. When Justice Robert Jackson of the United States Supreme Court took leave so as to prosecute Nazi war criminals at Nuremberg he was mocked by his colleagues. The Chief Justice thought Nuremberg was a "high grade lynching party." Today, Justice Jackson is heralded as a pioneer of international criminal justice. Few even remember the name of the dismissive Chief Justice.

What about the Universal Declaration of Human Rights, an instrument whose significance and relevance seem to grow over time, even more than six decades after its adoption? By contrast, other texts of the time in the field of human rights, such as the European Convention on Human Rights, appear somewhat antiquated, with anachronistic language and norms that have passed their sell-by date. What led extraordinary individuals like Eleanor Roosevelt, John Humphrey, René Cassin, Charles Malik, and P.-K. Chang to invest their energies in the project of codifying fundamental rights? They grasped the importance of the project; others did not.

In Canada, to be sure, there was a lack of genuine understanding about the significance of what was taking place during this decisive period in the codification of human rights. The Canadian academic John Humphrey played a major role, but it was as an international civil servant rather than as a representative of his country. He was kept outside of the Ottawa loop and apparently had little influence there. Nothing in the archives suggests that Canadian diplomats tried to profit from what was potentially a very privileged relationship with a senior United Nations official.

The result was a terrible miscalculation, the decision to abstain in the vote in the Third Committee of the General Assembly on December 7, 1948. Three days later, when Canada changed its mind in the plenary General Assembly and voted in favour of the Declaration, Minister of

External Affairs Lester B. Pearson provided an unconvincing explanation for the faux pas. To those who had followed the debates, Canada's abstention was hardly an anomaly. The mediocre level of participation in the drafting stood out by comparison with other small and middle powers, like Australia, New Zealand, Belgium, Lebanon, and Cuba, all of whom showed that they had grasped the importance of the Declaration.

The same Canadian absence was visible in international criminal justice at the time. Unlike most of the other Commonwealth states, Canada did not participate actively in the meetings of the United Nations War Crimes Commission, where plans for the postwar prosecutions were made. At Nuremberg, the judges underscored the universality of the great trial by pointing to the fact that more than twenty states had ratified the London Agreement and its annexed Charter of the International Military Tribunal.[4] Canada was not among them. We do not know why. Probably, as with the Universal Declaration of Human Rights, it was lack of interest. According to Fannie Lafontaine, "Canada's post-war policy was little concerned with the war crimes issue and almost entirely focused on asserting its own autonomy."[5] Lester Pearson and the senior officials in the Department of External Affairs were more interested in Canada's role in the establishment of NATO than in the drafting of the Universal Declaration of Human Rights or international criminal justice. There were a few perfunctory trials of war criminals, and Canada sent a judge to the Tokyo Tribunal, but little more. The scandal of impunity finally broke in the 1980s, prompting the establishment of the Deschênes Commission and the adoption of war crimes provisions in the Criminal Code.

A decade or so ago, when interest revived in the Universal Declaration of Human Rights on the occasion of the fiftieth anniversary of its adoption, astonishment was sometimes expressed about the little-known fact of Canada's abstention during the vote in the Third Committee. Under Foreign Affairs Minister Lloyd Axworthy, Canada was at the zenith of its international activism, a paragon of human rights. It was basking in the glory of the successful stewardship of the negotiations leading to adoption of the Rome Statute of the International Criminal Court, and the dominant presence of Canadians at the International Criminal Tribunal for the former Yugoslavia. There was much boasting about the contribution of John Humphrey to the drafting of the Universal Declaration of Human Rights. The Department of Foreign Affairs made exaggerated claims about Canada's contribution that simply did not correspond to the official record of the negotiations or with ugly details in the archives. The Standing Senate Committee on Human Rights, in its 2001 report, said that "Canada was at the table and played a key role in the drafting of the *Universal Declaration of Human Rights* . . . "[6] As Jennifer Tunnicliffe points out in her chapter in this collection, the myth lives on: there is a reference on the Foreign Affairs website to "our central role in the drafting of the Universal Declaration of Human Rights in 1947/1948."

But if the notorious abstention in 1948 appeared out of character from the viewpoint of the late 1990s, it seems more plausible today. Since the 2005 election, Canada's international human rights profile has become increasingly tarnished. Canada has even broken ranks with close allies and traditionally like-minded states. In 2007 Canada was one of a tiny minority of states that voted against the Declaration on the Rights of Indigenous Peoples. Two years later, it conspired to undermine the Durban Review Conference. In 2012, the government closed the International Centre for Human Rights and Democratic Development, known in its later years as Rights and Democracy. The centre, which had been established by Parliament in 1988 and was initially led by Ed Broadbent, brought Canada great prestige and made important contributions to the promotion of human rights in many parts of the world.

Yet the fluctuations in the Canadian government's attitude to human rights cannot readily be reduced to the see-saw of red and blue party politics. It was a Liberal government in 1948 that faltered in the Third Committee. Subsequently, in the 1950s when the International Covenants were being negotiated, there is evidence in the archives of opposition not only from diplomats and bureaucrats but also at the political level, within the Liberal government, as Jennifer Tunnicliffe explains in her chapter in this book. The Liberals were especially chary of economic, social, and cultural rights, viewing this as the preserve of the more left-wing Co-operative Commonwealth Federation. The great personalities in promoting human rights law, whether at the international level or domestically, cannot simplistically be categorized by their party affiliation: John Diefenbaker, Frank Scott, Andrew Brewin, Brian Mulroney, Pierre Trudeau, Lloyd Axworthy, Ed Broadbent. Each of the main parties is represented with distinction.

At the bureaucratic level, the role of institutional cultures should not be neglected, although further research in this area is required. The archives do not reveal many champions of human rights within the Department of External Affairs in the 1940s. One exception was Escott Reid, the "radical mandarin" who proposed a draft charter of the future United Nations in the hopes Canada might promote this at the San Francisco Conference. The first chapter of his text was headed "The rights of every man." The proposal was not taken up. Hume Wrong apparently considered it a "wasted effort" although the department allowed Reid to publish his proposal anonymously.[7] It was in fact circulated to the delegates at San Francisco in a pamphlet issued by the Free World Research Bureau entitled "The Constitution of the United Nations."[8] In February 1947, Reid also managed to slip references to his human rights proposals into a speech he drafted for then Minister of External Affairs Louis St. Laurent.[9]

Some of the latent hostility to the Universal Declaration of Human Rights within Canada's foreign policy establishment can be seen almost immediately following its adoption. On December 13, 1948, Thomas A. Sutton, Chairman of the Eldorado Shareholders' Committees, send a copy of the Universal Declaration to the Department of External Affairs in the context of complaints about the expropriation of the company's capital stock, which was effected by an order-in-council in January 1944. A few days later, a memorandum to the legal adviser noted cynically: "The attached correspondence from the Chairman of the Eldorado Shareholders' Committees represents the first fruits of them that slept and brought forth the Declaration on Human Rights."[10]

From the earliest days, the United Nations received many complaints about human rights in Canada. Perhaps naively, victims of violations had understood that the references to human rights in the Charter of the United Nations implied that the organization was actually interested in complaints about the behaviour of its member states. In the 1940s, the secretary general had no interest in such petitions, no matter how meritorious. He simply forwarded them to the relevant diplomatic missions, including that of Canada. These early submissions concerned a broad range of issues, including police brutality, prohibition of press freedom in Quebec, Doukhobors, indigenous peoples, and discriminatory immigration polity. The chapter by James W. St. G. Walker provides considerable insight into the postwar human rights environment in Canada that spawned so many of these grievances.

When a petitioner from Georgetown, in what was then British Guiana, complained he was being denied entry to Canada because his wife was "Asian,"[11] the director of the Immigration Branch, C.E.S. Smith, wrote: "[Entering Canada] is a privilege and Canada is perfectly within her rights in selecting immigrants whose admission will contribute to the economic and/or cultural well-being of the Canadian people."[12] A complaint that the African-American singer Paul Robeson had been prevented from leaving the United States and coming to Canada referred to articles 13(2) and 19 of the Universal Declaration of Human Rights. A sinister note in the file says: "I don't think we should reply. Perhaps RCMP would like a copy of her letter."[13]

Eventually, the treatment of such petitions to the United Nations was institutionalized, but at the time there was much uncertainty about their status. Confronted with a petition by Canadians of Japanese descent who complained that more than three years after the end of the war they were still being denied the right to vote, the United Nations Division asked for advice from the Legal Division, questioning whether the petitions should be circulated to the relevant departments.[14] Disappointed by advice from London, officials turned to Washington for guidance where they were told of "the lack of power of the Commission on Human Rights to take any action in regard to complaints concerning Human Rights."[15] Anticipating the expiry of the offensive order-in-council sometime in 1949, J.W. Holmes recommended that no answer be provided to the United Nations until the regulations had lapsed, "when the Canadian leopard will have partially changed his spots so far as the Japanese are concerned." A.R. Menzies made a pencilled notation to the file: "No action taken."[16] Some years later, Saul F. Rae of the United Nations Division confirmed that Canadian policy was basically to ignore such communications.[17]

By the 1980s, the human rights culture within the Department of Foreign Affairs had improved. A new generation of officials was at the helm. Human rights training became a requirement for foreign service officers. But the enthusiasm of many of them for human rights was more than just a job requirement; it manifested a personal commitment. In some cases, professionals were recruited directly from the NGO sector. There were many more "radical mandarins" than in the 1940s, although this time around inspired officials often found themselves pushing on an open door at the political level. When they sensed that the minister was more focused on business and trade than rights promotion, some lost heart and contemplated leaving government altogether, only to have their spirits revived when Lloyd Axworthy, whom they adored, took up the reins of the department.

Mary Robinson begins her recent memoir with a famous quote from Eleanor Roosevelt: "Where, after all, do universal rights begin? In small places, close to home—so close and so small that they cannot be seen on any maps of the world."[18] The former United Nations High Commissioner for Human Rights is a big fan of Eleanor, as well as of the Universal Declaration of Human Rights. One of the elements of the drafting of the Declaration that more cynical observers seem to miss is the enormous and unprecedented presence of women. As the first Chairman of the Commission of Human Rights, a charismatic presence with an emblematic surname, Eleanor Roosevelt stands first and foremost. But there were many others involved at the time, including Hansa Mehta of India, Minerva Bernardino of the Dominican Republic, Jessie Street of Australia, and Bodil Begtrup of Denmark, to name only a few. Alas, there were no Canadians. This was the most significant involvement of women that there had ever been at the international level. In the past, their role had been largely confined to participation in NGO delegations. Four women signed the Charter of the United Nations, in June 1945, but the feminist contribution was confined to a reference to gender equality in the preamble and the requirement of non-discrimination in employment in article 8. By 1947, women had become full participants in the codification of international human rights standards. Eleanor Roosevelt was the first woman to lead an international body.

Samuel Moyn would probably reject such an observation as yet another naive manifestation of the "celebratory attitude" of contemporary historians to the emergence and progress of human rights.[19] He has his own enthusiasms, of course. Moyn's insistence on sobriety about the accomplishments of the 1940s is replaced with its own euphoria about the 1970s, which he picks as the real turning point. Here, the highlights are the award of the Nobel Peace Prize to Amnesty International, the election of Jimmy Carter as president of the United States and the stirrings in Central and Eastern Europe manifested in the establishment of Charter 77. Yet such an understanding is in no way incompatible with an appropriate recognition of the seminal law-making of the 1940s. The 1970s renaissance could not have taken place outside of the normative framework of the Universal Declaration of Human Rights. Nor, in all probability, could the Declaration have been drafted as quickly and effectively and with as much unanimity in the 1970s as it was in 1948. Like other documents of comparable importance—the Magna Carta, the Declaration of Independence, the Déclaration des droits de l'homme et du citoyen—its impact cannot be accurately assessed within a time frame of only a few years.

Professor Moyn is not the first to have underestimated the importance of the Universal Declaration. Of course there was the lukewarm Canadian position, already discussed above. At the time of its adoption, some eminent international legal scholars like Hersch Lauterpacht were similarly dubious about the Universal Declaration.[20] John Humphrey was furious with Lauterpacht. Years later he said that it was "only fair" to note that Lauterpacht's comments were made "shortly after the adoption of the Declaration, before it began to have any real impact and before the subtle processes began to work which would make it part of the customary law of nations."[21] And indeed, if Lauterpacht were alive today he would probably be among the first to proclaim the profound significance of the Declaration.

Hersch Lauterpacht's contrariness resulted only from disappointment that the Declaration seemed to lack legal teeth. Lauterpacht, who died in 1960, did not live to see it grow them. This was a gradual process that took many years. In 1972, the Security Council condemned "the recent repressive measures against African labourers in Namibia" and called upon "all States whose nationals and corporations are operating in Namibia . . . to use all available means to ensure that such nationals and corporations conform in their policies of hiring Namibian workers to the basic provisions of the Universal Declaration of Human Rights."[22] In 2007, the Universal Declaration of Human Rights was confirmed by the United Nations Human Rights Council as one of the principal bases for its systematic monitoring of observance of international standards by states known under the title Universal Periodic Review.[23]

The international law of human rights is immensely more complex than it was in 1948, at its beginnings. There is now a web of international treaties at both the global and regional levels, accompanied by various mechanisms for their enforcement (most of them invoke the Universal Declaration in the preamble). But the treaties are dependent upon ratification, which is sometimes uneven and almost never universal. They are subject to various forms of reservation, allowing states to cherry-pick obligations. There is considerable resistance from governments and courts—including those of Canada—to any direct application in national law. The treaties only apply to governments and do not speak directly to the variety of non-state actors, such as transnational corporations, who are involved in the business of violating human rights.

None of these shortcomings exists with the Universal Declaration of Human Rights. A trite formulation of law lecturers distinguishes the Universal Declaration from the subsequent treaties by characterizing the former as "non-binding." This both understates the significance of the Universal Declaration and exaggerates the impact of the treaties, which, while "binding" in principle, are often difficult if not impossible to enforce.

Lord Acton famously described the French Déclaration des droits de l'homme et du citoyen as "a single confused page . . . that outweighed libraries and was stronger than all of the armies of Napoleon."[24] The Universal Declaration of Human Rights, like its French ancestor, also takes up only a single page although, thanks to the work of Eleanor Roosevelt, John Humphrey, and René Cassin, it is a page that is far from confused.

NOTES

1. Treaty of Peace and Friendship between France and Great Britain, signed at Utrecht, April 11, 1713, Dumont VIII, Part 1, 339, art. 14; Definitive Treaty of Peace between France, Great Britain and Spain, signed at Paris, February 10, 1763, BFSP I, pp. 422, 645, art. IV.
2. 1793 SUC (2nd session), c. 7.
3. Mark Mazower, *Governing the World, The History of an Idea* (London: Allen Lane, 2012), 68.
4. *France et al. v. Göring et al.* (1949), 22 IMT 411.
5. Fannie Lafontaine, *Prosecuting Genocide, Crimes Against Humanity and War Crimes in Canadian Courts* (Toronto: Carswell, 2012).
6. The Senate: *Promises to Keep: Implementing Canada's Human Rights Obligations* (Ottawa, December 2001), 14.
7. Escott Reid, *Radical Mandarin: The Memoirs of Escott Reid* (Toronto/Buffalo/London: University of Toronto Press, 1989), 192.
8. LAC MG 31, E 46, Vol. 3.
9. Escott Reid, *On Duty, A Canadian at the Making of the United Nations, 1945–1946* (Toronto: McClelland & Stewart, 1983), 18–23.
10. Memo of December 17, 1948, signed H. Hay, NAC RG 25, Vol. 3690, 5475-W-4–40, Part 1.
11. UNSG Letter SOA 317/02 to PermRep, Oct 4, 1954, NAC RG 25, Vol. 6282, 5475-W-6–40, [Pt. 1.2].
12. Letter 1–54–7082 from C.E.S. Smith, Director, Immigration Branch to USSEA, November 17, 1954, NAC RG 25, Vol. 6282, 5475-W-6–40, [Pt. 1.2].
13. Letter from Jean Carlson, Lake Cowichan Peace Council, Feb 6, 1952 to External Affairs Department, NAC RG 25, Vol. 3690, 5475-W-4–40.
14. Memorandum for Legal Division from United Nations Division, October 28, 1948, NAC RG 25, Vol. 3690, 5475-W-4–40, Part 1. Also: Letter No. 3387 from George Ignatieff for the Acting

SSEA to High Commissioner for Canada, London, December 6, 1948, NAC RG 25, Vol. 3690, 5475-W-4–40, Part 1.

15. Letter of G.L. Magann, February 19, 1949, NAC RG 25, Vol. 3690, 5475-W-4–40, Part 1.

16. "J.W. Holmes to A.R. Menzies, March 1, 1949," LAC RG 25, Vol. 3690, 5475-W-4–40, Part 1.

17. "Memorandum from S.F. Rae, United Nations Division, to Consular Division, January 13, 1954," LAC RG 25, Vol. 6282, 5475-W-6–40, [Pt. 1.2].

18. Mary Robinson, *Everybody Matters: A Memoir* (London: Hodder & Stoughton, 2012), 1.

19. Samuel Moyn, *The Last Utopia, Human Rights in History* (Cambridge, MA: Belknap Press, 2010), 5.

20. Hersch Lauterpacht, "The Universal Declaration of Human Rights" *British Yearbook of International Law* 25 (1948): 354.

21. John P. Humphrey, *Human Rights & the United Nations: A Great Adventure* (Dobbs Ferry, NY: Transnational Publishers, 1984), 74. See Stephen P. Marks, "From the 'Single Confused Page' to the 'Decalogue for Five Billion Persons': The Roots of the Universal Declaration of Human Rights in the French Revolution," *Human Rights Quarterly* 20 (1998): 459.

22. UN Doc. S/RES/310(1972).

23. Institution-building of the United Nations Human Rights Council, HRC/RES/5/1, 5/1, Annex, I.A.1(b).

24. Cited in A.H. Robertson and J.G. Merrills, *Human Rights in the World, An Introduction to the Study of the International Protection of Human Rights* (Manchester: Manchester University Press, 1996), 4.

Select Bibliography

Adam, Barry D. *The Rise of a Gay and Lesbian Movement.* rev. ed. New York: Twayne Publishers, 1997.

Adams, Eric. "Building a Law of Human Rights: Roncarelli v. Duplessis in Canadian Constitutional Culture." *McGill Law Journal* 55, no. 3 (2010).

Afshari, Reza. "On Historiography of Human Rights. Reflections on Paul Gordon Lauren's *The Evolution of International Human Rights: Visions Seen.*" *Human Rights Quarterly* 29 (2007): 1–67.

Amos, Jennifer. "Embracing and Contesting: The Soviet Union and the Universal Declaration of Human Rights, 1948–1958." In *Human Rights in the Twentieth Century*, edited by Stefan-Ludwig Hoffman. 147–65. Cambridge: Cambridge University Press, 2011.

Backhouse, Constance. *Colour-Coded: A Legal History of Racism in Canada, 1900–1950.* Toronto: Osgoode Society and University of Toronto Press, 1998.

Bailey, Peter, and Annemarie Devereux. "The Operation of Anti-Discrimination Laws in Australia." In *Human Rights in Australian Law: Principles, Practice and Potential*, edited by David Kinley, 292–318. Sydney: Federation Press, 1998.

Bangarth, Stephanie D. "'We are not asking you to open wide the gates for Chinese immigration': The Committee for the Repeal of the Chinese Immigration Act and Early Human Rights Activism in Canada." *Canadian Historical Review* 84 (2003): 395–422.

Bangarth, Stephanie. *Voices Raised in Protest: Defending North American Citizens of Japanese Ancestry, 1942–49.* Vancouver: UBC Press, 2008.

Barsh, Russel Lawrence. "Aboriginal Peoples and Canada's Conscience." In *Hidden in Plain Sight: Contributions of Aboriginal Peoples to Canadian Identity and Culture*, edited by David R. Newhouse, Cora J. Voyageur, and Dan Beavon. Toronto: University of Toronto Press, 2005.

Bartlett, Richard H. "Citizens Minus: Indians and the Right to Vote." *Saskatchewan Law Review* 44, no. 2 (1979–80).

Bashevkin, Sylvia. *Women on the Defensive: Living Through Conservative Times.* Toronto: University of Toronto Press, 1998.

Behiels, Michael. "Canada and the Implementation of International Instruments of Human Rights: A Federalist Conundrum, 1919–1982." In *Framing Canadian Federalism: Historical Essays in Honour of John T. Saywell,* edited by Dimitry Anastakis and P.E. Bryden, 151–84. Toronto: University of Toronto Press, 2009.

Blackburn, Robin. *The American Crucible: Slavery, Emancipation and Human Rights.* New York: Verso, 2011.

Block, Sheila, and Grace-Edward Galabuzi. *Canada's Colour Coded Labour Market: The Gap for Racialized Workers.* Toronto: Wellesley Institute, 2011.

Borgwardt, Elizabeth. *A New Deal for the World: America's Vision for Human Rights.* Cambridge MA: Belknap Press, 2005.

Bothwell, Robert. *Alliance and Illusion: Canada and the World, 1945–1984.* Vancouver: UBC Press, 2007.

Boyd, Susan, and Claire F. L. Young. "From Same-Sex to No Sex? Trends towards Recognition of Same-Sex Relationships in Canada." *Seattle Journal of Social Justice* 3 (2003): 757–93.

Brownlie, Robin [Jarvis]. "'A better citizen than lots of white men': First Nations Enfranchisement—an Ontario Case Study, 1918–1940." *Canadian Historical Review* 87, no. 1 (March 2006).

Burke, Roland. *Decolonization and the Evolution of International Human Rights*. Philadelphia: University of Pennsylvania Press, 2010.

Byrnes, Andrew, Hilary Charlesworth, and Gabrielle McKinnon. *Bills of Rights in Australia: History, Politics and Law*. Sydney: UNSW Press, 2009.

Cain, Frank, and Frank Farrell. "Menzies War on the Communist Party, 1949–1951." In *Australia's First Cold War, 1945–1953*, edited by Ann Curthoys and John Merritt, 80–136. Sydney: George Allen & Unwin, 1984.

Cairns, Alan C. *Charter versus Federalism: The Dilemmas of Constitutional Reform*. Montreal and Kingston: McGill–Queen's University Press, 1992.

Cairns, Alan. "Citizenship and Indian Peoples: The Ambiguous Legacy of Internal Colonialism."In *Handbook of Citizenship Studies*, edited by Engin F. Isin and Bran S. Turner. Thousand Oaks, CA: Sage Publications, 2002.

Carter, Sarah. *Lost Harvest: Prairie Indian Reserve Farmers and Government Policy*. Montreal and Kingston: McGill–Queen's University Press, 1990.

Chappell, Louise, John Chesterman, and Lisa Hill. *The Politics of Human Rights in Australia*. Cambridge: Cambridge University Press, 2009.

Churchill, David S. "Transnationalism and Homophile Political Culture in the Postwar Decades." *GLQ: A Journal of Lesbian and Gay Studies* 15: 1 (2009): 31–66.

Clarke, Frank K. "Debilitating Divisions: The Civil Liberties Movement in Early Cold War Canada, 1946–8." In *Whose National Security? Surveillance and the Creation of Enemies in Canada*, edited by Gary Kinsman, 171–87. Toronto: Between the Lines, 2000.

Clarke, Frank K. "'Keep Communism out of Our Schools': Cold War Anti-Communism at the Toronto Board of Education, 1948–1951." *Labour/Le Travail* 42, no. 1 (2002): 93–121.

Clément, Dominique. *Canada's Rights Revolution: Social Movements and Social Change, 1937–1982*. Vancouver: UBC Press, 2008.

Clément, Dominique. "A Sociology of Human Rights: Rights through a Social Movements Lens." *Canadian Review of Sociology* 48, no. 2 (2011): 121–35.

———. "Human Rights in Canadian Domestic and Foreign Politics: From 'Nigardly Acceptance' to Enthusiastic Embrace." *Human Rights Quarterly* 34, no. 3 (2012).

———. "Human Rights Law and Sexual Discrimination in British Columbia, 1953–1984." In *The West and Beyond*, edited by Sara Carter, Alvin Finkel, and Peter Fortna. Edmonton: Athabasca University Press, 2010.

———. "'I Believe in Human Rights, Not Women's Rights': Women and the Human Rights State, 1969–1984." *Radical History Review* 101 (2008): 107–29.

———. "'It Is Not the Beliefs but the Crime That Matters:' Post-War Civil Liberties Debates in Canada and Australia." *Labour History* (Australia) no. 86 (2004): 1–32.

———. "'Rights Without the Sword Are but Mere Words': The Limits of Canada's Rights Revolution." In *A History of Human Rights in Canada*, edited by Janet Miron. Toronto: Canadian Scholars Press, 2009.

———. "The Royal Commission on Espionage and the Spy Trials of 1946–9: A Case Study in Parliamentary Supremacy." *Journal of the Canadian Historical Association* 11, no. 1 (2000): 151–72.

———. "Searching for Rights in the Age of Activism: The Newfoundland-Labrador Human Rights Association, 1968–1982." *Newfoundland Studies* 19, no. 2 (2003): 347–72.

———. "Spies, Lies and a Commission, 1946–8: A Case Study in the Mobilization of the Canadian Civil Liberties Movement." *Left History* 7, no. 2 (2001): 53–79.

Cmiel, Kenneth. "The Emergence of Human Rights Politics in the United States," *Journal of American History* 86, no. 3 (1999): 1231–50.

———. "The Recent History of Human Rights." *American Historical Review* 109, no. 1 (2004): 1–17.

Cohen, Stephen. *Australian Civil Liberties Organizations*. Sydney: International Business Communications Directory, 1990.

Cook, Ramsay. "Canadian Freedom in Wartime." In *His Own Man: Essays in Honour of A.R.M. Lower*, edited by W.H. Heick and Roger Graham, 37–54. Montreal and Kingston: McGill–Queen's University Press, 1974.

Creese, Gillian. "Organizing Against Racism in the Workplace: Chinese Workers in Vancouver before the Second World War." *Canadian Ethnic Studies* 19 (1987): 35–46.

Cushman, Thomas, ed. *International Handbook of Human Rights*. New York: Routledge, 2011.

Devereux, Annemarie. *Australia and the Birth of the International Bill of Human Rights, 1946–1966*. Sydney: The Federation Press, 2005.

D'Emilio, John. "Will the Courts Set Us Free?: Reflections on the Campaign for Same-Sex Marriage." In *The Politics of Same-Sex Marriage*, edited by Craig A. Rimmerman and Clyde Wilcox, 39–64. Chicago and London: University of Chicago Press, 2007.

Dershowitz, Alan. *Rights From Wrongs: A Secular Theory of the Origins of Rights*. New York: Basic Books, 2004.

Dobrowolsky, Alexandra. *The Politics of Pragmatism: Women, Representation, and Constitutionalism in Canada*. Toronto: Oxford University Press, 2000.

Dyck, Noel. *What is the Indian "Problem"? Tutelage and Resistance in Canadian Indian Administration*. St. John's, NF: ISER Books, 1991.

Eberlee, T.M., and D.G. Hill. "The Ontario Human Rights Code." *The University of Toronto Law Journal* 15 (1964): 448–55.

Egri, C. and W. Stanbury. "How Pay Equity Legislation Came to Ontario." *Canadian Public Administration* 32 (1989): 274–303.

Feldman, David. *Civil Liberties and Human Rights in England and Wales*, 2nd ed. Oxford: Oxford University Press, 2002.

Fingard, Judith. "Race and Respectability in Victorian Halifax." *Journal of Imperial and Commonwealth History* 20 (1992): 169–95.

Frager, Ruth, and Carmela Patrias. "'This Is Our Country, These Are Our Rights': Minorities and the Origins of Ontario's Human Rights Campaigns." *Canadian Historical Review* 82, no. 1 (March 2001).

Fudge, Judy, and Eric Tucker, eds. *Work on Trial: Canadian Labour Law Struggles*. Toronto: Irwin Law/Osgoode Society for Canadian Legal History, 2010.

Gearty, Conor. *European Civil Liberties and the European Convention on Human Rights: A Comparative Study*. The Hague: Brill, 1997.

———. *Principles of Human Rights Adjudication*. Oxford: Oxford University Press, 2004.

Gecelovsky, Paul, and Tom Keating. "Liberal Internationalism for Conservatives: The Good Governance Initiative." In *Diplomatic Departures: The Conservative Era in Canadian Foreign Policy, 1984–1993*, edited by Kim Richard Nossal and Nelson Michaud, 194–207. Vancouer: UBC Press, 2001.

Gillies, David. *Between Principle and Practice: Human Rights in North-South Relations*. Montreal and Kingston: McGill–Queen's University Press, 1996.

Gordon, Nancy, and Bernard Wood. "Canada and the Reshaping of the United Nations." *International Journal* 47, no. 3 (1991): 479–503.

Goutor, David. "A Different Perspective on the 'Labor Rights as Human Rights' Debate:

Organized Labor and Human Rights Activism in Canada, 1939–1952." *Labor Studies Journal* 36 no. 3 (2011): 408–27.

Grabham, Emily. "Law v. Canada: New Directions for Equality Under the Canadian Charter?" *Oxford Journal of Legal Studies* 22, no. 4 (2002): 641–61.

Graefe, Peter. "Political Economy and Canadian Public Policy." In *Critical Policy Studies*, edited by Michael Orsini and Miriam Smith. Vancouver: UBC Press, 2007, 19–40.

Headley, John, M. *The Europeanization of the World: On the Origins of Human Rights and Democracy.* Princeton: Princeton University Press, 2007.

Hobbins, A.J. "Eleanor Roosevelt, John Humphrey and Canadian Opposition to the Universal Declaration of Human Rights: Looking Back on the 50th Anniversary of the UDHR." *International Journal* 53, no. 2 (1998): 325–42.

Hobsbawm, E.J. "Labour and Human Rights." In *Worlds of Labour: Further Studies in the History of Labour*, edited by E.J. Hobsbawm, 297–316. London: Weidenfeld and Nicolson, 1984.

Hoffman, Stefan-Ludwig, ed. *Human Rights in the Twentieth Century.* Cambridge: Cambridge University Press, 2011.

Hochschild, Adam. *King Leopold's Ghost.* New York: Houghton Mifflin, 1999.

——. *Bury the Chains: Prophets and Rebels in the Fight to Free an Empire's Slaves.* New York: Houghton Mifflin, 2005.

Howe, Robert B. and David Johnson. *Restraining Equality: Human Rights Commissions in Canada.* Toronto: University of Toronto Press, 2000.

Hufton, Olwen, ed. *Historical Change and Human Rights: The Oxford Amnesty Lectures 1994.* New York: Basic Books, 1995.

Hunt, Lynn. *Inventing Human Rights: A History.* New York: W.W. Norton, 2007.

Ibhawoh, Bonny. "Stronger than the Maxim Gun: Law, Human Rights and British Colonial Hegemony in Nigeria." *Africa* 72, no. 1 (2002): 55–83.

——. *Imperialism and Human Rights: Colonial Discourses of Rights and Liberties in African History.* Albany NY: SUNY Press, 2007.

Iyer, Nitya. "Disappearing Women: Racial Minority Women in Human Rights Cases." *Canadian Journal of Women and the Law* 6: 1 (1993): 25–51.

Ignatieff, Michael. *The Rights Revolution.* Toronto: House of Anansi, 2000.

——. *Human Rights as Politics and Idolatry.* Princeton: Princeton University Press, 2001.

——. *The Lesser Evil: Political Ethics in an Age of Terror.* Toronto: Penguin Canada, 2004.

Iriye, Akira et al., eds. *The Human Rights Revolution: An International History.* New York: Oxford University Press, 2012.

Ishay, Micheline. *The History of Human Rights: From the Stone Age to the Globalization Era.* Berkeley, CA: University of California Press, 2008.

James, Matt. *Misrecognized Materialists: Social Movements in Canadian Constitutional Politics.* Vancouver: UBC Press, 2006.

Keck, Thomas. "Beyond Backlash: Assessing the Impact of Judicial Decisions on LGBT Rights," *Law and Society Review* 43, no. 1 (March 2009): 151–86.

Keenleyside, T.A., and Patricia Taylor. *The Impact of Human Rights Violations on the Conduct of Canadian Bilateral Relations: A Contemporary Dilemma.* Toronto: Canadian Institute of International Affairs, 1984.

Kent, Ann. "Australia and the International Human Rights Regime." In *The National Interest in the Global Era: Australia in World Affairs, 1996–2000*, edited by James Cotton and John Ravenhill, 256–78. Melbourne: Oxford University Press, 2001.

Kobayashi, Audrey. "The Japanese-Canadian Redress Settlement and its Implications for 'Race Relations.'" *Canadian Ethnic Studies* 24 (1992): 1–19.

Kome, Penney. *The Taking of Twenty-Eight: Women Challenge the Constitution.* Toronto: The Women's Press, 1983.

Korinek, Valerie J. 2003. "'The most openly gay person for at least a thousand miles': Doug Wilson and the Politicization of a Province, 1975–1983." *Canadian Historical Review* 84, no. 4 (2003): 517–50.

Lambertson, Ross. "The Dresden Story: Racism, Human Rights, and the Jewish Labour Committee of Canada." *Labour/Le Travail* Spring, no. 47 (2001): 43–82.

———. *Repression and Resistance: Canadian Human Rights Activists 1930–1960.* Toronto: University of Toronto Press, 2005.

Langer, Rosanna L. *Defining Rights and Wrongs: Bureaucracy, Human Rights, and Public Accountability.* Vancouver: UBC Press, 2007.

Lauren, Paul Gordon. *The Evolution of International Human Rights: Visions Seen.* Philadelphia: University of Pennsylvania Press, 1998, 2003.

Lee, Carol F. "The Road to Enfranchisement: Chinese and Japanese in British Columbia." *BC Studies* no. 30 (Summer 1976): 44–76.

Lenon, Suzanne J. "Marrying Citizens! Raced Subjects? Re-thinking the Terrain of Equal Marriage Discourse." *Canadian Journal of Women and the Law* 17: 2 (2005): 405–21.

Lépinard, Eléanore. "In the Name of Equality? The Missing Intersection in Canadian Feminists' Legal Mobilization Against Multiculturalism." *American Behavioral Scientist* 53, no. 12 (2010): 1763–87.

Levitt, Cyril, and William Shaffir. *The Riot at Christie Pits.* Toronto: Lester and Orpen Dennys, 1987.

———. "The Swastika as Dramatic Symbol: A Case-Study of Ethnic Violence in Canada." In *The Jews in Canada*, edited by Robert Brym et al. Toronto: Oxford University Press, 1993.

Luard, Evan, ed. *The International Protection of Human Rights.* London: Thames and Hudson, 1967.

MacLennan, Christopher. *Toward the Charter: Canadians and the Demand for a National Bill of Rights, 1929–1960.* Montreal and Kingston: McGill–Queen's University Press, 2003.

Madsen, Mikael Rask. "Legal Diplomacy: Law, Politics, and the Genesis of Postwar European Human Rights." In *Human Rights in the Twentieth Century*, edited by Stefan-Ludwig Hoffman, 62–81. Cambridge: Cambridge University Press, 2011.

Mahon, Rianne. "Child Care as Citizenship Right? Toronto in the 1970s and 1980s." *Canadian Historical Review* 86, no. 2 (2005): 285–315.

Manfredi, Christopher P. *Feminist Activism in the Supreme Court: Legal Mobilization and the Women's Legal Education and Action Fund.* Vancouver: UBC Press, 2004.

Mahoney, Kathleen. "Human Rights in Canadian Foreign Policy." *International Journal* 47 (1991): 555–94.

Mar, Lisa Rose. *Brokering Belonging. Chinese in Canada's Exclusion Era, 1885–1945.* Toronto: University of Toronto Press, 2010.

Maul, Daniel Roger. "The International Labour Organization and the Globalization of Rights, 1944–1970." In *Human Rights in the Twentieth Century*, edited by Stefan-Ludwig Hoffman, 301–20. Cambridge: Cambridge University Press, 2011.

Marshall, Dominique. "The Language of Children's Rights, the Formation of the Welfare

State, and the Democratic Experience of Poor Families in Quebec, 1940–55." *Canadian Historical Review* 78, no. 3 (1997): 409–42.

Martinez , Jenny S. *The Slave Trade and the Origins of International Human Rights Law*. New York: Oxford University Press, 2012.

Mazower, Mark. "The Strange Triumph of Human Rights, 1933–1950." *The Historical Journal* 47, no. 2 (2004): 379–98.

McEvoy, F.J. "'A Symbol of Racial Discrimination': The Chinese Immigration Act and Canada's Relations with China, 1942–1947." *Canadian Ethnic Studies* 14 (1982): 24–42.

McIvor, Sharon. "Aboriginal Women Unmasked." *Canadian Journal of Women and the Law* 16 (2004): 107–36.

McLaren, John P.S. "The Early British Columbia Supreme Court and the 'Chinese Question." *Manitoba Law Journal* 20 (1991): 107–47.

McRoberts, Kenneth. *Misconceiving Canada: The Struggle for National Unity*. Toronto: Oxford University Press, 1997.

Mertus, Julie A. *Human Rights Matters: Local Politics and National Human Rights Institutions*. Stanford: Stanford University Press, 2008.

Miki, Roy. *Redress: Inside the Japanese Canadian Call for Justice*. Vancouver: Raincoast Books, 2004.

Miller, J.R. "Owen Glendower, Hotspur, and Canadian Indian Policy," *Ethnohistory* 7, no. 4 (Fall 1990).

———. "Cultural Insecurity in the Peaceable Kingdom: Assimilation Policy and Government Propaganda." British Association of Canadian Studies, University of Birmingham, 6 April 2011.

———. *Lethal Legacy: Current Native Controversies in Canada*. Toronto: McClelland & Stewart, 2004

———. *Skyscrapers Hide the Heavens: A History of Indian-White Relations in Canada*, 3rd ed. Toronto: University of Toronto Press, 2000.

———. *Shingwauk's Vision: A History of Native Residential Schools*. Toronto: University of Toronto Press, 1996

———, ed. *Sweet Promises: A Reader on Indian-White Relations*. Toronto: University of Toronto Press, 1991.

Moores, Christopher. "From Civil Liberties to Human Rights? British Civil Liberties Activism and Universal Human Rights." *Contemporary European History* 21, no. 2 (2012): 169–92.

Moravcsik, Andrew. "The Paradox of U.S. Human Rights Policy." In *American Exceptionalism and Human Rights*, edited by Michael Ignatieff, 147–96. Princeton: Princeton University Press, 2005.

Morsinck, Johannes. "World War Two and the Universal Declaration." *Human Rights Quarterly* 15 (1993): 357–405.

———. *The Universal Declaration of Human Rights. Origins, Drafting, and Intent*. Philadelphia: University of Pennsylvania Press, 1999.

Moyn, Samuel. *The Last Utopia: Human Rights in History*. Cambridge, MA: Belknap Press, 2010.

Mutua, Makau. *Human Rights: A Political and Cultural Critique*. Philadelphia: University of Pennsylvania Press, 2002.

Nolan, Cathal J. "Human Rights in Canadian Foreign Policy." In *Human Rights in Canadian Foreign Policy*, edited by Robert O. Matthews and Cranford Pratt, 101–14. Kingston and Montreal: McGill–Queen's University Press, 1988.

———. "The Influence of Parliament on Human Rights in Canadian Foreign Policy." *Human Rights Quarterly* 7, no. 3 (1985): 373–90.

———. "Reluctant Liberal: Canada, Human Rights and the United Nations." *Diplomacy & Statecraft* 2, no. 3 (1990): 281–305.

Normand, Roger, and Sarah Zaidi. *Human Rights at the UN: The Political History of Universal Justice.* Bloomington, IN: Indiana University Press, 2008.

Nossal, Kim Richard. "Cabin'd, Cribb'd, Confin'd: Canada's Interests in Human Rights." In *Human Rights in Canadian Foreign Policy,* edited by Robert O. Matthews and Cranford Pratt, 23–45. Kingston and Montreal: McGill–Queen's University Press, 1988.

———. *Rain Dancing: Sanctions in Canadian and Australian Foreign Policy.* Toronto: University of Toronto Press, 1994.

O'Neill, Nick, Simon Rice, and Roger Douglas. *Retreat from Injustice: Human Rights Law in Australia.* Sydney: The Federation Press, 2004.

Olzak, Susan. *The Global Dynamics of Racial and Ethnic Mobilization.* Stanford: Stanford University Press, 2006.

Patrias, Carmela. "Socialists, Jews, and the 1947 Saskatchewan Bill of Rights." *Canadian Historical Review* 87, no. 2 (June 2006).

Patrias, Carmela. *Jobs and Justice. Fighting Discrimination in Wartime Canada, 1939–1945.* Toronto: University of Toronto Press, 2012.

Paul, Daniel N. *We Were Not the Savages: A Mi'kmaq Perspective on the Collision of European and Native American Civilizations,* rev. ed. Halifax: Fernwood, 2000.

Pegram, Thomas. "Diffusion across Political Systems: The Global Spread of National Human Rights Institutions." *Human Rights Quarterly* 32, no. 3 (2010): 729–60.

Pettipas, Katherine. *Severing the Ties that Bind: Government Repression of Indigenous Religious Ceremonies on the Prairies.* Winnipeg: University of Manitoba Press, 1984.

Pinker, Steven. *The Better Angels of Our Nature: Why Violence Has Declined.* New York: Viking, 2011.

Pitsula, James M. "The Saskatchewan CCF Government and Treaty Indians, 1944–64," *Canadian Historical Review* 75, no. 1 (March 1994).

Pross, A. Paul, ed. *Pressure Group Behaviour in Canadian Politics.* Toronto: McGraw-Hill Ryerson, 1975.

Puar, Jasbir K. *Terrorist Assemblages: Homonationalism in Queer Times.* Durham and London: Duke University Press, 2007.

Purich, Don. *Our Land: Native Rights in Canada.* Toronto: Lorimer, 1986.

Quataert, Jean H. *Advocating Dignity.* Philadelphia: University of Pennsylvania Press, 2009.

Ramos, Howard. "Aboriginal Protest." In *Social Movements,* edited by Suzanne Staggenborg, 55–70. Toronto: Oxford University Press, 2007.

———. "What Causes Canadian Aboriginal Protest? Examining Resources, Opportunities and Identity, 1951–2000." *Canadian Journal of Sociology* 31, no. 2 (2006): 211–35.

Randall, Melanie. "Equality Rights and the Charter: Reconceptualizing State Responsibility for Ending Domestic Violence." In *Making Equality Rights Real: Security Substantive Equality Under the Charter,* edited by Fay Faraday et al, 275–317. Toronto: Irwin Law, 2006.

Reid, Alan D. "The New Brunswick Human Rights Act." *University of Toronto Law Journal* 18, no. 4 (1968): 394–400.

Reif, Linda. "Building Democratic Institutions: The Role of National Human Rights Institutions in Good Governance and Human Rights Protection." *Harvard Human Rights Journal* 13 (2000): 1–69.

Regan, Paulette. *Unsettling the Settler Within: Indian Residential Schools, Truth Telling, and Reconciliation in Canada*. Vancouver: University of British Columbia Press, 2010.

Risse, Thomas, Stephen C. Ropp, and Kathryn Sikkink, eds. *The Power of Human Rights: International Norms and Domestic Change*. Cambridge: Cambridge University Press, 1999.

Ross, Becki. *The House That Jill Built: A Lesbian Nation in Formation*. Toronto: University of Toronto Press, 1995.

Roy, Patricia E. *A White Man's Province: British Columbia Politicians and Chinese and Japanese Immigrants, 1858–1914*. Vancouver: UBC Press, 1989.

———. "Lessons in Citizenship, 1945–1949: The Delayed Return of the Japanese to Canada's Pacific Coast." *Pacific Northwest Quarterly* 93 (2002): 69–80.

———. *The Oriental Question: Consolidating a White Man's Province, 1914–41*. Vancouver: UBC Press, 2003.

Russell, Ian. "Australia's Human Rights Policy: From Evatt to Evans." In *Australia's Human Rights Diplomacy*, edited by Ian Russell, Peter Van Ness, and Beng-Huat Chua, 3–48. Canberra: Australia Foreign Policy Publications Program, 1993.

Russell, Peter. "The Political Purposes of the Canadian Charter of Rights and Freedoms." *Canadian Bar Review* 61, no. 1 (1983): 30–54.

Russell, Peter H. *Constitutional Odyssey: Can Canadians Become a Sovereign People?*, 3rd ed. Toronto: University of Toronto Press, 2004.

Rutherford, R. Scott. *The Red Man's on the Warpath: The Image of the "Indian" and the Second World War*. Vancouver: UBC Press, 2004.

Sanneh, Lamin O. *Abolitionists Abroad: American Blacks and the Making of Modern West Africa*. Cambridge: Harvard University Press, 1999.

Schabas, William. "Canada and the Adoption of the Universal Declaration." *McGill Law Journal* 43 (1998): 403–41.

Schmidt, Vivien A. "Discursive Institutionalism: The Explanatory Power of Ideas and Discourse." *Annual Review of Political Science* 11, no. 1 (2008): 303–26.

Sellars, Kirsten. *The Rise and Rise of Human Rights*. Phoenix Mill: Sutton Publishing, 2002.

Scott, Frank R. *Essays on the Constitution: Aspects of Canadian Law and Politics*. Toronto: University of Toronto Press, 1977.

Simpson, Brian. *Human Rights and the End of Empire: Britain and the Genesis of the European Convention*. Oxford: Oxford University Press, 2004.

Smith, Miriam. *Lesbian and Gay Rights in Canada: Social Movements and Equality-Seeking, 1971–1995*. Toronto: University of Toronto Press, 1999.

Smith, Miriam. "Social Movements and Equality Seeking: The Case of Gay Liberation in Canada." *Canadian Journal of Political Science* 31, no. 2 (1998): 285–309.

———. "Social Movements and Judicial Empowerment: Courts, Public Policy, and Lesbian and Gay Organizing in Canada." *Politics and Society* 33, no. 2 (2005): 327–53.

———. *Political Institutions and Lesbian and Gay Rights in the United States and Canada*. New York and London: Routledge, 2008.

Snyder, Sarah. *Human Rights Activism and the End of the Cold War: A Transnational History of the Helsinki Network*. Cambridge: Cambridge University Press, 2011.

Sohn, Louis B. "A Short History of United Nations Documents on Human Rights." In *The United Nations and Human Rights*, 39–186. New York: Commission to Study the Organization of Peace, 1968.

Soohoo, Cynthia. "Human Rights and the Transformation of the 'Civil Rights' and 'Civil Liberties' Lawyer." In *Bringing Human Rights Home: A History of Human Rights in the*

United States, edited by Cynthia Soohoo, Catherine Albisa and Martha F Davis, 71–104. Westport: Praeger, 2008.

Spigelman, James. *Statutory Interpretation and Human Rights*. Queensland: University of Queensland Press, 2008.

Staggenborg, Suzanne. *Social Movements*, 2nd ed. New York: Oxford University Press, 2011.

Stammers, Neil. "Social Movements and the Social Construction of Human Rights." *Human Rights Quarterly* 21 (1999): 980–1008.

———. *Human Rights and Social Movements*. London: Pluto Press, 2009.

Stanley, Timothy J. *Contesting White Supremacy: School Segregation, Anti-Racism, and the Making of Chinese Canadians*. Vancouver: UBC Press, 2011.

Stone, Sharon Dale. "Lesbian Mothers Organizing." In *Lesbians in Canada*, edited by Sharon Dale Stone. Toronto: Between the Lines, 1990, 198–208.

Stone, Sharon Dale. "Lesbians Against the Right." In *Women and Social Change: Feminist Activism in Canada*, edited by Jeri Wine and Janice Ristock. Toronto: James Lorimer, 1991 236–51.

Sutherland, David A. "Race Relations in Halifax, Nova Scotia, During the Mid-Victorian Quest for Reform." *Journal of the Canadian Historical Association* 7 (1996): 35–54.

Tarnopolsky, Walter S. "The Historical and Constitutional Context of the Proposed Canadian Charter of Rights and Freedoms." *Law and Contemporary Problems* 44, no. 3 (Summer 1981): 169–93.

———. *Discrimination and the Law in Canada*. Don Mills: De Boo, 1982.

Tarnopolsky, Walter S., and William Pentney. *Discrimination and the Law in Canada*. Don Mills: De Boo, 1985.

Thomas, Daniel C. "Human Rights Ideas, the Demise of Communism, and the End of the Cold War." *Journal of Cold War Studies* 7, no. 2 (2005): 110–41.

Thompson, Andrew S. *In Defense of Principles: NGOs and Human Rights in Canada*. Vancouver: UBC Press, 2010.

Tillotson, Shirley. "Human Rights Law as Prism: Women's Organizations, Unions, and Ontario's Female Employees Fair Remuneration Act, 1951." *Canadian Historical Review* 72, no. 4 (1991): 532–57.

Titley, E. Brian. *A Narrow Vision: Duncan Campbell Scott and the Administration of Indian Affairs in Canada*. Vancouver: University of British Columbia Press, 1986.

Triggs, Gillian. "Australia's Ratification of the International Covenant on Civil and Political Rights: Endorsement or Repudiation?" *British Institute of International and Comparative Law* 31, no. 2 (1982): 278–306.

Tunnicliffe, Jennifer. "The Ontario Human Rights Code Review, 1975–1981: A New Understanding of Human Rights and Its Meaning for Public Policy." MA thesis, University of Waterloo, 2005.

Vickers, Jill, Pauline Rankin, and Christine Appelle. *Politics As If Women Mattered: A Political Analysis of the National Action Committee on the Status of Women*. Toronto: University of Toronto Press, 1993.

Vickers, Jill. "A Two-Way Street: Federalism and Women's Politics in Canada and the United States." *Publius* 40: 3 (2010): 412–35.

Vipond, Robert. "The Civil Rights Movements Comes to Winnipeg: American Influence on 'Rights Talk' in Canada, 1968–1971." In *Constitutional Politics in Canada and the United States*, edited by Stephen L. Newman, 89–107. Albany: State University of New York Press, 2004.

Waldron, Jeremy, ed. *Theories of Right*. London: Oxford University Press, 1984.

Walker, James W. St. G. *The Black Loyalists: The Search for a Promised Land in Nova Scotia and Sierra Leone*, 2nd ed. Toronto: University of Toronto Press, 1992.

———. *"Race," Rights and the Law in the Supreme Court of Canada: Historical Case Studies*. Toronto and Waterloo: Osgoode Society and Wilfrid Laurier University Press, 1997.

———. "The 'Jewish Phase' in the Canadian Movement for Racial Equality." *Canadian Ethnic Studies* 34 (2002): 1–29.

———. "Black Confrontation in 1960s Halifax." In *Debating Dissent: Canada and the Sixties*, edited by Lara Campbell, Dominique Clément, and Greg Kealey. Toronto: University of Toronto Press, 2012.

Warner, Tom. *Never Going Back: A History of Queer Activism in Canada*. Toronto: University of Toronto Press, 2002.

Weaver, Sally M. *Making Canadian Indian Policy: the Hidden Agenda 1968–1970*. Toronto: University of Toronto Press, 1981.

Winston, Morton. "Human Rights as Moral Rebellion and Social Construction." *Journal of Human Rights* 6 (2007): 279–305.

Yalden, Maxwell. *Transforming Rights: Reflections from the Front Lines*. Toronto: University of Toronto, 2009.

Zeleza, Tiyambe, and Philip McConnaughay, eds. *Human Rights and Economic Development in Africa: Establishing the Rule of Law*. Philadelphia, University of Pennsylvania Press, 2004.

Zuckert, Michael, "Natural Rights in the American Revolution: The American Amalgam." In *Human Rights and Revolutions*, edited by Jeffrey Wasserman et al. Latham MD: Rowman & Littlefield, 2000.

Contributors

STEPHANIE BANGARTH is associate professor of history at King's College, Western University. She researches and teaches in the areas of social movements, human rights activism, and immigration in Canadian history.

DOMINIQUE CLÉMENT is an assistant professor in the Department of Sociology at the University of Alberta. He is the author of *Canada's Rights Revolution: Social Movements and Social Change, 1937–82* (UBC Press, 2008) and *The Rise and Fall of the British Columbia Human Rights State* (forthcoming), as well as editor for *Alberta's Human Rights Story: The Search for Equality and Justice* (John Humphrey Centre for Peace and Human Rights, 2012) and *Debating Dissent: Canada and the Sixties* (UTP, 2012). Clément has written numerous articles on the history of human rights, social movements and women's history. For further information, visit www.HistoryOfRights.com.

RUTH A. FRAGER is associate professor of history at McMaster University. She is the author of *Sweatshop Strife: Class, Ethnicity, and Gender in the Jewish Labour Movement of Toronto, 1900–1939* (UTP, 1992) and co-author (with Carmela Patrias) of *Discounted Labour: Women Workers in Canada, 1870–1939* (UTP 2005).

DAVID GOUTOR is an assistant professor in the School of Labour Studies at McMaster University. He is the author of *Guarding the Gates: The Canadian Labour Movement and Immigration, 1872–1934* (UBC Press, 2008).

STEPHEN HEATHORN is professor in the Department of History at McMaster University. He is the author of *For Home, Country, and Race: Gender, Class, and Englishness in the Elementary School, 1880–1914* (UTP, 2000) and *Haig and Kitchener in Twentieth-Century Britain: Remembrance, Representation, and Appropriation* (Ashgate, 2013).

BONNY IBHAWOH is an associate professor in history and peace studies at McMaster University. He is the author of *Imperialism and Human Rights: Colonial Discourses of Rights and Liberties in African History* (SUNY Press, 2007) and *Imperial Justice: Africans in Empire's Court* (OUP, 2013).

MICHAEL IGNATIEFF teaches human rights and democratic politics at the Munk School of Global Affairs, University of Toronto and the Harvard Kennedy School. He is the former Leader of the Liberal Party of Canada.

DOMINIQUE MARSHALL is professor of history at Carleton University. She researches the history of children's rights at the League of Nations and in Canada, and the history of international humanitarian aid and of social policies, families, and poverty in Canada and Quebec. She is currently working on the history of Oxfam Canada.

JIM MILLER is the Canada Research Chair in Native-newcomer Relations and professor of history at the University of Saskatchewan. His research focuses on policies directed by governments and Christian churches at First Nations in Canada. He has published works on the history of residential schools (*Shingwauk's Vision: A History of Native Residential Schools* [UTP, 1996]) and treaties between the Crown and Aboriginal peoples (*Compact, Contract, Covenant: Aboriginal Treaty-Making in Canada* [UTP, 2009]).

CARMELA PATRIAS is professor of history at Brock University, with a special interest in Canadian immigration, labour, and women's history. Her publications include *Patriots and Proletarians: Politicizing Hungarian Immigrants in Interwar Canada* (McGill-Queen's University Press, 1994) and with Ruth Frager *Discounted Labour: Women Workers in Canada, 1870–1939* (UTP, 2005).

WILLIAM SCHABAS is professor of international law at Middlesex University, London; professor of international criminal law and human rights at Leiden University; and emeritus professor of human rights law at the National University of Ireland, Galway. He has an avid interest in the history of international law and especially in the development of such international documents as the Universal Declaration of Human Rights.

MIRIAM SMITH is professor in the Department of Social Science at York University. Her areas of interest are Canadian and comparative politics, social movements, and lesbian and gay politics. Among other works, she is the author of *Lesbian and Gay Rights in Canada: Social Movements and Equality-Seeking, 1971–1995* (UTP, 1999) and *Political Institutions* *and Lesbian and Gay Rights in the United States and Canada* (Routledge, 2008), and the co-editor of *Critical Policy Studies* (UBC Press, 2007).

JENNIFER TUNNICLIFFE is a doctoral student in history at McMaster University, examining Canadian attitudes and policy toward the development of international human rights from the 1940s to the 1970s. Her research interests include the intersection of domestic and international human rights, and the evolution of the definition of rights more generally.

JAMES W. ST. G. WALKER is professor of history at the University of Waterloo, where he specializes in the history of race relations and human rights. He is a former Bora Laskin National Fellow in Human Rights Research.

Index

Aboriginal and treaty rights, 252, 253–54
Aboriginals. *See* First Nations
African Canadians, racial discrimination, 37–38, 41, 45–47, 48, 154
African Charter on the Rights and Welfare of the Child, 206
African children's rights, 196–200, 204–5, 206
African National Congress (ANC), 74–75, 205
Afshari, Reza, 30
Akwesasne, 241
Allende, Salvador, 130
American Child Health Association (ACHA), 195–96
The American Dream series, 153
American Jewish Committee (AJC), 141–42
American Jewish Congress, 141
Amnesty International (AI), 9
anti-colonialism, 74, 75–78, 80–81
Anti-Defamation League of B'nai Brith (ADL), 141, 142
anti-discrimination: American Jews' approach, 147–48; Canadian *vs.* US campaigns, 156–58; legislation, 92, 96–97, 146–47, 149–53, 155–56. *See also* anti-semitism
anti-semitism: Canada, 41–42, 144–46, 154–55; legislation, 146–47, 149–53, 155–56; Quebec, 158; Springfield Plan, 144–45; United States, 141–43, 144–45
antislavery movement, 69–72
Argentina, 130
Australia: bill of rights, 92, 93–94; Cold War, 95–96; communism, 90–91, 95; international human rights, 92–93, 100–102; legislation, 103–4, 105–6; postwar debates, 90–92, 93, 95; rights revolutions, 88–89, 98–102, 103–5, 107; UDHR support, 90–91
Australian Council for Civil Liberties (ACCL), 91–92
Axworthy, Lloyd, 264

Ballantyne, Davidson and McIntyre v. Canada (1989), 14
Bandung Conference, 9
Bangarth, Stephanie, 42–43
Behiels, Michael, 167, 169, 171
Belgium, children's rights, 190, 191
Biafra conflict, 127–29, 134
Bill 101 (Quebec), 14–15

Bill C-31, 253–55
Bill C-71, 131–33
bill of rights (Canada), 92, 93–94, 98–99, 124–26, 181
Bill of Rights (Canada), 11, 12, 181, 221–22
Bill of Rights (Saskatchewan), 92
Bill of Rights of Children (USA), 195–96
Bliss case, 222
Blum, Sid, 152, 153, 154
Borgwardt, Elizabeth, 32
Brewin, Andrew F.: Biafra conflict, 127–29, 134; Bill C-71, 133; bill of rights advocacy and CBR, 124–26; biographical overview, 114; Chile crisis and refugees, 131–33; as Christian socialist, 115–16, 135n5; legal studies and practice, 116; political and civic activism, 116–17, 126–27, 134–36; Saskatchewan Trade Union Act, 117–19; work with Japanese Canadians and CCJC, 119, 121–24
Britain. *See* England and Britain
British Columbia, racial discrimination, 39, 44
British tradition and legal model, 3–7, 91, 93–94, 174
Brooke, Stephen, 16
Burke, Roland, 32, 35
Burnett, Hugh, 41, 45

Caiserman, H.M., 145
Canada and human rights: differences from US in campaigns, 156–60; disregard in 1950s, 265–67; international interest, 170–71, 181; literature and scholarship, 15–17; place of human rights, 2–3; promotion abroad, 92–93
Canada and the Biafran Tragedy, 128–29
Canadian Association of Adult Education, 149
Canadian Catholic Confederation of Labour (CCCL), 157–58
Canadian Civil Liberties Union (CCLU), 92
Canadian Council of Christians and Jews (CCCJ), 144
Canadian Human Rights Commission (CHRC), 255
Canadian Jewish Congress (CJC), 43, 145–46, 148
Canadian Museum of Human Rights (CMHR), 64–65, 81
Cartwright, J.R., 122

Charlottetown Accord, 252

Charte de la langue française, 14–15

Charter of Rights and Freedoms: Charte de la langue française, 14–15; and equality, 222–23, 224–25, 253; First Nations, 252–53; importance for human rights, 13, 103; lesbian and gay movement, 216, 225–27, 228–29; notwithstanding clause, 223, 253, 259n41; sections 15 and 28, 222–23, 224–25, 253; sections 25 and 35, 252–53; women's movement, 216, 222–26, 228

Charter of the United Nations, 167–68

Child Protection Committee (CPC), 198, 199–200

children's rights: African children, 196–200, 204–5, 206; Canada, 194, 195, 201–2; citizenship and empowerment, 204–5; diminished interest in, 203–4; health and birth registration, 198–99; individual rights, 200–201; International Year of the Child (IYC), 204–5, 206; origins, 191–92; popular support, 192–93; Second World War, 202–3; United States, 195–96; and war, 198, 199–200. See also Declaration of the Rights of the Child (United Nations); Declaration of the Rights of the Child (DRC) of the League of Nations

Child Welfare Committee of the League of Nations, 194

Chile crisis and refugees, 129–33

Chinese Canadians, racial discrimination, 38–39, 44

Chrétien, Jean, 250

Christie, Fred, 38

church and State separation, 158–60

Churchill, David, 215

civil and political rights. See individual rights

civil liberties: British approach, 3–5, 92, 93; Canada, 6–7, 89–90, 91, 166, 172; vs. human rights, 50; as origin of human rights, 3–5, 97–98; postwar debates, 90–92, 93, 95; in UDHR, 8, 166

Civil Liberties Association of Toronto (CLAT), 116–17, 120–21

Clark, Joe, and government, 251

Cmiel, Kenneth, 33, 50

Cold War, 8, 10, 79–80, 94–96

collective rights (economic and social rights): in draft Covenant, 170, 172–73; vs. individual rights, 8–9, 14–15, 76–77, 79–80, 173–74; and neo-liberalism, 229; origins, 45; protection, 13–14, 172–74; racial discrimination, 44–48; in UDHR, 8

Commission on Human Rights, 167–68, 170

Committee for a Bill of Rights (CBR), 124–26

Committee for the Repeal of the Chinese Immigration Act, 43–44

Committee on Jewish–Gentile Relationships, 144

communism, 90–91, 95–96, 156

Communist Dissolution Act (Australia), 95

Conference of the African Child, 197–200

Constitution (Canada), 220–21, 251–52. See also Charter of Rights and Freedoms

Convention of the Rights of the Child, 205–7

Cook, Ramsay, 89

Co-operative Committee on Japanese Canadians (CCJC), 42–43, 120–24

Co-operative Commonwealth Federation (CCF), 117–18, 119, 155–56

Dalhousie University, 46–47

Declaration of Independence (US), 3, 4

Declaration of the Rights of the Child (United Nations), 200–205

Declaration of the Rights of the Child (DRC) of the League of Nations: Britain, 190–91; Canada, 194, 195; entitlements and principles, 193–94; failures, 194–95; national legislations, 195–96; origins, 191–93; promotion, 194, 196

Declaration on the Granting of Independence to Colonial Countries and Peoples, 77

Defence of Canada Regulations (DOCR), 89, 116–17

Dembour, Marie-Bénédicte, 66

Desmond, Viola, 45–46

development of human rights. See origins of human rights

Dicey, Albert W., 5

Diefenbaker, John G., 11, 12, 126, 181, 249

discrimination, 6, 14. See also anti-discrimination

displaced persons, 160–61

distributive justice, 72

domestic jurisdiction clause, 90, 167

domestic rights, 1, 34–35, 50–51, 62

Donnelly, Jack, 72

Douglas, T.C. "Tommy," 117–18

The Dream series, 153

Duclos, Louis, 131–33

Dumbarton Oaks, 167

Duplessis, Maurice, 7, 158

East Nigeria conflict, 127–29, 134

Economic and Social Council of the United Nations (ECOSOC), 167

economic and social rights. *See* collective rights
education, 144–45, 158–60, 159, 248–49
Egerton, George, 169
Eisendrath, Rabbi Maurice N., 143–44
enfranchisement of First Nations, 235–37,
    245–46, 250
England and Britain: abolitionism, 69–70;
    children's rights, 190–91; development of
    civil liberties, 3–6; as legal model, 3–7,
    91, 93–94, 174; legislation, 99
English–French dualism, 157–58
Enlightenment, origins of human rights,
    30–31, 68–69
equality: Charter of Rights and Freedoms,
    222–23, 224–25, 253; First Nations, 253;
    legislation, 38–39, 42, 45, 47, 146–47
Ethiopia, 199
Evatt, H.V., 90
External Affairs (Canada), 170–71, 175–76,
    179–80, 181–82, 266

fair practices legislation, 149–52, 157–58
Fairweather, Gordon, 256
family allowances program, 201–2
federal state clause, 171, 176, 179, 182
Feinberg, Rabbi Abraham, 154–55, 159
feminism, 5. *See also* women's movement
First Nations: Aboriginal and treaty rights,
    252, 253–54; agricultural policy, 239;
    Charter of Rights and Freedoms, 252–53;
    coercion from government, 241–42,
    245–46; and constitutional reforms,
    251–53; education, 248–49; elections and
    voting, 240–42, 249–50; enfranchisement,
    235–37, 245–46, 250; equality, 253; and
    Euro-Canadians' view of human rights,
    247–52, 256–57; governance, 239–40,
    242; Indian status and band membership,
    253–55; kinship, 234, 256; Meech Lake
    and Charlottetown Accords, 251–52; pass
    system, 238; potlaches and Sun Dance,
    242–43; property rights, 237–39; protec-
    tion, 255–56; public awareness, 233;
    relationship with government, 234–35;
    residential schools, 243–45, 248–49;
    Second World War, 233, 246–47; women's
    discrimination, 236–37, 253–55. *See also*
    Indian Act (1876)
First World War, children's rights, 191–92
Ford, James W., 197
Ford v. Québec (1988), 14
foreign policy of Canada, 99–100, 101–2
Forsyth, David, 129

Fortier, Laval, 175
Franklin, William, 38
Fraser, Malcolm, and government, 102
French Canadians, and Jews, 157–58
French–English dualism, 157–58
Frost, Leslie, 45

Garson, Stuart, 93, 171, 175, 177–78, 181
gay movement. *See* lesbian and gay movement
gender movement. *See* women's movement
Global Human Rights Timeline, 65
global South, 9, 206
Goutor, David, 119
Gouzenko, Igor, and affair, 10, 89–90, 91, 95
governance, First Nations, 239–40, 242
Gradual Civilization Act (1857), 235
Gradual Enfranchisement Act (1869), 235, 236,
    239–40

Hasluck, Paul, 93
Held, Adolph, 158
Helsinki Accords, 10, 99–100
Hesse, H. Quarmina, 199
historical institutionalism, 216–19, 229; gender
    and sexuality movements, 217–18, 227–28
Hochschild, Adam, 69
Holmes, John, 184
Hoover, Herbert, 195
Horkheimer, Max, 147–48
human rights: concept in Canada, 172, 175; de-
    fined, 8, 33–36, 49, 61, 83; as entitlement,
    49–50; history and study of, 1–2, 17, 29,
    59–61, 81; as progress, 60; public display,
    61–62. *See also* origins of human rights
Human Rights Act (1977), 102, 255–56
Humphrey, John P., 11, 168, 263, 269; on
    Canada's response to UDHR, 88, 90, 92;
    children's rights, 200
Hunt, Lynn, 30–31, 33–34, 68

Ignatieff, Michael, 32, 66
Ilsley, J.L., 93
immigrants, 129–33, 160–61
Indian Act (1876): Bill C-31, 253–55; changes
    of 1951, 248; coercion from government,
    245–46; denial of rights, 233–34; enfran-
    chisement, 235–37; Joint Parliamentary
    Committee, 233, 248; origins, 234;
    property rights, 237–38; protection of
    First Nations, 255–56; treatment of First
    Nations as children, 234–35
individual rights (civil and political rights): for
    children, 200–201; *vs.* collective rights,

8–9, 14–15, 76–77, 79–80, 173–74; racial
discrimination as, 36, 37–44
Interdepartmental Committee on Human
Rights (Canada), 170
International Bill of Rights, 72, 166–67, 168
International Covenant on Civil and Political
Rights, 77, 170
International Covenant on Economic, Social
and Cultural Rights, 170, 173–74
International Covenants on Human Rights,
and Canada: collective rights, 172–73;
constitutional issues, 175–76; draft version comments, 171, 172–73, 175; federal
state clause, 171, 176, 179, 182; human
rights concept in Canada, 172, 175; and
legislation, 174; national sovereignty and
domestic policy, 174–75; pressure on
Canada, 178–79, 181; and provincial governments, 171, 176, 182–83; ratification,
182–83; resistance to, 167, 169–70, 173,
175–78, 181; support for, 171–72, 175–76,
178, 179–82, 183–84; and UDHR, 8, 169;
value of, 170–71
International Criminal Court, 10
International Prisoner-of-War Agency, 191–92
International Year for Human Rights (1968), 97
International Year of the Child (IYC), 204–5,
206
In the Matter of a Reference as to the Validity
of Orders in Council of the 15th Day of
December, 1945 (P.C. 7355, 7356 and
7357) in Relation to Persons of Japanese
Race (1946), 121, 122–23

Jackson, Justice Robert, 263
Jaeger, Hans-Martin, 192
Japanese Canadians, 267; CCJC and Brewin's
work, 120–24; deportation and expatria-
tion, 7, 42–43, 119–24
Jebb, Eglantyne and Dorothy, 191–92
Jewish Labor Committee, 106–7, 141
Jewish Labour Committee (JLC): and
American programs, 153–54; anti-
discrimination legislation, 146–47, 151;
displaced persons, 160; influence of
American ideas, 146, 148–50; Quebec,
158; role, 140, 143
Jews in Canada: academic links to US, 147–48;
American ideas and cross-border ties,
106–7, 139–41, 143–48, 153–54;
anti-semitism, 41–42, 144–46, 154–55;
Canadianization of materials, 153;
education and Springfield Plan, 145; fair

practices legislation, 149–53, 157–58;
influence on American activism, 153–54;
involvement with CCP, 155–56; labour
movement, 146, 147, 148–50; prejudice,
152; Quebec situation, 157–59; racial discrimination, 40, 41–42, 151; role against
discrimination and prejudice, 139–40,
144–45
John East Iron Works case, 118–19
Johnson, Reverend Ted, 128
Joint Parliamentary Committee on the Indian
Act, 233, 248
Joint Public Relations Committee (JPRC), 140,
144, 145, 146–47, 148–49
Jones, B.A. "Rocky," 46
Jones, Reverend Richard, 144

Kaplansky, Kalmen, 16, 146, 150, 155,
160–61
Kent, Ann, 101
Kenyatta, Jomo, 198
King, Mackenzie, 201

labour movement: black–white polarization,
156; Canadian Jews, 146, 147, 148–50;
Quebec, 157–58; Saskatchewan, 117–19;
United States and Jews, 142–43, 147,
148–50
Lafontaine, Fannie, 264
Lambertson, Ross, 116–17
land tenure, First Nations, 237–38
language laws of Quebec, 14–15
Laqueur, Thomas, 50
Lauren, Paul Gordon, 30, 33
Lauterpacht, Hersch, 269
Lavell case, 222
League of Nations, 92–93, 194. See also
Declaration of the Rights of the Child
(DRC) of the League of Nations
Léger, Jules, 172
legislation (Canada): anti-discrimination
and anti-semitism, 92, 96–97, 146–47,
149–53, 155–56; Bill of Rights, 181; early
developments, 11–12, 13, 14–15; expan-
sion from 1970s, 99–100, 102–3, 105–6,
107; fair practices, 149–52, 157–58; First
Nations, 233–34, 255–56; gender and
sexuality movement, 220–21, 222–23,
224–25; human rights in, 261–62;
International Covenants, 174; Quebec
language laws, 14–15; racial equality, 38–39, 42, 45, 47, 146–47. See also
Supreme Court

legislation (international), 10, 70, 99, 195–96; Australia, 103–4, 105–6

Lépinard, Eléanore, 225

lesbian and gay movement: Charter of Rights and Freedoms, 216, 225–27, 228–29; constitutional debates, 220–21; historical institutionalism, 217, 227–28; legal cases and mobilization, 225; origins and human rights, 214–16; political influences and developments, 219–20, 228–29; same-sex marriage, 227

lesbian feminism, 214

Lewis, David, 118

LGBT. *See* lesbian and gay movement

Liberal government of 1940–1950s, 174

liberties. *See* civil liberties

Ligue des droits de l'homme, 97–98, 105

local rights, 1, 34–35, 50–51, 62

Macdonald, Bill, 156–57

MacDonald, David, 128–29, 131–33

MacDowell, Laurel Sefton, 117

Madsen, Mikael Rask, 32

Mahoney, Kathleen, 95

malleability of human rights, 1

Manning, Ernest, 92

Marchand, Jean, 157

Maybank, Ralph, 171

Mazower, Mark, 31–32, 94, 263

McInnes, G.C., 178

Meech Lake Accord, 251–52

Menzies, Robert, and government, 90–91, 93–94, 100

Mertus, Julie, 94

Miron, Janet, 17

Morley, Terry, 115–16

Moyn, Samuel, 9, 11, 34–35; origins and history of human rights, 31, 59, 96, 262, 268–69

Mulroney, Brian, 205–6, 251–52

Mundell, David, 175

museums of human rights, 63–65, 66–67, 81–83. *See also* Canadian Museum of Human Rights (CMHR)

Mutua, Makau, 74

National Council of Civil Liberties (Britain), 6

national self-determination, 74, 75–78, 80–81

natural law theory, 67–68

natural rights, development, 3–4

neo-liberalism, and collective rights, 229

Newfoundland and Labrador, 225

1970s: gender and sexuality movements, 214–16; legislation and treaties, 99–100, 102–3, 107; origins of human rights, 9–10, 78–81, 96, 262, 268–69

Nolan, Cathal, 93

non-governmental organizations (NGOs), 9–10

Normand, Roger, 183

notwithstanding clause, 223, 253, 259n41

Nova Scotia, 37–38, 45–47

Nova Scotia Association for the Advancement of Coloured People (NSAACP), 46

Nuremberg trial, 262, 263, 264

Ontario, 42, 45, 97, 145, 146–47

Ontario Human Rights Code, 47

Organisation of African Unity, 206

origins of human rights, 30–33, 35–36, 60–61, 134, 262–63; and anti-colonialism, 74, 75–78, 80–81; and antislavery, 69–72; Canada, 3–7, 10–13, 36–38, 49–52, 261–62; and civil liberties, 3–5; Enlightenment, 30–31, 68–69; as global phenomenon, 7–10; in museums and public spaces, 61–63, 66–67, 81–82; in 1970s, 78–81, 96, 262, 268–69; and religion, 33, 67; Second World War, 71–72, 262; and UDHR, 72–75

Padlock Law, 7, 158

Park, Eamon, 161

parliamentary supremacy, 93, 98–99

pass system, for First Nations, 238

Patterson, Monica, 205

Peace of Utrecht, 261

Pearson, Landon, 204

Pearson, Lester, 168–69, 182, 264

Pegram, Thomas, 99

Pinochet, Augusto, 130

political and civil rights. *See* individual rights

political system, British origin, 3–7

potlaches, 242–43

prejudice against Jews, 152. *See also* anti-semitism

property rights, First Nations, 237–39

provinces and territories, 13, 45–46, 249–50; International Covenants on Human Rights, 171, 176, 182–83

public history: in museums, 63–64, 82–83; and origins of human rights, 61–63, 66–67, 81–82

Quebec, 14–15, 105, 157–59, 182–83, 195

R2P "responsibility to protect," 129
racial discrimination: African Canadians, 37–38, 41, 45–47, 48, 154; Chinese Canadians, 38–39, 44; as collective right, 44–48; denial in Canada, 154–55; as individual right, 36, 37–44; against Jews, 40, 41–42, 150–51; legislation, 38–39, 42, 45, 47, 146–47; South Indians, 39, 44
Racial Discrimination Act (Ontario, 1944), 42, 146–47
Red Cross, 191–92
Reed, Hayter, 239
refugees policy, 129–33
Reid, Escott, 176, 266
religion, 33, 67, 158–60
residential schools, 243–45, 248–49
Rethinking Human Rights workshop, 29
Rights of Man, The (Paine), 4
rights revolutions, 66; Australia, 88–89, 98–102, 103–5, 107; Canada, 48–49, 88, 96–105, 107
Riot at Christie Pits, 40
Robertson, Gordon, 171
Robinson, Mary, 268
Roosevelt, Eleanor, 268
Russell, Bertrand, 6

Saalheimer, Manfred, 147–48, 152
Salsberg, Joe, 147, 156–57, 161–62
same-sex marriage, 227
Saskatchewan, 92, 147, 151
Save the Children International Union (SCIU), 191–92, 196–97, 199, 200
Schabas, William, 37, 167, 169
Scott, Duncan Campbell, 236, 246
Scott, Frank R., 118, 124
Scott, Ian, 116
Scott, Rt. Reverend Ted, 115
Scott, S. Morley, 176
Second World War: children's rights, 202–3; family allowances program, 201–2; First Nations, 233, 246–47; impact on human rights, 40–44; and origins of human rights, 71–72, 262; racial discrimination, 40–42; violations of freedom, 7
Selassie, Haile, 199
self-determination, 9, 172–73
sexuality movement. See lesbian and gay movement
Shane, Bernard, 146
Shumiatcher, Morris, 147
Silcox, Reverend Edwin, 144
Six Nations Reserve, 242

Skinner, Quentin, 36
slavery, 69–72
Small, Frédérique, 199
Smuts, Jan, 90
social and economic rights. See collective rights
social inequalities, 14
social movements, 97–98, 216–19
South Africa, 101, 102, 204–5
South Indians, racial discrimination, 39, 44
Special Joint Committee on the Indian Act, 233, 248
Springfield Plan, 144–45, 159
Stammers, Neil, 29
St. Laurent, Louis, 90, 175
Sun Dance, 243
supremacy of Parliament, 93, 98–99
Supreme Court: Brewin and Japanese Canadians, 121–23; Charte de la langue française, 14–15; John East Iron Works case, 119; racial discrimination and equality, 38–39, 47; women's rights cases, 222
Sutton, Thomas A., 266

Taking Liberties workshop, 17–18
Trade Union Act (Saskatchewan), 117–19
trade unions, 142–43
Le Travail, 157
Treaty of Paris, 261
Trudeau, Pierre Elliot, and government, 98, 127–28, 182–83, 250–51

UDHR (Universal Declaration of Human Rights): adoption, 7–8, 72, 263; civil liberties in, 8, 166; domestic jurisdiction clause, 90, 167; and International Covenants, 8, 169; origins of human rights, 72–75; significance, 269–70; sovereignty of nations, 73–74; support from Australia, 90–91; Western focus of, 74–75, 76; women's role, 268
UDHR and Canada: civil liberties protection, 166; influence, 37; myth of central role, 166–67, 185, 265; resistance to and delaying tactics, 166–67, 168–69, 266; support for and signing, 90, 169, 263–65; views on creation of, 11–12, 88, 90, 263–64
UNICEF, 203
unions, 142–43
United Automobile Workers (UAW), 156–57
United Nations, 43–44, 93, 266–67
United Nations Human Rights Committee (UNHRC), 14–15

United Nations Relief and Rehabilitation Administration (UNRRA), 202–3
United States: anti-semitism, 141–43, 144–45; Canadian Jews' influence on, 153–54; children's rights, 195–96; differences from Canada in human rights campaigns, 156–60; gender and sexuality movements, 215–16, 217–18; influence on Canadian Jews, 106–7, 139–41, 143–48, 153–54; International Covenants, 170, 179; Jewish organizations, 141, 143; labour movement and Jews, 142–43, 147, 148–50; tradition of rights, 3–4
Universal Declaration of Human Rights (UDHR). See UDHR (Universal Declaration of Human Rights); UDHR and Canada
universal human rights: in definition of human rights, 33–35, 172; emergence and influence, 8–9; impact on Canada, 175; interpretation, 50; vs. local rights, 34–35; resistance of Canada, 166–67; use in claims in Canada, 43–44

"vernacularizing" of human rights, 62
visible minorities, discrimination, 48

war crimes, 10. See also Nuremberg trial
War Measures Act (Canada), 7
Western democracies, influence on human rights, 9–10
White Bear, 241
White Paper on Indian policy, 250–51
Whitlam, Gough, and government, 100–101
Winston, Morton, 33
women, discrimination, 236–37, 253–55
Women's Legal and Education Action Fund (LEAF), 223–24
women's movement: Bill of Rights, 222; Charter of Rights and Freedoms, 216, 222–26, 228; and constitutional debates, 220–21; historical institutionalism, 218; legal cases and mobilization, 221, 222–23, 224–25; origins and human rights, 214–16; political influences and developments, 219–20, 228
World War II. See Second World War

Yalden, Maxwell, 103
young people. See children's rights

Zaidi, Sarah, 183